The Mind's Provisions

NEW FRENCH THOUGHT

SERIES EDITORS
Thomas Pavel and Mark Lilla

TITLES IN THE SERIES

Vincent Descombes

The Mind's Provisions

A CRITIQUE OF COGNITIVISM

Translated by Stephen Adam Schwartz

 NEW FRENCH THOUGHT

PRINCETON UNIVERSITY PRESS · PRINCETON AND OXFORD

Library of Congress Cataloging-in-Publication Data

Descombes, Vincent, 1943–
[Denrée mentale. English]
The mind's provisions : a critique of cognitivism / Vincent Descombes;
translated by Stephen Adam Schwartz.
p. cm. — (New French thought).
Translation of: La denrée mentale.
Includes bibliographical references and index.
ISBN 0-691-00131-6 (alk. paper)
1. Philosophy of mind. I. Descombes, Vincent. Denrée mentale. English.
II. Title. III. Series.

BD418.3 .D4713 2001
128'.2—dc21   2001036380

This book has been composed in Adobe Bauer Bodoni

Printed on acid-free paper.∞

www.pup.princeton.edu

Printed in the United States of America

10 9 8 7 6 5 4 3 2 1

Contents

*subject's mind, not the real state of the world. This is what the
psychology of the computer-mind does: it detaches thought by
defining it as formal calculation. This defense of methodological
solipsism fails to account for the moment of appearances: the
Cartesian subject who has suspended judgment continues to
encounter appearances.*

The Complete Holist

IT IS FAIR to say that, in the English-speaking world, modern or contemporary French philosophy is always preceded by its reputation. Yet the content of this reputation depends on the prospective audience. Among specialists in most areas of the humanities, the reputation is a sterling one. Modern French philosophy is known in advance to be radical, transgressive, opening the constrained concerns of philosophy to philosophy's "Other": the "noise" or "violence" that philosophy purportedly excludes.[1] Radicality is clearly—and perhaps paradoxically—a core value in the English-speaking humanities today, and modern French philosophy is revered for having initiated many of those working in the humanities in the ways of radical thought. Yet among philosophers in the English-language tradition, modern French philosophy has a poor reputation at best and *for the very reasons it is venerated in the rest of the humanities*: its radicality, which is seen at worst as a kind of eccentricity, another manifestation of what the French themselves call "the French exception." At best, modern French philosophy is thought of as an individualistic endeavor focused on the endless and ever more radical and idiosyncratic reinterpretation of the philosophical tradition, an endeavor that rarely if ever takes the form of a collective project with real aims and some concrete achievements in the way that analytic philosophy so often does.[2]

There is no doubt some truth and error in both views. One is nevertheless entitled to wonder which modern French philosophers each group has in mind. Both groups, it would seem, think of modern French philosophy as synonymous with a skeptical and irrationalist current that unquestionably predominated during most of the twentieth century. This is the current that could be said to originate in Pascal and to have taken as its watchword his famous claim that "the heart has its reasons which reason knows not." This self-styled liberatory current is one that sees reason (even in the minimal sense of the simple avoidance of contradiction) as both limited and limiting and therefore as something to be thrown off, overturned, or simply gotten beyond. It includes the ways of thinking associated with French Romanticism and Symbolism, Bergson, and the two waves of twentieth-century French thinkers inspired by Heidegger and Nietzsche. For these latter thinkers, one of the primordial facts of human existence is that reason is a form of alienation or estrangement from the true functioning of the world by which it is conditioned: this is implicit in the idea, for example, that, to the extent that they are rational, all of our concepts might be false and inadequate to a world which is fundamentally contradictory. The first of these waves in the 1930s and 1940s included not only existentialists like Sartre and Jean Beaufret who explicitly acknowledged their debt to Heidegger, but also thinkers like Alexandre Kojève, best known for an interpretation of Hegel that drew much from Heidegger. This wave also included difficult-to-classify thinkers like Maurice Blanchot and Georges Bataille, who drew much from both Heidegger and Nietzsche. The second wave of Nietzscheo-Heideggerianism is perhaps the one most closely associated with modern French philosophy and is characterized, broadly, by a willingness to see everything—concepts, desires, beliefs, duties, etcetera—as, at root, relations of force, whether mechanical or not, and, therefore, once again, as contradiction. It includes the major structuralist and post-structuralist thinkers of the 1960s and 1970s: Derrida, Foucault, Deleuze, Lyotard, and Lacan (a philosopher *honoris causa*, as Descombes once referred to him[3]), among others.

There is, of course, another tradition of French philosophy that tends to be neglected when the subject of discussion is modern French philosophy: the tradition of rationalism that runs from Descartes through the thinkers of the Enlightenment (Voltaire, Diderot) to the late-nineteenth- and early-twentieth-century neo-Kantians (Renouvier, Brunschvicg). The success of the twentieth-century neo-Hegelian, Heideggerian, and Nietzschean critiques of Kant and rationalism in general did have as a result that this current became less conspicuous (which often means it retreated into French universities) and certainly less visible in the English-speaking world. Yet, recently, it has undergone a minor resurgence, with a "return to Kant," for example, being advocated by French philosophers like Luc Ferry and Alain Renaut.[4]

Vincent Descombes is certainly a stern critic of the irrationalist bent in French philosophy in its Nietzschean, decisionist, and poststructuralist guises. But he is no straightforward rationalist. He is probably still best known in the English-speaking world for *Modern French Philosophy* (1980), his masterful survey of the then-dominant irrationalist line running from the discovery (or revival) of "the three H's" (Hegel, Husserl, Heidegger) in the 1930s to that of the three "masters of suspicion" (Marx, Nietzsche, Freud) in the 1960s and 1970s.[5] Indeed, the thinkers discussed in that book—Kojève, Sartre, Merleau-Ponty, Lacan, Serres, Foucault, Althusser, Derrida, Deleuze, and Lyotard—are those that most people think of when the subject turns to modern or contemporary French philosophy. However, in its original French form, Descombes's book was called *Le même et l'autre: Quarante-cinq ans de philosophie française (1933–1978)*

(The Same and the Other: Forty-Five Years of French Philosophy [1933–1978]). There is in the French title an acknowledgment of the historical limitations of the survey that is not present in the English title, where the philosophers covered could be misconstrued as embodying modern French philosophy as such. Indeed, in the English-speaking world, the philosophers discussed in Descombes's book and their preoccupations *have* come to be taken as synonymous with modern or contemporary French philosophy as such. This is so despite the fact that almost twenty-five years have passed since the end of the period covered in the book and that almost all of the philosophers in question (Derrida and Serres being the exceptions) are no longer with us.

Yet French philosophy has continued and, indeed, flourished in the years since 1978. Those years have been marked by a return to themes and topics that had been neglected or abandoned during the years in which the skeptical, irrationalist, and antihumanist tradition predominated. French philosophy today is as diverse as at any time in its history, as readers familiar with the other titles in the New French Thought series will be aware. Most striking about its recent evolution is that, alongside the various resuscitations carried out through the typically French immanentist move of the "return to" (not just the "return to Kant" but, for example, the recent revival of Husserl), there has been a veritable explosion of interest since 1978 in what is called, for want of a better term, analytic philosophy. After almost fifty years of almost unqualified philosophical—indeed, *a priori*—skepticism concluding in philosophy's own impotence and obsolescence, the question of what philosophy is capable of has recently come to underlie many of the efforts in the field. Where, for prior generations, philosophy was often presented as a hopeless (yet inevitable) undertaking, always rewriting and reworking itself while awaiting its own "overcoming," for current French philosophers, the question of what philosophy can do is not one that can be declared to have been answered in advance. One actually has to see what can be done, to see whether previously "insoluble" paradoxes, contradictions, and conundrums can be resolved rather than simply highlighted. Doing so has, for many, involved abandoning the "grand style" of the "master thinker" equipped with "transcendental arguments" for why, say, conceptuality is nothing but "relations of power" or why human communication is ultimately impossible. "In the face of skepticism," as the title of a recent French book describes the current situation,[6] what has replaced these kinds of negative speculative declarations in the work of thinkers like Jacques Bouveresse, Christiane Chauviré, François Recanati, Pascal Engel, and others working in the analytic tradition is a form of what Descombes calls "elementary critique," one that "asks us not to understand any more than we are capable of explaining and applying in some way."[7] For this way of doing philosophy, paradox and contradiction may well be where philosophy begins; they cannot be where it ends. This requires the embrace and revival of a certain form of rationality, although, in the case of Vincent Descombes at least, such rationality is more broadly and anthropologically defined (in terms akin to those of Baudelaire) as one in which there is "a legitimate and mysterious reason for all customs"[8] and where the justification by means of tradition proper to many cultures can be as rational as the justification by appeal to rules of argument.[9] Indeed, Descombes is what could be called an "anthropological rationalist": one who differs from other varieties of rationalist by placing ways of life in the anthropological sense (and the hierarchies of status they entail) at the center of what reason and thought are. This also entails a certain self-limitation of the field of the philosopher's competence.

It is certainly not my intention to write a sequel to *Modern French Philosophy* here. However, if one were to write such a sequel with the aim of covering developments in the years since 1978, it is certain that one would have to include a chapter on Vincent Descombes himself. For Descombes is quite simply among the most brilliant and original philosophers working anywhere in the world today. His work is encyclopedic in its scope, profound in its implications, and systematic in its ambitions. Descombes works broadly in the field of what could be called "the philosophy of society," but the necessity for such a catchall phrase highlights the wide range of his concerns. From the workings of language and society to the role and possibilities of the social sciences to the philosophy of political judgment to aesthetics and the philosophy of literature, Descombes seems to take an interest in everything. But he is no dilettante, and his contributions to each of these fields are at once extraordinarily insightful and refreshingly modest.

Modesty and circumspection are certainly not qualities often associated with French philosophy. By calling his contributions "modest" I do not mean to suggest that Descombes's claims are simply incremental adjustments to work already in place or positions already established. Modesty here consists in eschewing the assumption—one that is virtually constitutive of the modern conception of what it means to be a philosopher on the continent—that originality and, yes, truth are always and only the result of a rush to extremes or a radicalization of thought.[10] In Descombes's case, the modesty of his claims and of his very language can also be seen to be of philosophical import. By refusing grandiloquence and writing in a straightforward and often witty manner, Descombes has taken a position against one form of solipsism. For is not a grandiloquent style, as Clément Rosset maintains, one that bypasses the real, attempting to render the real "by words that have clearly lost every relationship with it,"[11] enclosing itself in its own verbiage and thereby confirming the solipsistic hypotheses

it so often serves to present? Conversely, does not the refusal of grandiloquence already make the point that the meaning of words is not something
yet to be discovered but must be the meaning that they have publicly? In
other words, linguistic meaning—and, in Descombes's view, meaning of
all kind—is not something determined, let alone decided or discovered, by
each of us individually (Humpty Dumpty: "My words can mean whatever
I want them to mean"), but necessarily a product of rules and institutions
that are, by definition, collective or, more specifically, common. One who
believes and argues precisely this, as Descombes does, will seek to present
his arguments in as generous and clear a way as possible. Descombes once
responded to the question of what meaning "philosophy" has for him by
writing:

> It would . . . appear legitimate that I should be asked *what meaning philoso-*
> *phy has for me*. And yet I have no intention of replying to a question put in
> this way. I am in no way disposed to concern myself about some meaning that
> the word "philosophy" might have especially for me, or even that it might in
> any case have for me, whether it had the same sense for others or not. This
> would be to accept my own responsibility for "giving a meaning to it," as they
> say; whereas I maintain, rightly or wrongly and certainly until I see proof to
> the contrary, that the meaning, for me, of the word "philosophy" is exactly
> the meaning which it ought to have for everyone. There is nothing extravagant
> in itself about such a claim: it is only a way of saying that I myself wish to
> understand the word "philosophy" in the sense that it should have for every-
> one. . . . Hence the question "what sense does it have for me?" is ambiguous.
> If this sense refers to the meaning of the word, it is not so much my business
> to give it as to discover it in order to conform to it.[12]

A recurring theme in much of his work is accordingly what he has called
"the paradox of precarious communication."[13] This paradox is, as Descombes points out, the inopportune consequence of any number of theories
in the philosophy of language and mind, and not just French ones. It is
therefore a possible beginning for elementary critique. Indeed, this paradox would seem to be a consequence of both the version of semantic holism
presented (and criticized) by Jerry Fodor and Ernest LePore in *Holism: A*
Shopper's Guide and of what would appear to be its opposite, for example,
the solipsism that one finds expressed throughout Proust's *A la recherche*
du temps perdu and that Descombes has analyzed masterfully in his book
on that author.[14] If holism—the idea that signs, for example, only have
meaning given the entire system in which they function—entails the rejection of atomism, "the idea that a language might be constituted by providing a sign for one thing, then another sign for another thing, and so on,"[15]
then it would seem that

the meaning of a sentence pronounced or written by an individual depends
on the meaning of the other sentences that this individual has produced or
could have produced. Something that is materially the same sentence could
not have the same meaning when pronounced by different mouths, unless all
the other sentences produced by the two speakers were also identical.[16]

It would follow from this that "ordinary facts of communication begin to
take on the appearance of improbable events, perhaps even miracles."[17]
Furthermore, to the extent that mental semantics is also holistic, the very
possibility of a psychology would seem to be in jeopardy, since we could
never identify anyone's beliefs, desires, etcetera. The solipsistic view of
meaning arrives at a similar result in a different way, maintaining that, in
order to speak, each of us must translate our personal representations into
a common language and, in order to understand, we must translate that
public language back into our idiolect. Proust expresses this throughout
the *Recherche* in statements like: "Man is the being who cannot take leave
of himself, who only knows others within himself and who is lying when
he says differently."[18] In this view, one never really communicates one's
thought because thought is irretrievably private, while the means for its
expression are incommensurate because public. It follows that interpretation is not only unavoidable and ubiquitous but utterly inadequate. This
is by no means a point of view unique to literary figures, and one finds it,
as Descombes points out, among any number of reputable philosophers in
both the continental and analytic traditions.[19]

Finding a way to rescue the banal yet mysterious fact of human communication and, indeed, the very possibility of a psychology from these opposing perils—i.e., to understand them—has been part of Descombes's
project for over twenty years now. It is in many ways the theme of the book
you are about to read and its as yet untranslated sequel, *Les institutions
du sens* (The Institutions of Meaning). The two volumes in fact form a
whole, to which Descombes has given the collective title *Les disputes de
l'esprit* (The Mind Debates), although *The Mind's Provisions* can certainly
be read independently of the later volume. This volume is, first and foremost, a critique of the solipsistic and causalist position in the philosophy
of mind. More specifically, it is a critique of cognitivism, the latest philosophical incarnation of the project for a "scientific psychology." Cognitivism is here taken to task for the Cartesian "detachment of the mind" from
the world that it requires in order to think of the mind in causal and mechanical terms by taking the computer as its model. The second volume is
correspondingly a defense of holism against the charges made by many
that it necessarily renders the identification of thought (and thereby also
communication) precarious. Carrying out that defense will involve coming
up with criteria for the identification of thoughts that do not rely, as Des-

combes claims the cognitivist's criteria do, on a metaphysics of states of mind (as representations) that has been illegitimately imported from a naturalistic metaphysics of states of things. For representations or significations (in the sense of signifieds, not signifiers) can no more be picked out and identified or enumerated one-by-one in the mind than they can in, say, a painting. As Descombes argues, "it is quite impossible to say how many significations or representations there are" in, for example, a figurative painting like *The Raft of the Medusa* because the concept of a signification "manifests no identity criterion" (p. 241 below).

Descombes calls the doctrine that he defends in this book and its sequel "anthropological holism" or "structural holism." As the first of these names implies, this is not merely a position in semantics or the philosophy of mind but something much broader. It is essentially the view, derived from Wittgenstein, that meaning of any kind (and therefore thought) inheres first and foremost in a whole network of practices, institutions, mores, and "forms of life": in a word, a set of normative rules. This is a holistic position because it maintains that meaning is only given in a totality rather than in a one-to-one relation between a representation and its object. It is anthropological, not because it would seek to engage in properly anthropological work that is better left to the anthropologists themselves, but because the totality in question is one made up of the human institutions and practices that anthropologists study. And it differs from the sort of semantic holism discussed and criticized by Fodor and LePore in that it does not merely hold that meaning is the sort of thing that "if anything has [it] *lots* of other things must have [it] too."[20] It maintains this, of course, but adds a further qualification: lots of other things must have it and *there must be an order* among those things, a set of internal relations that gives them their meaning. The concept of an order, of a structure of relations and, above all, *rules* (in the normative rather than the mechanical and causal sense), is thus crucial, and broadens the considerations of the philosophy of mind into a philosophy of society, renewing a sociological and anthropological tradition leading from Montesquieu through Durkheim to Louis Dumont. Descombes seeks to provide this tradition with a philosophical undergirding by means of an explicit concept of what he calls, following Hegel, *objective mind*, or, following Montesquieu, an *esprit des lois*.

Anthropological holism is also historical: over and against the solipsistic positions of cognitivist philosophers like Jerry Fodor, who maintains that thoughts may be identified as brain states without regard for the world in which they take place (for example, that two subjects who are physically identical "down to the last molecule" have the same thoughts regardless of their past histories), Descombes insists upon what he calls the "principle of narrative intelligibility": "psychological attribution imposes a historical context: a particular past must have taken place, a particular future must be conceivable. Barring which, the present attribution is quite simply inconceivable" (p. 183 below).[21] In other words, thoughts can only be determined in a historical context and only attributed to appropriate entities within those contexts. If I remember my appointment at the bank, I must inhabit a context where there are banks and appointments and I must have made such an appointment; if I remember going to the seashore, it cannot logically be claimed that my brain remembers it any more than it can be claimed that my hand is writing a letter to my sister (see sections 8.5 and 8.6 below). In making this claim, for which he argues brilliantly, Descombes revives a long-standing tradition in scholastic philosophy running from Aristotle through Thomas Aquinas to more modern thinkers like Leibniz to much more recent philosophers like Gilbert Ryle, according to which it is a category mistake (an error in "philosophical grammar," as a Wittgensteinian might put it) to attribute actions to parts rather than to individuals. To the extent that this "intentionalist" line of thinking for which Descombes argues also subsumes the philosophy of mind within the philosophy of action, it follows that thought as well is properly attributed to persons, not brains.

The Mind's Provisions is certainly focused on positions and debates within the analytic tradition of the philosophy of mind. This might come as something of a surprise for readers who know Descombes only through *Modern French Philosophy* and who might be led to conclude that the concerns of so-called "continental thought" no longer interest him. And it is true that in France, Descombes has a reputation for being an analytic philosopher, although in the French context this is an entirely relative term. Yet one of the many merits of this book, one that sets it apart from most other works in the philosophy of mind, is its constant contextualization of the debates with which it engages. Descombes continually reminds us that many of the ideas—and indeed the underlying metaphysics—of contemporary cognitivists were not born with the computer but have a long heritage; that, for example, the project for a scientific psychology has roots in Mill's nineteenth-century associationism or that the "representational theory of mind" has been with us since Descartes (as its chief proponent, Jerry Fodor, is also ready to admit). In the course of *The Mind's Provisions*, Descombes will also remind us of both antecedents and correctives to the positions of his opponents in the current debate: in Aristotle, Aquinas, Descartes, in Leibniz, in the nineteenth-century debate about the specificity of the social sciences, in Lévi-Strauss's notion of a "symbolic effectiveness of myths," in Lacan's notion of "psychical causality," and even in the works of Alexandre Dumas. But this is not simply a matter, as some have maintained, of rendering complex and often technical debates in analytic philosophy palatable for a French audience. Nor is it simply a matter of enriching a debate that otherwise risks being too abstract or scholastic (in the pejorative sense of the term). Here again, to insist on such contextualization—to do philosophy in this way—is to take an implicitly philosophical position.

> Philosophical activity produces critical effects in that it confronts mere opinions with a rational ideal. This ideal must in turn assert itself in the discussion, failing which it would remain a prejudice. But such an ideal can never be a consequence of discussion; indeed, we have just used it in a positive definition of the latter. It remains to define it as a purely formal *a priori*: the ideal of rationality is the pure form of discussion, that is to say the whole set of rules of free debate.[22]

Consider the way in which analytic philosophy is often conducted. For many, this style of debate is held to be exemplary in its rationality, and in just the way suggested by the above passage. There is certainly much to be said in its favor. The world of analytic philosophy is seemingly a purely intersubjective one, not unlike a discussion club where communication is unconstrained and where any and all are able to contribute arguments and refutations. Yet, as Descombes points out, this "free discussion presupposes collective silence; it is a social relation in which the social aspect has been neutralized."[23] It is important to note that Descombes's point here is not that of the irrationalist scorning the barbarity and violence on which such civilized institutions purportedly rest. Descombes is here making a sociological point about the "naivety" of seeing social relations as purely intersubjective relations but also, perhaps more importantly, a political point about the futility of upholding such intersubjective relations as the model for what a society should be and for how political judgment should be exercised (as Jürgen Habermas's notion of "communicational rationality" can be said to do). A human society cannot be a discussion club, precisely because such a club is predicated on the evacuation of all relations of subordination (of priorities, of ends) "so that only the purely rational subordination of 'particular' to 'general,' of 'consequence' to 'principle' and of 'theorem' to 'axiom' remains."[24] The very existence of such a discussion club presupposes those social relations: "the emergence of societies permitting free discussion is never itself the consequence of such discussion, and . . . their peaceful operation implies a world outside, one in which social relations are not those of free discussion held in a context of collective silence."[25] Yet the intersubjective model for the way to do philosophy—whatever the branch of philosophy in question—can lead to the illusion that the world is but a discussion club and humans nothing but its participants, pure minds devoid of any particular status or aims in the world:

> Mental philosophy [which is what Descombes calls the theory of mind de-
> tached from the world] is, in a sense, a psychology, but a psychology of beings
> who never display anything even resembling *psychic life*. Animation—the spe-
> cific behavior of an animal system in its environment—is not its concern. It is
> instead concerned with representation, a phenomenon of presence to mind [p.
> 10 below]

For Descombes, this "encroachment of cognition upon the entirety of psychic life" [p. 127 below] is the result of a similar severing of the mind from society: "if the philosophical speculations on the origin and structure of psychological concepts became aberrant, it is because it was thought possible to cut mind off from society."[26] In the face of this, he insists that "the psychology of intellectual functions must take on the problem posed by institutions that are properly intellectual, by cultural styles of thought, and by techniques for reflection and meditation. It will have to be a *histori-cal* psychology" (p. 157 below).

To see philosophy as rooted in the here and now and divorced from its own history—which is always the danger for philosophy in the analytic style, though one avoided by its best practitioners—is also to cut mind off from society. It is to treat that history (i.e., how we got here) as inconse-quential, in much the same way that modern science does. It is perhaps not surprising, then, that one of the dominant perspectives on the mind in the analytic tradition is one that maintains that a brain struck by lightning so that its molecules were scrambled into the same configuration as my brain when I am thinking "I must go to the bank" would also be thinking "I must go to the bank" even if the brain in question belonged to a cave-man. The point here is that just as "I must go to the bank" requires an entire narrative context that includes banks, rules governing our interac-tions with them, and any number of other things in order to be a meaning-ful utterance, so too does philosophical discourse require its own narrative context for its intelligibility. This is both a stance and a style of doing philosophy that is highly original: neither strictly an immanentist illumi-nation of problems in the history of philosophy for their own sake (or for the sake of a simple radicalized "return to") nor a set of claims and posi-tions detached from every historical mooring.[27] There is a consonance of aims, positions, methods, and, yes, style in Descombes's work that makes it almost seamless, indeed: complete, whole.

It is important, however, to forestall a potential source of misapprehen-sion. Descombes's holism must be distinguished from two alternative pic-tures of objective mind—of the human mind in its relation to the (social and historical) norms of thought—that differ around the following ques-tion, one which has been crucial in the social sciences: "Do the agents know what they are doing?"

On the one hand, there are all of those theories that treat the agents' own understandings of their actions (including their verbal and mental actions)—their *reasons* and the rules governing their thinking and acting—as mere epiphenomena of deeper *causes*, whether internal or external. For these theories, the agents ultimately do not know what they are doing, and the reasons for their thoughts and actions are something other than what they think they are. One might class among these theories the Freudian "scientific psychological" theory of the unconscious (internal) or the Marxist theory of the economic base (external). One might also put in this category the externalist theories of French structuralists, who also put forward a version of holism (since, for them, it is the system that provides its elements with their meaning). But theirs is a "causal holism" strongly criticized by Descombes for having "taken the rules of an intellectual activity for mental causes" and "the structures of the mind for psychical mechanisms."[28] In this regard, the cognitivist position, one which is both solipsistic and causalist, is, as Descombes shows, an unlikely bedfellow for French structuralism and, especially, the Freudian (and Lacanian) project for an internal "scientific psychology." Cognitivism's Cartesian solipsistic principle, which frequently takes the computer as a model for mind (so that it makes no difference whether the computer-mind is installed in a robot-body or not; see chapter II below), also requires that we accept that humans know not what they do in the world, incapable as they are of escaping their own representations. Cognitivism's causal principle asks us then to believe that they themselves are not doing and thinking what they are doing and thinking: their brains are. These theories would seem to have the advantage of collapsing the social sciences into the natural sciences, allowing us, the third parties, to uncover the causal laws governing human behavior but at the price of having us inhabit a fundamentally mysterious world, one in which we are mere puppets of forces that exceed us.

On the other hand, there are rationalist, intentionalist, and individualistic theories (including those of dialogical rationalists) that see the shared rules governing thought and action as the result of a freely given consensus, that see, for example, social rules as an amalgamation of individual intentions to which we, collectively, assent. Here again the model of the discussion club asserts itself. This view rescues the actor's self-consciousness, but at the price of a false, voluntarist picture of institutions as the work of one or several Legislators. "By this view," Descombes writes, "we imagine a group of *orators* who, in a spirit of free deliberation, pronounce *eloquent speeches* for the consideration of the *assembled people*." He then asks: "But where did the orators learn the art of rhetoric? Who taught them to speak? How was the assembly convened? How was the matter for debate decided upon?"[29] Any picture of institutions as the work of

Legislators must be a false one, because it presupposes at least some of the institutions it is meant to explain.

Descombes's position differs from these in that it thinks of the normative conditions on action and thought as kinds of grammatical constraints that are not unknown to the actors. These constraints are to be uncovered by what he calls, following Wittgenstein, "philosophical grammar."[30] He shares with the structuralists and also philosophers in the English-speaking tradition like Hilary Putnam and Tyler Burge[31] their externalism, the view that the locus of meaning is outside, in the world and not in the individual's head, while fleshing out this theory with a properly anthropological and humanistic conception of how meaning is instantiated as objective mind. Yet grammatical constraints and normative rules are different from the rules the structuralists hoped to uncover in that they are explicit norms and not occult rules in the natural scientific sense, i.e., "principles of functioning" that we would have to uncover.[32] He shares with the rationalists the view that individuals act and think and that the reasons they give for what they do are not delusional: "The voluntarist explanation at least has the virtue of taking into account the fact that the institution exhibits a meaning in the eyes of those whose institution it is, and that it must therefore be comprehensible" (p. 58 below). But he differs with them in his refusal to see objective mind as merely an accretion (i.e., as intersubjective) or as anything other than primordial.

It should be clear, in any case, that Descombes's work marks, if not a revolution (the practice of proclaiming a revolutionary break having itself been broken with in recent French philosophy), a profound transformation in the aims and procedures of French philosophy, one that can fruitfully enter into dialogue not only with philosophers in the English-speaking traditions but with those in the English-speaking humanities whose point of reference is French structuralism and its aftermath. Will this dialogue occur? If an individual "wants to communicate his thought to anyone at all, he will have to accomplish an act of discourse and, thus, establish a social relation of interlocution."[33] If the conditions for this cross-cultural social relation of interlocution—not least between French thought and its English and American counterparts—show signs of having finally been put in place, it will no doubt be in large measure thanks to the mediation of Vincent Descombes.

The Mind's Provisions

CHAPTER 1

The Phenomena of Mind

The mental commodity, like any other,
indispensable, maintains its price.

—MALLARMÉ, *Variations on a Subject*

THE PHENOMENA of mind are also called mental phenomena. The question in what follows will not be whether there are such phenomena but rather where they are to be located.

That there are mental phenomena is not an empirical thesis in need of support. It is simply a question of definition. "Phenomenon" here means whatever may contradict our speculations and lead us to correct our initial descriptions. There are phenomena if there are facts that could result in the overthrow of even the most entrenched dogmas or in the rejection of the conclusions of even the soundest line of reasoning. "Phenomenon" certainly does not mean: what it is that will reveal to me what I am talking about at any given moment. What I am talking about is something I must have already understood or decided. Rather, phenomena are what I must inspect in order to know more or in order to discover anything at all about the things I want to talk about. If this is how we understand mental phenomena, the question of their existence need never be raised. Even those who utterly reject the idea that the mind is distinct from the brain or who maintain that the mental itself is merely a hypostatized entity do not go so far as to contest the difference between a pebble and, say, a high-school senior. They have no difficulty accepting that the difference between these things is manifested by various phenomena that can be examined. The difference is neither a speculative hypothesis that one might choose not to embrace nor a result that needs to be established by some sort of special investigation. No special acuity or methodical research is required in order to recognize this difference.

But the fact that there are, incontestably, mental phenomena in no way suggests that there is agreement about the correct way to understand them. In fact, the question of mind is the epitome of a contested philosophical problem. For there is indeed a point that cannot be decided simply by examining how things in fact happen, a point the determination of which cannot be exempted from philosophical disputes: the way in which to express and account for the difference between a pebble and a high-school senior. What should be emphasized? What sorts of distinctions should be drawn between things that are held to have a mind and things that are not? The entire debate regarding the phenomena of the mind bears in fact on the conception of these phenomena and preeminently on their place in a macrocosmic system.

The words "phenomena of mind" inevitably call to mind the illustrious tradition of the phenomenologies of mind, of which the most famous is that put forth by Hegel in his work by that name. And, in many ways, it is precisely the question of a phenomenology of mind that will be asked in what follows, provided that the phenomenology of mind is seen as an attempt to understand mind as it manifests itself. As it manifests itself: but where does mind manifest itself and how does it do so? In a person's innermost soul in a private form that is difficult to communicate? Or, rather, within public space and, therefore, in a historical and social form?

Every philosophy of mind must begin as a "phenomenology of mind" in at least one sense: we expect such a philosophy to tell us where we can find its chosen subject. "Where do you locate the mind?" is a question asked of philosophers who refer to the mental. There have traditionally been two responses: within or without. Within, according to the mentalist heirs of Descartes, Locke, Hume, and Maine de Biran and among whom one can also place the phenomenologists and the cognitivists. Without, according to the philosophers of objective mind and the public use of signs, for example, Peirce and Wittgenstein. I have two aims in this book. First, to support the thesis of the externality of mind: mind must be located outside, in exchanges among people, rather than inside, in the internal flux of representations. Second, to comprehend the difference between these two responses from the point of view of the moral sciences or *Geisteswissenschaften* [*sciences de l'esprit*].[1] Doing so will require a reassessment of the debates surrounding the human sciences that have persisted for a century: hermeneutics versus positivism, the philosophy of the subject versus structuralism, methodological individualism versus the holism of the mental. I believe that these debates must not be limited to methodological questions but should instead be considered ways of putting a philosophical conception of mind to the test in the terrain of anthropology.

1.1. Mental Things

The mental commodity: when Mallarmé uses this somewhat unusual expression, it is understood that he is referring to books.[2] The poet relates that he had just taken a morning walk in the streets of Paris. This allowed him to ascertain that the public had not stopped reading, contrary to the rumor then circulating that there had been a "crash" in the book trade. In bookshop displays, merchandise meant to nourish the mind was displayed in abundance. The price of the mental commodity had not collapsed.

Is it only an audacious stylistic turn of phrase that allows the adjective "mental" to be associated here with voluminous and heavy things, the books that the booksellers pile into columns resembling, according to Mallarmé, the architecture of a bazaar? At first glance, Mallarmé's expression seems to match his intentions perfectly: it seems self-explanatory and requires nothing in the way of annotations. Yet, if one is to believe the proponents of "cognitivism," the most recent philosophy of mind, a book could not be described as a mental thing. This new philosophy of mind is a kind of *mentalism*. According to the explanations offered by its adherents, mentalism consists in the rejection of behaviorist psychology, which sought to explain the behavior of people without appeal to their mental life, that is, without attributing to them a mind lodged somewhere between the stimulations provided by the world and the responses of the organism. In the eyes of a mentalist philosopher, the mental commodity cannot, strictly speaking, be a book, because that is something given outside of human heads. Rather, it would have to be the set of operations concerning the book that must have been carried out in the author's head or the set of those by which the reader will come to know it. After all, they point out, books do not write or read themselves. Without customers, a bookstore risks bankruptcy. The case of the book itself is even more serious: without readers, this book is nothing more than a stack of paper stained with printer's ink. These sheets do not become the pages of a book until they happen to be represented as such in the mind of a reader.

It might well seem that the new mentalism thus supports the so-called "philosophy of the subject" (or of the *cogito*), which has always maintained, contrary to the various prophets of the "death of the author" or the "end of man," that books do indeed have authors and readers. There are no books unless they are books for subjects, and precisely in virtue of this subordinate relationship. The confidence of the philosopher of the subject on this point has proven to be unshakable: if you tell him that a book exists, he assures you that *at least* one subject exists, namely the person who wrote the book. The philosopher of the subject is certain to have the public's approval on this, even in situations where that public dare not admit it, having been intimidated by the vociferous "critiques of the subject."

Like the philosopher of the subject, the mentalist also believes that books—and signs in general—have a subordinate mental status: the book would contain neither language nor meaning if these things did not exist in someone's head. The attribute of mentality belongs first and foremost to what happens inside someone and only secondarily to what happens outside: words, gestures, and written signs. For such a philosopher, "mental" is a synonym of "intrinsically meaningful," precisely because this word refers to whatever it is inside us that allows a meaning to be attached to external things which are otherwise devoid of meaning, like the sounds of a voice or the traces of a pen on paper. In order to be intrinsically mental or meaningful, the phenomena of mind must be internal and not external. They must be sought inside people and not in the world.

Yet it would be a mistake for the philosopher of the subject to hastily assume that the mentalist's position bolsters his own. For the mental operations located within a person should not necessarily be held to belong to a subject, at least in the strict sense in which philosophers define the term "subject" as the origin of our meaningful utterances, that is, as the person who can claim recognition as their author and say, "I and I alone am speaking." The new breed of mentalists—the cognitivists—differ from most of their predecessors in their adherence to a strict materialist doctrine. They make clear from the outset that, in their eyes, mental life is a physical process and that the mind that they seek to reestablish over and against behaviorism is a material system: quite simply, the brain. The new philosophy of mind, like the associationism that preceded it, sees itself as a mental mechanics. What keeps these new mentalists from calling a book a "mental thing" is not that a book is too material, physically heavy, ponderous, and subject to various kinds of physical deterioration. All of this, in their eyes, is just as true of the mind: it has a certain weight, it takes up space in the cranial cavity, it is vulnerable to excessively violent shocks and other deleterious actions. In fact, for these philosophers, the only reason that the merchandise for sale in the bookstore cannot be literally described as "mental" is that it is located on shelves and in displays and not inside people's heads. So it is that, in their view, a division has been established: if what you are looking for is mental, you must seek it inside the skull. If, on the other hand, the object of your inquiry is outside the head, it is also external to mental life. The motivation behind this division is that, as long as the book remains outside of me, it can tell me nothing. In order for it to become thoughts for me to ponder or information from which I might benefit, the bookish commodity must first literally become a mental one. The intelligible content of the book must be detached from its material support in the printed pages and transferred, so to speak, into an internal support: that is, into a support that is sufficiently close to me that it can be said that I have *come to know* what the book says. Thus the new mentalist, who presents himself as the partisan of a doctrine called "cognitivism," will point out that I cannot claim to know what a book says if my relation to it amounts to nothing more than having bought it at the bookstore and placed it on my bookshelf. As long as the book has not passed, partially or entirely, into my memory, it is not sufficiently close to me to enter into my mental operations. The mere possession of a book does not allow one to answer questions about its content or to conduct oneself according to its teaching. One is here reminded of the old but still pregnant image of the zealous reader who goes so far as to literally devour the sacred text in order to be all the more certain of carrying it in his heart and not just in his baggage. Had it even the slightest cognitive merit, this sort of transfer by physical incorporation would be a conventional way of reading books. If a student could succeed brilliantly in his exams simply by eating his crib notes rather than by committing them to memory, then eating a textbook would be an acceptable variety of the cognitive transfer known as "memorization." In order for a cognitive transfer to take place, we are told, the key is that a thing laden with meaning—a cognitive entity, a representation—be transported to a point within the person where it can play an effective role in the control of his conduct.

The new mentalists, particularly the theorists attached to the cognitivist program, would deem the preceding considerations mere platitudes hardly worth mentioning at all but for the fact that powerful anti-mentalist prejudices have for a long time been widespread not only among the scientific public but also among the philosophical public under the influence of thinkers like Wittgenstein and Ryle. I cannot agree with them on this point. There is nothing banal or obvious in any of this. The idea that the mental must be something internal to a person is hardly a basic and obvious fact. Rather, it is an exacting thesis. To accept this thesis, we would have to modify profoundly our ordinary conceptions and ways of speaking. I assume that, for a neo-mentalist, the expression "mental commodity" could be applied to things that might be put on the market such as information, knowledge, techniques of calculation, and software programs. When the expression is applied to a book, it can only be through a figure of speech, since a book only has mental or semantic properties in a derivative way. Such a figure works through an expansion of the applications of a vocabulary that refers first and foremost to the mind itself. We are expected to concede that we *know*, through the science of physiology, that the mind is located in the brain and that we must conclude, according to this philosophy, that the mind is thus identical to the brain, unless we are prepared to admit that two active powers can effectively occupy the exact same place.

Notice, however, that all of the vocabulary of semantic verbs applies equally well to books and other such products of the mind. It is easy to imagine a librarian helping us in our research by pointing to different books in his department and saying: this book *upholds* such and such a proposition, this book *professes* such and such a doctrine, here is another book that *shows* that the first is in error, here is a book that *refutes* all of the others on the shelf. It might be claimed that, in this case, the vocabulary has been transferred from its original field of application to a secondary one. Indeed, it may well be that our understanding of these semantic verbs takes place in a derivative way: when we say that a book upholds a doctrine, it may just be a way of saying that the author of the book upholds the doctrine. But, in such case, the derivation would go from persons to books. The primary use of these verbs would be to say, when standing before Raphael's painting of the School of Athens: "This is the philosopher who upheld such and such a doctrine while this one over here sought to refute him." By contrast, it does not seem at all possible to apply these same verbs not to people but to *brains*. One cannot say: This brain *professes* the Platonic doctrine but has been *refuted* by this other brain. Such attempts to apply semantic language directly to brains must be immediately counterbalanced by a change in the application of the substantive "brain" so as to mean "person" rather than an organic part *of* a person. Moreover, it is worth noting that the same thing would be true of the direct application of such verbs to minds. "I am the mind that always negates": we understand that it is Mephisto who always negates and not simply a material or immaterial part of his person.[3]

Such considerations of vocabulary are of course incapable of establishing anything from a philosophical point of view. We may well find we have excellent reasons for reforming our ordinary ways of speaking and may even decide to treat the brain henceforth as a subject to which we can attribute the cognitive properties that had hitherto been reserved for people. But to do so would be a major philosophical revision and not a simple return to common sense.

Another way to take stock of the conceptual revision recommended by mentalists is to consider in a more direct way the location of mental operations. We have no trouble admitting that knowledge of the contents of a book is to be located in the person who has read the book and not in the book itself sitting on the library shelf. Imagine, for example, that we belong to a team of explorers following the instructions given in a book written in an ancient language and that only one member of our team has proven able to read this book. The most important thing for our team would not be to know where the book is at any given moment but to know the whereabouts of our colleague who has understood its meaning and remembered the directions it gives. Our knowledge of the contents of the book moves with our colleague and not with the book itself. In other words, to the extent that the group's knowledge of the book's contents is located anywhere, it is located in the space occupied by our associate who has read it rather than wherever the book happens to be. If we were somehow to maintain possession of the book after having lost our knowledgeable companion, we would also have lost our knowledge of the book. Yet the reverse is not true: to lose the book is not to lose the knowledge, as long as our colleague remains with us. Thus, knowledge of information that is avail-

able somewhere is itself available somewhere, in another place, namely, in the knowing subject and, if one insists, "in his head." In general terms, the place in which signs are actualized is not the place of their intellection (or of what Peirce called their "interpretant").

Up to now, the role played by the topographical precision that locates a given mental resource "in so-and-so's head" has been perfectly clear, since we have only been discussing ways of referring to the person who can give us the information we seek. Yet we should bear in mind that, rather than being a mental operation, knowledge is the condition of such operations. Thus it is that the knowledge of the meaning of the book can be contained "in our colleague's head," while the answers to our questions—for which this knowledge is the condition of possibility—can be given neither "in his head" nor, for that matter, "in our heads" by some sort of inexplicable telepathy. Rather, those answers are given through intelligible communication between him and us and thus take place wherever we happen to be at the time. What is more, the knowledge that our colleague possesses is the result of his having read the book. This is another operation, one which would seem to take place wherever it was that he read the book—the National Library, for example—and not inside his head. The knowledge about the book travels along with the person who has assimilated its content, but the activity of reading the book must take place wherever the book happens to be. If the book is moved, the act of reading it must move with it.

These observations are obviously not sufficient to clear up the disputed point. My aim in making them has only been to point out the special nature of questions of place when they are asked regarding the mental. It may well be that topographical and chronological qualifications have a different status depending on whether they are applied to physical facts or to mental ones. The question "where is X located?" may well change its meaning depending on whether it bears on the location of a book or of a mental commodity: in the latter case, we will have to distinguish between the performance of the act of reading and the competence of the reader who has understood what he has read. Yet in any case, the mentalist view is a *thesis* and not a reminder of something incontestable. This thesis holds that *the operation of reading a book takes place in one's head* and not on the surface of the work itself, because only the text *represented* as a meaningful text can be what is read, and representations have their place in the head.

Texts written on paper do not compose themselves. But the new mentalist philosophy argues that the situation is quite different for the text composed in one's head. It could well be the case that this "mental" text has composed itself in the mind in reaction to an impulsion by the various subsystems or "modules" that make up the author's mental organ. This

happens in the mind and therefore, we are given to understand, in the brain, since that is the only place within the subject that we can imagine locating the mind. This is why philosophers who uphold the idea that books are written by their authors will have more or less the same reaction to the new mentalism that they did to the doctrine once called "structuralism."[4] The only difference to their eyes is that the previous critical doctrine sought to dispossess the author of his status as author of the work in favor of a whole or system of which the individual person whose name graces the book would be little more than the executing agent or amanuensis (whether this whole be a *Zeitgeist*, an "epistemè," or some sort of "ideological apparatus"). By contrast, the new mentalism transfers authorhood from the whole of the person to a part thereof. In this view, the production of a book, like any mental activity, consists in a set of mental processes by which representations are transformed or combined, without this being, strictly speaking, the action of a subject. Whether the philosophy is that of the structural unconscious or of the mind as a cognitive machine, the result is the same. The paradigmatic example of this in the French context has always been the production of a literary work: the book is often held to be written in virtue of mechanisms at work either above or below the level where people usually claim to locate their activity when they set themselves to writing.

The new philosophy of mind maintains that the subject of thinking is not the book, which is an external object containing nothing but printed signs, entities whose meaning and cognitive power are derived and secondary. The book by itself says nothing, thinks nothing, means nothing. There are no intentional phenomena whose substratum or "subject of attribution" can be located in the book itself.[5] The subject of attribution is the mind and therefore, from the naturalistic point of view, the brain. This philosophy therefore seeks to show how such a subject's inner life can account for the external phenomena of mind.

I have just alluded to the two principal debates in the philosophy of mind in the twentieth century: the psychology of autonomous mental life versus the psychology of external behavior; the philosophy of the subject versus the philosophy of anonymous process. The first dispute took place primarily among American and British philosophers, which is why there is no word in French for "behaviorism." The second debate played a major role in the intellectual life of countries like Austria and France. It is not surprising that the two doctrinal oppositions in question do not overlap. Yet these two disputes have something in common: both are expressions of the same sense that modern philosophers confront a difficulty in defining the place of mind in the world. A modern philosopher is one who has decided to understand the world in the light of modern science, or rather, in the light of the natural philosophy that he believes must necessarily

accompany our natural science. It is only once this natural philosophy has been formulated that he begins to wonder how to complete it with a philosophy of mind.

In order to understand the initial question of every philosophy of mind— Where are the phenomena of mind located?—we will need to get a better sense of the oppositions I have just mentioned between the various possible positions. More to the point, it will be useful to be able to point out the lines of derivation and affinities among these points of view. For example, it would be helpful to know in what way cognitivism is not so very far from the classical philosophy of the subject and in what way it is also close to behaviorism. The sort of synoptic overview that we need, however, cannot be the direct result of a historical inquiry but will instead have to serve as a guide for just that sort of historical research into the evolution of ideas in this domain. It follows that we should now equip ourselves with a conceptual classification of the possible positions for a philosophy of mind (see below, § 1.3). In order to come to an understanding of the principle of this classification, we will begin with the following question: What distinguishes the position of the question of mind in a modern philosophy?

1.2. Mental Philosophy

"Much of cognitive science," writes Jerry Fodor, "is philosophy rediscovered—and, I think, rehabilitated."[6] Fodor shows that this philosophy, which has regained a measure of currency thanks to the cognitivist program, is a version of what, in the nineteenth century, was called "representationism."[7] Cognitive psychology has rediscovered what Fodor calls a "Good Old Theory" according to which, as in the classic works of associationism, the mind is seen as a reader or operator of representations.

The traditional vocabulary of British philosophers also has a name for the type of philosophy whose rehabilitation (through the somewhat surprising metaphor of the computer) Fodor welcomes: they called it "mental philosophy." John Stuart Mill, for example, wrote that Auguste Comte had rejected "Mental Philosophy."[8]

I am similarly going to use this expression to designate a current in the philosophy of mind that comes out of Locke. This philosophy seeks to discover the laws governing human understanding, and even human nature. In doing so, it oscillates between two positions: a Cartesian one by which it reflects on what it is that is "present to mind," namely "representative ideas," and a naturalistic one the ambition of which is to formulate the laws governing the passage from one idea to another and, more generally, from one mental state to another. This philosophy of mind seeks validation through introspective reflection, yet conceives of itself as a mechanics of the mind. I believe that one finds a similar sort of vacillation today.

Why is mental philosophy a post-Cartesian project rather than a discipline that would have to be included in any philosophy with the ambition to be comprehensive? Why is there, strictly speaking, no Aristotelian mental philosophy? The reason is that mental philosophy can conceive of no other way to insure the autonomy of psychology than for it to take as its object a mind utterly separate from the world. For a mental philosopher, psychology has a justification precisely in the fact that the psychological subject does not have a direct relation to things but only to its *representations* of things. In order to study someone's mind—to understand, say, his behavior—the essential thing is not to know who he is, where he lives, and who his teachers were. The key is rather to know who he *thinks* he is, where he *thinks* he lives, and so on. That is mental philosophy's basic doctrine: the separation between the mental sphere and the world.

Mental philosophy is, in a sense, a psychology, but a psychology of beings who never display anything even resembling *psychic life*. Animation— the specific behavior of an animal system in its environment—is not its concern. It is instead concerned with representation, a phenomenon of presence to mind.[9]

What distinguishes a theory as mentalist is not, of course, the fact that it is put forward in language that includes the word "representation." In itself, this word is innocuous. It is likely that *any* philosophy of mind will have to refer to representations, whether it uses the word itself or an equivalent. I do not count myself among those critics who seem to think that this word has some strange magnetic power that explains the entire orientation of modern thought, as if one could explain many aspects not only of modern thought but of our history itself by the fact that representations are, etymologically speaking, *re*-presentations. The difference between mental philosophy and other sorts of philosophy has nothing to do with whether or not they use the word "representation." Instead, the difference lies in what they mean by this word and in the conceptual systems that undergird its use. Among mental philosophers, representation is not a vital activity and in this regard differs from other activities like extracting information from the flux and variation of one's environment or drawing up a plan of action so as to be ready to move within a milieu whose complete contours can only be guessed at based on the partial information at hand. Representation, for a subject or "intelligent system," involves entering into a certain relationship with a cognitive entity: for the mentalists of the past, a representational idea; for those of the present, a real and physical symbol located within the organism.

There is, however, one aspect of mental philosophy that makes it firmly post-Cartesian rather than Cartesian. As Bréhier emphasizes, the philosophy of mind of the post-Newtonian classical thinkers is fundamentally unstable.[10] Like Descartes's philosophy, it is opposed to natural philosophy. However, unlike Descartes's philosophy, it does not subsume the opposition between natural philosophy and mental philosophy within a rational system. Mental philosophy continually oscillates between proclamations of the autonomy of the science of the mental, on the one hand, and awkward imitation of the scientific paradigms of the day, on the other. Neither of these solutions is satisfactory. The autonomy of the mental is perhaps comforting for mental philosophers in that it gives them their own field of research, but it does so by excluding them from natural philosophy, thereby rendering their entire enterprise suspect. The condition for the existence of this philosophy would seem to have been the delimitation of a mental sphere impervious to the incursions of the elements and forces of the "external world." The external world, as this philosophy conceives its relation to mental activity, exists only in the form of representations. The autonomy of psychology thus devolves into a glorious isolation. Yet, this situation could not continue, for the secession of mental philosophy would also seem to threaten the division on which the autonomy of the physical is founded: the initial division between natural philosophy and philosophy of mind. The world external to the mind is a world that is *represented* as being external. Mental philosophy might therefore be suspected of preparing the way for an idealistic physics, a physics in which it would be known in advance that the physicist's conclusions will conform to certain *a priori* truths and that these truths will be those that the philosophy of mind discovers through its reflection on the conditions governing the representation of an external world by a representing subject. If philosophy proves unable to "naturalize" psychology, then natural science risks finding itself once again subordinate to the demands of a mind that prescribes laws, if not to the real external world, at least to the world represented as being external. This debate between those philosophers who want to naturalize psychology and those who want to make it into a (transcendental) first philosophy is at the heart of modern philosophy. And it is a debate internal to the tradition of mental philosophy.

1.3. Taxonomy of the Philosophies of Mind

It is today considered good form to declare that "Cartesian dualism" has finally been overcome. Yet experience shows that declarations of anti-Cartesian monism are not enough to establish a coherent unification of the two branches of philosophy: both the branch whose success has been universally admired, natural philosophy, and the branch that has not yet been so blessed, mental philosophy. Moreover, it is not unusual for one and the same author both to declare himself a materialist and to advocate rehabilitating the representational psychology of Descartes's first heirs.

In order to get a clearer view of all this, it will be useful to ask what makes a philosophy of mind a mental philosophy. Not all philosophies of mind are mental philosophies in the way we are using this phrase here, namely: a mental philosophy is one that starts off by detaching the mental from the (material) external world, thereby ensuring the autonomy of the mental, one that only subsequently raises the inextricable problem of the *interaction* of the mental and the physical.

Using two criteria, I will construct a synoptic table that classifies philosophies of mind according to their phenomenologies. For two different questions must be asked: (1) *where* is the phenomenon under consideration, i.e., the mind, given?; (2) *how* does this phenomenon make its manifestations known? On the one hand, the phenomena of mind can be seen as phenomena that are either internal or external to the person: they are either given *inside* (in a mind that is detached from the world) or *outside* (in the world itself). On the other hand, the phenomena of mind can be held to be *direct* manifestations of mind or manifestations that are merely *indirect*. This latter distinction serves as a reminder that the notion of a "manifestation" can be taken in two distinct ways. It can be said that a thing manifests itself if it lets its presence be known even if it does not actually appear. In that case, it has manifested itself in something else or by means of something else, in the way that fire reveals its presence through the production of smoke. But one can also say that a thing manifests itself when it simply shows or reveals itself, in which case, the thing's manifestation is accomplished in its own activity and not merely in the *effects* of that activity. The difference can be made clearer by means of the distinction Wittgenstein draws between criteria and symptoms.[11] "How do you know what is the case in a given situation?" We answer this question by adducing phenomena. Our answer, however, will not have the same meaning when we take the phenomena we adduce to be *symptoms* of what is the case in the situation in question, that it will when we take them to be *criteria* for what is the case. For example: How do we know whether cats dream while they sleep? We will have to seek out *symptoms* that can provide our theory with a basis in induction. How do we know whether a student knows Latin? We ask him to translate a page of *De viris illustribus*. If he translates correctly, he knows Latin. There are two philosophies of this capability. For the mentalist, the external activity of translating is the symptom of the presence in the student of a mechanism or a cognitive state that explains his performance. Wittgenstein contested this conception. For him, the very notion of attributing a mental ability to someone—for example, the ability to understand Latin—is inseparable from the possibility of

giving one or more criteria for that ability: in our example, the manifestation of the ability in an act of translation. The relation between the im-
puted ability and its possible exercise is not one of cause to effect (or symptom) but an internal relation in which the application of one of these
concepts logically requires the application of the other.[12] To translate necessarily shows, in the very act of doing it, that one *can* translate, and to
be able to translate is precisely what we mean by knowing the language
whose sentences one translates. The cognitive attribute thus does not apply
to something in the mind of which we can only observe the external effects.
It applies to something that manifests itself or is expressed directly in a
public act.[13]

Applying these two dichotomies will allow us to contrast four different
philosophies and to draw out the lines of opposition among them.

	internal	*external*
direct	Philosophy of consciousness	Philosophy of intention (Intentionalism)
indirect	Theory of the unconscious	Theory of mental causes (Mentalism)

We should first verify that these theoretical possibilities resemble doctrines that have actually been put forth. Among the four conceptions, two
deserve to be elaborated. In our table, the philosophy of consciousness,
like the others, is allotted only one square, a quarter of the space. Yet this
is not commensurate with its importance in the history of ideas, where the
philosophy of consciousness, far from being one among many varieties of
mental philosophy, is the principal one. The theories of the unconscious
and of mental causes can be seen as attempts to correct the philosophy of
consciousness: first, by abandoning the idea that the phenomena in which
mind is manifest are its direct expressions, then, by taking a further step
and abandoning the so-called "first-person" perspective. These two conceptions may well call into question certain of the claims made by the
reflexive philosophy of consciousness. They nevertheless should be included, like the philosophy of consciousness, within mental philosophy.

The same cannot be said for the fourth possibility on our table, which
I've called "intentionalism." Intentionalism is the only possibility in the
contemporary philosophy of mind about which it can be said that it avoids
the paradoxes of (classical or recent) mental philosophy, for it is the only
one that rejects the idea that the basis for the autonomous reality of the
mind is its detachment from the world. This position is less familiar than
the three others. Since it is the position that I intend to defend in what
follows, it deserves a section of its own (see below, § 1.6).

1.4. The Philosophy of Consciousness

A philosophy of consciousness holds that the phenomena of mind manifest themselves directly: that the mind is given to itself in the self-presence called consciousness. These phenomena are, therefore, only given internally, i.e., in the interiority of a subject whose mental life may represent the external world but is otherwise unaffected by it.

It may seem normal or somewhat obvious to us that the principal characteristic of the mind (*mens*) is cogitation, i.e., the activity of directing its attention to various things. Yet, this idea was found to be surprising the first time it was put forth. Moreover, the first French translators of Descartes were reluctant to use the French word "*conscience*" [consciousness] to translate the Latin text where he claimed that "we are conscious." It is as if they saw the eccentricity of this usage. For example, the definition of "thought" (*cogitatio*) proposed by Descartes was rendered by his French translators as follows[14]:

> In the noun "thought," I include everything that is inside us in such a way that we are immediately cognizant of it. Thus, all of the operations of the will, the understanding, the imagination, and the senses are thoughts. But I included the word "immediately" in order to exclude those things that follow from and depend on our thoughts: for example, voluntary movement has, in truth, its principle in the will, yet it is nevertheless not a thought.[15]

This definition of thought is as remarkable in what it excludes as in what it includes. It excludes action (voluntary movement) from thought. Yet it includes in thought both willing and sensation. Thereafter, to think that I am walking is mental, to want to walk is mental, but the action of walking with the aim of arriving where I've decided to go is only an effect of the mental. To walk is not "to think." On the other hand, to will is an act of thinking. Even feeling—the experience of pain, for example—is an act of thinking.

The novelty and strangeness of the conditions that Descartes placed on consciousness become immediately obvious when one considers the misinterpretations to which they gave rise among his first readers. Gassendi, for example, in his objection to the second *Meditation*, asks why Descartes privileged an intellectual act. Why did Descartes feel the need to use "all this apparatus"[16] in order to prove his existence? Without a doubt, if I think, I exist. But, according to Gassendi, *any* action could have provided the required premise: for example, if I am walking, I exist. Descartes protested that Gassendi had completely misunderstood his reasoning, going so far as to write:

I may not, for example, make the inference "I am walking, therefore I exist," except in so far as the awareness [*conscientia*] of walking is a thought. The inference is certain only if applied to this awareness, and not to the movement of the body which sometimes—in the case of dreams—is not occurring at all, despite the fact that I seem to myself to be walking. Hence from the fact that I think I am walking I can very well infer the existence of a mind which has this thought, but not the existence of a body that walks.[17]

But is it right to say that the conclusion of the inference "I am walking, therefore I exist" is not a good one? At first glance—and even after having thoroughly considered the question—Gassendi would seem to be right: the inference that moves from "I am walking" to "I exist" is an excellent one. Yet it ought to be clear that Descartes's response to his critic is not given from an exclusively logical point of view. Gassendi's error, in Descartes's view, is to have failed to take methodical doubt seriously (a mistake made by many of Descartes's readers, and not always the least attentive among them). Gassendi does not see that the meditative subject cannot use the premise "I am walking" precisely because he had rejected in advance any premise that could lead him into error. If, for Descartes, Gassendi's conclusion is incorrect, it is because the fact of walking does not have the kind of certainty required by the Method's extraordinary strictures.

Whatever an exegete might say to explain Descartes's response, it is nonetheless the case that Gassendi is right on the logical point. The inference "I am walking, therefore I exist" has the same logical force as does "I am thinking, therefore I exist." In both cases, there is an action that presupposes an agent. Yet the dispute between the two philosophers helps us better understand that only by becoming a mental phenomenon—a thought—can the act of walking enter into Cartesian reasoning. Not, of course, that taking a walk is somehow tantamount to thinking (or, more precisely, that walking is the embodiment of the thought of a possible walk) but in the sense that to be conscious of walking is to think that one is walking, regardless of what the fact of the matter is. This is the source of the troubling quality of a Cartesian consciousness for us. If I am consciously walking, and not sleepwalking, I am conscious of the fact that I am walking. No one will be surprised that the philosopher of consciousness expresses himself in this way. Indeed, he seems to derive his philosophy from simple common sense. But, when this same philosopher of consciousness goes on to claim that to *dream* that I am walking is also to be conscious that I am walking, he talks in a disconcerting way. Of what am I conscious if I can be conscious of taking a walk when I am not actually walking, i.e., when there is no walk of which I can be conscious? In order to serve as a premise in the argument of the *cogito*, it need only be consciousness or, as the translator chose to put it, an internal "awareness." Is taking a walk in thought or in a dream just a different way of walking? One may as well maintain that meals eaten in thought or solutions worked out in dreams are the equivalents—at least from the perspective of a thinking consciousness—of meals eaten at tables and solutions worked out in reality. How is one to distinguish between *consciousness* that one is walking and an *illusion* that one is walking? Descartes stresses the fact that his conception of the thinking consciousness was never meant to vouchsafe the fact of taking an actual walk (a physical event) but only of the presentation to the mind of something that is taken to be a walk (a mental event). Whether I am indeed walking or just deluded, a representation of myself in the act of walking will be given to me as my intentional object (*cogitatum*). And that is all that can be immediately present to the mind. It clearly follows that consciousness of walking is never consciousness that a walk is actually taking place, even in the case where my body is in fact taking a walk at the same time that I experience a representation of myself walking. Such is, in the end, the meaning of the separation between the internal world of the mind and the external world of bodies: the object of knowledge is not the walk I take but the mental phenomenon of consciousness of walking.

If cognitivism is, as Fodor suggests, the philosophical descendant of Descartes's philosophy of representational consciousness, the consequences for it are immediately obvious: the psychology of a representing mind is a cognitive psychology but *without cognition proper*. What it calls "cognition" is not something that would be expressed by a sentence like: "I know what I am doing: I am walking." Its conception of cognition is modeled on the Cartesian idea of consciousness as a pure "internal cognizance": a system is the locus of a process of cognition because its structure allows it to be immediately aware of the presence within it of cognitive entities, i.e., internal representations. What makes these entities "cognitive" is not that they make known to the system that it is walking. For they do not do this. Rather, they are cognitive because they give the system the *representation* of what would be the case if it were walking. In order for it to be the case, the system would have to be associated with a body, and this body would have to be in the state indicated by the representation communicated to the mind. Is it? Whether it is or is not cannot be directly represented to it. The mind of an organism cannot ascertain whether the organism's representation of walking is real or a dream, just as a computer cannot recognize whether the stroll, of which it is calculating a function, is real or a simulation.[18]

For all its flaws, the fact remains that the cognitivist philosophy of mind freed psychology of the first-person perspective. This was undeniably a step forward. Does this mean that the philosophy of consciousness has today disappeared? Hardly, for it is alive and well, sometimes in the systematic form of a philosophy of the subject, sometimes in the identification that many researchers automatically make between the mental and the data of introspection. Jean-Pierre Changeux, for example, in a book that aims to acquaint the reader not only with the current state of scientific research into the nervous system but with his own theory of "epigenesis by selective stabilization of synapses," takes up just such a perspective in order to raise the question of the relationship between the "neural" and the "mental."[19] This is the aim of Changeux's chapter 5, entitled "Mental Objects." It is interesting to note that this book, which is rightly celebrated for the great clarity of its presentation of difficult subjects, nevertheless contains one section whose obscurity frustrates even the most attentive reader: precisely the chapter where the author has moved from discussion of neurons and the organization of the brain to what he calls "mental objects," i.e., mental images and concepts. When Changeux talks of identifying "mental units" with "states of physical activity in neuronal assemblies,"[20] the reader has an understanding of the physical activities involved because the preceding chapters have explained them to him. But what are "mental units"? Where are we supposed to look for an understanding of this notion? Since when is a concept a mental entity with a corresponding neuronal configuration? The answer is apparently that the notion of a mental object is derived from the "introspective information." In short, the only philosophy of mind considered in this book is the old psychology of introspection, whose failings have often been noted.[21]

1.5. The Reforms of Mental Philosophy

Mental philosophy has not left in place its entire Cartesian inheritance. Among the elements that have been repudiated is the requirement that the mind's manifestations be given both directly and internally. Two reforms were needed, both of which are more correctly referred to as "theories." Because the mind is no longer given directly, it becomes what, in the philosophy of science, is called a "theoretical entity," i.e., an entity whose (hidden) presence and efficacy the theory invites us to postulate in order to account for observed phenomena. But the reader may find surprising the claim that there is a kinship between the theories of the unconscious or of the calculating mind, on the one hand, and the Cartesian legacy, on the other. This point merits a brief review here.

Are the *theories of the unconscious* critiques of consciousness? Do they call mental philosophy into question? On the contrary, it would appear that they are one of the most dynamic areas of mental philosophy. Thanks to certain spectacular controversies, we have grown accustomed to setting in opposition the philosophy of consciousness—the philosophy of the *co-*

gito—and the theories of the unconscious. These theories expressly present themselves as fostering ideas that subvert one of the founding orthodoxies of the established order. Yet the opposition between the philosophers of the *cogito* and the critics of consciousness is an optical illusion. The "critics of consciousness" are more like moralists or "psychological" writers (in the sense in which Nietzsche uses this term, i.e., in the same way that, in French, one refers to "moralists," who are observers of character and passions). What their critique calls into question is not the metaphysician's *cogito* but the good conscience of the acting individual who believes himself able, through sincere self-examination, to provide an accurate account of the real motivations of his conduct.

Theories of the unconscious call into question the discernment of the mental insight attributed by the philosophy of consciousness to all creatures endowed with apperception. But to challenge the idea that everything mental is conscious is to do nothing more than put forward the hypothesis that there are, beyond the field of consciousness, other mental events and operations about which the conscious subject knows nothing directly. This hypothesis does not exclude the possibility that a psychologist might indirectly learn something about those events and operations. Those unobserved operations and unconscious representations need do no more than make their effects evident within conscious life itself, manifesting themselves in the form of perturbations (for example, either the sudden emergence of incongruous elements or the unexpected absence of elements of which traces remain). Such perturbations allow the theory to reconstitute, by means of its explicative models, what goes on in the furthest reaches of the subject's mental life. For this theory, then, the phenomena of mind are internal but divided into two categories: the "superficial" phenomena that are immediately known to the subject, and the "deep" phenomena, which must be inductively inferred if one is truly to account for what is happening on the surface.

For the new *mentalist* philosophers, the phenomena of mind are also indirect: we observe behavioral phenomena and seek their satisfactory explanation. The behaviorist answer would be the right one if it were able to provide explanations without making hypotheses about the events taking place within the "black box" of the system whose behavior is being studied, between the external stimulation and the visible reaction. But the complexity of the behavior generated by the "black box" goes beyond anything that can be explained by the control exerted on the organism by the external environment. So hypotheses about the internal events of the system are required, and the new mentalist philosophy aims to provide them. For it, mental activity has nothing to do with a flux of consciousness experienced by a subject. Mental activity is the object of a theoretical hypothesis regarding the mental causes of the behavior of a physical system. It is as if this philosophy had inverted Descartes's perspective: I see a body that is walking and, as I am unable to explain its movements using theories applicable to billiard balls, I postulate that there is within this body a complex system which controls its observable movement. This system is called "mind." The problem for the theorist is then to find a satisfactory model for the mental, i.e., one that would allow him to conceive of an interaction between the physical and the mental.

It turns out that today's mentalist philosophy relies on the same conception of observable conduct as does the behaviorism it is at such pains to denounce: that behavior is a physical phenomenon whose cause must be sought. But it has the same conception of this cause as did yesterday's mentalist philosophy: that this cause is a mental process. Above all, this philosophy rehabilitates the theory of representative ideas, all the while insisting that these ideas are not ideal constructs but real cerebral entities.

1.6. The Philosophy of Intention

In our table of philosophies of mind, what I called "intentionalism" is the conception of mind characterized by the following phenomenology: the origins of the phenomena of mind are not internal, and the phenomena of mind are given directly (i.e., they are expressions, and not effects, of what they make manifest). The convergence of these two traits leads to the conclusion that a book, for example, is literally a mental commodity—and not in any derived sense. This obviously does not mean that a book thinks, reflects, draws conclusions, or in any way behaves like a thinking subject. Books are mental commodities because they express thoughts. In general terms, the relation between thought and language is not one of efficient causality. When we read a book, we do not proceed from the printed signs to the author's thought as we would from an effect to its cause. Whatever causality is at work is *formal* causality. The expression of thought in language and in action is not a mere index of mental life or the starting point of a deduction. It is, rather, the paradigmatic example of mental life.

That the phenomena of mind are not internal in origin does not exclude the possibility of their being internalized. Mental life can become an internal life. But that requires discipline. One can keep one's thoughts to oneself, read silently, or avoid expressing one's opinions. It is not clear, however, that these possibilities are open to every intelligent being. The experience of playing poker would suggests that this power is acquired through practice and maturity. Whatever the case, the fact that one can keep one's opinion secret or calculate in one's head offers no support to the doctrine of the interiority of mind, because such exploits are more complex than the corresponding ones of simply forming an opinion or carrying out a calculation.

Yet it may have been misleading to give the name "intentionalism" to the fourth possibility in my table of phenomenologies of mind. The fact that this possibility is called "the philosophy of intention" could be taken to suggest that other schools do not appeal to the concept of intention in their definition of the mental. Such a conclusion is obviously false. The phenomenological doctrine of the Husserlian school, for example, can legitimately claim to be a "philosophy of intention." Its partisans might rightly extol the crucial role that this philosophy has played in the revival of the philosophical theme of intention within contemporary thought. The phenomenological doctrine, as presented by Husserl in the *Cartesian Meditations*, is and seeks to be a philosophy of consciousness. For Husserlian phenomenologists, mental phenomena are the "lived experiences of consciousness" and have the structure of Cartesian consciousness described by the schema *ego-cogito-cogitatum*.[22] This school practices what it calls "phenomenological reduction": the separation of the mind (one might even say its "absolutization") in relation to the given. In much the same way, John Searle is today working out an analysis of the intentionality of the mental explicitly within the context of a definition of mind as consciousness.[23]

I will have to clarify the way in which the term "intentionalism" is here understood in order to account for the varied philosophies of intentionality. I borrow the term "intentionalism" from the contemporary philosophy of action.[24] Georg von Wright has distinguished two conceptions of practical intention, i.e., of the sort of intention by which one carries out an action. For the causalist, the concept of intention is that of a mental cause of the actor's behavior: to know the actor's intentions is to know the internal causes of his action. For the intentionalist, an intention cannot be understood as the cause of an action or a mental event distinct from the movements and gestures of the actor and which would then be their necessary and sufficient antecedent. Instead, for the intentionalist, a practical intention is *nothing other* than the action itself described in its mental aspect, i.e., in its distinctive teleology. As von Wright explains, the intentionalist sees an internal—conceptual or logical—relationship between the subject's intention and his action. But to speak of an internal or conceptual relationship between the two is another way of agreeing with Wittgenstein: an intentional action is not an *effect* of the actor's thought, it is an *expression* of it.

I will therefore reformulate my thesis as follows. My thesis is not that any philosophy for which the mental is defined by intention will in virtue of this fact occupy a distinct position in the table of phenomenologies of mind. Most contemporary philosophers, at least the analytic ones, have accepted what is called "Brentano's Thesis": that the mental is characterized by intentionality. My thesis is rather that a philosophy of intention is only complete if it can account for the relation between the logical and practical uses of the term "intention." The logical use originates in the technical vocabulary of scholastic logic.[25] This is the definition that Brentano took up and that was passed on to the Husserlian phenomenologists. The practical use is that elaborated by jurists and moralists in their analyses of the *actus humanus*. In both cases, the logical and the practical, the word "intention" is used in a technical sense, even where the practical usage also shows up in ordinary language. So my thesis ends up being the following: intentionalism, as the analysis of the different forms of intentionality, must take the practical usage of the word "intention" as its point of departure. This is why it must call into question the way that mental philosophy secures the reality of the mind, namely through the disassociation between things and their representations in a person's head.

The notion of *intentionality* was first used by the scholastics and then regained favor in the work of Brentano and his successors, notably the Husserlian phenomenologists. Only later was it adopted by philosophers in the analytic style, and then more in reference to Brentano than to Husserl. In contemporary writings, what is known as Brentano's Thesis is the following proposition, that can indeed be gleaned from his work on psychology: *Everything mental is intentional and everything intentional is mental.*[26]

The short passage from which Brentano's famous Thesis has been extracted is generally acknowledged to be exceedingly obscure.[27] All that can be derived from it are images that are themselves in need of interpretation. Mental phenomena are held to have as their distinctive trait the fact of being "oriented" toward something other than themselves, of having a "direction" or of possessing a kind of significance or capacity to refer to something else. The distinction drawn is apparently between physical phenomena, which are what they are and do not refer to anything, and psychical phenomena, which are what they are by being about something else.

Unfortunately, when we ask Brentanians or Husserlians what concept of intentionality we are supposed to derive from this passage, the answer is invariably couched either in misleading explanations or in images that are too vague to be of much help. Their analyses of mental intentionality are constructed along the lines of the famous saying according to which "all consciousness is consciousness of something." Thus, the intentionality of perception would correspond to the following: to perceive is always to perceive something. Similarly, the intentionality of love could be expressed thus: all love consists in loving something. Such formulas are in fact ambiguous. If we apply them not to mental acts or states of mind but to the *descriptions* of those acts and states, the formulas are irreproachable and provide the starting point for any analysis of intentionality. They highlight a fact about the language in which we ascribe mental action to someone: this language cannot contain just a verb, but must also have a direct or indirect object specifying the content of the verb. To say that "someone is imagining" is elliptical until one has specified *what* is being imagined, the object of the person's imagination. What conclusion can we draw from this analysis of the language of the mental regarding the analysis of the mental itself? It is in making this step that formulas like "Every *cogitatio* is a *cogitatio* of a *cogitatum*" become misleading. They have the flaw of covering up the decisive issue by conflating the intentionality of acts or mental states with a certain grammatical *transitivity* or property by which certain verbs require a direct object. Yet the notion of intentionality is useful precisely to the extent that it allows us to avoid conflating the grammar of psychological verbs (like "to perceive" or "to love") with those of ordinary transitive verbs. From a purely linguistic point of view, the grammar of the verb "to seek" cannot be distinguished from that of the verb "to find." Both require an object. But, from a logical perspective, the philosopher cannot help but notice the following difference: it cannot be true that someone has found something unless there is a something that he has found; but it can be true that someone is seeking something without there being any real entity that is what he seeks. For example, someone can seek the solution to a problem that is in fact insoluble. Or he can seek a dog's owner when the dog is in fact a stray. As a result, in our example, the formula for intentionality would have to be the following: Every finding is surely the finding of something, and that is why the verb "to find" *is not* (or not entirely) intentional. For one cannot find unless there is something that is the object that one finds. By contrast, one can easily seek without there being anything at all that is the object of one's seeking. Thus every case of seeking *is not* about something else, and this is what makes the verb "to seek" fully intentional.

The classic formulas for intentionality construe it as a complication of the relationship between subject and object. They thereby mask or attenuate what should really be emphasized: that intentionality is in no way a kind of transitivity.[28] But if we reject the misleading formulas that present intentionality as a transitive quality of mental acts, we are left with little more than the images that accompanied that definition. These images, though often brilliant, give us no purchase on the analysis of intentions. They have nothing but a polemical force: they set in opposition, for example, the "openness" of a mind characterized by intentionality and the "closed" quality of the classic representational subject's mental world, with the latter being incapable of moving beyond the compass of its mental

images or ideas. Or they draw a contrast between the disquiet and enthusiasm that are constitutive of the subject of intentions, on the one hand, and
a kind of torpor or dazed satisfaction with things, one that can never be
drawn "outside of itself" (or "torn," as is also said, out of its "imma-
nence"), on the other. Such images should not be taken to be analyses,
though it must be acknowledged that they provide a forceful expression of
the expectations of those they inspire. The explanation for the enthusiasm
demonstrated by several generations of French philosophers for the ideas
of Husserl and Heidegger seems to me not to lie in any profound assimilation of the technical and conceptual aspects of the difficult doctrines propounded by the masters. Rather, this enthusiasm can be better explained
by their prior adherence, based on such suggestive stylistic figures, to a
philosophy whose rationale was far from being grasped but about which
it was understood that it promised to overcome the psychologism and representationism inherited from classical philosophy. So it was that Jean-
Paul Sartre, in his famous article on intentionality in Husserl, won an
entire generation of young philosophers over to the cause of phenomenology by presenting Husserl's thought as a doctrine of life in the wide open
spaces, which he skillfully contrasted with the reclusive existence that academic idealism would force us to adopt.[29]

If we are going to take an image as our point of departure, we might as
well return to the one that lies at the origin of the philosophical acceptation
of the term "intention." The image is that of the archer who aims his arrow
at a target, a deer, say. This is still only an image, but one that at least
allows us to sketch out a preliminary analysis to illustrate the main conceptual oppositions. The situation of the archer aiming at a deer is characterized by the *distance* that separates him from the animal. This distance has
not yet been traversed, and there has not yet been contact between the two
in the way that there will be if the arrow is released and hits its mark. It
is not even certain that the distance will ever be traversed, given that the
archer may well miss his mark. Are we ready to say that the distance is
traversed in the mind, or in the archer's intention? To do so would be to
hastily assimilate the archer's thought to a kind of mental arrow that has
in some way already hit its mark and that is immediately in contact with
the target, while the physical arrow still has some work to do in order to
reach its destination. Moreover, it may well be that the archer has not
properly aimed his weapon or that he has not gotten a clear view of what
he is aiming at.

In a word, the language of intention ushers in the distinction between
failure and success, between correct and flawed orientation. The question
of whether the archer has properly aimed his arrow is answered when the
arrow hits something. Has the archer hit what he was aiming at? If we

consider the question from outside, without taking his intentions into account, we will have to answer that, by definition, he has hit what he aimed his arrow at: what he was aiming at is the first object we find that intersects the line describing the direction of the arrow. Such description could be called "external" or "material." It leaves aside the intentionality of the archer's behavior because it sees things from what, in logic, is called an "extensional" point of view. In other words, this description is an answer to the question, what is in relation with what in this case?

If we assess the situation from the point of view of the intentions or meanings at work, we will make a distinction between successes and failures: is the thing that the archer in fact hit what he intended to hit when he drew his bow as he did? Or did he make a mistake? It should be noted that there are several ways of making a mistake, for example by shooting the arrow someplace other than where the deer is located or by hitting, say, a dog when he thought he was shooting at a deer.

The same could be said of linguistic activities. Someone can write a letter addressed to the Director of the Opera and in so doing believe that he is writing to X when his letter will in fact be received by Y who, unbeknownst to the letter writer, has replaced X as Director of the Opera. The letter is here like an epistolary arrow. Someone can also speak of the Director of the Opera and believe he is speaking about X when he is in fact speaking of Y. Finally, someone can think (either out loud or to himself) about the Director of the Opera. The problem of intentionality is then one of knowing whether he is thinking about X, about Y, or about neither of them in particular. The solution is that thought is not a mental arrow. Therefore, a thought about the Director of the Opera is about nobody in particular and, in this sense, *has no object*, since it bears on whichever person happens to occupy the position at the moment in question. When somebody thinks about the present Director of the Opera, there is no relationship between a subject and an object but simply the determination of the act of thought by an intellectual content.[30]

The main lesson to be drawn from these observations is that the problems raised by the intentionality of action are not essentially distinguishable from problems raised by the intentionality of language or the intentionality of mental acts.[31] Solving analogous difficulties will thus require similar analyses.

The consequence of this is that a philosophy of mind that defines the mental by intentionality will have to be a philosophy of action as much as a philosophy of purely intellectual operations. Many philosophers have, as it happens, come to this conclusion. In *Content and Consciousness*, for example, Daniel Dennett is reluctant to treat the verbs "hunt" and "search" as what he calls "mental terms."[32] He prefers to call them "psychological terms," with the result that Brentano's Thesis applies to both the mental and the psychological. Donald Davidson, by contrast, is not troubled by such considerations. Intentional action is part of the mental because it successfully passes the "test of the mental" proposed by Brentano's Thesis.[33] Lion hunting is mental just as is representational painting, not because it takes place entirely in one's head or because painting is not done on a canvas but because both require sustained attention, calculation, and an order of operations that allows one to make adjustments, corrections, and coordinations that render the result the work of an agent.

These remarks on intentionality would obviously be inadequate if our aim here were to articulate the logic of intentional grammatical constructions. They nonetheless provide us with a first sketch of intentionalism, a doctrine that not only defines the mental by intentionality but includes action itself within the mental, rather than construing it, in the Cartesian way, as a consequence or effect of mental processes. Descartes's philosophy of mind presupposes a definition of thought (*cogitatio*) that excludes action itself from the mental, in order to retain only the will. Intentionalist philosophy, by contrast, escapes from the gravitational field of mental philosophy precisely by conceiving the philosophy of mind as a philosophy of action.

The principal trait seems to me to be this: if both gestures and mental acts are intentional in an analogous way—in that both "aim at" something—then one cannot continue to conceive of intentionality as a relation between subject and object. Indeed, the word "object" is ambiguous if we are supposed to believe that thinking of Pierre is a relation between a subject and an object (Pierre) and that planning a trip to Italy is also a relation between a subject and an object (a trip to Italy). If we say that these are different types of objects within a more general category of objects in general, we would be doing nothing more than insisting that the conceptual scheme based on transitivity be applied in all cases: not only in cases of ordinary transitivity, but also in cases of intransitivity, which will have to be held to be cases of extraordinary transitivity. In fact, if we were to take at face value the apparent transitivity of intentional verbs, we would have to say that the act signified by such verbs *always has an object even when it doesn't*. When I plan to take a trip to Italy, my planning has an object even if, in the end, I abandon my plans and even if, as a result, there is no trip to Italy that I planned to take.[34]

In order to understand intentionality, it is more worthwhile to follow the lines of analysis suggested by the metaphor of the archer. If the arrow has a direction, and if the bow is drawn in a position so that the weapon is pointed at something, it is because the archer has given his bow this direction for a reason. Drawing his bow is indeed a transitive action, but the object to which this act transitively applies is the bow, not the deer. On the other hand, the way that the bow is drawn is dictated by the goal, which is to hit the deer by releasing the arrow.

More generally, intentionality is the mark of the mental because it is a *phenomenon of order*. The archer carries out his movements in a certain order, whether viewed from a synchronic or diachronic point of view. The coordination of these movements is intelligible and can be explained by a rational principle: his movements are carried out one after another (or simultaneously) so that the arrow will go toward the target.

Now imagine that you return home and find a strange object in front of your door, a package, say. If it is there by chance or has simply been forgotten by someone, then its presence at your door has no particular significance: it is a brute fact of physical presence. If, however, you understand that the package has been left there so that you will notice it on your return home, or if you understand that it is there so that the plastic explosives it contains will destroy your apartment, you will conclude that the package is in its proper place where it is. It is in its proper place for whoever left it there for you, even if it is not in the place where you would prefer that it be (in which case, you will probably try to move it). An intentional phenomenon is at work whenever a disposition of things can be seen not as the result of the history of each of these things taken separately, but as the result of a thought that embraces an entire set of facts.

Understood in this way, "mind" is not primarily defined by consciousness or representation but by order and finality. *Mentality*—what makes it the case that something or someone has a mind—is then conceived as the power of producing an *order of meaning* somewhere. The important thing is not the place where this order is realized: it may be within, in the interiority of immanent activity; or it may be without, on paper, for example. The multiplicity that is to be ordered may be a flux of mental images or perhaps a set of memorized data (as in the activity of reflection). The multiplicity can be a set of gestures and operations to be carried out with the arms, legs, and torso (as when one serves the ball in tennis). In any case, the notion of intentionality refers to a power of mind. We might follow Leibniz here in calling this power an "architectonic" capacity. Many philosophers of mind think of the mind in Hobbesian terms according to which to think is to calculate.[35] Leibniz proposes an alternative image of the mind as a constructor rather than a calculator. To think may well be to manipulate symbols, but it is above all to invent an order in which they take on a meaning or to find an arrangement in which they offer a solution to a problem we have put to ourselves.

> For, not to mention the wonders of dreams, in which we invent without effort (but also without will) things we could only discover after much thinking when awake, our soul is architectonic in its voluntary activities also, and,

discovering the sciences in accordance with which God had regulated things (*pondere, mensura, numero*, etc.), it imitates in its own sphere, and in the little world in which it is allowed to act, what God performs in the great world.[36]

This text calls for two clarifications, however. First, it would have been better to say that a *man* can organize his conduct relative to a goal, in order to avoid suggesting that the architect of the actions a person accomplishes is not the person himself but a separate subject (the soul). Second, Leibniz's theological analogy seems to reverse the order of things, for the idea of an order imposed on things is entirely anthropomorphic. Man is not thought of in theological terms by being endowed with an architectonic power. Rather, divine power is conceived in human terms when it is compared to that of an architect.[37] Yet Leibniz nevertheless splendidly highlights the fact that the problem of the mind is a problem of architecture.

．　．　．

In this chapter, I have maintained that a philosophy of mind must begin with a phenomenology of mind in the modest sense, i.e., with a response to this preliminary question: Where are mental phenomena given, and how do they manifest what they manifest? The conflicts among the various philosophies of mind are primarily about what is appropriately called a "mental phenomenon."

Accepting the classification of the conceptions of mind that I proposed earlier allows us to restate the entire philosophical problem of mind as a question regarding the relationship between the mental and the practical. In what way can a walk be characterized as mental? Is a mental stroll one that is carried out only "in thought" in the same way that a mental calculation is done in one's head rather than on paper? To calculate mentally counts as calculating just as surely as does calculating with a pencil on paper, yet a walk taken only "in thought" is no walk at all. Reflections of this kind may lead us to call into question the Cartesian division between thought (consciousness) and action (movement). A walk is a mental phenomenon if it is carried out with an objective and a goal. The movements of a walker are mental, not in the Cartesian sense in which these movements are what the walker is conscious of doing (whether rightly or wrongly), but in the intentionalist sense that they are what the walker thinks he must do in order to carry out his intention to walk. In this light, a walk is a mental act because the fact of walking is intentional. Yet the intentionality of walking is not to be found in a relationship between the walker and an intentional object: in, say, a purported relation of belief with the proposition "I am walking." Such a claim takes us back to the representationism we have already rejected. The intentionality of a walk must be sought in the intelligible order given to all of the gestures and undertakings that make up the walker's tack. These movements are governed by the thought of the walk to be taken and not, for example, by the thought of having to get to one's place of business.

There is, of course, a dissident strain of phenomenology which has sought to work out a philosophy of intention outside of the framework put in place by the philosophies of representational consciousness.[38] One cannot but applaud the motivations behind this dissidence: the notion of intentionality cannot be of a *relation* between a subject and an object. But this brand of phenomenology, which at one point was called "the phenomenology of existence," has, in my view, failed to live up to its promise precisely because it reinstated in an enhanced form the very subject/object schema that it was at such pains to reject. It has continued to assume that intentional verbs are *transitive* verbs.[39] In so doing, the phenomenology of existence has only added to the considerable difficulties faced by a conception of intentionality that sees the mental act as one that transcends the sphere of the subject.[40] Those difficulties are compounded by a doctrine that sees intentional verbs as transitive ones yet whose direct object resembles nothing that can be designated *as* an object. That said, it is true that it is often difficult to determine who has and has not understood the theses of the "existential analytic." I make no claim to have grasped the intricacies of this doctrine, and would ask only to be enlightened by those who have been convinced by it, assuming they are willing to explain it.

We have seen how the determination of the phenomena of mind is a function of how one sees the relationship between someone's mental activity and his behavior. If action is exterior to the mental, the relation is that between apparent effect and latent cause: the corporeal movements of a subject are then symptoms of his mental life. If, however, action is included within the mental, the behavior is rather the *expression* of mental life. I have attempted to show that the discussions of this issue in contemporary philosophy of mind derive from a tradition of thought that goes back to the origins of modern philosophy. The novelty of today's terminology and arguments ought not disguise the enduring nature of the problem.

The subject of these discussions is essentially this: What do we expect from an explanation of someone's conduct in terms of his thoughts and intentions? In other words, what sort of explanation do we expect a science of mind to provide? Here again, the contrast is clear. It is as if mental philosophy feels itself duty bound to work towards the creation of a science of mind. If it ever establishes the principles of such a science, it will have accomplished for the mind what natural philosophy achieved long ago. Though the partisans of mental philosophy readily acknowledge that we do not yet have a science of mind that meets their expectations, they often seem to believe that its appearance is imminent. By contrast, intentionalist philosophers believe that there is no need for speculation about what a science of mind will be or ought to be. Our concept of mind does not exist in a void: it is the general name of a vast network of concepts used by people to explain themselves and to talk to one another. Moreover, these concepts have already been subject to a certain systematization, particularly in the rhetorical arts as used by judges and lawyers, political orators, and historians. The application of these kinds of concepts to the material furnished by historical experience is the daily bread of the *moral sciences*, so called because they are the study of mores, the ways of doing and thinking of various people. For the intentionalist, the sciences of mind are to be found nowhere else.

Two Sciences?

2.1. The Sciences of the Mind

Over the last twenty years or so, the mention of a "science of the mind" in a program of study or the title of a scholarly work has usually referred to the "cognitive sciences" and thus to the utilization of analogies between human intelligence and artificial intelligence. A contemporary reader devoid of ideological baggage might wrongly believe that there is no relation between this sort of science of the mind and what German writers usually call the "sciences of the mind" (*Geisteswissenschaften*), namely, other than psychology, such disciplines as anthropology, political economy, law, history, philology, and aesthetics. In fact, it is impossible to accord psychology a place among the sciences without at the same time ordering all of these other disciplines relative to one another, thereby determining which of them are to be excluded from or included in the domain of science properly so-called. This is the case not because psychology must be seen as the foundation or point of entry into the sciences of the mind, but because the status of psychology is necessarily a disputed one, to such an extent that the mere fact that someone calls himself a "psychologist" tells us very little about the kind of researcher he might be. We wait for him to add a qualification: Gestalt psychologist, depth psychologist, cognitive psychologist, or perhaps something else again.

We know that the word *Geisteswissenschaft* was used, if not for the first time then at least for the first time in a systematic way, to translate into German the term "moral sciences" used by John Stuart Mill in his *System of Logic*.[1] The book's sixth part concerns "The Logic of the Moral Sciences." It contains a discussion of the classification of the sciences proposed by Auguste Comte, who had himself taken up and systematized the Enlightenment project of a positive science of the human mind, but rejected the idea that psychology might be that science. Against Comte, Mill sought to reinstate psychology as a real science of the mind. He thus remained faithful to the ideas of his father, James Mill, who had defended the theory of associationism in his *Analysis of the Phenomena of the Human Mind* (1829). Dilthey, in his *Introduction to the Human Sciences [Geisteswis-*

senschaften], applauded John Stuart Mill for having moved beyond Comte's narrow empiricism, but remained unsatisfied with the methodological monism that Mill adopted from Comte.[2] Dilthey replaced their positivistic monism with a dualism divided between naturalistic and hermeneutic disciplines, with psychology serving to bridge the gap between them.

The expression "moral science," which exists in English, also has a long history in the French tradition, since it is one of the names given to the science of man heralded at the end of the eighteenth century. The law of the 3 Brumaire, year IV (October 25, 1795), which founded the Institut de France,[3] envisioned a second division for the "moral and political sciences," to fit between the physical and mathematical sciences (first division) and the combination of literature and the beaux-arts (third division). This division is itself divided into the following sections: "analysis of sensations and ideas, morals, social science and legislation, political economy, history, geography." Henri Gouhier, from whom I have taken these details, points out that Napoleon was quick to eliminate the second division (in 1803), perhaps because he saw it as nothing more than philosophy, which he sought to eliminate, "disguised as moral and political science."[4] Gouhier's comments on the "academic philosophy" of the Ideologues are worth dwelling on. He reminds us that the project of a scientific psychology is, as we would say today, a research program, one that is born with what might be called, following Gouhier's excellent suggestion, the second Modernity.

> For there is an academic philosophy whose meaning is suggested by the names that were given to the second class in the Institut de France and its sections. The terms "moral sciences," "political sciences," and "social sciences" call to mind the dream of that century: to make the knowledge of man as scientific as the knowledge of nature. Above all, by getting rid of the word "philosophy" and substituting for it the "analysis of sensations and ideas," the legislator gave official recognition to the idea that the scientific study of the human mind began in France with Condillac following the historic break that made Locke the father of modern thought and that made the century of Descartes, Malebranche, Leibniz, and Spinoza into a second Antiquity.[5]

What better way to say that the expression "moral science," here and later on in Mill's work, was not at first distinguished from the sciences of nature? Rather, it initially suggested the project of extending the methods of the physical sciences to the study of man and his mind. In other words, reference to "moral sciences" did not imply, as it later would, that one had staked out a position in the debate about the unity or duality of scientific methods, a debate about *explanation* and *understanding*. The designated program of the section of the Institut that ended up replacing philosophy is what we have been calling a "mental philosophy," whose aim is indeed to develop an "experimental physics of the soul."[6]

My aim in this brief historical contextualization is not just to temper the feeling of novelty or originality that has often accompanied the successive projects for a scientific psychology. I also want to stress that these projects are necessarily responses to a profound need of those living in the "second Modernity," since no failure or disappointment seems able to put an end to them. So it is that even today one can read books in which the successive failures of several generations of philosophers to present even an intelligible "materialist theory of the mind" is presented as the onward march of a discipline in the process of formation, one which, even if it has no results as yet, is nevertheless endowed with a rich scientific bibliography.

In this chapter, I will present what I see as the current state of the question. Since my aims are not historical, I will not discuss the earlier stages in the debate surrounding the ideas of a science of man or a science of the mind. The current state of play can be described through a comparison of the terms in which the distinction between "explanation" and "understanding" was discussed at the turn of the century with the terms in which this distinction is currently debated. At the end of the nineteenth century, at the stage of the debate just previous to the current one, the contrast was drawn between the hermeneutic method of the moral sciences and the positivist method of the natural sciences. For our part, we are already able to draw several lessons from the most recent stage of the debate, which has been expressed in the idiom of analytic philosophy.

2.2. Intentionalism

The term "intentionalism" was used earlier to designate a school in the philosophy of mind. I borrowed this term from Georg von Wright, who draws a contrast between "intentionalist" and "causalist" philosophies of action.[7] In order to understand this distinction, we must first briefly recall the terms of the question that divides philosophers with regard to the causation of action.[8]

The basis of the dispute can be put as follows: Causalists do not see how an action can be explained by the intentions of the actor unless this intention itself is part of a causal chain that results in the production of the gestures and movements by which the action is carried out. In other words, the causalist requires that explanations by means of aims, or teleological explanations, be translated into explanations by means of antecedents, or causal explanations. Otherwise, the causalist maintains, it will have to be admitted that an aim—a state of things that the actor seeks to produce and that therefore does not yet exist—can produce effects. The future would be able to make the present transform itself so as to assume the desired configuration. Consider, for example, an architect who plans to build a house. Because the house to be built does not yet exist, it has no purchase on the present factors of its production other than that afforded by the architect's vision. This vision is at the moment given only in the architect's mental activity. Teleological explanation therefore must be a short way of appealing to the causality of representations: the project of building the house must have won out in the architect's mind over other possibilities for the use of his time. Here again we encounter the classic way of accounting for actions carried out in pursuit of a goal: they are actions carried out *under the effect* of a previously formed representation.

By contrast, the intentionalist does not see how an intention could be a mental cause of the action. In order to be a mental cause in the required sense of the word "cause," the intention with which I carry out my action would have to be a mental event prior to the accomplishment of the action. But this gives rise to two objections. First, it is not necessary for the intention with which an action is carried out to give rise to a mental event distinct from the action itself. Of course it often happens that one forms an intention through prior reflection and then moves into action. But, still more frequently do we intentionally carry out movements without having first planned out these movements through some prior calculation. Second, and this is Wittgenstein's main objection, it is a grammatical category mistake to conceive of intention as a kind of event or mental episode. When we say that someone intends to become a doctor, we are not referring to a mental act that took place at a given moment and by which his conduct is caused. We are referring to the continuous subordination of his efforts and decisions to a goal, one that need not, in order to be *his* goal, be constantly present to his mind. For the intentionalist, this order that subordinates means to an end provides the concept of intention with its content.

The debate over intentionalism and causalism is one about the structure of action. In his now-classic book *Explanation and Understanding*, von Wright showed that analytic philosophy of action had taken up and recast in its own style the nineteenth-century debate regarding the unity or duality of scientific method. The resemblance is obvious: Are the teleological explanations usually offered by historical and social disciplines real explanations, or are they instead elliptical ways of alluding to explanations by means of mechanisms? The first response is reminiscent of the hermeneutic school's methodological dualism; the second of the positivist school's methodological monism. Which is why von Wright chose to title his book as he did. At the time of its appearance, this book did much to reopen lines of communication between national traditions of contemporary philosophy that had remained isolated from one another after the First World War. In it, von Wright offered a taxonomy of the major strands, revealing hitherto unnoticed affinities among them. We have for some time, he points out, set logical positivism and idealistic or phenomenological currents of thought in opposition to one another. Yet positivism was positivist before it became logical: in many ways it is a matter of historical chance that an alliance was formed in Austria between the positivist ideal and modern logic.[9] It is therefore misleading to define analytic philosophy as positivism and to act as though non-positivist thought must *ipso facto* be non-analytic thought.[10] In reality, von Wright explains, it has become increasingly clear that there are two poles of analytic philosophy: the heirs of the Vienna Circle and those of the second Wittgenstein. At the end of the 1960s, when von Wright was writing his book, it had become customary to set two analytic philosophies of language in opposition: one that continues the project of a "formal semantics" (in the tradition of Carnap), and Oxonian "ordinary language philosophy."[11] In hindsight, this opposition now appears to have been a local one. The claim that it was the expression of a deep tension within the philosophy of the time was itself somewhat provincial. The polarity that von Wright uncovered, however, was much more instructive. For it is clear that the debate between causalists and intentionalists is indicative of a profound difficulty not only for professional philosophers but for our entire culture. Which is why that debate makes it possible for us to envisage the instruments of philosophical analysis being used to consider and clear up real problems in several domains and, in particular, the classic problem of method in the sciences of the mind. This also explains the title of his book, which is an allusion to the debate over method within late-nineteenth-century German philosophy.

Who are the intentionalists, outside of von Wright himself? Among works that had then been recently published, he cites as particularly representative those by Elizabeth Anscombe and Charles Taylor.[12] The two books were in many ways complementary. Anscombe's book extricates the concept of intention from the causalist psychology of mental events, using reflection on the *logic* of practical inference—which moves from the desired end to the means to be employed—to uncover the characteristics of the concept of intentional action. For his part, Taylor showed how all of the attempts to treat behavior without applying forms of teleological explanation to it have failed. When a behaviorist thinks he has done so, he has merely hidden the teleology of the object under consideration by, for example, shifting it into the experimental situation itself. He has not dispensed with it. The very concept of a psychological comportment is teleological. The behaviorist claims to have eliminated from his conceptual apparatus all of the shadowy notions "from a bygone era," by speaking of nothing but observable behavior. He avoids saying that the rat *believes* it will find sugar at the end of the passageway or that the rat *hopes* to escape from the maze. If such a psychologist were to show even greater consistency and rule out saying that the rat *is looking for* sugar or behaves in such a way as to *avoid* electrical shocks, animal psychology would have nothing left to study.

2.3. Explanation and Understanding

What is striking about von Wright's characterization of the intentionalist school is the surprising—some might say incongruous—alliance between Aristotle and Wittgenstein. Wittgenstein provides the idea that intention should be studied in its expressions, in the description of intentional action. Aristotle provides the ideas of practical rationality and finality. Is this anything more than the fortuitous confluence of two different sources of inspiration in the work of a few philosophers, both Aristotelians who happened to be students of Wittgenstein and his heirs and Wittgensteinians who took the time to read Aristotle?

I hope to convince the reader that this alliance, far from being explained by the biographies of those who promote it, has solid grounds in a philosophical principle. But in order to demonstrate this, I will have to move away from the position defended in von Wright's book. Von Wright chose to underline the affinities between intentionalism and the ideas of the hermeneutic school, reminding us of the idealist (Hegelian and Neo-Kantian) origins of that school. This perspective allows him to suggest that the philosophical family tree could be revised in the following way: instead of drawing a border between analytic philosophers and phenomenologists, the border would run between a positivist school and a hermeneutic one, the latter made up of two wings (or two parts), the dialectical hermeneutics of Gadamer, Apel, and Habermas, and the analytic hermeneutics that comes out of Wittgenstein.[13]

The problem with this classification is that it leads to an overestimation of certain affinities (like those that are often held to comprise the "linguistic turn," as if all the alleged participants were speaking about language in the same way, or even in related ways). As a result, we lose sight of something decisive that von Wright himself has done much to bring to light. The methodological dualism of explanation and understanding pertains to a distinction to be drawn between the natural sciences and the sciences of the mind. But the question of teleology is not limited to one or the other of these disciplines: it arises in nature as it does in history. In other words, the central question raised by the distinction between the natural and hermeneutic sciences is one of knowing whether we are looking for laws, as we are in astronomy, or meanings, as we are in philology. But, for an intentionalist, this is not the crucial question. The question is rather one of knowing whether a teleological system exhibits a natural teleology or an intentional teleology.

The difference, if it exists, is considerable. What is at stake is the very sense of the contrast between two modes of apprehending something. In order to understand this point, we need only ask the partisans of hermeneutic dualism the grounds for their distinction. Here I will only consider the canonical version of the distinction, without taking up its many variants. I take my representative formulation from the version given by Raymond Aron, which has the advantage of being an exposition of the hermeneutic distinction by one of its partisans, one who takes it on himself to bring out the doctrine's strengths in his usually clear way.

The two domains of scientific inquiry are delineated as follows: natural phenomena are not directly intelligible, whereas the phenomena of human behavior are. In the first case, we will seek natural laws. In the second case, we are able to understand the meaning of a particular human action without the mediation of a general principle. The notion of understanding is thus held to have a negative relation to the notion of explanation: outside of that relation, it might be said to be immediately comprehensible. But we might well ask whether such an opposition is coherent.

Since the distinction drawn by the hermeneutic school does not correspond to a difference reflected in ordinary language, it is important that we concentrate on the examples given by the defenders of methodological dualism. Here is an example put forth by Aron:

> In the case of human behavior, comprehension is, in a sense, immediate: the teacher understands the behavior of the students in his class. . . . I understand why the driver stops in front of a red light; I do not need to observe how often drivers regularly stop at red lights in order to understand why they do it. Human behavior is intrinsically intelligible due to the fact that men are endowed with consciousness.[14]

If we replace the word "consciousness" with the word "mind" in the last sentence, the distinction is the one that concerns us. What is the intelligibility proper to a phenomenon that we seek to explain through intentional explanation?[15] The answer given is that the intelligibility of a meaningful phenomenon is intrinsic, while the intelligibility of a natural phenomenon is indirect and mediated, or, as we might say today, nomological.[16] In order to understand why the driver stopped at the red light, there is no point in invoking what other drivers regularly do. One need only consider this driver and understand what the red light means to him. The perspective of understanding is, as they say, the perspective of the meaning things have "for a subject."

Such a distinction between explanation and understanding is commensurate with a positivist conception of natural science. Of course hermeneutic theories are formulated so as to resist what their partisans see as the movement of the natural sciences. But since positivism defends the universality of the naturalistic method, many are too quick to conclude that hermeneutic philosophers are implacable critics of positivism in every domain. To do so is to forget that the hermeneutic conception of natural science is identical to that of the positivists. More to the point, the hermeneutic philosopher derives his conception of what a natural science is from the positivist himself. Having taken from positivist doctrine the idea that natural sciences seek the laws of nature and that they explain natural phenomena through general truths, the hermeneutical theorist makes plain that the historical sciences proceed in an entirely different way.

Yet, if the positivist's description of the explanatory practice of the natural sciences were a good one, we would no doubt be forced to accept the validity of methodological monism. Positivist philosophy of science does not require that the phenomena to be explained be natural ones. What it insists on is the idea that one provides an explanation by bringing to light universal invariants and consistent correlations. And there is no reason why constants of this sort cannot be sought in historical phenomena.

In fact, it would seem that what the hermeneutic school distinguishes are not two types of intelligibility but rather cases that are intelligible and others that are not. What is it that is distinguished in the distinction between explanation and understanding? Clearly, the difference in the intellectual satisfaction provided by an explanation, according to whether it is natural or intentional. But what justifies this distinction for the partisan of a hermeneutic specificity of the human sciences? We will better understand this if we go back to Jaspers, from whom Weber took his notion of understanding (*Verstehen*). Aron gives the following elucidation of Jaspers's thought:

> We determine that syphilis results in paralysis through the regularity with which the one follows from the other: we do not understand it. Yet the fact that a man under attack grows angry, or that a disgraced and weak man tends to detest the strong: these are things that we understand, regardless of their frequency.[17]

If this is so, the difference is not between two modes of intelligibility but between a perspective in which it is possible to make what happens intelligible (the man is angry because he is being attacked) and another perspective where this is not possible (the man is paralyzed because he is sick). In the latter case we observe a state of affairs that is always so, but we cannot say that we understand why it is so. Normally, we would be tempted to say that, having failed to understand it, we are all the less capable of explaining it. The hermeneutic philosophy of explanation in the natural sciences, however, asks us to believe that, when we are unable to understand, we can always make do with an explanation in the form of a general observation (bearing on a set of cases none of which has been understood).

Aron's example illustrates the drawbacks of adopting the positivist philosophy of science for only some domains while denying its applicability to others. If we uphold the hermeneutic distinction between explanation and understanding, we will not need to provide an explanation wherever it is possible for us to come to an understanding. Having understood that the taxi driver has stopped because he saw the red light, why would I need a nomological explanation? What could such an explanation tell me? Even if we happen to be in a city where it is not true that all taxi drivers obey the red lights, we nevertheless understand why those who stop at red lights do so. By contrast, according to the proposed dualism, "explanations" are to be sought for cases where understanding is not forthcoming. Yet, bizarrely enough, the explanations would not have the effect of rendering those cases more intelligible. If giving an explanation amounts to saying that what has just befallen this sick person has also befallen others, we could "explain" why the sick person is sick even though we would still be unable to understand what is happening to him. The incomprehensible remains just as incomprehensible, even after having been explained.

In fact, it is not the case that the difference between understanding and explanation is that the former is not mediated by a universal. It is indeed probable that a passenger who sees his taxi driver stop at a red light immediately *understands* why the taxi is stopping, without needing a general observation of the consistent, or even usual, behavior of other taxi drivers. He understands it at once, immediately, but only if he is cognizant of local practices. In this case, the driving of a car is subject to a code, so that there are explicit rules (that can be invoked in order to impose a fine on those who break them). There is thus a mediation through one of the rules of the road that must be learned if one is to become a competent driver.

Thus, Aron's illustrative example brings to light the inadequacy of the positivist approach to the philosophy of physics. If sociology does not seek to explain by means of "laws," this is not because it is a science of significations rather than a "social physics." Rather, it is because physics itself could not claim to explain natural phenomena if the only explanations it had to offer were laws like the following: every X in circumstance Y will have behavior Z. Let us imagine for a moment that the piloting of a taxi by its driver is a natural phenomenon for which we are seeking a purely naturalistic explanation. My taxi comes to a stop in the following circumstance: there is a red light in front of us. A social physics devised by a strictly positivist physicist explains to me that, in the country in which I happen to be, taxis have always been observed coming to a stop whenever there is a red light. Where is the explanation here? However much this positivist physicist insists that this is a natural law, his invocation of Nature will seem to us to be nothing more than a superstitious formula. His account offers no explanation whatever, whether physical or intentional. Let us change the example slightly: my taxi stops whenever it passes in front of a bakery. I am told that this has always been the case for the taxi I am riding in and even for all taxis. Where is the explanation? How does the presence of a bakery precipitate the stopping of the taxi? What needs to be found is obviously the connection between the regularly associated events. Does the light, by changing from green to red, somehow act upon the car's machinery? Does the taxi, when it passes in front of a bakery, succumb to the attraction of chocolate éclairs?

A real naturalistic explanation, of course, does not limit itself to relating a particular fact observed here to a general truth observed everywhere. In taking note of such a coincidence—that, say, between the turning red of traffic lights and the stopping of taxis—we have done nothing but increase the opportunities to ask for an explanation, since all of these agents are merely similar to one another and their movements are therefore independent from one another: when one stops moving, nothing happens to the others. The naturalistic explanation assumes the discovery of a *mechanism* by which event number 1 precipitates event number 2. Intentional explanation assumes that event number 1 provides someone, the taxi driver, with a *motive* to cause event number 2, the stopping of his vehicle.

And here we see the principle underlying the alliance between Aristotelian ideas and Wittgensteinian ones. The distinction between *causes* and *reasons* in Wittgenstein suggests that intentional explanation has nothing to do with the deductive logic invoked by positivism in defining nomological explanation, and that its philosophy should instead be sought in the form of practical inference. Aristotle showed that, beside the demonstrative syllogisms of the deductive sciences, there are also practical syllogisms. From these practical syllogisms we derive our concepts of means and ends and thereby the resources necessary for teleological explanation even in the natural sciences (see below, § 2.5).

2.4. Explanation by Natural Laws

In reality, it is unclear whether the positivist's "laws of nature" have an empirical or realist status. If they are just statements of regularities that have been observed up to now, they speak about *what is* or of what has been, but explain nothing: they do not even allow us, on this hypothesis, to foretell *what will be*. On the other hand, if they have some explanatory value, then they are much more than general truths. As Fred Dretske has shown in a remarkable article, the positivist conception of a law of nature is ambiguous.[18] This conception is logistical in that it believes knowledge can be accounted for by the logical form of scientific statements. For positivism, laws are distinguished by their logical status: they are universal propositions. For example, a law states that *all metals conduct electricity*. Such a doctrine of science is quite common and can still be found within any number of philosophy textbooks. But it has two flaws, one that is vulnerable from a logical point of view, another from an epistemological one.

As Dretske points out, from a logical point of view, the form of a nomological statement cannot be that of a general truth; otherwise every proposition of the following form could be considered a law:

> *For every x, if x is of type F, then x is of type G.*

The above propositional schema is extensional. The semantic values of the letters "F" and "G" matter little, so that in interpreting them one can substitute for a property another property coextensive with the first. Here is Dretske's example: Let us assume that there is a law according to which diamonds have a refractive index of 2.419, and let us assume that the property of *being a diamond* applies to the same set of things as does the property of *being mined in kimberlite* (a dark basic rock). Under this hypothesis, there is indeed a general truth: Everything mined in kimberlite has a refractive index of 2.419. But even if this general truth has been partially derived from a law, it is still not a law. It could be a mere coincidence. This implies that the statement of a law is not about things, but must rather be about their *properties*. In order to give a general observation the force of a law, a nomological operator must be added to it that says something like "it is a law that. . . ." Such an operator changes the logical regime of the expression to which it is applied. Instead of the propositional schema above in which "every *F* is a *G*," we now have: "It is a law that every *F* be a *G*."[19] In other words, what is declared to be linked in the statement of the law are properties: it is impossible to be an *F* without being a *G*. The logical regime of our speech has ceased to be one of strict extensionality.

Things are no better for the positivist doctrine of laws from the epistemological point of view. Why should a law, conceived as a universal truth, have any explanatory power? The explanation is held to lie in the possibility of subsuming the particular case under a general truth. Perhaps the idea that this is explanatory comes from the habit of referring to such truths as "rules" under which we subsume the particular case by means of a "determinative judgment." But this suggestion derived from the traditional philosophical lexicon does not add an ounce of necessity to the particular case. Every man is mortal; therefore Socrates, who is a man, is mortal. Where is the explanation in this? By saying that every man is mortal, we imply that they all are, including Socrates, Plato, you and me. But in making that claim, we have still not even alluded to a possible explanation of the mortal condition of any of us. Only if we added that "it is a law that . . ." would there be, if not an explanation, at least an indication that a *link* must be sought between the fact of being human and the fact of being mortal.

To objections of this sort, positivists usually respond by adding a few epicycles to their system. A law of nature, they admit, is not a simple uniformity; otherwise it would be nothing but a grand coincidence. Rather, it is a general truth accompanied by a complement that provides it with both its necessity and its explanatory power. They then invoke counterfactual conditions that would account for the predictive power of laws and thereby guarantee that the uniformity raised to the status of a law of nature is not a fortuitous coincidence. Yet these counterfactual implications only deepen the mystery. The logical schema for the statement of the law is then no longer simply "every F is a G" but has added to it "if x were an F, it would be a G." But where is the guarantee? Dretske gives the following example: if we are told that all the dogs born at sea until now have been cocker spaniels, we have still not been given a reason to believe that, if this dachshund had been born at sea, he would be a cocker spaniel and not a dachshund, or that, if we took some dachshunds out to sea, their offspring would be cocker spaniels.[20] In reality the general proposition claims to say what *is* the case, but does not bear on what *would be* the case in other circumstances that we can imagine that are contrary to the situation as it is. To say that the law would be broken if the counterfactual assertion were not obeyed is to admit that a law must state much more than a mere observation of uniformity. To add counterfactual assertions to general truths is to assume implicitly that there is a reason for the uniformity that has been raised to the importance of a law: if it were a law that every dog born at sea were a cocker spaniel, there would have to be something out there that prevents other canine species from reproducing.

We thus return to the conclusion sketched earlier: by recording a regular succession or a constant correlation, one has still not explained anything. In order for a correlation to explain anything at all, it must make clear what sort of link exists between the phenomenon to be explained and the explicative factors. The problem of the duality of modes of intelligibility arises from the fact that this link sometimes takes the form of a mechanism (i.e., of a generative system that need only be set in motion), sometimes the form of a motive.[21] Without such a connection, there is no explanation, and this is as true of (efficient) causal explanation as it is of intentional explanation.

2.5. Functional Explanations and Intentional Explanations

So it turns out that Dilthey and his followers were right to set in opposition the modes of intelligibility of the moral and natural sciences. But the terms of this opposition must be understood in an entirely different way, so as to avoid making authentic intelligibility the sole preserve of the sciences of the mind. In order to revise the formulation of the duality that concerns us here, von Wright borrows from Kurt Lewin the idea of a grand opposition between the Galilean tradition (with its Platonic roots) and the Aristotelian tradition.[22] Galileans respond to the question regarding the forms of explanation that teach us something by citing forms of mechanical explanation, while Aristotelians add to those mechanical explanations (which they by no means scorn) teleological ones.

For a positivist, the teleological form of explanation belongs to a bygone era of human intelligence. To explain something by its end is to give in "abstract" form an explanation that is in fact animistic, one according to which the thing possesses a sort of will or appetitive force that makes it seek its goal (whether its natural place or its developed form).

But the intentionalist sees the debate as having been decided by the practices of the scientists themselves. The animistic explanation derided by the positivist *is not* a teleological explanation. It is a *pseudo*-explanation by efficient causality, since what it calls a "soul" is a kind of active power inside the thing that represents the goal to itself and directs the thing toward that goal. By contrast, the functional explanations of biology or cybernetics are teleological explanations, even if we sometimes feel obligated to call them something else precisely in order to distinguish them from animistic pseudo-explanations. Teleological explanations do not replace (mechanical) causal explanations, nor do they contradict them. They satisfy a different kind of curiosity and are carried out from a different point of view. Specifically, teleological explanations do not invoke a power of intervention that the future would have upon the present, that is, the impossible production of an (efficient) cause by its effect. If a system is functional, then its parts are there to carry out certain tasks, and the teleology consists in saying what they must do in order to discharge their functions (and not *how* they will do so mechanically). In order to avoid taking "final causes" for efficient powers, one need only recall that an approach that fails is just as teleological as one that succeeds. Since, in the case of failure, the result sought is not secured, it is difficult to see how one could explain an intentional approach that fails by the causal power of a result that, under this hypothesis, will not come to exist.

Armed with this reference to the classical conflict between the two sciences, von Wright is able to set up several conceptual contrasts, which can be illustrated by the following table:

Aristotelian Science	*Galilean Science*
teleology	efficient causality
finality	mechanism
understanding	explanation

This table makes immediately clear the decisive point of this reformulation of the problem of the sciences of the mind. It seems that the intelligibility associated with *understanding* falls into the column of natural science in the Aristotelian mode. Indeed, the two columns correspond to two conceptions of physics and have nothing to do with any opposition between the natural sciences and the humanities. What is opposed to Galilean physics is not Aristotle's rhetoric but his physics. It remains to be seen how a distinction between the different forms of explanation used in the natural sciences can tell us much about the status of the explanations given in the sciences of the mind.

The first conclusion that emerges from von Wright's analysis is that explanation and understanding are involved in all science. In order to provide an explanation, one must find a comprehensible link among the various elements of what is to be explained. The difference between the natural and moral sciences cannot be understood as a difference between mechanism and teleology once teleological explanation has been rehabilitated in the form of functionalism. It follows that the *idealist* conception of finality must be rejected. This conception holds that teleology is always mere appearance or simply a way of talking, except in the domains governed by consciousness. This restriction of teleology to consciousness results from the assumption that an explanation in terms of ends must be an explanation of the present state of things by means of a state yet to come, with the result that this future can only be incarnated in a representation and a desire. This is what allows Kojève, for example, to claim that there is only one authentically teleological phenomenon: human acts—actions where the actors are conscious of their goal.[23] In order for teleology to be denied to nature in this way and reserved for the mind, it must be defined in terms dictated by the philosophy of consciousness: in order for there to be teleology, the future must already be actively present (represented) so as to be able to intervene in the present. Here, the confusion between finality and the use of a generative mechanism by a subject seeking to attain a goal would appear to be total.

In a realist conception of teleology, this form of explanation is not the exclusive province of desiring creatures.[24] Teleological explanation applied to natural systems is not simply a way of talking (in a conditional, "as if" mode), but it is certainly a way of representing or describing these systems to oneself. One moves to a teleological description precisely when one is interested in the fact that a system is precisely that: a system, an organized whole.[25]

All of which takes us back to the distinction between theoretical and practical syllogisms. Can deductive syllogisms provide us with the logical form of the natural sciences? They can do this only if we remain within a positivist philosophy of physics. In fact, consistent positivists *criticize* the very idea of causality, precisely because the concept of a cause requires that we *go beyond appearances* in order to find a real connection that will allow us to understand the regularity in a sequence of events. But in order to conceive of such a real link, we need a *realist* conception of causality, a concept provided by the agent's point of view.[26] Causality understood as a generative mechanism is causality understood by an agent seeking to intervene in the course of things. This conception of causality takes us out of the linear relation between cause and effect and rests on the idea of an intervention: the idea of a difference between the state of things that will come to be if I intervene and the state of things that will come to be if I do not. But this contrast between two contingent futures in turn assumes that one is able to determine the physical system upon which the agent is contemplating intervention. For example, an agent knows that the window is set into its frame in such a way that it can be opened but that it will not (ordinarily) open by itself. In order to open it, he will have to go to the trouble of opening it himself or he will have to get someone else to open it. Thought about action is therefore, for the agent, a representation of his immediate environment as comprising various systems that are (more or less) closed but that also offer protrusions or holds that allow external intervention to be envisaged. Now, the notion of a natural system that is relatively closed to the influences of its environment but that can be perturbed from outside is the notion of an *organization* of the system's different components. What naturalist explanation here puts to work is therefore a teleological concept, that of a division of labor among parts each of which has a function to carry out, but without assuming that the system has a psychological organ charged with overall planning. The logic of explanation is derived from the psychology of social agents, but it goes without saying that it has been completely depsychologized before being applied to nature.

There is then indeed a relation between functional (teleological) explanation and practical reasoning. And it would be wrong to think that this somehow gives functional explanation an anthropomorphic cast. The relation does not consist in imagining that functional systems contain an organ whose task is to manipulate the means at its disposal in light of an end that must therefore be represented and thus represented by or to someone. Rather, practical reasoning involves a certain *abstraction from individual matter*, and this aspect of practical syllogisms is also found in functional explanation. Indeed, the major difference between deductive syllogisms and practical syllogisms is that the former conform to what is often called a "monotone" logic in which the conclusion follows necessarily from the posited premises and continues to follow from them regardless of new data. Practical inferences are nothing like this: the syllogism indicates the means to be employed, but does not tell us that it is necessary to employ *this specific means and no other*. For example, a line of reasoning tells me that, in order to go to Orly airport, I must take some kind of transportation— for example, this taxi that is willing to take me—but the same reasoning does not exclude the possibility that I might just as validly go there by means of a different taxi or by train. The contingence of the practical world, from which it results that the conclusion follows from the premises *all other things being equal*, is reflected in a certain dematerialization of the means employed. What matters is not the matter or the individuality, but the function. Of course the means to be used are material ones; yet what counts for the line of reasoning is not that the useful thing be made of a particular portion of matter, but that it be able to provide the required services. If some other thing proves to be able to fill the same role, this other thing will do just as well, even if it is entirely different in its constitution.

The problem of the sciences of the mind is thus one of knowing if they apply the same sort of teleological explanation as do the natural sciences when they study the functioning of systems, or whether the sciences of the mind instead rely on some other sort of teleology.

On this point it becomes possible to fill out the synoptic table of possible contemporary philosophies furnished by von Wright. The author astutely noticed a tension at the heart of analytic philosophy, one that could be exemplified by the difference between Wittgenstein's early and late philosophy, one part governed by the purest logical atomism, the second by what has been called "anthropological holism" (see below, § 12.1). Yet, in the philosophy that developed outside of the analytic sphere, von Wright sees only the idealistic and hermeneutic strand, one in which no similar tension is to be found. In order to derive a more complete synoptic table of twentieth-century philosophy, one would have to be able to find, on the continental side, a tension analogous to that between positivism (atomism) and intentionalism (holism). I believe that a tension of this type can be found in another attempt to renew the sciences of the mind, one that von Wright does not mention, namely structuralism and, more specifically, structural anthropology. The tension to which I refer is not, however, the one that has gotten most of the attention (i.e., that between thinkers who emphasize the subject and those who emphasize structures, e.g., between Sartre and Lévi-Strauss). Rather, this tension is one inherent in the structuralist project itself insofar as it refers both to a possible reduction (not unlike that effected by cybernetics) of mind to mechanisms and to a necessary structural explanation (in the holist sense) of social institutions. But this point merits a separate elaboration.

CHAPTER 3

The Anthropological Investigation
of the Mind

STRUCTURAL ANTHROPOLOGY's true importance lies, I believe, in its rekindling of the Durkheimian heritage of French sociology. For a Durkheimian, the study of a society cannot be detached from the study of its collective representations. Conversely, investigation of the mind must encompass habitual ways of doing things and the rules of social life. It follows that the moral sciences, or social sciences, are indeed, as they are called in German, sciences of the mind. This is a fitting title, since the study of social mores is precisely study of representations and ways of thinking.

This sociological insight is no doubt not what comes to most people's minds when they think about structuralism. It is likely that, for most readers, the word "structuralism" refers to theories that have in common certain explanatory models taken from the linguistic theory of the first part of the twentieth century. More generally, structuralism is associated with various attempts to apply semiotic models of analysis to various cultural phenomena using concepts like code and message, signifier and signified, statement and utterance. That is not what this chapter is about.[1] Although it made constant reference to linguistics, structural anthropology remained far removed from the real problems of linguistic analysis. At the same time, it elaborated a method for the analysis of institutions that presupposes a particular philosophy of mind. Moreover, Lévi-Strauss has never stopped insisting that the object of ethnological and mythological study is nothing other than the human mind. But in order to understand this claim, we will first have to consider the very idea of an anthropological science.

3.1. Anthropology's Two Sources

Dan Sperber has pointed out that the discipline of anthropology, in its social component (as opposed to its physical component), carries within it the marks of a conflict—or at least a tension—between two different propositions.[2] The split in question is, at root, a philosophical one. The presupposition of any anthropological science is that there is, in a sense that will have to be specified, one human mind and not a diversity. It is true that we distinguish among different forms of mind: the Chinese mind or the bourgeois mind, for example, are not the same thing as the Madagascan mind or the warrior mind. We also often speak of "mentalities." But the study of mentalities would no longer be anthropological if the forms of mind were not forms of the same human mind. One must therefore postulate, behind the obvious diversity of styles and forms of life, a set of anthropological universals.

How do we know that there is only one human mind? This is not a factual question. Sperber says as much: "What are the common and specific attributes of humans? This question, central to anthropology, can only be answered in a speculative fashion."[3] The answer to the question will not be provided by research in the field, since one must already have answered the question in the affirmative for the "field" to have been defined as an "anthropological field," in keeping with the rules of this discipline.

The question of anthropological universals is a philosophical one. More precisely, from a philosophical point of view, it is the application of a philosophy of universals (in the sense in which this term has given rise to philosophical debate) to the attempt to clear up the following problem: How is it that humans are all equally human (in accordance with the substantial concept of humanity[4]), even though they are differentiated in the ways that they incarnate this humanity through languages, mores, and organizations whose principles differ from one another? How can there be several anthropological types of a single humanity? These are questions the philosophy of mind must answer. For only the philosophy of mind can provide the distinctions necessary to a satisfactory expression of the thesis by which the human mind is in principle uniform yet diverse in its historical forms. Here I will recapitulate and modify Sperber's exposition.

Sperber explains the current divided state of anthropology by the fact that anthropology has two philosophical sources. The consequence of this dual intellectual genealogy is a disagreement regarding the discipline's very object. "Today, most anthropologists acknowledge the legacy of Durkheim, Max Weber, or Marx rather than that of William James, Wundt, or Freud, and going further back, that of Hobbes or Montesquieu rather than that of Hume or Kant."[5] Anthropologists think of themselves as more like (Durkheimian) sociologists than as psychologists, closer to the tradition of the philosophy of right than to that of the philosophy of mind. But, Sperber adds, this situation could well change. Were anthropology to abandon the comforts of cultural relativism and thereby rediscover its object, anthropological universals, it would recognize that its place is among the sciences that the cognitivist program brings together under the name "sciences of the mind."

Sperber's diagnosis is clear: anthropology must decide whether the formal objects of its research are institutions or, rather, ideas and cultural representations taken as a subset of the entirety of mental representations.[6] In the latter case, anthropologists will have to explain why some "mental representations" and not others manage to acquire public expression and, thereby, gain the status of cultural representations. Sperber is here outlining a program for a cognitivist anthropology, one that would consist in studying the circulation of representations from one subject to another, just as one studies the circulation of a virus: an "epidemiology of ideas." The ethnological discipline should, in his view, become one of the cognitive sciences. For it does in fact form part of a vast theoretical enterprise whose object is the *functioning* of the system called "the human mind"; or, put differently, one whose goal is the discovery of the "internal constraints" of a natural kind by which all intelligent activity is limited.[7] Just as linguistics must, according to Chomsky's disciples, redefine itself as psycholinguistics (the study of the mental organ responsible for linguistic performance), so to, one might claim, social anthropology should become more the study of mental mechanisms than of social systems.

But the proposed alternative presupposes the necessity of choosing between the philosophy of right and the philosophy of mind, between the study of institutions and the study of representations. Sperber here uses the term "philosophy of mind" in the English sense of a philosophical psychology and perhaps also of a doctrine of human nature. This is why the philosophical forebears recognized by these anthropologists are Locke, Hume, Kant, William James, and Freud. Yet the great Durkheimian and Maussian principle was precisely that one cannot separate the study of ideas from the study of institutions. Nor can one separate the study of institutions from the study of ideas. Moreover, the proposed alternative takes it for granted that the heirs of the philosophy of right must be cultural relativists, while the heirs of "rationalist" philosophy will be universalists. Sperber suggests that, if cultural anthropology does not adopt a cognitivist basis, it will necessarily highlight the differences among humans and thereby put the emphasis on cultural relativism. This would indeed be the case if the only conceivable anthropological universals were internal constraints of a natural kind. But is this the only way in which to raise the question of anthropological universals?

Though I recognize that there are two philosophical reference points for an anthropologist today, I believe that both of them belong within the philosophy of mind, provided that one has not decided in advance that the philosophy of mind must take the form of a mental philosophy in the sense in which I have been using this term. Doctrines of human nature make up one of these reference points. They enjoin us to seek out the mental mechanisms and functional principles behind comportments. The other reference point does indeed have something to do with the philosophy of right, but that does not mean that it cannot also be a philosophy of mind in a crucial sense of the term. For what interested Hobbes and Montesquieu was the human capacity to *institute* an order of laws, a capacity that undeniably also merits being called "mind." Moreover, Hobbes in the end explains the exercise of this instituting capacity by means of a theory of human nature, while Montesquieu does so using the notion of collective mind.

Montesquieu refers to a "spirit of the laws," and this expression has often been taken up by anthropologists.[8] His object is not just legislation— law in the strict sense—but the institutions taken together as a whole.[9] His thought is thus well and truly part of the philosophical tradition out of which sociology sprang. But Montesquieu stresses that his concern is the *spirit* of the laws. Is it so obvious that this use of the word "spirit" [*esprit*] is utterly foreign to the philosophy of mind properly so-called?[10] It is true that, in current English, one cannot translate the word "esprit" in Montes- quieu's title by the word "mind," but this is perhaps more indicative of a gap within English philosophical vocabulary than of the polysemy of the French word. Indeed, Montesquieu explicitly links what he calls "the spirit of the laws" with the individual subject's way of thinking. "Peoples, like each individual, have a run of ideas, and their entire way of thinking, like that of each individual, has a beginning, a middle, and an end."[11] What better way to say that the (sociological) study of a people is the study of an intellectual system, a "run of ideas," and that this study, far from being extraneous to the philosophy of mind, is an indispensable part of it?

But this reference to Montesquieu also belies any seemingly necessary association between social anthropology (conceived as the study of a given society's "total way of thinking") and cultural relativism. Such a relativ- ism would be unavoidable if we limited ourselves to observing the irreduc- ible diversity of ways of thinking. In Montesquieu, every "run of ideas" is intelligible and, in this sense, rational. This would be relativism only for theorists of a natural law that bars any adaptation of institutions to the varied and complex circumstances of life as well as to the various possible apprehensions of that complexity according to the intellectual and moral habits of the subjects that confront it.

Yet the fact that Sperber was able to put forward his diagnosis in 1982 indicates a relative failure of structural anthropology, at least from a philo- sophical point of view. Indeed, the philosophical importance of Lévi- Strauss's work was to have proposed a way of overcoming the alternative according to which one must either insist upon the ultimate unity of the human mind at the risk of underestimating the profound differences among various types of culture, or study that diversity while adopting a perspective that leads to relativism. In hindsight, the structuralist solution appears to have been ambiguous, reproducing within itself the conflict it had initially set out to resolve. As a result, the question raised remains unanswered: Is the study of institutions, by the very diversity of its objects, already the study of the human mind? Or does it only become the study of the human mind by reducing ethnology to psychology?

Structural anthropology seeks at one and the same time to be a cultural anthropology (a theory of mind) and a social anthropology (a theory of institutions). One might well be able to account for the diversity of anthropological types (i.e., for the variety of cultures) within a universalist theory of the human mind. But the status of this theory of mind remains to be determined: Is it a psychology or is it an anthropological contextualization?

3.2. Structural Explanation

In fact, Lévi-Strauss has always presented structural anthropology as a science of the mind. The structures used to account for systems of kinship are "structures of the human mind," mental structures whose universality he seeks to establish.[12]

How can institutions and mental structures both be studied at the same time? We will perhaps better understand this by looking at a passage where Lévi-Strauss is explaining how the notion of structure, which was in part inspired by Gestalt psychology, makes possible a new solution to a problem confronted by ethnologists. This problem happens to be that of explaining a form of marriage that often surprises Western observers: preferential marriages between cross-cousins. In the kinship system in question, the subject's "parallel cousins" (the children of paternal uncles or maternal aunts) are like brothers and sisters, while "cross-cousins" (children of maternal uncles or paternal aunts) are seen as possible, even desirable, marriage partners. We find this way of thinking surprising because we are aware of the identical biological proximity of both groups. The system's rationality escapes us. Before having understood the rational motive for it, a Western researcher might be tempted to interpret this institution as the result of facts that are extrinsic to it. "There has been no intrinsic reason isolated for the peculiar cross-cousin relationship, and from this it has been concluded that the whole institution must have been the indirect consequence of a different order of phenomena."[13]

Needless to say, the problem raised here goes far beyond this particular example. The general difficulty is one of knowing how to account for the apparent meaning of human institutions (when they seem to have such a meaning) or their apparent irrationality (when at first we do not understand them). Lévi-Strauss explains that, when faced with the problem of explaining the rationale of a custom or institution, the human sciences of the early part of the twentieth century saw only two possibilities:

A human institution has only two possible origins, either historical and irrational, or as in the case of the legislator, by design; in other words, either incidental or intentional. Consequently, if no rational motive can be found for cross-
cousin marriage it is because it is the result of a series of historical accidents
which in themselves are insignificant.[14]

This alternative is essentially one suggested by common sense. It is much
the same as the choice put forward by traditional eighteenth-century theories of finalism: if there is organization, it must either be attributed to an
intelligent craftsman (the watch proves the existence of the watchmaker)
or be seen as the chance effect of a blind chain of events. The only two
conceivable explanations are providence and chance.

It is remarkable that, in both cases, what is sought is an efficient cause:
either a legislator or a chain of events. There is no sense that what needs
to be explained in institutions is an *order* rather than a simple accumula-
tion of events. Yet the real anthropological question is that of an institution's meaning and not its origin: why do people *persist* in marrying in
accordance with these rules?

This is where Lévi-Strauss appeals to the "new psychology" as a way
of contesting the traditional assumptions of the human sciences. The old
psychology, he explains, was based on a prejudice analogous to the one
just mentioned: either concepts are acquired through experience (empiricism), in which case they are the product of an "automatic process of
association," or they do not have their origin in such chance empirical
encounters, in which case they must be of transcendental origin (rationalism). Lévi-Strauss believes that this alternative has been refuted by Gestalt
psychology. "This antinomy was resolved once it was realized that even
the lowly fowl can apprehend relationships. Once this was acknowledged,
both associationism and idealism found themselves non-suited."[15]

The following is Lévi-Strauss's characterization of the intellectual revolution that he felt would allow anthropologists to escape the alternative
between historical chance and conscious intention in the social sciences
(though he claims merely to be an observer of this revolution, one gets the
feeling not only that he welcomes it but that he intends to set himself to
completing it as well):

> The same change in attitudes is beginning to appear in the study of human
> institutions, which are also structures whose whole—in other words, the regu-
> lating principle—can be given before the parts, that is, that complex union
> which makes up the institution, its terminology, consequences and implica-
> tions, the customs through which it is expressed and the beliefs to which it
> gives rise. This regulating principle can have a rational value without being
> rationally conceived. It can be expressed in arbitrary formulas without being
> itself devoid of meaning.[16]

This text shows clearly how Lévi-Strauss's thought brings together a thesis about institutions and a thesis about the mind. The former, a Durkheimian thesis, posits the reality—and therefore the holism—of the social. The latter explains the status of collective mind through the idea, borrowed from certain linguists, of a structural unconscious (i.e., an infrapersonal mental activity). According to the view governed by the alternative between conscious action and historical chance, the meaning of institutions, if they have a meaning at all, must have first been present in an individual consciousness before becoming part of social reality. Conversely, if the institution is not a work of legislation, it can only be explained by happenstance, by unequal development, as a vestige, etcetera. The new way of thinking, which Lévi-Strauss attributes to Gestalt psychology, is thus holist. This holism is vigorously advanced in this text: *the whole can be given before the parts*. But how can this be so? How can the whole already be in place where the parts are not yet present? Considered historically, from the perspective of the actual transitory presence of the various stages through which a regulated practice must pass (e.g., the various stages through which one must pass in order to carry out a matrimonial alliance), the whole can only be given at the end, after all of the parts have themselves been produced.

Lévi-Strauss's solution is that the whole is given as a "regulative principle" before being given as a concrete whole or sum of various parts. It is therefore *in the mind* that the whole is given before being given in the social reality of institutions and customs. The whole is present from the beginning. It has not been engendered, whether by an individual intention or by historical circumstances, since the institutional agents are all of the *same* mind. Lévi-Strauss here appeals to a difference between two levels of the human mind. At the level at which the principle finds expression, it is entirely possible that we will find nothing but "arbitrary formulas" or "irrational conceptions." It is thus possible that the people concerned will be unable to explain the meaning of their institutions. But one must postulate another, infraconscious or impersonal, level of mental activity, a level at which the principle serves to regulate the parts (or to give a single structure to the "complex whole" of the parts, which includes the vocabulary of kinship, the beliefs relative to kinship, mores, etc.).

The problem is knowing whether this response is comprehensible. It is thus also a problem of knowing whether it is possible to develop a philosophy of mind in which we can understand the meaning of the claim that the whole is given as a regulative principle before its own parts, and that its mode of being is thus mental. What is the conception of mind that underlies the holist approach to institutions? Whatever the answer to this question, it is clear that it is not simply in virtue of a play on words that the philosophy of mind concerned with the psychology of actors and the philosophy of mind concerned with the spirit of laws have been brought together.

The third way perceived by Lévi-Strauss assumes a distinction between a level at which the whole is given and a level where it is not yet so given. Obviously, Lévi-Strauss himself hopes to find the solution in the idea of a *mental infrastructure*. True, he does not use this term. But he does refer, on the very same page, to a "subjacent reality" underlying social institutions.[17] To follow this suggestion is to be led towards a program for a kind of cognitivist anthropology. We will see that much of this program was in fact delineated by one of the strands of French structuralism, the strand that put forward the theories of the structural unconscious (see below, chapter 5). In the signifiers without signifieds postulated by these doctrines, we may duly recognize the precursors of the "internal representations" that, according to the theory of computational mind, are the objects of our elementary mental operations.

3.3. Formal Psychology or Sociology?

The passages we have been discussing are elliptical in their meaning. In order to better understand them, we should turn to a text about French sociology that Lévi-Strauss wrote for an anthology in 1945.[18] It is clear from this text that the structural solution proposed above grew out of a critique of Durkheim's method. In the 1945 text as in later work, Lévi-Strauss disagrees with Durkheim regarding the relationship between psychology and sociology.

Lévi-Strauss points out that Durkheim is far from denying "the mental side of social processes"[19]: he is opposed only to the reduction of society to its individuals by means of psychological explanation. But once the autonomy of the social is recognized, Durkheim is willing to admit that the social is made up of the mental. He writes, for example, that social facts are psychic, "since they all consist of ways of thinking or behaving."[20] For Durkheim, this means that, as institutions, collective representations cannot be grasped by individual psychology.[21] By contrast, for a partisan of methodological atomism, the mental character of society must be understood differently: in reality, there are only individuals and, in the heads of these individuals, certain representations bearing upon their various relations and the foundations of these relations. This is precisely the conception of the mental character of society that Durkheim contests.

Lévi-Strauss's critique of Durkheim focuses on two points. First, Durkheim does not grant any validity to functional explanation. For him, the only truly scientific explanation is genetic. In his view, to claim to explain the existence of an institution through its purposes is to fall into a naive finalism. Second, Durkheim is unable to account for symbolism, seeking as he does to give a genetic explanation by means of social life. But this explanation is in fact circular, since social life presupposes, in Durkheim's own view, symbolism (here, the word "symbolism" designates every activity that makes use of signs, whether linguistic or nonlinguistic, from tattooing and art to discourse and magico-religious classifications).

The link between these two critiques is not a straightforward one. Lévi-Strauss's objections could, however, be understood in the following way: Durkheim's reasoning is that of philosopher trained in neo-Kantianism in that it opposes finalism and mechanism. Genetic explanation, which provides the efficient causes of an institution's existence, is on the side of mechanism. Functional explanation—explanation by means of the benefits provided—is on the side of finality understood as something conscious, i.e., as the intentional pursuit of a goal by an agent who is consciously able to organize means towards that goal. We can understand why Durkheim rejects explanation in terms of finality, for it would turn institutions into the ways and means used by individuals to arrive at their personal ends.[22] But if one rejects explanations through the function accomplished, i.e., through *social meaning*, then all that is left is mechanical explanation through historical circumstances. These are the two terms juxtaposed by Lévi-Strauss in his work on kinship: the antinomy for which Durkheim is unable to see a solution is one that opposes "the blindness of history, and the finalism of consciousness."[23] As early as this article, the solution for Lévi-Strauss is to be found in the new psychology: "Modern sociologists and psychologists solve such problems by calling upon the activity of the unconscious mind; but at the time when Durkheim was writing, the main results of modern psychology and linguistics were lacking."[24] But this allusion to "modern psychology" is hardly enlightening, since it is difficult to see it as anything but an amalgamation of concepts of the unconscious borrowed from both psychoanalysis and linguistics, a double reference that explains nothing. In the case of psychoanalysis, what is unconscious is what has been repressed. The fact that it is unconscious is explained by a kind of censorship or by some mechanism of expulsion out of the field of consciousness. In the case of linguistics, however, unconsciousness corresponds to the fact that a speaker is usually unable to provide the rules (whether of pronunciation or of sentence construction) of his native language, even though he is obeying them while speaking and has no need to *consult* those rules in order to speak his language correctly. We might say, if you will, that "linguistic structures" are within him in an "unconscious" way. But even this claim is still equivocal in the current context, which is largely dominated by the dissemination of Freudian ideas. All that one is trying to say in referring to the unconsciousness of the principles of language is that they are present as capacities (*habitus*). A speaker proves that he possesses these principles by speaking correctly. It would be odd to turn these principles into mechanisms or causal powers that, unknown to the subject, control his expressive activity.

Why does Lévi-Strauss see the structural unconscious as the solution to the problem he has raised? His text tells us: the mind's unconscious activity seems to provide the impersonal finality that sociology requires in order to account for social symbolism. Lévi-Strauss agrees with Durkheim that there is no sociology without a critique of artificialist theories of society. Appeals to the finality of a self-conscious subject—for example, of a legendary legislator or of a citizen entering freely into a social contract—are therefore ruled out. Yet, in this text, Lévi-Strauss defends functionalism (even though he will later come to criticize it).[25] What functionalism means here is the study of something as a whole or a system. Thus, he writes, when Mauss advocated the study of "total social facts" he was essentially recommending an approach that would subsequently be called "functionalist."[26] Taking into account the criticisms later leveled at functionalism, primarily by Lévi-Strauss himself, we might prefer to speak of an approach that is "holist." For what is truly at issue here is the holism of the social: by rejecting all functional or finalistic explanations, Durkheim denied himself the very means of his own holism. This would appear to be the substance of Lévi-Strauss's critique: "If finalism is to be abandoned, however, it has to be replaced by something else making possible an understanding of how social phenomena may present the character of meaningful wholes, of structured ensembles."[27] The solution is then to preserve finality while detaching it from individual subjects through the notion of an "unconscious activity of the mind." This conception of the mind, which we are supposed to have adopted from the most advanced psychological sciences, is really a combination of two other conceptions, and allows for a "dialectical" solution to the antinomy.[28] The notion of mind guarantees that there is finality—functions fulfilled within a systematic whole—while the notion of the unconscious guarantees that we are not returning to the naive notion of a "finalism of consciousness."

One may well doubt that this "dialectical" solution, as the author calls it, will resolve the antinomy. Indeed, it would appear to be entirely unstable. As Pierre Bourdieu points out, one might well see the invocation of the unconscious as an invitation to *naturalize* the mind, so that the rules of social life become a kind of "unconscious *regulating* by a mysterious cerebral or social mechanism."[29] But one might also see this unconscious as a way of *idealizing* social life, by replacing effective practices with a purely intellectual "unconscious activity of the mind" that is detached from "individual and collective history."[30]

Lévi-Strauss's two critiques of Durkheim are valid. On the one hand, if one claims that the study of the social is the study of a totality, a place must be made for a form of functional explanation. On the other hand, social symbolism cannot be explained by means of society, for society is itself above all a *symbolic* system and not, as naturalistic functionalism believes, some kind of organic system. Taken together, these critiques point the way toward a redefinition of functional explanation in terms of intellectual (or "symbolic") needs rather than in terms of "social" functions (in the crude sense in which the only needs satisfied by social rules are those of maintaining the cohesion and unity of the group). But by consigning all of that to psychology and even to neurology,[31] Lévi-Strauss has transgressed the great Aristotelian principle that Durkheim continually stressed, one that Durkheim claimed to have learned from his teacher, Boutroux: that each science must explain its phenomena by principles that are its own.[32] Lévi-Strauss would seem to have strayed from this precept, since the psychology he invokes, though not exactly individual, is certainly not collective, corresponding exactly to what Durkheim referred to as "formal psychology."[33] This brand of psychology studies the laws governing the association of ideas, without concern for whether these ideas are individual or collective, so that it does not matter whether they are personally developed (as in a dream or a poem) or collectively developed (as in a myth or a legend). Lévi-Strauss's structural unconscious is recognizable here, and he himself expressly refers to his own work using the term "formal psychology,"[34] one whose (purely theoretical) possibility Durkheim regarded with the deepest skepticism. The problem with assigning the meaning of collective representations to this sort of formal psychology is that the study of the mind is then dissociated from the study of institutions and practices, which is contrary to the very principle of social science according to the Durkheimian school.

Is there another way out of this impasse? There may be one, provided that we recognize that the functionalism of Lévi-Strauss's text is ambiguous. Indeed, Lévi-Strauss refers to two different things as "functional explanations." On the one hand, there is *naturalistic* teleological explanation in terms of needs to be met by an activity. On the other is the apprehension of a simple complementarity among various symbols whose sole "function" is to form a *meaningful* totality. Obviously, the second sense of the term is the one to be retained in defining structural anthropology as a science of the mind. Durkheim perhaps foreshadows this distinction when he comments, with regard to the method that explains institutions by their social usefulness, that "to show how a fact is useful is not to explain how it originated or why it is what it is."[35] In other words, there is more than just explanation by means of efficient causes (mechanism) and explanation by means of function within a whole that has certain needs (teleology): there is also explanation by means of the formal traits that result in a reality being constituted as it is. We may well conclude that such explanation by means of "formal causes"—explanation that says "how the thing is what it is" and why it falls into a given class—is as close to a recipe for structural explanation as one is likely to get.

3.4. Structural Explanation and Radical Comparison

It is clear how the answers given by anthropologists become questions for philosophers. The anthropologist has to provide himself with something like an impersonal collective mind, otherwise he remains at the level of common sense, somewhere between explanation by means of consciousness and explanation by means of the play of historical circumstances. But this notion of impersonal mind requires a philosophical clarification. We have just seen how Lévi-Strauss, the philosopher of the structural mind, elaborated the positions of Lévi-Strauss, the anthropologist of kinship systems, by invoking a theory of the structural unconscious (one which was to remain largely programmatic).

Before considering these problems in the forms that they have taken in recent times as a result of the development of models of artificial intelligence, we should note that Lévi-Strauss's solution is not the only one conceivable, even from within structural anthropology. In a chapter of his book on the caste system in India, Louis Dumont raises the same problem in similar terms. His response, however, is one that could be called *intentionalist* rather than *mentalist*. Dumont distinguishes three possible attitudes a researcher might take when confronted with a social institution that is incomprehensible to us (in his case, the Indian caste system).[36] "Voluntarist or artificialist explanation" sees the institution as the work of a legislator or sacerdotal group. If the institution has meaning, this meaning is to be explained by the wisdom of the legislator. And if the institution seems irrational to us, this senselessness is also to be explained by the prejudices, superstitions, and ignorance of the legislator. On the other hand, "historical explanation" sees the institution as the effect of "the more or less unique confluence of circumstances or factors."[37] These are exactly the same terms of the alternative criticized by Lévi-Strauss.

The voluntarist explanation at least has the virtue of taking into account the fact that the institution exhibits a meaning in the eyes of those whose institution it is, and that it must therefore be comprehensible. But it has the same flaw as the political doctrines of Enlightenment thought: it confuses social institutions and legislative codes and forgets that there can be no formal rules where there are no preexisting practices and customs.

Historical explanation, on the other hand, abandons the idea of providing any explanation whatever of the spirit or meaning of an institution, seeing the ideology of the actors themselves as a mere epiphenomenon. What we require, then, is an explanation that provides the institution's intellectual principle, but without seeking it in an individual consciousness.

Like Lévi-Strauss, Dumont indicates that the very idea of a structural approach is that of a third kind of explanation, one that explains neither by means of a self-conscious individual legislator nor by means of historical happenstance. Dumont's third possibility, which opens the way to a different surmounting of the false opposition between conscious will and the concourse of circumstances, does not appeal to a *psychic unconscious* but rather to the *socially implicit*. Indeed, Dumont's attitude consists in trying to link the institution that is at first incomprehensible (for us) but that is manifestly meaningful (for them) to the "known features of the society with which we are familiar" (i.e., to our own social milieu).[38] For example, a Western observer who has not entirely forgotten the "aristocratic mentality" of the French *ancien régime* will be able to put this part of his education to use in understanding the caste system as a "limit case." He can, more easily than, say, a Jacobin could, see it as the radical form of implementation of a holistic or hierarchical ideology.

Dumont himself, like Evans-Pritchard, to whom he refers on this point, compares the ethnographer's work to that of a translator. One could then characterize the attitude of the "limit-case scenario" as that imposed on a translator faced with the problem of rendering the meaning of an original text that makes use of particular linguistic resources for which the target language has no equivalents. One need only recall the difficulties faced by the translators who first attempted to render Aristotle in medieval Latin. Not that ancient Greek was any less suitable than another language to be rendered in Latin. The difficulty was rather due to the fact that Greek philosophers had developed in their schools a special idiom, different from ordinary or even literary Greek both lexically and syntactically. The solution for these translators was therefore to develop, using the existing resources of Latin, comparable means of expression. One could call this kind of work *idiomatic translation*: it is not an ordinary translation (for ordinary language has no way of translating what is idiomatic in the original text), nor is it an admission of failure (as it would be if the foreign word were kept and accompanied by historical and philological footnotes). Idiomatic translation is a particular variety of limit case: within what is familiar to me and that I understand, there is always something that allows me to enter into a foreign intellectual and linguistic world; but the familiar elements that allow me to establish such a connection are not immediately available in such a way as to allow simple translation or transposition.

This is why they require an elaboration or development like the "limit case" (for the anthropologist) or the "constitution of a specialized idiom" (for the translator).[39]

Thus, Dumont's answer is not a mentalist hypothesis about the structural unconscious, but rather a principle of "radical comparison" between forms of life and thoughts that are quite different from one another. Radical comparison involves confronting the way things stand for them (the object being studied) and the way they stand for us. The problem is clearly one of translation, but this translation is more complex than the linguistic operation that goes by this name, for we cannot be certain that they will share our categories or that we will share theirs. The two systems of categories will have to be compared and in order to do that, these two systems must first be given in explicit form. In other words, the translator may well be dealing with a text that is idiomatic in its original language, but at least he is working on an articulate expression; by contrast, the ethnographer takes as his task the description of ways of acting and of doing things. Mores are expressed first of all in conduct itself and only subsequently in rhetorical or pedagogical commentaries. And even if the locals have elaborated codes of etiquette and manuals of proper conduct, it is still not certain that these explicit elaborations provide us with the principles of that conduct. As a result, idiomatic translation must include—over and above its development of the resources of the target language—an explicit expression of the thoughts that the people display yet have not necessarily formulated explicitly for themselves. The ethnographer is in much the same position as a translator who, in addition to translating, must derive a grammar of the original language, where those whose native language it is are unable to provide one.

Returning to Mauss's teachings, Dumont gives the following formula for an understanding based in comparison, a comparison that is radical because it forces the investigator to put his own common sense into play: "In the last analysis, in order to truly *understand* we must be able on occasion to ignore this partitioning [among general classifications like morality, politics, economics] and to search, in the whole field, for what corresponds on *their* side to what *we* acknowledge, and for what corresponds on *our* side to what *they* acknowledge. In other words, we must strive to construct on both sides comparable facts."[40]

The reader might be tempted to conclude that to adopt such a view is to abandon the idea of uniting the study of institutions and the study of the mind. But to do so is to forget that, within the perspective of social anthropology, the human mind is first and foremost a social mind rather than a natural mind. In Dumont's view, anthropological inquiry, whose very principle is radical comparison, does indeed have the human mind as its object, and it is in fact the only means by which to uncover real universals. He writes, in a passage that provides the answer to the very question we have been asking:

> One can speak of "the human mind" only when two different forms of it are subsumed under a single formula, when two distinct ideologies appear as two variants of a single broader ideology. This process of subsumption, ever in need of renewal, designates the human mind both as its principle and as its asymptote.[41]

Where Lévi-Strauss deployed a new psychology that proposed a theory of the unconscious activity of the mind, Dumont invites us to take a comprehensive approach. In fact, we are here presented with two versions of the universalism constitutive of the structural anthropological project. These two versions are indications of incompatible philosophies of mind.

. . .

Structural anthropology has propagated a profound idea: that the teleology proper to our minds is not only manifested in individual instances of instrumental rationality (something no one disagrees with) but also in cultural phenomena. In the latter case, the rationality is not as easy to grasp, unless one is willing to return to the myth of the primordial Legislator whose wisdom explains the institutional system's coherence.

Lévi-Strauss has frequently stressed the distinction that must be drawn between functionalism and structuralism.[42] Functionalism postulates that all institutions serve a purpose, which is to produce social cohesion. But the problem confronted by structural anthropology is not the problem of social cohesion so much as it is the problem of intellectual cohesion. It is curious that this distinction between two types of proper ordering or coherence is constantly forgotten. Why is it so easily misunderstood? The answer is to be found in a look back at the strengths and weaknesses of structural anthropology. With the advantage of hindsight, it is easy for us to make such an assessment today.

Structuralism had as its ambition to surpass the classical opposition between scientific explanation (the preserve of the natural sciences) and the subjective understanding proper to the humanities. In his Inaugural Lesson at the Collège de France, Lévi-Strauss referred to this as a "false dichotomy,"[43] one outstripped by anthropology's combination of causal explanation and experiential understanding.

We have seen why the traditional hermeneutic formulation of a duality of the sciences was untenable. In it, the natural sciences could be called "objective," but at the price of abandoning intelligibility properly so called. For their part, the moral sciences could provide a meaning to human life, but it could never be known whether it was the correct meaning, since it is a function of the investigator's historical perspective and intellectual choices. This may explain why the idea of a structural explanation of anthropological facts had such an impact. Such a form of explanation seeks to be objective, like the explanations given in the natural sciences, but it also seeks to account for the meaning and rationality of institutions, as is fitting for a moral science.

Today, we recognize that the claim that structuralism would outstrip hermeneutic dualism remained unfulfilled. The preceding discussion shows why. In fact, hermeneutic dualism can be contested from opposing directions. One may find that the opposition between an explanation that does not lead to understanding and an understanding that is simply empathetic is not the correct way of characterizing the difference between the modes of intelligibility of natural scientific explanations and of anthropological ones. What one has then called into question are the very terms in which the opposition is expressed. But one can also reject hermeneutic dualism precisely because it is a dualism, i.e., because it posits that the moral sciences cannot be reduced to natural sciences.

By setting nature and culture in opposition, Lévi-Strauss seemed to be proposing a reformulation of that dichotomy. But in fact, it was the dichotomy itself that he was rejecting. In his view, the opposition between the natural and the cultural must be considered to be both methodological and provisional: in reality, the study of culture must seek to be the study of the natural conditions on culture. The goal is "the reintegration of culture in nature and finally of life within the whole of its physico-chemical conditions."[44] Structural explanation would then be a step in the direction of physical explanation, since by moving from institutions to their psychological foundations, we move closer to the brain and therefore closer to the natural infrastructures of the mind. Structuralism's philosophical significance, in this view, lies in having used the recent renewal of our natural philosophy to overcome the dichotomy of nature and mind. Structural explanation is thereby drawn in the direction of natural functional explanation. The idea is that hermeneutic dualism might have seemed inevitable as long as natural philosophy rejected every kind of teleology. In this view, the nineteenth-century incorporation of mind in nature was basically premature. Today, however, things are held to be different: we are witnessing the formation of a new physics of meaning, a natural science able to recognize that the material universe has not only "physical properties" but also "semantic properties."[45]

With hindsight, we can see that the context in which Lévi-Strauss formulated his methodological program was one marked by the ill-founded expectation that the social sciences and the natural sciences would be brought together by means of cybernetics.[46] Today, researchers would be more likely to expect a "formal psychology" from the disciplines involved in Artificial Intelligence (or "AI"). But if the model of the computer is to provide the cognitive psychology that, in the recent past, was expected to come from devices like the thermostat, Lévi-Strauss's program was simply ahead of its time. The hopes placed in both the psychology of the unconscious and information theory will have finally been realized by the "cognitive sciences." The unification of the sciences of the mind can then be well and truly carried out on the basis of a "formal psychology," that is, on a naturalistic basis rather than a sociological or historical one.

In fact, the practice of structural explanation has taken an entirely different direction. The invocation of the "structures of the human mind," taken to mean "mental mechanisms," has remained an empty gesture, a stance that is purely speculative. When anthropologists work, they do indeed study the human mind, but one that manifests itself either in the form of a population whose matrimonial alliances take place within a kinship system that is to be understood by comparing it to other such systems, or in the form of a mythological and ideological corpus whose principle it will have to provide. Structural explanation consists in treating as symbolic systems these forms in which the human mind is manifest, i.e., in treating them as systems of an intellectual sort that are to be understood by means of principles.

Structural anthropology does indeed overcome the rough opposition between explanation and understanding. But it does not do so by proposing naturalistic explanations of social and ideological facts (in the way that the philosophy of the structural unconscious seeks to do). It does so because its practice makes plain that the opposition between the natural and the moral sciences must be understood in a different way. All sciences seek to explain, and every explanation seeks to make comprehensible or intelligible something that is not immediately so. Some explanations help us understand phenomena by revealing the *mechanisms* responsible for their production. Other forms of explanation do so by identifying the *representations* and the *rules* of those who act in a certain way. The dichotomy is thus one of mechanisms and representations. To seek to go beyond it is to seek the means of reducing representations to mechanisms or to provide them with a physical causality. From a philosophical point of view, it might be said that cognitivism covers the same ground as structuralism conceived as a theory of the mind's unconscious activity, precisely because it also claims to have the correct reductive procedure.

These conclusions regarding the strengths and weaknesses of structural anthropology provide us with a way of approaching the question of the mind, taken as an inquiry into the status of the moral sciences.

Whatever the correct answer to the question regarding the duality of the sciences, we are already in a position to know that it will not consist in an opposition between explanation and understanding, or, if you will, between an "objectivist" point of view and the point of view of consciousness. In this regard, I believe that the general critique of the philosophies of consciousness is one of the achievements of twentieth-century thought and that the question is closed, even if certain equivocal formulations of this critique in the work of structuralists and others may have given false hopes for its revival.

The Achilles' heel of the project for the anthropological study of the mind was not that it failed to understand consciousness or subjectivity. We now see, with hindsight, that the "structures of the mind" meant to serve as explicative principles were equivocal. These structures were defined in *psychologistic* terms: they were presented both as rules, i.e., as normative principles governing activity, and as natural laws or principles governing the mind's very functioning. It is as if there were no difference in the meaning of the word "principle," whether used to refer to the principle of identity or to the principles of thermodynamics. Lévi-Strauss drew a distinction between the rules that subjects believe they are following (in their reasoning and their discourse) and the real principles of their activities. These "unconscious principles" are hybrids: while they are still rules, i.e., *intellectual principles*, we are nevertheless supposed to discover them through observation and use them in order to give causal explanations, as if they were *natural principles*.

All of this could be put in another way. Philosophies of mind diverge when it comes time to propose a concept of *objective mind*, by which I mean a concept of impersonal mind. No philosophy of mind can do without a definition of this concept (whether under this name or another). Indeed, every philosophy of mind will have to provide a status for what is called "tacit knowledge." People follow rules and act in the light of representations without those rules and representations being present as explicit expressions in their consciousness. That is why, for example, a speaker may judge a sentence to be incorrect, to be something that "one does not say," without necessarily being able to indicate the rules of his language in virtue of which the sentence is poorly formed. Similarly, people know who their parents are and who they may wed without having to refer to a general theory of their kinship system. The notion of objective mind must explain this gap between the actors' intellectual capacities and their consciousness. Are the rules part of the (tacit) knowledge of the actors or not?

There have traditionally been two ways of accounting for this gap and thereby of developing a philosophy of objective mind. The first of these is to posit a natural objective mind as a theoretical entity: rules and representations are then in reality mental structures that are physically present in the organism. This is the account given by the new mental philosophy on which the contemporary cognitivist program is based.

The other account defines the objective mind as a social mind. Objective mind, by which we measure the gap between the actor's intellectual abilities and his consciousness, consists in an *order of meaning*, one that is presupposed in every manifestation of intelligence on the part of a subject. This is the intentionalist route: mind is present in its phenomena and therefore in the world, in symbolic practices and institutions. Within people's heads, there are literally only the personal (and therefore physical or physiological) conditions for participation in these practices and institutions. The mental, however, is everywhere that it manifests itself, therefore in both discourse and action, whose conditions of existence are of a holistic nature. This account is that provided by the anthropological holism of the mental.

CHAPTER 4

The New Mental Philosophy

4.1. Prospectus for the New Science of the Mind

Wᴇ ᴡɪʟʟ ꜱᴏᴏɴ witness the establishment upon solid foundations of a scientific psychology. Its imminent arrival can be adduced from the fact that we are beginning to understand how a mechanical model might be provided for the way things take place in the mind."

So goes the communiqué that mental philosophy has been expecting to publish ever since it set itself the task of equaling, in the study of the mind, the successes of natural philosophy in the study of physical phenomena. The recent past has of course seen several premature announcements of such a scientific psychology. In each case, it had to be admitted subsequently that the theory had given rise to nothing but a pseudo-explanation (as was the case for the theory of the association of ideas) or that the doctrine initially presented as a great scientific discovery in fact derived its authority from something other than science (as was the case with psychoanalysis). Today, the program for a scientific psychology is called "cognitivism." In this chapter, my sole consideration will be the reasons that are given in support of the belief that this program constitutes a fundamental revision of all of our philosophical perspectives on the mind.

Before proceeding any further, we must distinguish between the scientific program and the philosophy that, according to some, supports it or, according to others, merely accompanies it. I will follow the usage recommended by several authors and make a distinction between the *cognitive sciences* and *cognitivism*.[1] The cognitive sciences are quite simply the sciences of the mind. By this I mean that the "cognitive sciences" to which the program appeals are those whose research bears upon behavior in which mind is exhibited. But the fact that one calls a given discipline—linguistics or anthropology, say—a "cognitive science" means that one has taken a particular position regarding both its object and its method. This position *is* cognitivism. If the sciences called "cognitive" were simply those whose objects are intellectual ones like language or culture, then the word "cognition" would be understood in the ordinary, precognitivist way, an understanding to which notions like the treatment of information and artificial intelligence are utterly alien.[2] Yet, when cognitive theorists include various already-existing disciplines among the cognitive sciences, they do so in order to propose that these disciplines redefine themselves in the light of a new conception of the mind. Thus construed, cognitivism is the program that seeks to change the sciences of the mind into cognitive sciences. For example, if linguistics counts among the cognitive sciences, it is not because it studies languages, which are intellectual systems. Rather, linguistics counts as a cognitive science because it could, we are told, be redefined or reconstructed as psycholinguistics, the study of the linguistic capabilities of a mental system endowed with the "organs" necessary for the understanding and production of sentences.

One might well believe the new concept of the mind to have been derived from cognitive psychology, particularly from that branch that has broken with behaviorist strictures by seeking to find out what happens within the infamous "black box." It is well known that the emergence of cognitive psychology was linked to the invention of the computer. The basis of cognitivism would in that case be a new psychology, itself the result of a technological innovation. In reality, however, the cognitivist conception of mind has been derived not from cognitive psychology but, as we shall see, from a particular philosophy. As early as 1976, the psychologist Ulric Neisser cautioned his readers against an excessive enthusiasm for the comparison between our cognitive abilities and those of the computer. He pointed out that the analogy with machines had served above all to reassure psychologists regarding the existence of a mental life to be studied. Why does the computer matter to psychologists? The important thing about the computer is that it works with information, that it manipulates symbols, that it stores and looks up elements in its "memory," that it classes messages, recognizes physical shapes, and so on. It matters little whether the computer proceeds as we do when it carries out such operations. For a psychologist, the crucial point is that the computer is able to do these things. As Neisser writes, the reason that psychologists have been so impressed with the performance of the computer is that before its advent they were not sure they had the right to believe in the reality of cognitive processes (in the pre-cognitivist sense of the term).[3] The objections of the behaviorists had sown the seeds of doubt. But if a computer engages in activities of a cognitive sort, what is there to stop a human being from doing the same? The computer offers, as is often said, a model. The fact that computers are machines—physical systems—provides what would seem to be this model's principal virtue. For the cognitivist hypothesis does not require that the specific operations of human psychology be exactly the same as those of the computer. What matters above all is the assurance that at no point has one taken leave of the physical world.

In the same text, Neisser asks what the real contribution of this model has been. In his view, the real contribution has been techniques and models whose psychological meaning is not clear, for they concern systems studied in laboratories. "There is still no account of how people act in or interact with the ordinary world. Indeed, the assumptions that underlie most contemporary work on information processing are surprisingly like those of nineteenth-century introspective psychology, though without introspection itself."[4] This is, once again, the point of view frequently put forward by Fodor: cognitivism is the rehabilitation of the representational theory of mind. The difference is that, by abandoning the first-person perspective, mental philosophy can present itself as a theoretical science of behavior.

If this is the case, we should not expect the sciences to which the adjective "cognitive" has been applied to explain its import. We should, rather, expect this of philosophers. If there has indeed been a "Cognitive Revolution," to use Howard Gardner's phrase,[5] I believe it lies above all in the reversal in which philosophy must provide, based on its own requirements, a concept of mind apt to provide the sciences of the mind with the "paradigm" they must follow in order to take shape as such.[6] In the debate regarding the *Geisteswissenschaften*, philosophy had always taken the opposite tack: the philosophy of the moral sciences sought to articulate a concept of mind able to encompass the phenomena of the mind as described, classed, systematized, and ordered within the existing moral sciences. Yet it is true that, by asking mental philosophy rather than the moral sciences as they are currently practiced to provide us with a concept of mind, the cognitivist does little more than reproduce the approach taken by philosophy in the era dominated by the "scientific method" before the question of methodological dualism was ever raised.

There is no shortage of introductions and initiations into the cognitivist philosophy of mind. The portion of these works intended to pique our interest in cognitivism is invariably divided into three parts, which develop the following three ideas:

1. It is once again permitted to have a mental life; behaviorism is finished.
2. Why is mentalism again respectable? Because it can no longer be suspected of having spiritualist leanings. It sees itself as vigorously materialistic and insists upon a monistic ontology.
3. How was mentalism's rehabilitation achieved? Through the adoption of the correct model. The mental philosophers of the past compared the mind to things like delicate watches and steam engines. But it is difficult to talk about the psychology of a watch or a thermodynamic system. By contrast, a computer can be said to function physically at the same time that it can also be said to carry out a calculation.

In short, mental philosophy became respectable the day that it was able to provide assurances of its naturalism and materialism. From this perspective, cognitivism seeks to succeed where behaviorism failed: in naturalizing the intentional. Behaviorist theorists were unable to translate psychological concepts into simple types of overt—and therefore *external*—behavior. But the cognitivist program proposes to translate these same concepts into internal events of a physical sort and whose presence the theory adduces so as to account for visible behavior.[7]

In order to understand this debate, one must have a sense of the debate regarding materialism in the philosophy of mind. This dispute, which is as old as mental philosophy itself, is an expression of its fundamental conceptual difficulty.

4.2. Remark on Materialism

In the philosophy of mind, materialism is opposed to spiritualism. Spiritualism maintains that mental abilities should be attributed to an immaterial part of the person, the soul. The opposing doctrine maintains that all of the parts of the person are material.

Is this opposing doctrine really materialism, though? One might well believe it to be, since all philosophy textbooks refer to this opposition between two prominent philosophies of mind. Yet the definitions often given of materialism leave aside the most important point: before deciding whether mental abilities are rightly attributed to an immaterial or to a material part of the person, one must first decide whether it is not a mistake to attribute the abilities of the whole to a part of that whole, whether material or not.

If we were to follow the usual definition of the conflict of the two philosophies of mind, we would characterize the two positions as follows: spiritualism maintains a real distinction between the body and the soul, whereas materialism rejects such dualism. Yet it is obvious that this explanation is inadequate. What does this definition say? That there are two conceptions of the *subject* of thinking. Where for the spiritualist the subject of thinking is immaterial, for the materialist this subject is physical. Let us apply this definition to the inaugural episode of the *cogito*. Who is the thinking subject in Descartes's *Meditations*? According to the text, it is not the material subject. The answer is thus a spiritualist one. It follows that this thinking subject is not Descartes, for the individual named Descartes is assuredly a physical subject, endowed with a physical history. The name "René Descartes" was bestowed on a newborn during a baptismal ceremony. If we follow our definition, we conclude: spiritualism maintains that it is not the person who thinks but an immaterial part of that person (the soul). Is materialism then merely the negation of spiritualism? It would seem to be so since, as is so often repeated, the materialist thesis is that *matter can think*. It is certain that Descartes, who is certainly a living—and therefore material—being, can think.

Yet it quickly becomes apparent that the materialist is not satisfied with the conclusion that because Descartes thinks and Descartes is a physical subject (rather than an angel or an immaterial substance), the portion of matter called Descartes can in fact think.[8] In fact, the materialist position maintains not that Descartes thinks but that Descartes's *mind* is material. The thinking subject is here again not Descartes but his material mind (his brain).

Since this point is usually not made explicit, it bears further amplification. There is a conflict, we are told, between "dualism" and "materialism." If it were enough merely to oppose dualism in order to be counted a materialist, this conflict would be between the following two conceptions:

(I) When Descartes writes that he is going to suppose that whatever things he sees are illusions, it is Descartes who makes this supposition.[9] More generally, when Descartes reports in his text that he is carrying out a mental act, the subject of that act is Descartes.

(II) When Descartes writes that he will suppose that whatever things he sees are illusions, it is Descartes who does the writing (by hand, on paper) but it is Descartes's mind that makes the supposition. It is also Descartes's mind that sees all of the things about which it is written, in Descartes's hand, that they are seen by him; generally speaking, we call "Descartes" the man—the physical subject—without worrying too much about the distinction made by the thinking subject between what he now judges himself to be (*res cogitans, id est, mens, sive animus, sive intellectus, sive ratio*) and what he used to think he was (someone with a face, hands, arms, etc. and who feeds himself, walks, and so on).

The opposition between conceptions (I) and (II), however, does not do justice to the conflict between materialists and spiritualists. Cognitivist theorists will be unlikely to give us credit for our orthodox materialism if we are willing to say only that all of the *parts* of Descartes's person are indeed material. Even in so rejecting the idea of a "unity of body and soul," we may still have set aside a role for the way in which these parts are integrated with one another, as living parts, within a complete whole. In other words, our "materialism" may still be laden with Aristotelian residues insofar as it seeks to distinguish not between material and immaterial parts of the person, but between the material parts of the person and the form in virtue of which these parts are the parts of a whole. Now, the materialist philosophy of mind wants to be able to continue to speak about the interaction of the mind and the body. Its position is supposed to be a *response* to the mind/body problem, and in no way a *rejection* of the very terms of the venerable question. In order to express the materialist position, we will then have to maintain that:

(III) When Descartes writes that he is going to suppose that whatever things he sees are illusions, Descartes's hand does the writing but Descartes's brain is what has this thought and consequently causes the action of writing. This thought must therefore be attributed to Descartes's brain as must the vision of things, for it is Descartes's brain that constructs the mental representations of his visual experience.

There are, then, two stages in the dualism debate. The first stage is an attempt to answer the question: Should one make a distinction between the subject of physical actions (I eat, I walk) and the subject of mental ones (I see, I think)? In other words, should one make a distinction between the mental subject and the person? To answer in the negative implies that one believes that psychological vocabulary includes both immanent intentional activities (like reflecting about something) and transcendent intentional activities (like searching for someone in a crowd). And to believe this is already to have rejected the point of view of mental philosophy. On the other hand, to answer in the affirmative requires that one move to the second stage of the problem, in which one will have to determine the nature of the duality of mind and body. Is this distinction to be understood using a dualism of kinds of substance (the soul and the body) or is it to be formulated within a monism? Only at this second stage is there a dispute between the Cartesian mentalist, who distinguishes between the immaterial subject of thinking and the material subject of physical movements, and the materialist mentalist, whose distinction runs between the material system of the mental apparatus (the brain) and the material system of the external behavior (the body).

At this point, a materialist is likely to raise the objection (no doubt in the world-weary tone of someone constantly obliged to point out the obvious) that a move to the second stage, of determining whether the organ of thinking is material or immaterial, cannot be avoided. Everyone must come down on one or the other side of this question, as a materialist or a spiritualist. If you claim that one can think without a brain, you are a spiritualist; if you recognize that one cannot, then you are a materialist like us.

To ask this question is once again to insist that we make no distinction between the abilities of Peter or Paul (persons) and the (external and internal) conditions in which they possess these abilities. The fact that it is here a question of *mental* abilities changes nothing. Can Paul think without a brain? The question bears on the circumstances in which it can be said that someone possesses a given ability. If Paul's brain is destroyed, Paul will definitively lose the ability to think as well as the ability to be Paul. If Paul's brain is temporarily put into a state of hibernation, Paul once again loses the ability to think. He is, for example, no longer able to reply to his mail. But the conditions in which we can do something are not these abilities themselves: the fact that Paul ceases to be Paul if we remove his brain proves neither that Paul is a brain nor that, in reality, his brain and not him is the subject of attribution of psychological predicates. For it is Paul, and not his brain, that answers the mail that Paul receives.[10]

In one of Peirce's more vibrant passages, he explains that one of the reasons that we locate the mind in the head is that we identify the mind with consciousness.[11] Consciousness, in the most ordinary sense of the term, manifests itself in the experience or sensation of impressions, which vary according to changes in the external milieu. That is why we believe that the mind lies within the nervous system. For Peirce, by contrast, the mind is not to be sought *inside*, in internal events of an experiential kind, but *outside*. For those who see consciousness, in the form of feeling, as an essential attribute of mind, Peirce responds that "feeling is nothing but the inward aspect of things, while the mind on the contrary is essentially an external phenomenon." Peirce's claim is that mental phenomena should not be sought within our heads but without, for example in intelligent behavior or communication through signs. The psychologists Peirce has in mind are those who sought to locate the various mental faculties in specific parts of the brain. For example, they declared it to have been proven that the linguistic faculty was precisely located in a certain cerebral lobe. As proof, they adduced the fact that, if a psychologist cuts away a certain lobe of my brain, I find myself suddenly unable to express myself. The psychologist will say: "Clearly your linguistic faculty was located within that lobe." This view requires that the capacity to do something, in this case to speak, be localized within a part of the body that can be shown to be indispensable to the exercise of that capacity. Peirce rejects the proof outright for, he claims, if the psychologist had simply taken away my ink-well, I would similarly have found myself unable to express myself or pursue discussion before having acquired another one: "Yea, the very thoughts would not come to me."[12] It follows that the linguistic faculty is equally present in the inkwell, with the result that the manifestation of this faculty requires an ontologically remarkable description: the capacity for language can be found in two different places at the same time.

Peirce explains that it would be better to say that language resides in the tongue and that the thoughts of a living author are found in his books, rather than to say that all these things are lodged in his brain.

Peirce's psychologist interlocutor might well reply that it is easier to replace an inkwell than a brain. The latter therefore occupies a central place. This, of course, goes without saying. But in saying this we accept that we are in the process of arranging the empirical conditions for the possession of certain capacities in an increasing order of necessity (in the sense of "need"). The physiological conditions for psychological phenomena are in the brain. That is something we have learned from scientific research and not from any "neurophilosophy," i.e., the pretension to study the brain through philosophical speculation.[13] But these phenomena of mind are only phenomena *of mind* insofar as they exist outside, in the public world.

4.3. Charter of the New Mental Philosophy

What is it that makes the mentalist conception plausible for contemporary philosophers? In order to come to an understanding of this, we will need to look at the language used by mentalists to express themselves. Our starting point will be a text in which Fodor admonishes his fellow mentalists for their timidity in advancing their own doctrine. Fodor's position is in many ways that of an *ultra* on a crusade among middle-of-the-road mentalists. As is always the case, the ultra provides a more coherent version of the position espoused, since he need not worry about making concessions or compromises with reality or the appearances accepted by common sense.

Addressing his mentalist colleagues, Fodor summarizes their dogma in three points (before inviting them to add to these three the properly Fodorian thesis of a "language of thought"). Here are the three articles of the mentalist dogma:

(1) The first article posits the reality of the mental: "There are beliefs and desires and . . . there is a matter of fact about their intentional contents; there's a matter of fact, that is to say, about which proposition the intentional object of a belief or a desire is."[14]

The first part of the first article is an assertion of existence which provides psychology with its own domain. This ontological thesis seems obvious: if psychology has something to study, it can only be because people do indeed have beliefs and desires.

The second part of the first article is more enigmatically expressed and requires some elaboration. What Fodor means is that it is not enough to attribute belief or desire to someone. One attributes particular and identifiable beliefs and desires that can be distinguished from one another. How does one identify desires and beliefs? Here again the answer seems trivial. In order to distinguish the particular beliefs of someone, we act as if they were expressed in a *credo*. In other words, we attribute to him the mental attitude of belief with regard to a certain number of objects of belief called "intentional objects," objects of the attitude of mind that consists in be-

lieving. These intentional objects are quite simply the different articles of
the credo to which the person in question subscribes or could subscribe.
Thus, the question of knowing the contents of someone's belief is in principle a question of fact: one need only have an opportunity to ask the person
whether he assents to a given proposition.

In short, the starting point of this first article is a postulate that is difficult to deny: *People have beliefs and desires*. From this the article derives
an assertion of existence: *There are beliefs and desires*, and infers from
that assertion a philosophy of mind that can be expressed by the thesis:
People have relations to sentences expressing what they believe and desire.

(2) According to the second article, a mentalist theory of mind is conceivable: "It may be that believing and desiring will prove to be states of
the brain."[15] In other words, the materialist hypothesis is intelligible: we
understand what it proposes.

The article recognizes that philosophy cannot replace empirical research
(in this case, neurological research): how someone's brain system works
as he passes through a particular mental state is an empirical question. In
other words, there is no reason for a philosopher to prefer one empirical
hypothesis to another, for a philosophical line of argumentation cannot
free us from the obligation to study how things actually happen in the
world.[16]

3) The third article posits that mental entities, whose reality has just
been posited, have a causal function: "beliefs and desires have causal roles
and . . . overt behavior is typically the effect of complex interactions
among these mental causes."[17] This is the especially "mentalist" thesis.
Obviously, this is the thesis for which the others merely prepared the way.

There is in these three articles something that seems to hinge on a rhetorical maneuver or even the art of salesmanship.[18] At first, the mentalist
dogma is presented as something exceedingly ordinary, something like the
mere recognition of the existence of a psychological dimension to human
affairs. Who, other than an outmoded, narrow-minded behaviorist, would
dare deny that people have opinions and desires (article 1)? What obscu-
rantist would go so far as to dispute the psychological interest of neurological research into behavioral or mental disorders (article 2)? Who is willing
to reject the platitude according to which people act on their beliefs or
towards what it is they seek to achieve (article 3)? Yet, in the end the
reader is surprised to learn that, by assenting to these obvious truths, he
has gradually embraced the elements of a particular metaphysics of
mind,[19] one that will require radical revisions of his concepts.

Let us take up the articles in turn. Far from being expressions of obvious
and inconsequential truths, each of these articles requires us to replace a
commonplace notion with a canonical mentalist formula that will allow

psychology to accomplish the promised master-stroke of *naturalizing intentionality*. Since this canonical formula departs from our usual ways of talking about human psychology, we are within our rights to ask that it be explained and justified.

First article (on the reality of the mental). Our point of departure is a proposition that would seem of little account from a philosophical point of view. We claim that people have opinions and desires. This initial proposition could be a reaction expressing our surprise and disbelief about the claims made by behaviorists. Only subsequently does this proposition take on a metaphysical cast. The first article of mentalism asks us to adopt the following canonical phraseology: when someone has an opinion—when, for example, he believes that the government will lose the election—he is in a state that consists in having a particular attitude with regard to an "intentional object": i.e., the representation of the government as being destined to lose the election. The object with which he has this relation is a proposition. In other words, by the end of the first article, we have unwittingly subscribed to a doctrine of "propositional attitudes" according to which to believe something is to be in a state of having a certain *relation* (one of "believing that," rather than, say, one of "doubting that" or "wondering whether") with a certain entity, namely the proposition rendering the represented object. Now, the key point for all of the subsequent discussion will be precisely the notion of a *state of mind*.

Second article (on the possibility of assimilating states of mind and states of the brain). The mentalist formulation redescribes beliefs by bringing into play the category of states (of mind). The translation of the mental into the physical seems then to be on the right path. Believing something is a state of mind. Believing something *could* well turn out to be a state of the brain. The materialism of this thesis is what attracts our attention, like a red flag waved in front of those philosophers anxious to avoid being suspected of spiritualism. But the decisive point lies elsewhere, in getting us to take the attribution to someone of a belief or a desire (this gentleman running toward the railway platform believes himself to be late and wants to catch his train) for an attribution of a state (he is in the state of believing himself to be late; he is in the state of wanting to catch his train). The notion of a mental state has thus been introduced without having been put forward as such and *in a sense that is comparable to the notion of a state of the brain*, the goal having been to prepare the way for a psychology able to discover the laws of the mind and thus to discover regular sequences in the succession of the mind's states.

Note that once this metaphysical preparation of the ground is accomplished, the doctrine of a "language of thought" has a role to play and seems plausible. This doctrine is meant to provide an answer to the question of what exactly a "state of mind" might be, by adding to the ordinary mentalist doctrine the idea that the brain of someone who has an opinion the content of which can be articulated in a sentence, will in its turn contain a corresponding material symbol, one that has been constituted as a sentence according to the rules governing the writing of the "cerebral code."

Third article (on the causal function of beliefs and desires). Here again, there is a leap between the point of departure, which seems inconsequential, and the conclusion. If our traveler is running toward the railway platform, it must be *because* he is afraid of being late for his train. This is a starting point that no one would seriously dispute unless he had an ideological system to defend. Who would be willing to claim that there would be no change in the traveler's behavior if we informed him that his train had already departed or that, due to a delay, his train had not yet arrived in the station? Beliefs must therefore make a difference. In this case the appropriate formulation in the mentalist dogma runs as follows: if the traveler's legs move rapidly so as to give him a running gait, it can only be because there has taken place within his head a complex interaction between his beliefs regarding the train schedule, the time of day, the time necessary to cover the distance to his goal, and his prevailing desire not to miss the train. (Here, the doctrine of a language of thought adds that the causal role of a mental reality—for example, the presence of a belief in someone's mind—must be assigned to the physical symbol inscribed in the brain).

Taken together, these three articles provide the core of mentalist philosophy. Fodor concludes that "psychological explanations need to postulate a network of causally related intentional states."[20] Thus have we moved from commonsense platitudes to the theoretical hypothesis of a mental machinery. The first thesis is ontological: there are beliefs and desires. But that claim serves only to ward off the paper tiger of a doctrine that would claim that there are no such things. In fact, the important point is the associated metaphysical thesis that a belief bears upon a proposition and therefore, ultimately, on a sentence. Though this second thesis seems to be a kind of scientific prognostication, it in fact aims to model the metaphysics of mind on the metaphysics of physical systems that pass through various states. The third thesis is directly psychological: in order for there to be a psychology in the mentalist sense of the term, the psychological phenomenon must be divided into a purely exterior part and a purely internal one (the latter being postulated in order to explain the former).

On this point a distinction should be drawn between classical mentalist philosophy and the new variety. One way of doing this is to stress the kinship between today's "cognitive revolution" and certain philosophical ideas of the seventeenth century. In an introductory presentation of these topics, Chomsky goes so far as to refer to *two* cognitive revolutions: that of Descartes and his successors (which put an end to the dominance of the scholastic conception) and that of today (which abolished the hegemony of behaviorism).[21] The first of these revolutions established the "representational theory of the mind."[22] So it was that Descartes explained that the subject of visual perception is like a blind man with a cane. Whenever this man touches a cube, for example, with his cane, he constructs a mental representation of that cube. The perception of the cube results from the cognitive process by which sense data are treated and which results in the mental image. The second cognitive revolution coincides with the development of computer science, which provided plausible models of mental activities and their structures by presenting them as "cognitive processes," i.e., computational processes performed upon the system's internal symbols.

But what authorizes Chomsky to claim that in studying a person's linguistic capacities he is studying the person's *brain*? One thing is clear: he is studying the capacities of a physical system, for only physical systems can speak and understand. But do linguistic capacities depend on cerebral structures? Such a thing is possible, but the linguist, *qua* linguist, knows nothing about it. When Chomsky talks about studying the brain from the perspective of those cognitive capacities responsible for the use of language, he does so, as he himself admits, at a very high level of abstraction. In fact, this level of abstraction is so high that the word "brain" will have to be understood as something like "whichever part of the organism happens to underpin the capacities in question." Only from a distance is tribute here paid to neurology. In fact, nothing in Chomsky's generative grammar would change if we were to learn that, in the end, the kidneys and the heart sustain our linguistic activity rather than the brain.

Has the representational philosophy of mind been rehabilitated? It is to this question that we must direct our attention. In order to do so, we will have to take up the tenets of the new mentalist philosophy in an analytical order.

The aim of the new mentalist philosophy is to provide psychology with the means to formulate causal explanations. But does psychological explanation, in the way this expression is used currently, require mental states and internal representations? This is the problem of *psychical causality* (discussed in chapter 5 below).

The second cognitive revolution prides itself on having rendered intelligible the idea that mental states are physical states or, more precisely, states of an organism's brain. When we think, we do what computers do when they calculate, and no one doubts that computers are entirely physical machines. Here we face the problem of the psychology of the computer (chapters 6 through 8).

The two cognitive revolutions have a point in common: the idea that believing and desiring are two internal mental states. To adopt this hypothesis means, at least in principle, taking an entirely different approach to determining what people actually believe and desire (chapter 9). The solipsistic disposition of both the new and the old versions of mental philosophy has its origin in the metaphysics of mental states (chapters 10 and 11). This solipsism, however, can only be abandoned if one (formulates a satisfactory version of the "holism of the mental" (chapter 12), a formulation that I delineate in greater detail in my *Les institutions du sens*.

NOTE ON THE CONCEPT OF METAPHYSICS

In the context of the philosophy of mind, the word "metaphysics" might cause some confusion. One might well believe that a discussion is more likely to become "metaphysical" when it concerns the mind—an entity whose status is problematic if not entirely suspect due to the fact that it is intangible or hidden—than when it is about more palpable things like cauliflowers, the glycogenic function of the liver, or the rules of table tennis (to take examples from a variety of categories). It would be an error to think so. The most useful meaning of the word "metaphysical" is that which directs our thinking not toward speculative entities but toward the status, within our conceptual system, of classes of utterly familiar things. To ask such questions, one need not even use the word "metaphysics." Wittgenstein, who rarely used the traditional philosophical vocabulary (preferring to speak of what he called "philosophical grammar"), provides a perfect illustration of the meaning of metaphysical inquiry in the example he gives of a difference in categories. The context for the comparison he makes is his discussion of the confusion that arises from the fact that we persist in talking about different "kinds of objects" where in fact we need a distinction more radical than a mere difference in kind. For example, theorists of sense data draw a distinction between objects that are different in kind: a physical tree and a phenomenal tree. Wittgenstein explains the confusion as follows: "They think they are making such a statement as 'A railway train, a railway station, and a railway car are different kinds of objects,' whereas their statement is analogous to 'A railway train, a railway accident, and a railway law are different kinds of objects.'"[23]

It is true that the word "metaphysical" has several meanings among philosophers and that this may give us reasons to prefer less historically loaded terms. Yet it is difficult to do without this term. Moreover, the "ethics of terminology" (Peirce) requires that we restrict ourselves, as far as is practicable, to the vocabulary most apt to facilitate communication within the profession and therefore to use the traditional meaning of terms whenever possible.

In one of the (historically derived) senses of the term, the word "metaphysical" applies to what is immaterial, supra-sensible, a reality whose existence has no physical conditions. If the word were always understood in such a way, we would have to say that spiritualism has a metaphysics whereas materialism does not. This leads to an obvious terminological difficulty: how are we to qualify the declarations of the materialist who refers to his "physicalist ontology"? This is why I believe the word must not be used in a *dogmatic* sense but only in an *operational* one.

The operational sense of the term must be a neutral one that neither privileges nor excludes any particular school of thought. It seems to me that these requirements are met by one of the traditional meanings of the term "metaphysics." Every philosophy is required to make great conceptual distinctions like those made by Aristotle in the treatise called *Metaphysics*: between the actual and the potential, between independent existence (substance) and dependent existence (accident). The fact that a philosopher ponders such distinctions says nothing about his doctrinal affiliations. The use of the word "metaphysical" to qualify his thought is therefore not a dogmatic one. By contrast, a theorist who carefully avoids having undertake the examination of these sorts of distinctions demonstrates by this very fact that he is unwilling to commit himself seriously to the ways of philosophy. This is so whether the examination is *called* "metaphysical" or something else. What matters is whether there is a place in his thinking for the clarification of the category distinctions on which our understanding of a domain of inquiry or discussion rests.

A few references here will suffice to show that the operational sense of the term "metaphysical" is just as vital in philosophy as is the dogmatic one. Descartes's idiom provides an excellent example of this. In theory, the dogmatic sense should predominate in Descartes's work: the *Meditations* are metaphysical because they take immaterial things (God and the soul) as their subject. Yet it is also worth pointing out that the object of the *Meditations* does not exclude the physical, since it discusses the soul so as to establish a *real distinction* between the soul and the body. Likewise, it discusses God in order to demonstrate that there is one and only one universal Cause of things. As a result, Cartesian metaphysics also sets down the principles of *physics*. From an operational point of view, what is metaphysical in Descartes's *Meditations* is that it reaches its conclusions for reasons that revolve around the use of concepts like that of a "real distinction" (as opposed to a "distinction of reason" or a "modal distinction") or of "formal reality" (as opposed to "material reality" or "objective reality"). In the preface to the *Principles of Philosophy*, Descartes does in fact use the term "metaphysical" to mean "immaterial," but he also uses it in a way that is closer to what I have been calling the operational sense. He distinguishes that part of philosophy containing "the principles of knowledge" from another containing "the principles of material things." The first of these is *metaphysical*, the second is *physical*. But the principles of knowledge in question here are "first notions" and "eternal truths." Now, we know that for Descartes, first notions (notions that enter into the composition of all our thoughts regardless of their object) are divided into four classes[24]: (1) general notions (existence, number, duration, substance, accident, mode); (2) notions specific to the consideration of bodies (extension, figure, movement, disposition of the parts, divisibility); (3) notions specific to the consideration of minds (thought, perceptions of the understanding, the inclinations of the will); (4) notions specific to the consideration of the composite of the soul and the body (appetites, passions, feelings). Among the "common notions" are also found truths like "effects are proportionate to their causes" and "it is impossible that something both be and not be." Here we are thus again confronted with the idea by which the objects of metaphysical inquiry are such grand conceptual distinctions rather than a particular domain of reality.

In general, the operational sense of the technical term "metaphysical" is to be found whenever a philosopher is required to fix in advance the possibilities for classification and explanation offered by a general conceptual system. For example, Kant, in his "metaphysical exposition" of the concepts of space and time,[25] makes use of a classical division of categories when he asks whether space and time are things (substances) or determinations of things (qualities) or relations among things (Kant's innovation was to add a surprising fourth possibility to these). More recently, Russell enumerated the "metaphysical convictions" expressed by the symbolism proposed in the *Principia Mathematica*: "This symbolism assumed that there are 'things' which have properties and have, also, relations to other 'things.'. . . I employed small Latin letters for 'things,' small Greek letters for classes, and capital Latin letters for relations."[26] What I have been calling the "operational sense" of the word "metaphysics" is the one that is currently used in English-language philosophy today.

In the nineteenth century, questions about the status of the sciences of the mind were held to be questions of method. These were discussed as part of what was called "the logic of the sciences," where "logic" means the study of forms of explanation. It was on these grounds that positivism was challenged by hermeneutics. But this view of the problem is too short-sighted. Indeed, it adheres to a positivistic conception of science. Lying behind the reduction of the question of mind to questions of method, we find the old prejudice according to which scientific activity consists in the concoction of general theories compatible with the observed facts. This way of looking at the problem is flawed, however, for it is well known that one can always offer several theories that account for the same set of facts and that are equivalent from a logical point of view. How are we to decide among them? Positivist epistemology is obliged to add supplementary "constraints" of an aesthetic or economic kind (the simplicity of the explanation, the small number of principles and postulates). In fact, theories differ in their *ontologies*: for example, mentalist psychology sees the mind as having the same ontological structure as nature itself, which is why mentalists speak of changes in someone's state of mind as they might speak of a change in the state of the water in a kettle. In other words, it is not logic that decides this question, it is metaphysics. The fact that a theory is satisfactory in its logical (hypothetico-deductive) form is not enough for it to carry the day or even for it to be plausible. The problem is rather one of knowing whether the models a theory proposes respect the ontological conditions of a description of the mental. These ontological conditions must be fixed as matters of principle and, thus, through a philosophical process undertaken by the psychologist or anthropologist. In this way, the dogmas of positivism have today been largely and irrevocably overcome, it seems to me, in English-language philosophical writing. In general, contemporary philosophers of mind—whether materialist or not—take pains to make explicit the metaphysics of the conceptual models they are proposing, a sure sign that they see the need to justify those models from an ontological standpoint and thus from the standpoint of the categories of being to which they appeal. Moreover, even if these philosophers do not feel the need themselves, it is unlikely that their critics will fail to point out this weakness in the presentation of their theses.

These clarifications allow us to return to the tangled question of the "monism" that is usually contrasted with Cartesian "dualism." Here, there are really two questions that have been conflated into one. And the most important question is not necessarily the more sensational of the two, the question that Mersenne put to Descartes of whether a body can think. On the one hand, those who speak of reducing the mental to the physical consider their position to be a "materialist monism" opposed to "dualism." On the other are those who make a distinction between mental and physical states. But is the word "state" used in the same sense for each of these? If there is to be a dualism of substances or a "Cartesian dualism," the word "substance" will have to have the same meaning when applied to the body and the mind. Otherwise, it would be impossible to move to a *classification* of the two types of substance. It follows that the word "state" will also have to have the same meaning (with the same consequences) when one ascribes states to extended and thinking things. In terms of the categories it uses, Cartesian *dualism* must be underpinned by a *metaphysical monism*.

Metaphysical monism properly so-called is not about setting about counting the number of substances or existences and discovering that there is only one (determining that the Whole is One and not Many, as Russell put it at the end of the nineteenth century). Monism consists in saying that there is a single ontological class within which our inventory will be carried out. I will therefore use the phrase "metaphysical monism" to refer to the following presupposition: A single system of metaphysical concepts is all that is needed. By "metaphysical concepts" I mean general notions like *substance, state, process, capacity, operation, mode, attribute, relation*, and *intrinsic property*, notions that have been studied in metaphysical treatises since Aristotle. These are the concepts that must be used when moving forward with the distinctions, classifications, enumerations, correlations, and so forth in one's chosen domain of inquiry (the phenomena of mind, for example).

In Descartes's case, the dualism for which he is famous assumes that substances can be counted: the term "substance" is thus used with a particular meaning that makes enumeration possible. Descartes speaks of a real difference between the soul and the body only because he assumes that these two things can be conceived as separate, that one could exist without the other. That is why he concludes that the subject of attribution of mental operations must be deemed a separate substance. There is then no paradox in asserting that the Cartesian dualism of the mind and the body presupposes a metaphysical monism, since substances, whether material or spiritual, can be enumerated. A single system of categories allows us to describe everything that is, and in every domain.

Historians of philosophy have recognized this point. Guéroult points out that, though Descartes is famous for his "dualism," there is in fact in his work a complete parallelism between the science of material things and that of the mind. A single philosophy grounds rational physics and rational psychology. In other words, there is a neutral metaphysical structure that one finds both in discussions about extended bodies and in discussions about minds. As Guéroult puts it:

> The same concepts govern the true science of physical things and that of clear and distinct thought. The *Regulae* seem to confirm that thought, like movement, can be accounted for using notions inspired by analytic geometry, notions which, though they differ from our ordinary perceptions of things, are precisely meant to account for those perceptions. Just as each indivisible instant of simple movement (all of which are concatenated to comprise real, i.e., temporal, movement) contains within itself no assigned trajectory and is, in the end, an instant of rest, the individual intuitions whose accumulation con-

stitutes my thought over time are also atemporal rests that contrast with the "continuous movement of thought" [*Regulae*, Regula 3, A. T., X, p. 370] which is "always temporal like my actions."[27]

This monism of the general conceptual system is more consequential than the subsequent divisions between the properties of the body and those of the soul. The fact that Descartes applies the same schema of subject and attributes (properties) to both is confirmation of his tendency to make every description dependent upon a single general metaphysics.

Among twentieth-century philosophers, metaphysical monism largely predominates, irrespective of whether the philosophers support or contest the reduction of mind to nature. One finds it in Husserl's idea of a "formal ontology" that goes beyond the "regional ontologies"; one finds it in the idea of a "unity of science" put forward by the logical positivists. Today, it is found among those who believe that everything must be describable in terms of set theory and first-order predicate calculus.

Among the philosophers who contest metaphysical monism one finds above all Heidegger (with his distinction between categories and what he calls "existentialia") and Wittgenstein, whose "philosophy of psychology" rests on a critique of the prevalent ideas about "mental processes" and "mental states." More recently, several philosophers have taken up this Wittgensteinian theme, some in an Aristotelian context,[28] others in the context of the philosophy of science.[29]

In France, the weight of the Cartesian legacy and the prestige of mathematical formalism have hardly provided a favorable climate for the critique of metaphysical monism. One can nevertheless single out Cornelius Castoriadis's critique of the illusion of a general metaphysics. In Castoriadis's work, the critique of the philosophers' pretensions to draw up a universally valid system of categories is combined with a critique of the idea that authentic reality is determinate reality. Precisely because one is convinced that set theory furnishes a general ontology, one deems to be "unreal" everything that does not conform fully to the conditions of an extensional (or "set-identical") description, everything, therefore, that seems vague or indeterminate.[30]

In the context of the study of the mind, the metaphysical problem is not one of counting the varieties of substance (within the unique category called "substance"). It is to know whether the sciences of the mind are to work with the same system of categories as do some or all of the sciences of nature or whether, on the other hand, they should not instead take their metaphysical system from disciplines that deal with human affairs like law, rhetoric.

CHAPTER 5

The Doctrines of Psychical Materialism

5.1. What Is a Psychological Explanation?

EVERY ENDEAVOR to set up a "scientific psychology"[1] presupposes the possibility of formulating explanations that exhibit three traits at once: they will be *psychological* explanations, they will be well-formed *causal* explanations, and they will be explanations of a *mechanical* sort. While it would seem simple enough to bring together two of these traits, it remains to be seen whether it can be done with all three.

The first thing to notice is that an ordinary psychological explanation can be both psychological and causal without being part of any "scientific psychology." Why is that child crying? Because his friend took away his toy. This is a causal explanation: the child is crying (psychological phenomenon) because someone made him cry (causation of crying through the intervention of the agent who unleashed the crying by seizing the toy against the child's will). But this explanation is not of the form required for us to be able to impute its explicative value to a psychological science. What I mean by this is that such an explanation is not, for example, physiological or chemical. It says nothing about the mechanism of the lachrymal glands. Nevertheless, this psychological explanation is appropriate to a historical inquiry, not a natural one: once one has understood who made the child cry and how, one has understood all of the facts necessary for an explanation of the incident.

Is this explanation, as is often claimed, merely a crude natural explanation? Are so-called commonsense explanations really hypotheses that implement vague and uncertain laws that are one day destined to be replaced by real scientific explanations, in much the same way that scientific medicine replaced popular medicine and witchcraft? Fodor believes that the type of causal explanation given by what he calls "the psychology of beliefs and desires" is so essential that we do not understand what it would mean to abandon it. If you tell me, he writes, that it is not because we want something (a piece of fruit, say) that we extend our hand toward a piece of fruit or that it is not because it itches that we scratch precisely where it itches, then "practically everything I believe about anything is false and it's the end of the world."[2] As he also puts it, to abandon this psychology of intentions would be "the greatest intellectual catastrophe in the history of our species," a much more profound cataclysm than that caused by "the collapse of the supernatural."[3] There is much that is right in Fodor's observation, but his very way of expressing it betrays a certain confusion on his part regarding what is fittingly called the "psychology of common sense," a confusion between ordinary explanations and those of a theoretical sort (whether the theory in question is occultist and animist or enlightened and scientific). The aim of the present chapter is to clarify this point and, in doing so, to arrive at a better understanding of the conditions that a mechanistic science of the mind will have to fulfill. To fulfill those conditions would be to satisfy the principles of what might be called "psychical materialism" (by analogy with historical materialism, which credits itself with having put forth laws of history grounded in dynamic mechanisms like the "conflict between the growth in productive forces and the continuity of relations of production").

It is perfectly correct to say that we cannot imagine what it would be like to do without what we call psychological explanations. Why has my associate told me that it is three o'clock when it is really four o'clock? One possible explanation is that my associate is wrong. Unbeknownst to him, his watch has stopped and he really believes it to be three o'clock. He has told me that it is three o'clock *because he believes* that it is three o'clock. Unless of course he has told me it is three o'clock *because he wants* to make me believe that it was neither knowingly nor willingly that he arrived late for our appointment. This use of "because" is indeed beyond revision and is impervious to any change in our explanatory paradigms. We are incapable of understanding what the philosopher would have us do when he tells us that this sort of explanation will eventually be replaced by a more satisfactory one. The explanatory practice by which we clarify someone's statement through reference to the motives he has for putting it forth is not an optional or local practice that could be excised from the whole of our practices without affecting the others. This way of explaining is omnipresent and therefore impossible to isolate or even correct.

But if this is so, if we really cannot imagine replacing these explanations by others, then these explanations do not form a body of theoretical doctrine. Everything theoretical or hypothetical must be capable of being discussed, tested, and confronted with other ways of accounting for the same facts. To be theoretical is to be subject to revision and correction and eventual replacement by more satisfactory forms of explanation.

One must therefore choose: either ordinary explanations are the result of our applying to the facts a (commonsense) theory, in which case such explanations are liable to be improved or even eliminated by scientific research, *or* they are irreplaceable, in which case they do not have the status of hypotheses about the causes of observed phenomena. It seems to me that Fodor is right not to take seriously the materialists' prediction that intentionalist psychology will one day vanish in the face of the progress of Enlightenment: on that day, they claim, people will *cease to believe* in the value of explanations in terms of belief, and that will be because they *believe* in the superiority of a purely natural explanation that does not rely on beliefs. This very claim thus unwittingly confirms the view that ordinary explanations make no appeal to any theory and that their intelligibility does not depend on any particular hypothesis.

This is not Fodor's understanding of the problem. For him, commonsense psychology "takes for granted that overt behavior comes at the end of a causal chain whose links are mental events—hence inobservable— and which may be arbitrarily long (and arbitrarily kinky)."[4] If common sense explains things through causal chains whose existence is hypothetical, then common sense does indeed offer explanations of a theoretical sort. I believe, though, that the word "explanation" is being used equivocally. Common sense offers psychological explanations and these psychological explanations are causal. But they are not theoretical. A terminological distinction will help to illuminate this equivocation.

Because its origins are Greco-Latin, our philosophical vocabulary often has pairs of terms that are lexically equivalent. In such cases, it is possible to give a specialized meaning to each of the two terms—which are in themselves equivalent—in order to mark a distinction that is not yet expressed in ordinary language.[5] I propose to take advantage of the existence of two expressions within our lexicon, "mental causality" and "psychical causality," to mark a distinction between, on the one hand, the ordinary practice of psychological explanation for human behavior and, on the other, the construction of psychological theories that aim to satisfy naturalistic conditions of formulation and verification. Now it happens that the expression "psychical causality," which seems so scientific, was used by Jacques Lacan (in a text discussed below) as an equivalent of "psychogenesis" and thus to designate the scientific hypothesis of a purely psychological etiology of certain disturbances of personality or behavior.

I will use the term *mental causation* to refer to all explanations that are "psychological" in the way in which that term is used by biographers, diplomats, businessmen, and lawyers. And I will use the term *psychical causality* to designate theoretical hypotheses put forward by those seeking to develop a scientific psychology. Theories of psychical causality all have one thing in common: they must identify a set of psychical elements (destined to form part of the explicative chain) and describe a small number of simple mechanisms (in order to account for the emergence of effect B whenever cause A arises). Thus, the associationist theory was meant to be a scientific theory. In its case, the psychical units were ideas, and psychical causation the property that ideas have to call to mind others, either through similarity or contiguity.

5.2. Commonsense Psychology

Contemporary materialist theorists often point out the existence of a "folk psychology." This commonsense psychology, according to them, is to future science what the faith healer's medicine is to scientific medicine: both psychologies share common objectives (to explain) but differ in their means to that end (since one gives explanations derived by ignorant people for the benefit of other ignorant people while the other provides explanations guided by the scientific method). In reality, this conception of things is highly questionable. If there were something like a popular psychology, then in order to know what it consisted in, one would have to study it in the same way that one studies popular medicine, popular pharmacology, popular religion, or popular arts and traditions. Something like a popular medicine certainly exists, but the healer's remedies cannot be guessed through the sole consideration of current ways of speaking. All that can be predicted is that popular medicine will undoubtedly not be the same from one country or tradition to the next. If there were a commonsense psychology, it would also be just as variable, since all cultures do not explain the motives for actions in the same ways. In short, it would seem that the real purpose of the phrase "folk psychology" is a polemical one in which this label is tacked on to every use of the psychological verbs of ordinary language.

Summarizing the views of American writers who use this notion, Pierre Jacob writes: "What contemporary philosophers call 'naive or everyday psychology' seeks to describe, explain and predict human actions and behaviors that are held to result from the interaction of the mental states—intentions, beliefs, desires—that adult human beings attribute to one another in a seemingly effortless way."[6] Here is the first example he gives of a naive or ordinary explanation:

> *X wants to get rid of his headache,*
> *X believes that, if he swallows an aspirin tablet, he will get rid of his headache,*
> *Therefore, X swallows an aspirin tablet.*

At first glance, this example resembles a third-person practical syllogism. What is naive about such an explanation? What about it is unsatisfactory?

The naivety is of course introduced into this explanation by the philosopher, who changes the practical line of reasoning into a description of mental events. Indeed, "naive psychology" is supposed to speak of events and interactions. If it did not, it would not qualify as a predictive theory. But what interactions? Is it that the desire to get rid of a headache acts upon the belief in the therapeutic benefits of aspirin? If the desire acts on the belief, it will have to modify the belief and, if it modifies it, the subject will no longer have the same belief. Or is it the belief that acts on the desire? In that case, the action of the belief would have to change the desire into something else, into, say, a desire to put one's slippers on or into a memory of having visited the British Museum. To this, the theorist of psychical causes is likely to respond that it was never a question of desires and beliefs but of states of the subject: the state of desiring to get rid of a headache enters into interaction with the state of believing in the benefits of aspirin. But how can the states of a single subject interact? How can the state of something act upon another simultaneous state of the same something?

The theorist of psychical causes may well respond that the psychological subject is in fact a complex system comprising different parts. One of the parts of the system handles beliefs and another is responsible for desires. The interaction of these parts would then bring about behavior. But this "modular" explanation is still incomprehensible. Whenever a part of a person interacts with another part, it is never a belief acting on a desire or the converse.

It might be proposed that the interaction among mental causes be understood as corresponding to phenomena like the following: the acquisition of a belief that it is going to rain changes my desire to take a walk into a desire to stay home. Yet if that were all that were going on, the interaction in question would reduce to a way of speaking. To say that the acquisition of a belief modifies my desire is then just a complicated way of saying that, in learning that it was going to rain I gave up the idea of taking a walk and preferred staying home to getting wet. The stylistic variation is of no ontological significance. In order for there to be the beginnings of a theory, one has to add that to believe it is going to rain is to construct an internal mental representation of rain as something that will soon be falling, and that to abandon the idea of taking a walk because it is going to rain is to construct, under the effect of the mental acquisition of a belief relation to the mental proposition "it is going to rain," an internal mental representation of the walk as now being inopportune. It goes without saying that this entire metaphysical armature has been added by the philosopher: the common sense that is so often invoked has said nothing at all about hypothetical internal events.

Does this mean that the ordinary explanation is a spiritualist one and that it assumes that the episodes of mental life occur with no material support or that there are no cerebral processes at work in them? Not at all. To make this claim is to ask of common sense (for example, that of the lawyer's plea or the historian's narrative) that it make pronouncements about things that are not its concern. In saying that Achilles is enraged, the narrator says nothing about the state of Achilles' brain or his heart. That does not mean that the narrator maintains that a description of the physiological and neuronal state of an enraged man is impossible. The narrator cannot have taken a position on a question that he in no way considered. To claim that he has is to fall victim to the fallacy that treats a partially indeterminate representation as though it were the representation of a reality reduced to its determinate part. The fact that my representation of someone's state does not include a given condition of that state in no way implies that my representation is of a state free of all conditions. If it were, we would have to claim that, for example, if I say I have seen a tourist and I fail to specify his country of origin, or if I say I saw a tourist but did not notice where he was from, in both cases I am claiming to have seen a tourist who had no country of origin. Of course, I am claiming nothing of the sort (*abstrahentium non est mendacium*).

The theorist who is preparing the way for a scientific psychology is perhaps not in the best position to defend a psychology that seems prescientific to him. It is nevertheless incumbent upon him to attribute an intelligible theory to common sense. How is it that the commonsense practical syllogism is intelligible, while the "explanation" it is purported to give makes no sense at all? The answer is that commonsense never referred to "interactions" between "states" of believing and desiring. Those terms belong to the theorist's language and serve to give ordinary psychological explanations the false appearance of being "theoretical." Someone who has a headache is in a state that is more or less unpleasant, but someone who wants to soothe his headache is normally considered to be someone suffering from a headache and who is looking for a way to get rid of it: we do not attribute to him a second state (the desire) in addition to the first (the migraine).

Here we come across a second difficulty: once they are transcribed into canonical theoretical forms, ordinary explanations give rise to a mystery. How can the representation that it is desirable to stop having a headache act at all? How can the representation that aspirin gets rid of headaches be said to act? By transferring the initiative from the agent (actor X in our practical syllogism) to the "components" of his state of mind, the theorist needlessly gives rise to a riddle regarding the causality of representations. But the very idea of a causality of representations belongs to a magico-religious perspective on things.

How indeed could there be a causality proper to representations when the name "representation" is reserved precisely for an activity that leaves things as they are? How can the activity of representing something change the state of anything at all? By accepting a profane or "disenchanted" view of the world, we have *decided* to call "mere representations" those of our activities that have no effect on our environment. Yet these activities, which are purely representative or, as they are often characterized, purely symbolic, must exert an efficient causality if the claims of the most prominent theorists of the newly respectable science of the mind are to be believed. Does this view not make plausible the boasts of those self-proclaimed "psychics" who claim to bend metal spoons or repair clocks "through the power of thought"?

Representation has two meanings here: the *act* by which a subject thinks of something or envisions it in one way or another, and the *product* of that act. In both cases, representations are understood to be harmless. If merely thinking of someone were enough to affect him in some way, we would have to believe in the claims of parapsychology. If drawing someone's portrait were a way of controlling him, we would have to believe in magic.

The immediate response to these observations is that the causality theorized by scientific psychology is one that works in the mental sphere but not in the external world. Psychical causality is action by the mental on the mental. In particular, it is the action of intentions upon the internal agency in control of taking action, of setting into motion the muscular routines that correspond to the planned movements.

Yet one might well wonder whether it is not rather the entire mental sphere that is thus bathed in a kind of magic or enchanted atmosphere— until, that is, scientific psychology reassures us by pointing out that it is all quite natural and that only "naive psychology" could give rise to the illusion of supernatural phenomena.

5.3. Psychology and Rhetoric

"Do you mean to claim," our theorist of psychical causes might well reply, "that common sense gives no causal meaning to the word 'because' as used in ordinary explanations? Is it enough to draw an opposition between *causes* and *reasons*? Is this distinction not merely a verbal one by which we refuse to give the name 'causes' to the motives for our actions and beliefs and insist on calling them 'reasons'? Yet reasons are given in explanations that seek to tell us *what makes* people act as they do or believe what they do. Covering over this causality by means of a verbal stipulation in no way eliminates it."

My response to this objection hinges on the distinction made earlier between mental causation and psychical causality. Every explanation that tells us what makes the subject behave as he does is indeed causal. If the adduced cause is a mental episode in the story, then the explanation appeals to mental causation. This is not particularly difficult to accept. However, the theory of mental causation—the causality invoked by common sense—is not a scientific psychology in the required sense: it is not put forth in terms of hypotheses, mechanisms, theoretical entities, and causal chains. In order to see this, we would do better to consult the only real philosophical theory of mental causation to have been put forward: rhetoric.[7] It is remarkable that, although classical philosophers from Hobbes to Adam Smith made use of this resource, contemporary theorists never even mention it.

One can act on another person either through physical constraint or through persuasion. Some of the actions meant to act upon the mind form the field of study of ancient rhetoric. The art of the orator consists in finding the means to persuade, i.e., proofs. Aristotle makes a distinction between proofs that are external to the art of rhetoric proper and oratorical proofs (*Rhetoric*, 1355b35 ff). The production of witnesses, confessions by the accused, written documents, and the like are all means of persuasion that are external to the art of rhetoric. Aristotle divides oratorical proofs proper into three kinds: those that depend on the *ethos* of the rhetorician, those that depend on the *pathos* of the audience, and those dependent on the demonstrative value of the *logos*. The speaker must exhibit a certain character in his discourse (so as to render him credible in the eyes of his audience); he must put his audience in certain frames of mind (indignation, pity, fear, etc.); finally, he must fashion his discourse in such a way that it will be taken to be demonstrative.

Whether the orator uses "external" or "oratorical" proofs, the goal is always to act upon the mind of the audience, for example, of the judge who must issue a verdict. This action is called "persuasion." The theory of rhetorical persuasion is thus the very theory of *mental causation* as common sense understands it. And here is the remarkable point: rhetoric is a theory, but it is not a theory whose objects are natural processes. It is the theory of a general practice—oratorical persuasion—in which some are more skilled than others. The goal of rhetoric is not to *explain by means of causal chains* why some orators are more successful than others before certain audiences. The goal is to provide *reasons for constructing one's discourse* in one way or another, depending on one's audience and the position espoused. In other words, rhetoric is an *art*, not a *science*.

Among the proofs listed by Aristotle, one in particular is closer to what we call "psychology." One persuades through the dispositions of one's audience, writes Aristotle, by giving rise to certain "passions" in them. The audience will judge a discourse differently depending on whether it is indignant or moved to pity, amicable or hostile. The art of the orator rests then on the recognition of a link between what one feels and the way in which one decides or judges. This link is of a causal nature, since the orator tries to make use of this tie in order to *act* upon his audience. If my discourse is not more persuasive than my adversary's, all other things being equal, the verdict will not be in my favor.

Thus there is indeed such a thing as mental causation, since certain events, certain changes in the public's state of mind, or certain mental acts like a jury's decision can all be accounted for as results of an orator's intervention. We adduce the composition of the orator's discourse in order to explain the fact that people's minds have been changed. Such an explanation is well and truly psychological in the intentional sense in that it is based upon the *content* of what is said and the content of the minds that have been changed. It is also well and truly causal: through his speech *act*, the orator succeeds in persuading the public. Moreover, to call this "causation" is not simply a way of speaking or a superstition, as it would be if it were the mere invocation of a proverbial correlation between two events of the "red skies at night, sailor's delight" sort. We thereby elude the vacuity of positivist proverbs that are pompously called "nomological generalizations." Indeed, in the case of rhetorical persuasion, a connection can be indicated that explains how it is that the event of the change to be explained was effectively the result of the intervention that has been isolated as its cause.

Nevertheless, the causal mechanism brought to bear in such cases in no way resembles the "mental mechanisms" sought by cognitive psychology. It is entirely external to the subject. Consider an orator who takes it on himself to provoke his audience to anger. The elements of the definition of anger given by the art of rhetoric are all taken from the moral and social situation of the audience. In his chapter on the pathos of anger, Aristotle explains that three elements of the situation must be accounted for: who it is that is liable to become angry, about what, and on what occasion. At no point is it a question of causal chains of events internal to those enraged. The original example is that of Achilles' rage at the beginning of the *Iliad*. Why is Achilles enraged? Neither Homer nor Aristotle attribute his rage to beliefs acting upon desires. The issue is not relations of causality between mental entities but relations of rivalry between chiefs at the moment when the spoils are to be divided up.

Yes, the psychological or rhetorical explanation tells us that Achilles *believed* himself to have been insulted. What matters is not Agamemnon's action but the fact that this action *appeared* to be a mark of disdain towards Achilles.[8] Are we then to say that it is not Agamemnon's gesture but Achilles' belief that counts here? Perhaps, but when our rhetorical explanation makes reference to what Achilles believes, it tells us what the incident meant or "represented" for Achilles. It does not tell us that Achilles constructed an internal representation of what had happened to him (the knowledge of which came to him through his sense organs) as falling into the category of the insult.

In fact, there is a familiar "mechanical model" of the rhetorical act: manipulation. But what is manipulated in rhetorical manipulation? We speak of acting upon someone's mind. But one cannot act upon the mind of a person by acting on just a part of that person (in order to affect his internal machine), contrary to what certain common images suggest (to speak to someone's head or to his heart). The image of manipulation is rather that of a marionette whose strings are skillfully pulled by the orator. If there is a mechanism, it would have to be *outside*, since the person to be persuaded, rather than containing within his skin a causal chain to be activated, is himself imagined as a piece of the machine. To act on someone is to manipulate him by taking for granted that the person is part of a larger whole and that this person can be led to decide in a certain way or to adopt a certain position through action on this whole. For example, a public speaker attempts to provoke a people to anger by showing them that their rank has not been respected by an arrogant neighboring people. The same thing goes for "proofs that are external to the art of rhetoric." The lawyer who acts on the minds of the jurors by presenting them with testimony or documents does so by modifying the world in which the jurors are located. For example, he manages to have introduced into the record certain facts favorable to his client, with the result that the jurors are left with a different perception of the entire case, not because they have been internally modified (as they would be if, say, they had been given a drug) but because they have had new documents and evidence put before them.

5.4. "Psychical Matter" (Lacan)

During a conference on "psychogenesis" (of mental disorders), Lacan gave a lecture which he later published under the title "Propos sur la causalité psychique" ["Remarks on Psychical Causality"].[9] This text is remarkable for putting in exceptionally lucid terms the question of the conditions under which there might be something like a mechanical science of the mind or, in other words, a "scientific psychology." At the time, Lacan was not yet a "structuralist" and he had no answers to propose to the questions he raised. He was, as a result, all the more comfortable describing what a theory that met the required conditions would look like.[10] In doing so, he delineated in advance the requirements that the dogma according to which the unconscious is "structured like a language" is meant to satisfy.

Lacan presents his lecture as a critique of the ideas of his friend and colleague Henri Ey (who organized the "psychogenesis" conference) who had espoused an "organicist" theory that makes much of the idea of levels in the integration of vital functions.[11] Lacan launches his critique by recalling the Cartesian split between matter, which is identified with extension (*partes extra partes*), and mind. Ey's organicism relies exclusively on physical interactions and not on significations. It is therefore, according to Lacan, an attempt to explain mental illness as a phenomenon of the *res extensa* and not of the *res cogitans*. Is such a reference to Descartes beside the point when the theory in question sees itself as an "organicism"? No, claims Lacan: since the subject of the conference is the "psychogenesis" of mental disorders, each of the participants is therefore confronted with a dilemma. The origin of mental disorders is either physical or psychical. According to the former theory, mental disorders are an *illness*. According to the latter, they are forms of *madness*.[12] One must therefore choose between seeing such disorders as problems of the body (comparable to aphasia) or of the mind. If one chooses the latter, the disorder should not be seen as a disturbance in function but rather as an *illusion*: the specificity of the hypothesis of a "psychogenesis" is to be able to explain such disorders through factors that have the bizarre quality of being present nowhere other than in the abnormal representation that the subject has of what surrounds him. These factors intervene whenever the subject is convinced of their presence and influence upon him. Lacan clarifies this distinction through a contrast between reality and truth. An insane person is not someone whose organs (regardless of which organs) do not function properly. An insane person is someone who is profoundly mistaken and content to remain so. Here one would have to adduce phenomena like hallucinations, delirium, and so on.

But even having said all that, Lacan has still done nothing more than oppose Ey's medical theory with a philosophical one. He has cited the lunatics of Descartes's *First Meditation*, whose madness consists in thinking they are kings or pottery. He has also cited Hegel, for whom madness is a manifestation of freedom, of the possibility of a meaningless choice, and thereby differs from organic disorders, which are by definition alien to the dimension of meaning. In short, Lacan's article confronts us with the outlines of a philosophy of madness but not with a psychological science. Anticipating the rest of Lacan's article, we might say that what is still missing is the key that will allow us to take what seems to us as philosophers to be *absolute freedom* and to transcribe it as a kind of *psychical automatism*.

Once he has rejected the medical theory of mental disorders and decisively chosen the mental theory, and seeking as he does to move away from the philosophical plane, Lacan has no choice but to seek a way to turn the mind into an element capable of producing such effects. Otherwise, he risks seeing the difference between psychoanalysis and philosophy (which could be rechristened "existential psychoanalysis" or *Daseinsanalyse*) effaced. And this is precisely what Lacan maintains in this text, though he also claims not to know how to proceed with it.

Lacan stresses that a scientific psychology should be able to account for the success of purely psychological therapies like psychoanalysis through a "psychical causality."[13] He then declares that we do not as yet have the slightest idea of what it is that allows such a causality to produce its effects: "I mean that we have not yet been able to posit any law regulating this efficacy."[14] What do we still lack? In an enigmatic declaration, Lacan replies that we still do not know enough about *psychical matter*. By this he seems to mean that we do not know how signs (words) can have effects (like curing someone of his afflictions).

> Things are at a point where, having caught sight of the operational meaning of the traces left on cave walls by prehistoric man, we might well conclude that we know less than he did about what I will deliberately call psychical matter.[15]

The notion of "psychical matter" is not just another way of referring to the mind or to meaning. It refers to the trace or the sign insofar as they are effective (as things). What psychology must have in order to be scientific is the ability to indicate how it is that the mind is not just mind (meaning) but is also at the same time matter (because these meanings are effectively at work in the world). Or, to put it another way, what has been missing from the project for a scientific psychology (including Freud's efforts) has been a way of showing how representations can form causal chains and insert themselves into the mechanisms responsible for behavior, or even those that control the functioning of a given organ. It should be noted that the insertion of symbols within the chain of physical actions is the very formula for magic. Lacan is clearly aware of this, as indicated by his allusion to the presumed efficacy of prehistoric man's paintings of bison on the walls of his cave.

It goes without saying that "psychical matter" would be of no interest if it were nothing more than a part of *physical* matter. At the time of this lecture, Lacan had not yet fully developed his "doctrine of the signifier."[16] He had thus not yet decided to integrate psychical matter into *phonic* matter, thereby making the signifying chain responsible for "meaning effects" analogous to the poetical effects of figures of style (metaphor, metonymy). In 1947, he was still seeking psychical matter in a theory of images and visual forms.[17]

What, then, is psychical matter? Or, rather, what can we point to and say: "here is some psychical matter, this is what endows with reality the mechanisms alleged by scientific psychology in the course of its causal explanations"?

As the name itself suggests, an authentically scientific psychology requires a *material* object, but one that is not purely and simply physical. Otherwise, physical science would be sufficient to describe and explain the phenomena in question, while psychology would be relegated to the study of epiphenomena.

Sometimes, the "materialist of the signifier" is driven to make ridiculous claims by his desire to show language to be material. For example, Lacan is led to claim that language takes up space, has a certain weight, and so on. In the course of his famous "Rome Discourse" in September 1953, Lacan insists that by "signifier" he means something material, not something ephemeral:

> Though it means I will be taken to be a materialist, I must insist on the fact that a material is what is at issue, and I do so in order to stress, regarding the question of place which is our topic, the space occupied by this material: with the sole aim of destroying the mirage that seems to prescribe by process of elimination that the human brain is the locus of the phenomena of language. Indeed, where else could it be? For the signifier, the answer is: everywhere else. On this table you find, more or less scattered, about a kilo of signifiers. So many meters of signifiers are rolled up in the tape of the tape recorder where my discourse has been recorded up to now.[18]

In what follows, it becomes clear that Lacan has fallen prey to the somewhat crude but common error of confusing what information theory means by "information" (which is measurable in "bits") and information in the everyday sense in which, say, journalists use the term. He assures his audience that "modern communication theory" has established that the signifier "can be reduced to insignificant units called 'Hartley units.'" It is today so obvious that this perspective is confused that we need not belabor the point. But even leaving this mistake aside, it is still odd to refer to "a kilo of signifiers." Needless to say, the weight of the magnetic tape is only that of the medium carrying the text. There is, though, a way in which signifiers lend themselves to being counted and measured: written works can be compared in terms of length. Anthony Kenny notes that what remains of Aristotle's written works contains about one million words, which is about twice as long as what we have of Plato's works.[19] The texts of Wittgenstein's *Nachlass*, he claims, are about double the length of Aristotle's works. The most productive of the authors Kenny mentions is Thomas Aquinas, who produced some 8,686,577 words. One could easily imagine other sorts of comparisons of the signifying "mass" produced by philosophers, taking into account, for example, the length of the words used, or the richness of the author's vocabulary. But the important thing in all of this is that these measures are utterly immaterial: the way the text is given to us makes no difference, as long as it is a text.

Nevertheless, this odd idea of a "kilo of signifiers" may well provide indications of the root of the problem perceived by Lacan when he warned his colleagues that, without "psychical matter," they would forever remain outside the promised land sketched for them by Freud and all mental philosophy: the continent of science.

5.5. The Weight of Thoughts

The problem would seem to be the following: in order for an explanation to be psychological, one must be able to provide a mental content to the state, event, or act that one will use to explain a given *explanandum*; yet, if this psychology is to be explanatory, one must find a way in which the *explanans* can intervene in a natural or physical way, without its signifying or intentional aspect playing a role. Here we are again confronted with the dilemma that drove the doctrines of "structural causality" to the point of paradox: if the signifier possesses an effective power by virtue of the signified it carries, then we remain outside the form of explanation we seek; if, however, the signifier possesses this power independently of any signified, then our explanation is no longer psychological. The solution to this dilemma adopted by the school of the structural unconscious is the most absurd, since it merely proposes a restatement of the problem: signifiers that act are "signifiers without signifieds" or "pure signifiers."

This difficulty and its proposed solutions can be brought into focus through an example taken from a wry story told by Jean Paulhan.[20] Paulhan recounts having brought the manuscript of Sartre's *L'être et le néant* to the office of Gaston Gallimard, head of the Gallimard publishing house. While recommending that the press publish the "great metaphysical treatise," Paulhan warned the publisher not to expect more than modest sales. And, indeed, sales were initially as expected. But then, according to Paulhan, they took off. "One hundred thousand copies were sold in a few months. People were buying them by the crateful. Especially women. We were astonished." The key to the story, if Paulhan is to be believed, is this: it turns out that Sartre's book weighed exactly one kilogram. It also so happened that, at that time, all of the brass weights had been taken by the German occupying forces, so mothers were unable to find such weights with which to weigh their babies. Hence the commercial success of Sartre's austere treatise.

At least in this story, Sartre's work offers a clear example of an "entity" subject to two different sorts of description, one "physical" or "physicalist" (as a physical object weighing one kilo), the other "intentional" or "semantic" (as a metaphysical treatise). It goes without saying that the weight of the treatise has nothing to do with its content and that this same treatise could be presented in another physical form (as an ultralight volume on onionskin, as a file on a computer diskette, as a cassette containing a version recorded by a well-known voice, etc.).

It is as if scientific psychology were obliged to turn the fortuitous coincidence of the two attributes (the physical and the semantic) into a correlation with explanatory powers. Because thought has a certain content, it has a place in explanations concerning the mind, which are psychological. But because thought presents itself in certain physical forms, it can act in a natural way. In other words, the mental and the physical are unrelated when we are talking about a volume published by Gallimard and a baby scale, but things would be different if we were talking about a mental-cerebral version of the metaphysical treatise and a mental-cerebral scale on which the book's thoughts would have their natural weight.

Why should something that is devoid of meaning in the external world become conceivable on the grounds that one has moved from the realm of physical matter to that of psychical matter? The solution obviously consists in discovering a *non-fortuitous* relationship between the semantic and physical properties of the entity that is to play a causal role. The weight of a book cannot have any relationship with the contents of what is printed therein (nor, for that matter, with the quantity of information in the physical sense). But perhaps there are more relevant physical properties. The fate of a mechanistic psychology rests on its success in finding what Lacan called "psychical matter": physical properties able to play a role in causal explanations but that are also directly linked to semantic properties. Or, in the terms of today's cognitivist: the mental engine must be "syntactic," thereby working by means of the physical configuration of the symbols with which it operates, and at the same time be amenable to redescription as a "semantic" engine when viewed in light of the external behavior it produces (see below, chapter 8).

Jacques Bouveresse rightly points out that Lacan never provided a solution to the problem he raised, and that this failure prefigures that of more recent theories that attempt to derive the emergence of the mental from a combination of mechanical operations. The problem is to give a mechanistic account of an unconscious activity described in intentional terms. The various hydraulic or thermodynamic solutions of classical psychoanalysis all fall apart when confronted with the following challenge: "to account for personal intentionality and intelligence by trying to derive them from a combination and cooperation of constituents and agents that belong to the subpersonal level and are, in principle, nonintelligent and blind."[21] Lacan's linguistic solution might at first glance seem better: if the unconscious is "structured like a language," it would seem that the level of representations and the level of psychical mechanisms have been brought closer together and even identified with one another. Yet the language that Lacan's dictum refers to is precisely language insofar as it is subject to mechanical manipulation as in, for example, the copying of one magnetic tape onto another. It follows that the problems of every mechanical psychology of mind are still intact: how are we to break down activities or states on the intentional level into lower-level, infrapersonal events whose relations with one another are causal?

As Bouveresse notes, the difficulty that Lacan's theory runs up against foreshadows the difficulties today encountered by cognitive theories of mind. What do they have in common? Both proclaim the necessity of introducing an intermediary level between the order of reasons (intentions, meanings) and the order of causes (mechanisms, physical actions). This intermediary level is supposed to be occupied by language (and thus a condition on the mind), but language in a physical or mechanical form (and thus language without self-conscious mind). For French psychical materialists of the 1960s, this intermediary level has its guarantee in the idea that phonology deals with "phonemes," units at a level below that of the minimal semantic units of a language. This idea allows us to see such phonemes as *signifiers without signifieds*, signifiers whose sole mission is to mark "formal" differences (i.e., having to do with external forms) and not to signify one thing rather than another. The signifier was the rallying cry of structuralists with psychical-materialist tendencies because they perhaps felt that this notion was a kind of philosophers' stone by which to transmute significations into causal forces. It is true that these signifiers without signifieds in many ways do prefigure the "cerebral sentences" dear to contemporary theorists of "the language of thought."

What is meant by "the primacy of the signifier over the signified"? If this notion is supposed to force us into a perspective where the only properties of language that matter are those that can operate mechanically (i.e., morphological or phonetic properties), then we certainly cannot, from this perspective, speak of signification. But, at the same time, this perspective precludes our referring to *rules to be followed* (i.e., rules determining the formation of correct expressions). It therefore precludes us from speaking about language itself in any useful sense of the word. This is so not because the notions of intentionality or signification are in some sense supernatural or miraculous. What is supernatural is a *physical effect* that requires a power superior to any natural power. The error here is precisely that of seeking to understand notions of meaning and intention in terms of cause and effect: if signification were a physical effect or an emergent physical property it would indeed be as miraculous as the cure of a paraplegic or the gift of prophecy. When we distinguish the realm of physical operations from the realm of signification, we are not adding an order of supernatural effects to the order of nature, we are merely marking the distinction, within our conceptual system, between the physical and semantic descriptions of a thing. We have established a system of physical notions that is indifferent to the meaning or content of things. In this system of description, a book has the weight of its physical matter and not of its "psychical matter" or its "signifiers."

What was missing from French structuralism was perhaps a genuine interest in linguistics. Having decided that the entirety of linguistics inheres in phonology, readers of Lévi-Strauss and, later, Lacan, were led to lose sight of the fact that a linguistic structure is primarily a syntax (as the Greek sense of the word reminds us) rather than a simple morphology. A similar criticism can be made of the so-called "computational theory" of cognitive mental processes.

Marie-Cécile and Edmond Ortigues consider structuralism to have been a new attempt to formulate, in the sciences of the mind, a "theory of composition," i.e., a theory that aims to show how high-order properties can be derived from the combination of various lower-order elements. Psychology would be a natural science if it were possessed of a theory of composition (i.e., a theory of the composition of complex entities out of simpler ones). "Psychologists have certainly attempted to make theories of composition more respectable, developing theories like Associationism, Reflexology, etc. . . . Certain French structuralists even maintained that the unconscious was structured like a phonology, but this gave rise only to puns. What was missing was precisely the distinction between levels, between phonology and syntax, which alone is responsible for the originality of language, the richness of civilizations, and the fallibility of the mind."[22] Nevertheless, a true science of the mind like linguistics does not in fact rely on a theory of composition but on a *structural* theory. As Lucien Tesnière points out, the object of structural syntax is not to study words but sentences, i.e., *connections*. What makes linguistics a science of the mind is that the connections are within the sentence without there being any external manifestation of them.

> 3. Every word that is part of a sentence automatically ceases to be isolated as
>   it is in the dictionary. The mind perceives connections between it and the
>   neighboring words. The totality of these connections forms the sentence's
>   framework.

4. Nothing indicates these connections, yet it is essential that they be perceived by the mind. Otherwise, the sentence would be unintelligible. . . .

5. It follows from all of this that a sentence like "Alfred speaks" is not made up of two elements—(1) "Alfred," (2) "speaks"—but of three: (1) "Alfred," (2) "speaks," and (3) the connection that unites them and without which there would be no sentence. To say that a sentence like "Alfred speaks" has only two elements is to analyze it in a purely superficial and morphological way while leaving aside what is essential, namely the syntactic link. . . .

12. It is, moreover, this notion of a connection that is expressed by the very idea of syntax, in Greek "setting in order, disposition." And this notion of a disposition that is usually purely internal similarly corresponds to what Wilhelm von Humboldt called the *innere Sprachform*, or "internal form of the language."[23]

Tesnière's principles are worth pointing out, for they give us a means of marking what distinguishes the conceptions of language put forward by the various psychical materialists—conceptions that are usually held to be typically structuralist—from an authentic structural syntax. The masterstroke of the brand of structuralism derived from phonology lies in its ability to dissolve such connections and syntactic links so as to deal only with words as they appear in the dictionary, with the set of their acceptations and uses. This dissolving maneuver is what allowed many literary critics to make the task of understanding look like an exercise in the interpretation of words, an exercise that is in principle unlimited. Certain theorists even attempted to descend to the level of the phonological signifier. But all of these attempts were too quick to assume that separating the semantic from the syntactic amounts to separating the mental/intentional (i.e., meaning) from the mental/physical (i.e., the putative "psychical matter"). In doing so, as Tesnière points out, they confused syntax and morphology. Syntax is indeed autonomous, but that does not mean that the syntactic point of view has nothing to do with the mind considered as an *intelligence* of connections. The simple contiguity of elements in a sentence by itself does not provide us with the subordinating links that these elements have within the unit of the sentence (where the verb governs the other elements). It should also be noted that Tesnière's formulation of the situation is debatable at best: when he refers to three elements in the sentence "Alfred speaks," he cannot mean that the connection between the elements is of the same order as the terms it connects. To put the connection and the two words all on the same level would be to see the former as a component when it is in fact a composition of other components. The form of a sentence is not part of the sentence. It is the way in which those parts (the groups of words) are placed relative to one another.

5.6. Symbolic Effectiveness (Lévi-Strauss)

The very title of Lévi-Strauss's article on "The Effectiveness of Symbols," presents us with the problem of bestowing a natural causality on representations.[24] The problem is one of knowing how "physiological disturbances" can be treated via "psychological representations."[25]

Lévi-Strauss's point of departure is his study of an incantation used in what the author calls a "shamanistic cure."[26] What interested Lévi-Strauss about this cure is the following original characteristic: the shaman's incantation can be said to consist in the symbolization of the difficulty the woman is experiencing. The originality lies in the relationship we see here between a certain symbolism and a reality. In most cures, Lévi-Strauss explains, this relationship escapes our attention. Sometimes, the shaman performs suction on the member or organ to be treated and later brandishes something (a feather, a thorn) that he claims to have extracted and that is taken to be the cause of the illness. In such cases, there is only a simulacrum of intervention. If the sick person is cured, it is not because she has been physically treated. At other times, according to a complex symbolic ritual, the shaman recites an incantation or engages battle with spirits with the result that "it is difficult for us to understand its direct bearing on the illness."[27] In the text that Lévi-Strauss is studying here, the incantation refers only to the locus of the "pathological state" and to the state itself. The interior of the woman's body is named, described, examined. "In our view, the song constitutes a *psychological manipulation* of the sick organ, and it is precisely from this manipulation that a cure is expected."[28] What does "psychological manipulation" here mean? At first, it would seem to mean that the healer does not touch the woman's body but only talks about it. If he enters her body, he does so only symbolically. He thereby administers "a purely psychological treatment." But in what follows, the author of the text in question leads us to understand that the woman's organ is *really* manipulated, albeit through psychological means (i.e., through the fact of symbolization) rather that physically (through an intervention like surgery, massage, etc.). How does the shaman manage to manipulate the organ by means of symbols? The formula is meant to suggest that the organ is in fact affected despite not having been touched. The second part of the article is an attempt to explain this effective power of the symbol.

The first part of Lévi-Strauss's study presents a commentary that is entirely anthropological and structuralist in its orientation. It is anthropological in that it takes up the text discussed from the perspective of its place in the life and customs of the Indian society to which it belongs. It is structuralist because it stresses the way in which the details of the "cure" can be understood in the general perspective of the restoration of an order that has been disturbed. When a birth is difficult, there is not only an organic disorder of the woman's body, there is also a social and even cosmological disorder that is everyone's affair. The role of the shaman is to restore order on all these levels and not simply locally, in the woman's body. This restoration is carried out through two operations: first, a linguistic procedure which consists in giving a name to each of the elements of the incident (e.g., the places, episodes, pains, and ordeals); second, a procedure by which the scenario of an action—in the dramatic sense of the word—is constructed. This scenario is supposed to lead to a felicitous resolution (i.e., childbirth).

In this part of Lévi-Strauss's commentary, the only "effectiveness" to speak of is psychological in a straightforward sense. First, the shaman must restore meaning by presenting the disturbance of order as an ephemeral episode within an intelligible sequence of actions, namely an abuse of power on the part of *Muu* (the spirit responsible for the formation of the fetus), who has captured the spirit through which the mother is to give birth. Thus, *Muu* has introduced disorder into the woman's body. After the intervention of the shaman and the attendant crisis, there is finally the resolution that the group awaits. Any therapeutic effectiveness of this return to order is due to the fact that all of the attention paid to her state and the entire mobilization of the group communicate a salutary rhythm to the woman giving birth, effectively helping her to relax and enter into the process of childbirth. We may well be impressed by the staging and the myth and all that accompanies them: such is the anthropological difference between them and us. But the psychological forces at work to this point are only those of what I have been calling "mental causality."

In what follows, Lévi-Strauss speculates on whether, within a strictly "scientific" conception of things, action of the mental or symbolic upon the physical can be countenanced. This is where his analysis veers into psychologism. Lévi-Strauss wonders why the shamanic cure works while, for us, a psychological cure that consists in telling the patient that his flu is due to a virus does not work at all:

> We shall perhaps be accused of paradox if we answer that the reason lies in the fact that microbes exist and monsters do not. And yet, the relationship between germ and disease is external to the mind of the patient, for it is a cause-and-effect relationship; whereas the relationship between monster and disease is internal to her mind, whether conscious or unconscious: It is a relationship between symbol and thing symbolized, or, to use the terminology of linguists, between signifier and signified.[29]

Lévi-Strauss here draws two distinctions: (1) a distinction between a *cause-and-effect* relationship and a relationship of *symbol to thing symbolized* (the first is a physical relationship, the second a semiotic relationship);

(2) a distinction between a relationship external to the mind and one that is internal to the mind (meaning that the microbe functions whether we perceive it or not, but that the symbol only works if the woman sees the link between the symbolizing monster and the symbolized affliction).

What struck Lévi-Strauss is apparently the idea that the monster can be *inside* the mind—since the monster is nothing at all in external, physical reality—that the relationship between the monster and the sickness is one between a representation and a thing represented. His thesis would seem to be: where the microbe is in the body, the monster is in the mind, and this is why the microbe's action on the organism is physical while the monster's action on the organism is symbolic. But where does Lévi-Strauss see an action on the organism by the *monster* (or by its symbol)? What on earth can the action on an organism of something symbolized, or of a symbol, consist in?

It is at this point that Lévi-Strauss makes the comparison to psychoanalysis, i.e., to a form of therapeutic treatment that seeks to heal not through psychological action in the ordinary sense of "psychological" (which, for psychoanalysts, amounts to nothing more than suggestion or even indoctrination), but through what Lacan called "psychical causality." Like the shamanic cure, psychoanalysis does not seek to give the patient knowledge (like the doctor who thinks he can cure me by explaining to me what sort of virus is making me sick) but to give rise to an experience. The theory of symbolic effectiveness that Lévi-Strauss advances springs from a comparison between these two forms of cure, the shamanic and the psychoanalytic.

What is sought, then, is the "mechanism" of this effectiveness.[30] The solution Lévi-Strauss proposes is to distinguish several levels of organization within a system like that of the patient's person (the woman giving birth, the neurotic on the couch). The causality of symbols comes into play at an intermediary level "between the organic world and the psychical one."[31]

There are, according to Lévi-Strauss, three levels of the living organism: the level of organic processes, the level of the unconscious mind, and the level of conscious thought. His hypothesis is that a process taking place at one of these levels can have the same structure as a process on another level, and that the one can therefore artificially induce the other. By making the patient intensely live out a myth—a collective myth in the shamanic cure, a private one in the psychoanalytic cure—both sorts of healers act on the unconscious and, through the unconscious, on the body.

> The effectiveness of symbols would consist precisely in this "inductive property," by which formally homologous structures, built out of different materials at different levels of life—organic processes, unconscious mind, rational thought—are related to one another.[32]

To speak about formally homologous structures that are built out of different materials is to choose to undergird the explanation in terms of structural causality with a pluralist ontology. Lived reality (experience) acts upon the unconscious mind (mythical structures) which, in turn, acts upon the body, and all of this happens as a result of the mysterious "inductive property" hypothesized by Lévi-Strauss. This solution clearly gives rise to all of the classical objections to doctrines that envisage interactions between physical and non-physical reality. Assuming that the same structure is realized in three different materials—let us say as a myth, as a palace, and as a symphony—can I repair the roof of the palace by changing an episode in the myth or by modifying the score of the symphony? To do so would be magic. Or, suppose I am a general and I have an army of toy soldiers to represent the forces with which I will be doing battle tomorrow: Can I take action against the enemy by modifying the structure of the figures representing the situation? Once again, we have entered the world of magic.

It might be preferable to see Lévi-Strauss's hypothesis as foreshadowing the cognitivist theory of the mind: There is but one reality, but it presents itself sometimes as an organism, sometimes as purely formal unconscious processes, and sometimes as lived experience. As a result, the palace is simultaneously a myth and, through its architecture, crystallized music. Which is why one cannot lay a hand on the roof without modifying the myth or disturbing the musical harmony.

Perhaps, but in such case we would be dealing with a fortuitous connection among the descriptions of this single reality. Let us suppose it to have been discovered that a certain fable by La Fontaine can cure migraines and that another fable has the virtue of aiding digestion. These fables would then be both fables and "medicinal texts," in the same way that there are medicinal plants. If we follow Lévi-Strauss's hypothesis, the explanation will have to be sought in the existence of an intermediary level: a level which is that of a mental activity but also a level of processes and activities that, like most of the processes of the body, are not only outside of our rational control, but beyond our consciousness as well. We are to imagine that located on this level is a mythico-poetic activity, an operation of the "symbolic function." It would follow from this that by reciting "Le laboureur et ses enfants" I would find myself to have, at the unconscious level of my mental life, a configuration that is homologous with that of my digestive processes. But in that case, it is obvious that the homology has no relation to the content of the fable. If the fable that can heal the stomach also happened to refer to the stomach, it could only be by chance (from a structural point of view) and would thus have no role in its symbolic effectiveness. Moreover, a "formally homologous" piece of music would have the same effect.

Thus, Lévi-Strauss's speculation—inspired by psychical materialism—in the second part of his study jettisons the fruits harvested in the first part. There is no longer any reason to be interested in the fact that the incantation in his example refers to the body of the woman giving birth. In fact, the presiding authority might just as well have recited *Goldilocks and the Three Bears* if it so happened that this were the exact myth that possessed the precious property of "inducing" the required organic structural reorganization.

.   .   .

The psychical materialism of the 1950s may seem to have aged poorly. It might be claimed that its scientific references and techniques are outmoded and that its models are primitive when they are not entirely speculative. The partisans of materialist philosophies of mind would, however, do well to see such psychical materialism as a remarkable forerunner of today's views. For a philosopher, the resemblances with more recent theories are all the more instructive: they indicate that the hope of squaring the circle—naturalizing the mind—is at root independent of any particular hypothesis. The appearance of a new technology did not give rise to this model. On the contrary, materialist philosophers *know in advance*, in accordance with their natural philosophy, that the mind is an element of nature and that it must have a physical model. Only the model remains to be found.

French psychical materialism never managed to explain how sounds (signifiers) might come to *act in function of their meaning* or how they could have the effects of their meaning. By definition, signification is not part of the physical description of things. By what miracle, then, could significations have any bearing on the physical course of things?

In general terms, the problem to be solved in order to justify the project of a "scientific psychology" is that of the causal power of representations. In order to act, representations must be physical. Let us suppose that every representation turns out to be physical in just the way materialists hope to prove through their criticisms of semantic idealism (i.e., the idea that there might be "signifieds without signifiers," pure mental signs, representations not borne by a physical support). That still is not enough to give them a symbolic effectiveness, as Paulhan's anecdote about the weight of Sartre's book aptly shows. It is not enough that representations take up space or that they act physically: for it is essential that they do these things *as representations* and *as a function of what they represent*.

If the theorists of the new mentalism are to be believed, the failure of previous materialist doctrines in no way indicates a philosophical error of principle. It is instead to be explained by the deficiencies of the physical models of the mind available to our ancestors. Now it happens that the last century has seen the development of logical machines. Our mathematicians have developed a theory of the procedures by which rational decisions are made, and this theory explains how to automate the calculation of certain functions. The relation between thought and matter has, these materialists claim, been clarified by these theories. For the first time, thanks to the analogy with the computer, we may be able to explain how symbols can have the effects of their meaning.

This is obviously a version of the second article of what I earlier called the Charter of the New Mental Philosophy. It is thus to this analogy with the computer that we must now turn our attention.

CHAPTER 6

The Psychology of Computers

THE SECOND ARTICLE of the Cognitivist Charter (see above, § 4.3) states: "It may be that believing and desiring will prove to be states of the brain."[1] Where does the philosopher's confidence that there is no principle that precludes the identification of the mental with physical states come from?

In the past, we are told, materialism was only able to *posit* that thought was a physical activity, a function of the brain. But materialist philosophers had great difficulty explaining what the identity between mental events and cerebral events might mean. One can easily understand that, for example, the act of raising one's hand can also be the act of asking to speak, since it so happens that it is by raising one's hand that one asks to speak. But how are we to fathom the idea that a certain cerebral agitation is also an act of judging that it is time to sit down for dinner? How can an arrangement of neurons have an intentional content? How can something that I do (in this case, judge) at the same time be a temporary state of my brain? This idea might be comprehensible if we could refer to *cerebrations*, i.e., actions of which the organ would be the brain, in the same way that we refer to *manipulations* for actions of which the organ is the hand. But the brain is precisely not an organ that we put to use in the way that we use our hands or our legs.

In the past, mental philosophers were unable to provide a convincing natural model for our mental processes (where "natural model" obviously means a model that will allow us to reduce mental life to physical and mechanical processes). It so happens that since the invention of calculating machines and artificial intelligence, such a model does exist. At least that is what the "cognitive revolution" would have us believe. According to this view, the philosophy of mind has recently ceased to be a speculative endeavor and will soon become a positive science. Because we are able to produce artificial intelligence, we need only find out the principles underlying the construction of such thinking machines in order to know what our mental abilities (or at least our intellectual or "cognitive" abilities) consist in.

My question in what follows will be this: Is this analogy with the computer comprehensible? This is an entirely philosophical question: throughout this philosophical discussion no real appeal to empirical discoveries or technical procedures is made. Instead, we are confronted with what is often called a "paradigm change." According to the cognitivist, we now dispose of the concepts that our predecessors lacked. These concepts allow us to render intelligible the identity of the mental and the physical that used to be mysterious. Our inquiry will therefore be entirely conceptual. This needs to be underscored, since works on this subject often fail to make the distinction between scientific research and philosophical analysis. There are even philosophers who disguise their dogmas as "empirical hypotheses" while failing to indicate how these supposed hypotheses might be evaluated in the field. Thus, before further examining the analogy between machines and humans, we need to take heed of the following: the brain referred to in the philosopher's theory is not really the same thing as the natural system studied by the neurophysiologist. The philosopher's brain is, as it were, a philosophical brain, a speculative entity, a hypostasis of certain mental operations, a hypostasis that the philosopher's principles require. It is a coincidence that this hypostasis bears the same name as the part of the nervous system that anatomists call "the brain." The philosopher generally knows no more about the organ called "the brain" than does the average person. In the end, he therefore has very little to say about it. His reasoning about the materiality of thought tells him nothing about the location of thought nor about the circuits of the living organism that are mobilized by such thought. Indeed, it would be unfair to expect him to answer these sorts of empirical questions when he makes no claim to have derived his materialism from an investigation into the biological systems of human beings. All that he in fact maintains is that if his brand of materialism is true, or if it is at least plausible, then the thinking subject can and must be material. Moreover, the philosopher understands that natural science and medicine have concluded that a part of the encephalon called the "brain" plays a fundamental role in the exercise of psychological functions. The philosopher, if he is a materialist, latches on to this name as the designation for his "thinking subject." But nothing that he has to say about it is based in the examination of the nervous system's activity. Note that if this were not the case—i.e., if being a materialist were all that were required of a philosopher in order for his theory of the mind to be an abstract neurology—then it would mean that the recipe for an *armchair neurology* had been found. To contribute to this science, one would no longer need to go through arduous training or undertake theoretically and empirically difficult research: one would only have to have something to say on any subject concerning humans. So, for example, someone studying Talleyrand's diplomacy would be doing neurology, since Talleyrand's ideas are, thanks to the materialist thesis, functions or aspects of Talleyrand's brain. To identify Talleyrand's guiding ideas is then to give the (rather abstract) description of his cerebral functioning. All that would be left for the specialists would be to describe this mental-cerebral activity in greater detail.

In short, the philosopher's status as a philosopher prevents him from proposing empirical hypotheses about the brain, for every hypothesis he might present as a philosopher becomes, *ipso facto*, a speculation bearing on the philosophical organ, one whose contours and functions are traced in a purely philosophical diagram.

The difficulty for materialist psychology in the past was that it was unable to explain the identity it posited between the mental and the physical. We are easily able to see the relationship, in appropriate circumstances, between raising one's arm and asking to speak: someone who raises his arm so as to be allowed to speak is doing one thing and not two. There is nothing mysterious about the identity between the act of raising one's hand and the act of asking to speak. In describing such an event, we remain within a single category, that of intentional action. By contrast, the materialist theory refers to an identity between a physical phenomenon (a cerebral agitation) and a thought that comes to me. The difference in categories is here glaringly obvious: in one case, we describe the brain by describing a state or a sequence of states; in the other, we describe a thought by saying *what* I thought about and not by saying *what state* I found myself in. To render the tenor of my thought one has to speak not about me, the thinker, but about the things thought about. It can of course happen that I am both the subject and the object of my thinking activity, but this has no bearing on the preceding point: reflexive thought is just as much identified by its object as is thought directed toward something other than oneself.

The analogy with the computer is at the heart of the new mentalist philosophy because it seems to offer the solution to this problem. It presents us with a machine that can be described in two ways, *as if* it were a Cartesian composite made up of a thinking system and a material system but that we know to be *nothing but* a material system. Such a model combines all of the advantages of the mentalist doctrine (the mind is disassociated from the world) and the naturalistic doctrine (the human person is made up of only one substance and not two).

6.1. Man and Automaton

The terms of the analogy are: the machine with its capacities and us with our mental capacities. Since the clarity of this analogy is not dependent on the particular technology used to build the machine, there is no room for the claim that the analogy will be even more powerful when new generations of computer are created. Better, then, to turn our attention to the argument made by Turing in his famous article on the intelligence of computing machines.[2] Turing tells us in this article that he would have preferred to present a direct argument in favor of his thesis but that, in the absence of such an argument, he was left to respond to various objections. We are given to understand that a direct argument would have maintained the following:

a) here is a machine;

b) this machine can compute and thus carry out intellectual operations as we do;

c) this machine can therefore think.

This direct and positive argument is not, however, available to the partisan of the thinking machine, because it rests on a presupposition that is precisely what is at stake in this debate: whether the machine *intelligently* carries out its calculations at the same time that it carries them out mechanically. Must one be intelligent in order to perform calculations, or are there not rather two sorts of calculators, intelligent ones (us) and mechanical ones? Turing contents himself with an argument that is dialectical (i.e., refutative): all of the reasons that are opposed to his thesis are bad reasons.

The famous "Turing test" defined at the beginning of the article is derived from a parlor game that requires the participation of three people: A, B, and C. The game involves isolating one of the players (C) within a room from which he communicates telegraphically with the other two players. Thus isolated, he is to guess which of them is a man and which a woman. The role of A, who is male, is to answer in such a way as to lead C to believe that he is a woman. The role of B, who is in fact a woman, is to help C to distinguish the real woman from the impostor. Turing proposes to replace the game of determining the sex of one's interlocutor with one where the goal is to distinguish the human from the mechanical.[3] If the machine can pass itself off as human by giving answers that seem intelligent, then the machine is intelligent like a human being.

This argument, which could be called an argument by simulation, is thus the following: if a machine is able to pass the Turing test (i.e., to pass itself off as a human being in the course of an exchange carried out in the specified conditions), it must be said to be intelligent. Yet it should be pointed out that this argument is quite ambiguous, which perhaps explains why it has been used in rather weak lines of reasoning aiming to prove that machines can think. Sometimes, for example, it is claimed that if a single player were to lose at the game in which a machine simulates intelligence, that would be enough to solidly authenticate the intellectual status of machines. This claim is apparently made on the basis of a phenomenalist postulate according to which a difference which is not apparent is a difference that does not exist or is otherwise inconsequential.

However, the entire interest of the game derives from the fact that mistakes are possible: part of the fun of the "man or woman?" game comes from the possibility that Player C, upon leaving his room, may find that the player he took to be a woman is in fact a man. The game is amusing precisely because a man who successfully pretends to be a woman is not, for all that, actually a woman. In other words, we do not use this game to decide the sex of human beings. From a philosophical point of view, then, this game is based on the *opposition* between appearance and reality, and not on their phenomenalistic identification. One cannot attain the status of womanhood simply by expressing oneself as a woman might or by producing a feminine text. Does it not then follow that the analogy between the parlor game and the Turing test should instead be this: the mere fact of being able to produce appropriate responses in the course of a conversation does not make a playing partner intelligent? A player who is not a woman can pass himself off as one. Similarly, in the Turing test, the player who is meant to guess may well be mystified, in which case he will believe he has spoken with a person when he was in fact dealing with a machine.

The words "imitation" and "simulation," which loom large in this argument, risk calling to mind illusions or hoax-like phenomena. In fact, nothing is proven by the fact that an automaton can, in certain conditions, be mistaken for a person. Nothing is established about the psychology of the machine. Indeed, the fact that it gives the impression of being intelligent is not one of the *machine's* psychological properties. Rather, it is a psychological property of the machine's *observers* to be duped or confused by a clever manipulation of appearances.

The Turing test is thus valid only if we provide it with a different interpretation. In the parlor game, the idea was to judge the femininity of one's interlocutor. Is Player C so sure of being able to recognize a woman by her way of expressing herself that he is willing to commit himself to go to a ball with whichever of his interlocutors seems really to be a woman during the game? In the game involving the machine, the idea is not to judge its humanity, but its rationality and rationality defined, as in Descartes, as the ability to maintain a conversation. The problem is therefore one of knowing whether the questioner, having learned that he has been speaking with a machine and not a human, would lose all desire to continue conversing with such a partner or whether, on the contrary, he would continue to take an interest in his partner's psychology, knowing full well that it is a machine's psychology. This is the real comparison to make between the game of imitation and the game of intelligence: the feminine style of a response is not sufficient to establish the femininity of the respondent, but the intelligence of a response may well be enough to establish the intelligence of its source.

Correctly understood, the Turing test presupposes not some form of verificationism, but a principle governing the classification of beings into natural kinds. This principle could be expressed as follows: Beings that belong to a class of functional equivalents are, by this very fact, of the same "nature." Or, if one prefers, they form a real class, meaning that they really have certain properties in common and which constitute their "nature." If a machine does something as well as a human being, it has the same abilities with regard to this particular operation as does a human being. But what we are here calling "nature" are precisely the operational abilities of a thing. This principle has nothing in particular to do with computers, it does not betoken some scientistic fad, and it is in no way dependent on future technologies. It might even be claimed that this principle is not at all modern, since it does nothing more than draw a (conceptual) link between performances and competences. When an operation is proper to a certain kind of agent, one need only observe that the operation has in fact been carried out in order to know that one is dealing with an agent of that type.[4] *Mutatis mutandis*, if computation is proper to a class of creatures called "intelligent systems," then one need only catch a system in the act of computing in order to class it with the other intelligent creatures. Such a classification, based on these beings' *modus operandi*, will not necessarily coincide with classifications based on their material constitution or its breakdown into more basic structures. Here, then, we are faced with a tension between two concepts of *nature*, a tension that might well devolve into a conflict. On the one hand, things can be ordered into classes of functional equivalence and without our having to take their internal structure into account. On the other, things can be ordered into natural kinds on the basis of these internal structures, i.e., on the basis of the mechanisms undergirding their abilities.

The principle governing the reality of classes of functional equivalence can be expressed as follows: if x acts as does y and if the action is typical of y, then x is of the same nature as y. According to this principle, every entity that passes the Turing test can join the class of "cognitive systems," the class that is sometimes referred to as the class of "cognizers,"[5] or of systems driven by a "semantic engine."[6] All of these systems can, for example, perform arithmetical calculations: because they carry out the same operations, they are equivalent from a functional point of view. It is irrelevant how these systems carry out these operations, how they are constructed and out of what materials. If calculation requires thinking (or, rather, if thinking is calculation), then the class of calculators is also the class of thinking beings.

I believe this principle is, in itself, a perfectly appropriate one (later we will have to account for John Searle's objections to it). For example, if a system were invented that was capable of composing the speeches and

declarations of politicians, it would have to be held to be as much a speechwriter as is the writer who today fills that function. And if the productions
of artificial speechwriters were of the same quality as those of human
speechwriters, we would have to see each of them as having the same
abilities. This point allows us to make more precise the notion of "simulation" which is so frequently used in arguments about the two sorts of intelligence, natural and artificial.

What counts is not that the machine successfully *passes itself off* as a
human being, since that tells us nothing about the machine's abilities (as
opposed to the perceptive abilities of those who are fooled by it). Yet it is
an event of capital importance if one is able to put a machine *in the place*
of a human being to fill a certain function. In short, the notion of imitation
(and, even more so, that of simulation) can be understood in two ways.
Does the simulator pass itself off as capable of a certain kind of work when
in fact it is not capable of it? That is imitation in the sense of a deception
or hoax. Or does the simulator pass for the normal occupant of a position
because it does his job in his place and just as satisfactorily? In this case,
the "counterfeit" is just as good as the real thing, and only snobbery leads
us to prefer the real to the fake.

But this means that every comparison between machines and people
must be made from a particular point of view. Thus, if there existed the
possibility of being indifferent to whether one is dealing with a human
or an artificial speechwriter, it would only exist for someone who uses a
speechwriter's services. It would remain to be demonstrated that a speechwriter able to write a politician's public speeches could also write other
types of speeches or other texts: love letters, New Year's greetings, administrative memorandums. All of which boils down to saying that, under the
(purely fictitious) hypothesis that there are artificial speechwriters, we
would have to conclude that the activity of producing political speeches is
much more specialized than had hitherto been believed.

The above comparison was not between a machine and a human but
between a mechanical speechwriter and a human being who had himself
been transformed into a speechwriter. It goes without saying that, if a
system were able to behave like a human in every respect—or, at least, in
every area that is properly human—this system would be a human being,
regardless of its origin or even its external appearance. But here we should
perhaps use a more circumspect formulation: If a system were able to behave like a human being—i.e., accomplish the operations that are charac-
teristically human—this system would be *at least* a human being.

It results from all this that the interest of the Turing test lies more in the
questions it forces us to ask than in the answers it is alleged to provide.
The principle according to which functional equivalence makes real classification possible dictates that, for conceptual reasons, whoever is able to
carry out the operations of a certain kind of being thereby belongs to the

same functional class as that being. Moreover, this class is held to be real, one that corresponds to real properties (i.e., precisely the abilities required by the operations under consideration). Yet this is imprecise. If x can do something as well as y, x belongs at least to the same class as y with regard to this ability. However, the test does not rule out the possibility that x can carry out different operations of which y is incapable. In that case, x would belong to a *superior* class: the class of those who can replace members of class y yet cannot be replaced in all of their functions by members of class y. Now, the Turing test necessarily bears only upon limited abilities: holding a conversation, playing chess, adding numbers. It follows that in some ways the test reveals to us something that we already knew: that a human being is at least equivalent to a system able to play chess or add numbers. If we hold such systems to be rational because they carry out operations governed by rational principles, then we are left with the problem of distinguishing their rationality from human rationality.

The problem is that we have great difficulty in distinguishing rationality and humanity. It is not that we lack imagination: we have never had any difficulty imagining intelligent creatures not of the human species (be they angels or Martians). But when we ask ourselves what makes such creatures seem intelligent to us, we can come up with nothing other than the fact that they speak to us and that we are able to converse with them. It is here, in this manifestation of mind, that intelligence plain and simple tends to be confused with a human form of life.

In this regard, Turing's proposed test tickles the reader's imagination precisely because the ability involved is that of exchanging questions and answers. We cannot see how one could refuse to see a conversation partner, if not as a human being, at least as a being capable of taking on the intellectual appearance of a human being (regardless, as Turing stresses, of its physical appearance). But for this very reason, Turing could not have made a more unfortunate choice of domain to test his thesis. In fact, the automatons that have been constructed up to now make no claim to be able to carry out anything but highly specialized tasks like "medical diagnosis" or games of chess. At most, they are able to simulate the role of a therapist in a "non-directive" interview. But a computer is precisely the sort of evasive "therapist" whose express goal is to have nothing but an empty exchange with his "patient."

6.2. Rules and Programs

The principle by which we order beings into classes based on functional equivalence can be applied in any domain. It can be applied to physical agents, to medicines, for example, or to fertilizers or detergents. Or it can be applied to the subjects of intellectual operations. In what follows, we will be asking how we might use this principle to derive a class of "cognitive systems," capable of carrying out work that requires intelligence.

There are really two questions that need to be answered: one regarding the very meaning of a test of intelligence, the other about the notion of programming or about how an equivalence of competences is to be understood.

Descartes, as we know, proposed the criterion of conversation in the *Discourse on Method*.[7] Why is this an excellent criterion? In order to participate in a conversation, one must be able to share the interests of others. We cannot expect others to be spontaneously attentive to the things that interest us: they have different goals, different experiences, and different tastes. Manuals of etiquette teach that there are only two ways to chat with others: either by giving the things that interest us an amusing or provocative form capable of holding their interest, or by taking it upon ourselves to pay attention to the subjects that interest them. This latter method amounts, if you will, to a certain sort of simulation: it is the element of play, of false camaraderie and hypocritical civility that penetrates the very character of the courtly man and that all Misanthropes scorn. One might say, then, that a well-programmed machine might (perhaps) successfully simulate interest in the subjects I want to talk about in a conversation. But this simulation would be nothing more than a disappointing mystification if, in taking an interest in what interests me, the machine did not also have to *share* those interests. What I mean is that the only partners with whom one can want to engage in the exercise of conversation are those who are able to recognize, whether sincerely or out of simple civility, my subjects of conversation as their own. But, if a partner has no such interests, and therefore no subjects of conversation, then the automaton is not the one simulating a conversation with me. Rather, I am pretending to chat with someone, in much the same way as does the stroller of the ancient fable who hears the responses of Echo.

A machine cannot have its own interests if it does not have a form of life, aims that can appear to be in harmony or in conflict with those of other machines, as well as a set of institutions. All of this will have to be attributed to the machine if we are to speak about a general intelligence displayed in its operations. The measure of the intelligence at issue here is the extent to which the subject takes part in an intelligent communal activity. Here we have done nothing more than reiterate the reason why a science of mind is also a moral science. By taking conversation as our model of a phenomenon of mind, it becomes evident that the measure of mind is the *pertinence* of an initiative. To evince mind is to respond pertinently, i.e., by taking into account the subject, the thread the conversation has taken until now, and, above all, the established customs.

What happens if we make our required activity more specialized? An automaton can play chess (the game of chess being noteworthy as the epitome of a closed system that is entirely isolated from the outside world). Even here, a distinction is needed. On the one hand, there is the intelligence presupposed by the fact of playing the game. This intelligence has nothing to do with the success of this or that operation; it is a *status* that is granted from the beginning of the match. (In a chess class for absolute beginners, each player will be conceded the status of "chess player," while the early signs of incompetence will be treated as *errors* rather than as proof of a player's intellectual incompetence). There is no particular test for the conferral of this status. But it should be noted that, because intelligence is a status, it is an all-or-nothing matter: either it makes sense to say that *x* is a playing partner (even if he is a very bad one or one in need of instruction) or it does not.

On the other hand, there is the sort of intelligence that can be measured, that admits of gradations (like the idea of "strength" in a chess game). This is not a general status but a ranking of people who have the same status. What we measure is not the fact of participation in a social activity—this fact is assumed—but the level of that participation. If our partner does not participate at all, his status will not change, but we will say that his participation is "worthless" and of zero value: i.e., we will still be giving him a grade! The first kind of intelligence is of the same order as a Cartesian *bona mens*: it cannot be attributed by degrees but only all or nothing. The second kind of intelligence is the sort usually discussed: intelligence as something unequally distributed among the participants in a semiotic exchange.

This takes us back to our earlier question: When we learn that our partner is not what we thought, do we then think that it makes a difference? Is it entirely senseless to chat with an automaton? Nobody would refuse to pit themselves against a machine in a game of chess on the sole pretext that it is a machine. The only relevant reason would be that such a partner is too weak or too slow, i.e., too boring. But chess is a game. Could I take an interest in a simulated conversation? Yes, but doing so would be playing at conversation, in the same way that children have pretend tea parties. Conversation with this automaton would not be possible even where a game of chess with it is possible, given appropriate programming.

A mechanical chess player is really the functional equivalent of a flesh and blood player. The only issue is whether the former will beat the latter. By contrast, a mechanical companion (at a pretend tea party) and an automated chat machine (in a pretend conversation) are nothing more than simulacra. Here we have touched upon the most important point: the composition of a program corresponding to a rational activity. How are we to justify the definition of a real class of cognitive operators, one that includes both humans and machines? Turing's article provides a brilliant explanation of this in a passage that I believe to be the key to the entire question.

Take, for example, an operation that can be assigned to a human calculator (say, multiplying two numbers or deriving a square root). Turing postulates a human operator who must work under the following conditions: (1) the rules are given to him in advance in, say, a "rulebook"; (2) he is not allowed to deviate from them or use some other method[8]; (3) he is supplied with plenty of paper on which to calculate.

How will we then replace this human calculator with a mechanical one? The rules of calculation will be replaced by a list of instructions called a *program*. This program will be placed in the machine's "memory." In fact, according to Turing, this stock of information at the computer's disposal corresponds to the paper available to the human calculator, for the latter is given not only blank sheets of paper (to carry out his calculations) but also paper that has already been covered by signs (the rulebook). Like the machine, the human operator can place all of that in his memory by learning the rules by heart and calculating in his head.

Moreover, the machine's operations are subject to a control meant to guarantee that the instructions will be automatically applied: thus, the tentative and hesitating compliance required of the human calculator is replaced by an automatic control.[9]

How is the machine's list of instructions written out? It cannot be done unless one already possesses a rulebook for the human operator who lacks either the competence or the authority for the operations in question (as has already been specified). Once this book has been provided, it need only be transcribed. (Needless to say, the transcription from the language in which the rules are written into "machine language" bears no resemblance to translation, i.e., the passage from one language to another. Such transcription passes from language to non-language, from an intellectual operation to a sequence of mechanical operations. The art or talent of the programmer involves successfully carrying out the decomposition such transposition requires.)

We will have to begin, then, by acquiring a rulebook. Where do we get one? Turing's answer is that we should ask a human operator how he goes about the task and we should then take down his answer and call it a "rule." Of course, it will not do for the compiler of the rulebook to ask his questions of the sort of *incompetent* operator who is the intended recipient of the book. To the contrary, he will have to ask a competent operator, someone who knows how to calculate and has the authority necessary for the control of his own operations. The entire enterprise thus assumes that there is a calculator who calculates without consulting the rulebook and that this calculator will be able to explain how he proceeds for each one of the operations.

Turing himself notes that the "rulebook" is a convenient fiction. In fact, people do not consult rulebooks every time they want to carry out an operation involving a calculation or an inference. The programmer must therefore begin by getting the human calculator to make explicit the rules he in fact follows when calculating. We can summarize the situation by saying that the writing of a computer program presupposes that one has already carried out a psychological description of the operation to be assigned to the computer. But how are we to proceed in the task of psychological description? We will ask someone to teach us to perform the operation, i.e., to become our instructor. What does that imply for the philosophy of mind and the conflict between mentalism and intentionalism? Obviously, it would be hard to imagine a more extreme intentionalist point of view: *everything must take place externally.* The psychological description must be in every respect the description of an intelligent line of conduct. It will have to mention, on the one hand, the movements to be made (in this case, the inscriptions to be made on paper) and, on the other hand, the rules to be followed, rules that must be sought not in one's head but as they are linguistically expressed in the rulebook. *This explanation proposes no psychological mechanism*, if by "psychological mechanisms" one means regular phenomena produced "in the head" and of which the calculator would avail himself so as to obtain the result (by, for example, thinking very hard about "$257 + 893$" and waiting for the answer to come, perhaps by pressing a key on his mental keyboard). The calculation takes place on paper. The rules can be written out. Indeed, they must be. If the operator went on to say that there are still a few operations to be carried out mentally, he would be required to communicate them in an appropriate form *on paper.*

Turing clearly assumes that all of the rules that the human calculator in fact follows can be rendered explicit. Once they are laid down on paper, one need only transpose them into "instructions" for the machine. Up to this point, we have no difficulty following his demonstration. One may nevertheless wonder what, in the end, this demonstration actually demonstrates. The human calculator follows rules and, in order to explain how he goes about calculating, we need only give these rules expression without appealing to unexplained psychological mechanisms. The machine is provided with instructions that it carries out mechanically. All of its behavior can be explained by the program and the architecture of the machine itself. But, even if we accept all of this, the comparison between the two operators highlights a difference that militates against their being placed in the same class. In fact, when describing the principle governing the workings of the calculating machine, Turing explains that the machine is constructed with a physical structure that *determines* its operations. The machine is made in such a way that the presence of a symbol (an "instruction") in its current state (for example, in Turing's characterization, in the section of the "tape" that the machine is in the process of "reading") determines the passage of the machine into another state, i.e., the state determined by the instruction itself. The passage from one state of the machine to the next can therefore be explained physically. By contrast, the human calculator is not set into motion by the rulebook. The rule *does not act upon* his mind. The supervisor who is meant to ensure that the rules are being followed was presented by Turing as precisely that—a supervisor—and not as some sort of apparatus that would restrict the human calculator's freedom of physical movement. This comparison thus reveals a discrepancy between the human operator and the mechanical one, unless of course one assumes that the presence of a rule to the mind of a human being is the equivalent of an instruction in the "memory" of the machine. This assumption would have to be justified. Without such justification, we would be right in seeing this assumption as based on a sophism that plays on the meaning of the word "presence," as if "presence to mind" and "presence in the machine" were two varieties of a single sort of presence.

The reader will search Turing's text in vain for any justification for this metaphysical conflation. In the end, the following occurs: Turing asks us to compare the human control of the work of a human operator with the mechanical control of the work of a mechanical operator. As soon as we make this comparison, we cannot help but be struck by the difference between the two situations. The human operator works under the authority of another human operator who makes sure that the operations are carried out in the way that the rules prescribe they *must* be (and this "must" is logical and normative). The mechanical operator is ingeniously constructed: the movements it carries out *must* correspond to the "instructions" it has been given (and this "must" is that of a physical necessity rather than a logical one). Yet, strangely enough, Turing does not point out this difference. It is as if he were convinced that this comparison brings to light a functional resemblance between the two operators. But what sort of resemblance can this be? Let us assume that the human operator, having been dispossessed of all intellectual control of his own work, should be considered a "programmed" operator. Let us consequently assume that a human calculator working according to explicit rules and under the surveillance of a human controller is indistinguishable from a machine programmed to make the same calculations.[10] In that case, we will have to conclude that we are dealing with a human being (the controller) who is using a calculator (the "programmed" employee) to carry out his calculations. Yet it so happens that when we use an electronic calculator, we do not have to watch over its operations, because these happen automatically. And if the calculator did not work according to its instructions, it would have to be repaired: there would be no point in calling it to account.

6.3. The Exteriorization of Mental Operations

As long as Turing limits himself to explaining how to proceed in order to write out the rulebook, everything he has to say is perfectly compatible with the Wittgensteinian principle of the exteriorization of the mental. Wittgenstein consistently warns against the illusion according to which there are mental processes that are comparable to external processes like speaking or reading aloud, yet differ from them in that they take place inside the head. By this view, for example, thinking, like speaking, would be a process, but a private process that can be followed by only one person: the subject.

The mental processes that interest us here can take place inside a head or on a piece of paper. In the sense of the word "mental" that interests the philosophy of mind, so-called mental calculation or calculating in one's head is no more "mental" than are calculations carried out on a chalk-board or on paper. "We are not concerned with the difference: internal, external."[11] Wittgenstein means by this that this distinction is without consequence for descriptions of what happens when one applies oneself to an intellectual task. In fact, the criteria that allow one to say whether someone has calculated in his head the result of an operation are exactly the same as those one would apply to a calculation done on a sheet of paper. The same could be said about silent reading, about reasoning, about memorization: in each of these cases, one looks at whether the person has calculated correctly (i.e., whether he has found, through his "mental calculation" the result he was supposed to), whether he has read correctly (i.e., whether he has understood what the text says), whether he has come to the correct conclusion or whether he has remembered rightly.

It must be possible for everything that the classical psychology of mental processes situated inside the head to be put down on paper; and conversely, nothing that cannot be put in writing is of the least importance for the nature of the intellectual operation. If this is so, it is advisable to exteriorize all mental descriptions, i.e., to replace operations "in the head" with external operations.[12]

One might even say that the example Wittgenstein gives at the beginning of the *Philosophical Investigations* (§ 1) resembles the first stage in programming as described by Turing. Someone is charged with running some errands and is given a slip of paper on which the words "five red apples" have been written. He goes to the shopkeeper and hands him the piece of paper. What does the shopkeeper do if he proves himself able to understand what is being asked of him? In what does his understanding consist? It consists in handing over five red apples. But how does the shopkeeper get from the three words written on the slip of paper to handing over the apples? We are looking for a detailed answer, one that gives us the word-by-word progression of the operation. Here is Wittgenstein's explanation: the shopkeeper reads the slip, he opens a drawer marked "Apples," he consults a table showing the various colors and their names and spots the word "red" on it, finally he recites the sequence of numbers up to five while each time picking up an apple of the right color. Wittgenstein's example presents an operator who applies *explicit rules*: the word "Apples" is written on a drawer, a table of colors is made available to the operator as is the beginning of a list of the series of whole numbers. One might even imagine the shopkeeper as being in the process of writing out the rulebook for the correct understanding of the message "five red apples" (a book that might be, for example, intended for new employees who do not understand English well and to whom customers would be asked to submit their orders in writing so as to help the employees follow the above procedure).

Wittgenstein means to use this example in order to challenge our tendency to conceive of the understanding of a message according to the "Augustinian" model of a relationship established between each of the words and a corresponding object. According to the model of *De magistro*, each of the words must call to mind a mental object (an image of an apple, an image of a color, an image of the number five). Participation in the language game would accordingly require a set of internal operations: the evocation of the idea of an apple (upon reading the word "apple"), the evocation of the idea of red (upon reading the word "red"), and so on. But this model is misleading, for the message does not comprise three names, or three signs each of which—or all three together—is meant to elicit the emergence of a particular association in the reader's head. Everything can be exteriorized: everything can be expressed in terms of the use of the words in the course of a transaction with the customer. The shopkeeper demonstrates that he understands the message by carrying out the appropriate operations: he makes use of the words. His linguistic ability is above all a syntactic ability that is given full expression in the order of his actions: he begins by opening the apple drawer, then he seeks out those that meet the condition imposed by the red color sample, then he counts out five of them. In other words, linguistic comprehension is primarily the ability to apprehend the message as a syntactic unit whose elements have functions that are both heterogeneous and complementary. There is an *order* to be followed: the shopkeeper cannot begin by using the color red to identify the objects the customer wants. Similarly, he must have already applied the concept "Apples"—i.e., opened the apple drawer—in order to apply the concept "Five." This fact—that there is a logical or syntactic order to be followed in carrying out the various operations—is what renders the shopkeeper's comportment an intellectual one. The intentionality of the action is manifested in the way in which the different parts come together in an intelligible whole. Wittgenstein's analysis is meant to highlight what it is that deserves to be called understanding a message: grasping an order in the application of the different concepts. In what does the application of a concept consist? The above explanation is the *entire* psychological description of the operation: the words are used according to their meaning, i.e., according to the rules of their application (in the correct order). Understanding that the customer wants apples does not amount to reading the word and thinking about apples, nor does it amount to entering into a relation with the idea of apples: to understand is to open the apple drawer. This gesture is not an external effect indicating that the correct mental association has taken place in the shopkeeper's mind. Rather, it is a manifestation of the shopkeeper's ability to use the word "apple" correctly.

"But if that is the case," one might ask, "how does the shopkeeper know what to do with the words 'red' and 'five'?" Wittgenstein's answer is simple: we assume that he acts this way and we stick with that, for "explanations come to an end somewhere." In our example, the explanation comes to an end when we concede to our shopkeeper an aptitude to play this language game: he knows enough to keep shop and to serve his customers (provided that their orders are well formed).

Let us suppose that the shopkeeper knows to open the apple drawer without having to read the label that says "Apples" and that he knows how to choose red apples without having to consult a table of colors, and that he is capable of taking out five apples without having to count "1, 2, 3, 4, 5" out loud. Does this mean that he is carrying out *silently*, in his head, these same operations of consultation and recitation? Does it mean that he is doing them *very quickly*, so quickly that he does not even notice it himself? This may be the case, but it is not necessarily the case. Behind every exterior intelligent operation there does not necessarily lie an interior mental process. Indeed, according to Wittgenstein, one will at some point have to stop at an action that the subject can immediately carry out without having to consult, either in his head or in a book, the rule to be followed. It is in this sense that every explanation must come to an end somewhere: not because our explanations might in the end account for the facts to be explained by means of another set of ultimate facts that would themselves be inexplicable, but because, in our example, there is nothing left to explain. In other words, the entire explanation has *already* been given. The shopkeeper's operations are explained by reference to the rules that are made explicit by the rulebook, the labels, and the table of colors. Why open this particular drawer rather than another? Because it bears the label "Apples." Why exclude this particular apple? Because it does not match the color sample marked "red" and is therefore of some other color. The rules explain intelligent action to the extent that they provide the reasons for acting in one way rather than another. But the rules explain the actor's actions only if we assume that the actor has to *justify* what he does and that he is an actor capable of *doing* something. In our example, we assume that the shopkeeper has a book at hand that both guides his action and allows him to defend himself, a book that could be called "the book of justifications to offer," since it is the book of rules to be followed. The dimensions of this book are necessarily finite. It contains the answers to relevant questions, for example those of an apprentice asking what he should do in such and such a case.

When Wittgenstein says that the explanation must come to an end somewhere, he means that at some point the question "Why?" becomes pointless. In our example, the question of knowing why the drawer marked "Apples" must be opened is one that does not arise. This does not mean that this question could not be asked in *another* story, where the main character, a waiter, has received the order for "five red apples" and thus confronts the problem of knowing whether to look in the apple drawer or in the jar full of cooked apples: in this new scenario, the employee will have to be provided with a rule by the management of the restaurant.

Where does the series of explanations meant to provide the reasons for an act end? It varies depending on the situation. But in every practical situation there will be a point where explanations end. The fact that there is an end point—that there is a point at which everything problematic has been cleared up—never fails to scandalize the traditionally educated philosopher, who has acquired the habit of questioning not only the Why but also the Why of the Why, and for whom the principle according to which "one must stop somewhere" seems like nothing more than cowardice. Yet Wittgenstein points out that the chain of effective reasons for action *began* somewhere, since the subject did indeed bring himself to act.[13] The chain began when it came time to do something that the subject knew how to do, something that he was able to do without having to ask how to do it. The metaphysics of the infinite chain of reasons requires that we provide the reasons that might make a subject act who is still devoid of competence, of any grasp of things, and of all control over the situation. Needless to say, *in that case*—i.e., in the case where the subject under consideration does not have the status of a practical subject—the reasons *will* go on infinitely and with the result that this subject will never take action: one will never be able to give him a book of rules thick enough for him to know what he must do *now*. But that in no way proves that there is some paradox about rules or a mystery about their interpretation, since we began with the assumption that our subject was incompetent in every circumstance and in every way. In other words, this subject did not have the foundation necessary for understanding the rules given to him in the rulebook. Needless to say, it would be impossible to supply the practical abilities such a dysfunctional subject lacks by giving him a second book with the instructions for using the first one.

This may be expressed by saying that the point at which justification by explicit rules comes to an end is the point at which the operator's own *authority* is reinstated. Before reaching that point, the operator is in the position Turing describes: to deviate from the rules given to him by the rulebook is to fall into error. But eventually one reaches a point where the operator applies a rule, and therefore both understands it and demonstrates that he understands it. There is no longer any need to ask him the rule that allows him to correctly understand the rule as if, in order to understand how to apply a rule, he had to ask for instruction from an external or, what amounts to the same thing, internal authority. *He* is the one who understands, *he* knows that the drawer marked "Apples" is the drawer where he can find the objects the customer has asked for by the name "Apples."

As in Wittgenstein's example, programming as described by Turing rests on the idea that, in the end, one eventually gets down to operations that require nothing more of the operator than that he carry them out. The human calculator is given a rulebook. He is not authorized to deviate from the rules it contains, but we assume that he knows how to apply them. Turing tells us that the operator has been divested of all intellectual control over his work. Even so, he is perhaps a slave, but not a machine: he is asked to *read* the rules and to *apply* them. A supervisor is even put in place to keep him from taking liberties. This situation is then exactly the same as the one Wittgenstein describes. On the one hand, everything relative to a rule or an instruction has been made explicit or exteriorized: one might say that everything has been "formalized" in at least one of the senses of the word. Once this formalization has taken place, we no longer ask our calculator to make use of his theoretical knowledge, i.e., the tacit knowledge that he might have of other rules or other means of determining the thing to be done in a given case. His *cognitive* resources are no longer to be put to work. He has but one thing to do: comply. On the other hand, the rulebook to be applied has been given to him rather than installed in his memory (say, through some sort of nocturnal conditioning or implantation technique), as it is with the computer. Like Wittgenstein's shopkeeper, Turing's human calculator must read what is written and carry out the operation prescribed for the case at hand. Turing's calculator thus has practical abilities, since it could be just as easily said of him that "he *acts* as I have described. Explanations come to an end somewhere" (*Philosophical Investigations*, § 1).

Such cases allow us to refer to *primitive abilities*: a primitive ability is one that has already been acquired and can be put to use immediately.

Certain of the tasks assigned to an operator require nothing beyond such abilities. The rulebook of Turing's human calculator only assigns him operations that he can carry out without reflecting about them. It remains to be seen whether a satisfactory rulebook alone can form the basis for programming a machine.

The comparison between a man and an automaton makes evident a divergence between the working conditions of a human calculator and the conditions under which an automaton functions. The employee, whom we assume to be shackled to the rules, has no right to deviate from the prescribed procedure. However, this employee must be deemed to have what we have called primitive abilities to perform tasks. If he did not have such abilities, we would be in the paradoxical situation diagnosed by Wittgenstein where, even though instructions have been given, action cannot begin, because the way the rule is to be understood has yet to be justified, or, if you will, a method for the application of the method has not yet been provided. Needless to say, what is in question here is the structure of practical syllogisms: since we justify actions through reasons for acting, the *end point* of the justification is the same as the *starting point* of the action itself. Justification of the procedure one follows comes to an end when one arrives at the rule telling the subject concerned what to do here and now (for example: open the drawer marked "Apples"). In this example, the rulebook need not say *how* to open this drawer, for it is the job of the practical subject of our example, the shopkeeper, to keep shop. Yet if a psychologist sought to automate the operations of Wittgenstein's shopkeeper (as Turing sought to do with operations of calculation), he would not be able to stop there. He would not be able to count on the shopkeeper's primitive abilities and would have to replace them with explicit instructions. If this is so, then how is one to write out these instructions, since the rulebook we had envisaged to make explicit the correct understanding of the message "five red apples" says nothing about how to open a drawer, how to read the word "Apples" where it is written, how to grab an apple, etc.?

There are two possible attitudes one might take when confronted with this disparity between the rulebook intended for an apprentice shopkeeper and the list of instructions for a machine. The first is the attitude that takes account of the fact that, eventually, a point is reached where action is undertaken: since the rulebook has nothing to say about this point, these competences must be of another order. The competence required to open a drawer (and to open the correct one) is what one might call a "technique of the body" (to use Mauss's expression), acquired through motor training. What our example then shows, according to this attitude, is that the shopkeeper's language game presupposes a complex form of life that is shared by creatures who must have developed numerous practical abilities and techniques of the body as well as intellectual techniques (e.g., counting, classing colors, etc.) and numerous institutions, before being able to communicate even things as simple as "Give me five red apples."

The attitude of the cognitivist theorist is the opposite. The rulebook required in Wittgenstein's example has nothing to say about the rules to be followed in order to open a drawer and the rest, because these sorts of rules are not conscious. The subject has no "access" to them. They are for us to discover. These rules, which are applied unconsciously when the intelligent system knows what to do, make up the system's *tacit* knowledge. The task for cognitive psychology will then be to round out the rulebook by turning all of the tacit knowledge into explicit instructions. Only then will the programming be completed and the intelligent operation broken down into mechanisms. The theoretical price to be paid for this intellectualization of practical knowledge or "know-how" is that symbolization, cognition, and mind will be found at every level of the organism. Thus, in an example given by Fodor, knowing how to tie one's shoes becomes an intellectual competence and demands all kinds of calculations about representations.[14] Confronted with this encroachment of cognition— that is, inferential thought—upon the entirety of psychic life, one might well wonder if it is all just a way of speaking or whether it is meant to be a literal representation of what takes place.

Before taking up this crucial point (see below, chapter 8), we need to reconsider the principle underlying the entire comparison of humans to machines and deal with a principled objection raised by John Searle.

6.4. The Chinese Room Objection

Searle has contrived a thought experiment known to specialists as the "Chinese Room."[15] The Chinese Room argument is meant to refute the claims made by theorists of Artificial Intelligence. Searle holds that this argument discredits the very principle of a comparison between our mental abilities and those of computers.

By taking a closer look at Searle's objection, I do not mean to suggest that I find it convincing or even troublesome for those it is meant to refute. As we shall see, Searle's conclusion will have to be accepted, but not for the reasons he alleges. These reasons rely on a major assumption, which Searle seems to share with many of his adversaries. The value of the Chinese Room argument, to my mind, lies in having brought this assumption to light.

Although in this article Searle never explicitly refers to the Turing test, he is in fact proposing that we take the opposite point of view. Instead of replacing a player of the game with a machine, he replaces a machine with a player. The player will be Searle himself. Indeed, it would appear that, for Searle, the first-person perspective is indispensable when it comes to making a decision about who has a mind and who does not. In order to replace the machine with a man, one need only retranscribe the table of instructions (the program) into a rulebook (the instructions given to a human operator).

Searle asks that we imagine him locked in a room. He has been given sheets of paper bearing symbols that mean nothing at all to him, as well as a book of rules to be followed for the manipulation of these sheets of paper. Through a window, more sheets bearing various symbols are passed to him from outside. Searle, in the room, is assigned the task of handing back out the window, in exchange for these new sheets, a piece of paper from among those originally provided. The rulebook, which has been written in our philosopher's native language (i.e., English), tells him how to proceed: in exchange for a particular symbol, he is to hand out the sheet of paper bearing another particular symbol, and so on. Searle's entire task is to identify and compare configurations that are purely formal. In other words, Searle has taken the place of a computer: he manipulates objects that are individuated by their physical configuration, by their "form" or shape. It is just as if he were executing a program, calculating the "output" that corresponds to a given "input." And this is where Searle turns out to be unwittingly taking a Turing test of his knowledge of Chinese. Unbeknownst to him, the inscriptions that he is manipulating are Chinese ideograms and the rules that he is to follow are a Chinese conversation program: the sheets of paper that come in from outside are questions, those that he gives back are interpreted by people outside as the responses of the "Chinese Room." Because the room gives relevant responses to the questions asked of it, the Chinese Room successfully passes the Turing test. The philosophy of artificial intelligence asks that we accept that a system with which we can have a conversation in Chinese knows Chinese and is therefore intelligent.

Searle's objection is wonderfully simple, at least in appearance: Searle-in-the-Room no more knows Chinese than does Searle himself. I am quite sure, he might say, that I do not know Chinese, and that I am unable to read Chinese ideograms. You may insist for as long as you like that the Chinese-speakers outside the Room credit me with knowledge of Chinese, based on my performances in the Room: the fact is, I do not know Chinese. Yet the Chinese Room configuration puts Searle in the position and functional role of a computer program. It follows, he concludes, that the computer that he replaced no more knows Chinese than he does. Executing a program does not in itself allow one to understand or represent anything at all. More generally, it cannot be decided whether a given physical system is intelligent based solely on its behavior. How, then, does one decide?

Searle proposes two conditions: consciousness and a brain. Searle believes that his thought experiment has rehabilitated the perspectives of the philosophy of consciousness.

Taken by itself, Searle's conclusion is not problematic. It goes without saying that Searle-in-the-Room no more knows Chinese than does Searle in real life. The fact of being in the Room and in possession of the book of rules, written in English, for the correct utilization of the sheets of paper is not enough to inculcate in him knowledge of the Chinese language and system of writing. Nevertheless, the lessons that Searle seeks to derive from this argument are poorly founded.

First lesson: the first-person perspective is to be privileged. Outside the Chinese Room, people might be taken in and imagine that the contraption knows Chinese. By contrast, the subject in question need only consult his consciousness to know whether he can or cannot read Chinese ideograms. Searle therefore maintains that comprehension must be distinguished from comportment, that the former can only be determined from the first-person perspective. But this is an assumption on his part and not a conclusion entailed by his argument.

It is true that the Chinese Room device does not know Chinese and that the human operator inside it does not know Chinese either. But this is because there has never been any reason to attribute such knowledge to either of them. Searle is mistaken to suggest that people outside the room might be unable to distinguish someone who understands Chinese from someone executing a formal program. In fact, neither the device as a whole nor Searle-in-the-Room have engaged in linguistic behavior properly so-called. The man in the Chinese Room is more like an employee charged with distributing tickets than a speaker engaged in a conversation. No one denies that the distribution of train tickets can be automated, and no one would claim that intellectual effort is required of the automatic distributor in the carrying out of its tasks. In Searle's fiction, he answers questions but he does not produce questions of his own: he is restricted to a single role, and this prevents him from engaging in linguistic behavior in any interesting sense. If he were outside, he could not ask a question of the Chinese Room. If he went to China he could not order a bowl of rice, nor ask anything at all of a passerby. As long as no exchange of roles takes place between a speaker and his interlocutor, one can hardly refer to what does take place as "linguistic communication."

The other lesson that Searle derives from his thought experiment is even less convincing. Searle is a true materialist. He astutely criticizes the partisans of Artificial Intelligence for their tendency to dematerialize mental functions. Like a pre-Socratic philosopher, Searle aims to explain the human mind through material causes: we are able to think where computers do not because our brain is made of neurons while computers are made of silicon. Searle believes that this fact explains the following distinction: the Chinese Room gives the impression (at least to an external observer) that it "knows" Chinese and English (as we have seen, this is a point that need not be granted; let us here concede it for the sake of argument). Indeed, the operator responds correctly to questions in Chinese (because he is executing a program to this end) and he responds correctly to questions in English (because he knows English). How is it that Searle knows English but not Chinese even though he can give the impression (at least in this fiction) of being able to speak both? Searle's response is that he is made of different stuff than the computer: the fact of having a brain allows him to understand the language he has learned, while the computer, for want of such cerebral matter, cannot understand the program that it executes. Only a brain, or its material equivalent (as opposed to a merely *functional* equivalent), can give rise to the phenomena of mind.

The weakness of this line of argument is obvious. Were we to take it seriously, it would follow that I cannot be said to understand French until it has been confirmed that my cranial cavity contains a brain (rather than an electronic system). For it may well be that my linguistic behavior is not explicable by means of the material cause that Searle claims is indispensable to intelligence. Similarly, if a humanoid creature were to speak to me in French despite not having a brain in its head, Searle's requirement for a cerebral material cause would force us to conclude that the creature had not really spoken French.

It seems to me that a much simpler lesson should be drawn from Searle's fable. We have stipulated that the operator of the Chinese Room does not know Chinese. For him, the drawings on the pieces of paper he manipulates are not signs at all. The only question, then, is whether the manipulations carried out by the operator according to the instructions in his manual give the apparatus taken as a whole a knowledge of Chinese. Searle calls this objection "the systems reply." The cognitivist adversary Searle is here opposing grants that the man-in-the-Room does not know Chinese. But he points out that this operator is part of a system and that this system understands Chinese, since it manages to respond appropriately to the questions asked of it. Searle dismisses this response as simply ridiculous: "The idea is that while a person doesn't understand Chinese, somehow the *conjunction* of that person and bits of paper might understand Chinese."[16]

This is enough to reveal all of the underpinnings of the argument. It has been stipulated that the human operator does not speak Chinese or understand what is said to him, since he is prevented from having any contact with his interlocutors. If we were nevertheless to say that the Chinese Room engages in linguistic behavior, it cannot then inhere in the behavior of the human operator. If that is so, then the only possible candidate for having understood Chinese signs is the system formed by the combination of the Room and the operator. Yet the way in which Searle dismisses this possibility shows that the system also understands nothing for the simple reason that there is in this example *no system at all*. There is nothing but a *conjunction* of different elements. Moreover, in order to refute the systems reply more decisively, Searle proposes that we change our scenario: the operator is asked to learn the rulebook by heart and to work outside the Room. In such case, there is no longer a Chinese Room of which to be a part.

If it is so easy for the operator to internalize the "system," thereby ceasing to be "in" the Room, this can only be because in this fable there never was a role for the human operator that would be the part of a greater whole. There was thus never a behavior attributable to the entire Chinese Room—i.e., one that could be distinguished as that of the Room and separated from the behavior of the parts of the entire apparatus.

The Chinese Room argument has the unwitting virtue of drawing attention to an assumption common to Searle and his adversary who puts forward "the systems reply." The latter might be exemplified by Dennett's response to Searle to the effect that, indeed, the operator in the Room does not know Chinese but that this ability belongs to the whole apparatus.[17] Similarly, he maintains, Searle's brain does not know English, for only Searle himself can know English. "*I understand English, my brain doesn't.*"[18] This distinction drawn by Dennett, between personal attributes and infrapersonal ones—between the abilities of the person and those of the brain—is exactly what is needed here. Yet it is astonishing that Dennett does not seem to doubt that the operator inside his Room, who is meant to replace the computer, is analogous to a brain inside an organism.

The Chinese Room argument reveals a strange lacuna in contemporary reflection concerning the conditions of mind, whether physical or not: the question is never raised of how a man locked in a room in the conditions described in Searle's fable can play the role of the part of a whole, of a component in a system. Yet, as we saw earlier, it is impossible to make out a distinctive function proper to this operator, a function that would be his contribution to the activity of the entire system. Searle did no more than place an operator executing a program within a closed space, with two "transducers" (two instruments for receiving and emitting physical signals). The spatial arrangement is not to be confused with a relation of integration. What is missing is any sort of *subordination* of part to whole, a way for the activities of the part to depend, at least as regards their meaning, on the activities of the whole. The operations engaged in by the human operator are not partial operations. There is no interaction between this "part" of the system and other parts. In fact, everything seems to suggest that the overarching system in this case is the operator himself and that he has various instruments at his disposition with which to do his work. If there were any integration of parts within a whole, it would probably be the reverse, as Searle himself implicitly recognizes: the system of the Room is a part of the operator. Searle admits that his scenario is that of a *homunculus*, a little man whose intelligent operations explain the intelligent reactions of the machine. The main problem with a homunculus is that it is an entire little man, whereas it is expected to play the role of a human part working with other parts of the human-shaped whole. The man in the Room may be small in stature, but he has all of the abilities of a man.

· · ·

From this we can draw the following conclusion: what systems like that imagined by Searle are lacking is signs of their own. Neither the operator in the Chinese Room nor the entire system have any use for ideograms. The man-in-the-Room manipulates sheets of paper, he does not use signs (his own signs). Which is why his activity is not a symbolic one.

Alexandre Dumas tells a different imaginary story that we might well find preferable to Searle's thought experiment. As is often the case, the novelist here offers a more perceptive view of matters than does the philosopher. The count of Monte Cristo, seeking to ruin his enemy, the banker Danglars, has decided to plant a bit of misinformation in the Ministry of the Interior. He anticipates that the banker will not fail to engage in false speculation based on this misinformation, of which he is sure to be informed by his wife's lover, who is the secretary at the ministry. The stratagem requires that Monte Cristo be able to insert an apocryphal message into the channel used by the ministry to communicate with the various prefectures. This channel is the telegraph, which in those days worked through semaphore. The count need only pay an employee of the telegraph service to send a false message as if he had received it from his correspondent.

Of course, the telegraphic dispatches from the prefectures are coded, so as to be incomprehensible to the employees charged with transmitting them. Thus, the employee dealt with by the count of Monte Cristo is very much like Turing's human calculator. Here is their dialogue:

> "I have been told," said the count, "that you do not always yourselves understand the signals you repeat."
> "Certainly, sir; and that is what I like best," said the man, smiling.
> "Why do you like that best?"
> "Because then I have no responsibility; I am a machine then, and nothing else; and so long as I work, nothing more is required of me."[19]

The employee is very much *like* a machine. Moreover, optical telegraphs soon gave way to electrical ones. Yet the presence of human operators in the system of communication requires that some remnant of responsibility be left to the employees. Now and then, the telegraph employee stops being like a machine in much the same way that Turing's human calculator may stop acting like a mechanical calculator. How can we tell? By the fact that he starts using signs rather than simply passing them on. In order for the employee's work to be intellectual work, the signs must be addressed to him; they must be for his use. The conversation continues with Monte Cristo's question:

"And have you never tried to understand them?"
"Never. Why should I?"
"But still there are some signals only addressed to you."
"Certainly."
"And do you understand them?"
"They are always the same."
"And they mean—"
"*Nothing new*; *You have an hour*; or, *To-morrow*."

A machine does not communicate in anything other than a physical sense, and this is because it has no signs of its own. The same is true of a man whose duty is to use signs mechanically. The difference between the telegraph employee and a machine is that the employee *also* knows that the signals he is transmitting are signs for the minister and that he, as an employee, is not supposed to understand them. He himself does not *use* these signs in relaying them to his correspondent. By contrast, someone knows Chinese to the extent that he knows how to *use* Chinese, and this is so whether the someone in question is constructed like a living organism or like a machine, since we do not inspect that construction when deciding someone's linguistic abilities. He knows how to use Chinese if he is able to achieve various goals through the use of the Chinese tongue (or, as in the fiction of the Room, Chinese writing). Precisely what is missing from the system imagined in Searle's argument is the quality of *being a system*, and thus of having its own aims and operations. The Chinese Room does not speak Chinese for the simple reason that it has nothing to say. Devoid of aims and needs, the so-called system is nothing but a contingent assemblage of objects each of which maintains its own independence of movement.

For a philosopher, the story imagined by Alexandre Dumas is more instructive. The two have a point in common: the code used by the Ministry of the Interior is meant to allow the employee to transmit without understanding. The employee does not know, has no need to know, and does not seek to know what the signs mean. That is not his business. As a result, he transmits information in a physical sense but not in the sense of intelligent

communication. Things are entirely different when it comes time for him
to say that he is ready to receive a message or when he needs to tell the
colleague across the way to get ready: at those times, *he* is the one doing
the communicating, and what he is communicating are not merely physical signs but language.

Certain signs are for the use of the Ministry, others are meant to be used
by the employee for his own ends. A system must thus be provided with
ends and needs, at least if we want to continue to speak of a system capable
of having a conduct. All reasoning regarding men and rational automatons
rests on the possibility of asking whether a system's conduct is intelligent.
In order for a system's conduct to be intelligent, the system must first *have*
a conduct. It must therefore have a conduct that must be attributed to
it, a conduct that is the system's own and distinct from the autonomous
operations of its parts. And in order for it to have its own operations of
symbolic manipulation, these operations must bear upon symbols that are
its own symbols, those that it uses to achieve its aims.

CHAPTER 7

The Inside and the Outside

It is not enough to say what are the stuffs out of which an animal is formed, to state, for instance, that it is made of fire or earth. . . . For the formal nature is of greater importance than the material nature.

—ARISTOTLE, *Parts of Animals*, I, 640ᵇ22–29

7.1. Functionalism in Psychology

THE PRINCIPLE of the reality of functionally equivalent classes gives expression to an idea that, in the end, is quite simple: if various complex systems are able to do the same things, then, regardless of their internal constitution, they must have properties in common, namely those that will invariably be mentioned when describing the abilities that they all manifest. What psychology can be derived from this principle? Or, more modestly, how can this principle be used in a psychological theory? The time has come to turn to what is called "psychological functionalism." Unfortunately, this doctrine is somewhat muddled. Psychological functionalism is usually thought of as the first version of the conceptions that were later destined to be honed into the cognitivist theory. What could the common properties of behaviorally functional equivalents be, if not aptitudes for the physical treatment of information? From a purely historical point of view, the filiation is undeniable. Hilary Putnam was the principal promoter of the functionalism of mental states in the 1960s. In 1975, he provided a succinct definition of the functionalist position:

> According to functionalism, the behavior of, say, a computing machine is not explained by the physics and chemistry of the computing machine. It is explained by the machine's *program*. Of course, that program is realized in a particular physics and chemistry, and could, perhaps, be deduced from that physics and chemistry. But that does not make the program a physical or chemical property of the machine; it is an abstract property of the machine. Similarly, I believe that the psychological properties of human beings are not physical and chemical properties of human beings, although they may be realized by physical and chemical properties of human beings.[1]

From this it follows that the error of prior materialisms was to seek to match a given mental state with a corresponding physical one. This led to an impasse, since, as Putnam stresses, one would have to be able to characterize the difference between two thoughts as a difference between their physical and chemical makeup. Functionalism replaces this brand of materialism with one that defines mental states by their role, between the stimuli of the outer environment and the reactions of the organism. A mental state is "a functional state" of the organism.[2]

Yet Putnam's characterization of the idea of a functionalist psychology is ambiguous. It is thus not surprising to learn that Putnam later became the sternest critic of the doctrine that he himself formulated, a doctrine that was subsequently taken up and elaborated by the cognitivists, some of whom, including Fodor, were his students. There are two theses that can be derived from this description of functionalism, or rather, two notions of functional explanation. According to the first interpretation, functionalism is "causal." According to the second, functionalism is holistic, since it describes the functions filled by the parts within a whole.

In causal functionalism, mental states are seen as the missing link in the explanations given by behaviorists. For behaviorists, nothing lies between the stimuli of the external world and the physical behavior of the organism, which is why their psychological explanations have always been empty. By contrast, for the functionalist psychologist who would like to be able to provide causal explanations, an intermediary must be placed between external causes (stimuli) and external effects (behavior): namely, a mental state defined by its "causal role." According to this view, the mental state that plays this role in humans happens to consist in a particular physical and chemical state. Let us call it XYZ. But to be in this mental state is not defined by the fact of being in material state XYZ, since we can imagine a machine whose makeup would be entirely different also being in the same mental state (i.e., the machine would have the same type of behavior as a human in the same sort of situation). To be in the mental state in question is to be in a state that is equivalent in its causes and effects to the state XYZ among human beings.

This causal variant of psychological functionalism seems almost to have been invented as an illustration of Wittgenstein's critique of mechanical sorts of "psychological explanations." The psychologist feels the need to insert something mental into a partially known causal chain since, in principle, we already have a physical description of the outer environment (and perhaps even a physiological description of its effects on the organism) as well as a physical description of the organism's behavior. Only one link in the chain is missing: how can the activity observed at the beginning of the chain (using the sense organs and sensory nerves) be linked to the activity observed at the end of the chain (motor nerves, body movement)? Between the two lies a mysterious or occult mechanism, which for this very reason is called a "psychological mechanism."

The weakness of causal functionalism is evident in the very example that is usually given of a mental state defined by its "causal role": pain.[3] The popularity of this example would seem to be explicable by the fact that pain is clearly a state and that this state is easily connected to both ends of the causal chain: both to the prior stimulus and to the avoidance behavior that follows. Obviously, when an animal receives an electric shock, it feels pain and, feeling this pain, it takes action to make it stop.

But since when is pain a *mental* state? It all depends on what one means by "mental." If we give in to the recommendations of the philosophers of consciousness—recommendations that have by and large become part of informed common sense on these matters—we will claim that the state of suffering is the paradigm case of a mental state: men and animals suffer, rocks and galaxies do not. And, as for plants, we do not as yet know whether or not they have painful sensations when they are not well. Pain is the paradigm of what academic philosophy at the turn of the century called a "state of consciousness." Yet it is worth pointing out that a philosopher writing in Latin would be quite surprised to learn that pain was something mental: for him, mental things are by definition those dependent on the *mens*, i.e., intellectual things. To say that pain is a mental state then means that it is an intellectual state, a thought, like a judgment or an inference.

The reason we are not startled when someone claims that physical pain is the paradigm case of a mental state is that we have received and accepted the Cartesian heritage. For Descartes, the sensation of pain is mental precisely because, in his view, pain is a thought, a *cogitatio*, and therefore an intellectual rather than a physical matter. I have a toothache, therefore I exist, for the words "I have a toothache" give expression not to my physical state but to a thought.

There are two conceptions of pain at work here. One is psychological. We do not wonder whether plants, heads of lettuce for example, suffer. This is not because we lack imagination but because we see no way of extending to vegetal beings a conceptual system whose first area of application is the animal world and behaving systems.[4] Plants are without the locomotion and expression that would allow us to refer to pleasant or painful sensations when discussing their movements. Even more difficult to imagine would be the physical suffering of, say, an old chair, or a crystal, unless one is willing to adopt the perspective of a fable or a child's tale. The other concept of pain is the Cartesian one according to which pain is an event that has the characteristic property of not admitting a distinction between appearance and reality. If it seems to me that I am suffering from a toothache, I may know nothing at all about the state or even the existence of my teeth, but I am certain that I am suffering. The appearance of pain is by itself the reality of pain, just as the appearance of uncertainty is uncertainty, the appearance of doubt is doubt and, more generally, the appearance of any mental operation is the reality of the cognitive event. If it seems to me that I am seeing, I do not know whether I am seeing something, but I do know that I am having the experience of seeing (see above, § 1.4). This concept of pain could be called an *experiential* one: it is pointless to say that "you only have the impression of being in pain when in fact you are not," precisely because being in pain belongs to the class of impressions, and one need only have the impression of being in pain in order to be in pain, i.e., because the awareness of pain *is* pain, provided that it is internal awareness (*conscientia*).

By offering the example of pain, the causal functionalist introduces an incoherence into his system. One the one hand, he takes up the Cartesian identification of the mental (i.e., intellectual faculties) and the conscious. On the other hand, he seeks to give pain a psychological function: it is a state of an entire organism (and not simply of its consciousness, let alone its brain) within an environment. It is this second sense that is used to derive the functional definition according to which a human being endowed with a human nervous system is fully equivalent functionally with, say, a machine.

Right away, the partisan of the philosophy of consciousness will accuse our functionalist of having forgotten the most important thing, namely, the internal consciousness of pain, which is given in the first person. The system meant to be a functional equivalent of a human being has no need to experience painful sensations in order to act as we human beings would in a situation that is painful for us. Imagine a system that is my functional equivalent in the following situation: my bathwater is too hot. For me, the painful sensation leads to an appropriate reaction (I get out of the water and take steps to lower its temperature). One can easily imagine a system capable of engaging in equivalent conduct and that would have its own reasons for finding the water to be too hot for it (if, say, the heat risked damaging it). But nothing obliges us to attribute a painful *experience* to this system. It need only react as I do and "simulate" my behavior to be my functional equivalent. In short, the functional equivalent of a human being may well be able to think, as the human does, that the water is too hot, but it would think it without feeling it. This gives rise to the classic objection: functionalism has not accounted for consciousness, for the qualitative tenor of lived experience, for the "first-person" effect not of being plunged into a bathtub full of hot water (a situation that concerns only our behavior) but of having the lived experience of being so plunged (regardless of what is in fact happening). From this point of view, the machine that acts like a human would be, psychologically, a hypocrite: it would only *pretend* to be in pain. And if it did in fact feel something, we would be unable to conceive (*cogitatio*) what it really feels unless we were able to empathize with it (*Einfühlung*).

In what follows, the psychological functionalism with which I will be concerned is not this feeble theory of "functional states" conceived as the psychological links of a causal chain. The term "functionalism" will be reserved for a psychological theory based on the idea of a functional explanation. "Functional explanation" might at first be understood as something like: explanation of the function of a part within a whole. And it will be said: What do parts and wholes have to do with giving psychological explanations? But that consideration of the relation between part and whole is precisely what is so sorely lacking in the causal functionalism just discussed. The only totality taken into consideration by this theory is the whole of the causal chain. To counter this reductive view of things, we must start from an entirely different perspective. As soon as we talk about a psychology of behavior, we have in mind, in the terms of Merleau-Ponty's famous title, a *structure* of behavior. Even very simple behavior will present itself as a complex phenomenon: different elements present themselves in an order that is not random. This gesture must be completed before that one, this operation is incomplete without that one. Psychological description shows how these various movements contribute to the success or completion of a movement of the whole. Moreover, the behavior we want to study is not that of a material point or of a mere center of gravity: it is the behavior of a complex, animated system. This system must be an articulated one. For example, in order to act as it does, it must push on one part of itself so as to move another part of itself in the requisite direction. These observations are not, of course, psychological ones, but a way of reminding us that the very concept of behavior immediately puts us within an order of phenomena in which we will have to make use of concepts like *part* and *whole*, the *simple* and the *complex*, the *incomplete* and the *complete*, *success* and *failure*, and the *efficient* and *wasteful* use of energy. Correctly understood, functionalism is nothing more than the judicious use of these concepts.

One cannot imagine a better teacher than Herbert Simon to explain the original features of functional explanation and its place within a science of human behavior. Simon is one of the founders not only of the theory of Artificial Intelligence but also of its philosophical inflection toward cognitive science. It so happens that Simon is most frequently cited in the cognitivist literature for his work with Allen Newell on thinking machines. This work led to the theoretical elaboration of a mechanical reasoning machine, one that would have been able, for example, to demonstrate a theorem of the *Principia Mathematica*.[5] In fact, the aspirations of the time for such problem-solving machines turned out to have been misplaced. By today's standards, the General Problem Solver, as it was known, is not so impressive and seems downright stupid.[6] Simon's lectures on "Understanding the Natural and Artificial Worlds" and "The Architecture of Complexity" are less frequently referred to, at least among the philosophers that I have read.[7] Yet these lectures are most useful to us, for they bear precisely on the importance of the functional point of view for the study of phenomena, particularly of the phenomena that interest cognitive psychology.

As I mentioned, Simon is one of the founders of the program for the study of Artificial Intelligence and its later cognitivist development. It is thus all the more remarkable that his lectures on "The Sciences of the Artificial" introduce a functionalism that can be entirely dissociated from cognitivism. In order to support this conclusion, I will have to stray a bit from the letter and perhaps also from the spirit of what the author says. Simon himself does not seem to have noticed the dissonance between the functionalism he puts forth and the cognitivist explanation of human intellectual functions through the mental manipulation of internal symbols. I cannot therefore attribute to him the conclusions to which I have been led in reading him. Nevertheless, based on Simon's work (though without claiming that he has explicitly put forward this view), I hope to demonstrate that: (1) giving functional explanations in psychology in no way obliges one to adopt cognitivist hypotheses regarding *internal* mental processes; and (2) for this very reason, the cognitivist explanation is not just a functional explanation and that, for cognitivist theory, the functionalist explanation remains on the level of a simple simulation of the mind (see below, chapter 8). My conclusions assume that we take at face value the theorist's formulas meant to describe the conditions of existence of intelligent systems: that they have problems to solve, problems that arise for them in the environment in which they live (see below, § 7.4). If these same formulas were taken in a figurative sense or as nothing but a way of speaking, the functional explanation itself would become nothing more than a way of talking, and we would have no choice but to turn toward cognitivism in order to get back to the realities of mental life.

I am well aware that the thesis I am defending in this chapter may appear unorthodox to readers who have grown used to understanding functionalism in causal terms. Indeed, my thesis is that functionalism *properly understood* in no way supports mental philosophy, a philosophy for which mental life is somehow detached from the external world and consists in the manipulation, either by or within the subject, of internal mental representations. Functionalism in psychology should instead lead us to consider the activities of an animate system that must get by so as to achieve its aims in an environment that is both varied and variable. If this is so, the psychic life of a system is not the reflection of its internal construction but of the problems raised by the environment in which it lives. It will then have to be determined what place intelligence (*mens*) has in the work by which functional systems adapt to the conditions of their lives.

What, then, is functionalism properly understood? I believe it represents an attempt to complete naturalism in the modern sense by means of ideas that have recognizably been derived from the themes of ancient naturalism. This lineage is especially obvious in the triumph of structure (or formal causes) over the material of construction (or material causes), a primacy of form over matter that Searle, as a worthy representative of modern mental philosophy, is right to see as incompatible with the principles of the philosophy he upholds.

What makes this lineage sometimes difficult to see is the word "artificial." We must therefore begin by studying in greater detail what these sciences of the artificial in fact are.

7.2. The Problem of Artificiality

Herbert Simon tells us that the title of his lectures is to be explained by the widespread use of the term "Artificial Intelligence." He did not, however, use this term in his own research, speaking instead about "complex information processing" or "the simulation of cognitive processes."[8]

Simon recounts that, for him, the problem of the artificial arose for the first time when he was studying administrative organizations at the beginning of his career as an economist.[9] His aim was to develop a theory that would make it possible to understand the rationality of such organizations. The first artificial systems studied by Simon, those that were to offer the first illustrations of the idea of limited rationality, were social systems like large corporations, banks, and public services. In order to attain their objectives, which are normally limited in nature and thus amenable to explicit definition, such organizations typically proceed by distributing, in a "functional" or "rational" way, the work to be done among different departments, agencies, modules, etcetera. It is not insignificant that, where the cognitive psychology of human beings takes the computer as its model, for its part the psychology of computers might well take as its model the psychology of a supposedly rational collective endeavor.

The rationality that interests us here is an adaptive ability: a system is rational if it adapts intelligently to variations in the outer environment in which it must accomplish its tasks. A system demonstrates limited rationality if it lacks such flexibility. The limits of the rationality of all real systems can be explained either by the (inevitable) rigidity of their internal links or by the material breakdown (which is impossible to exclude) of some of their parts.

From these observations regarding bureaucratic rationality, Simon derives a more general notion of the artificial, one that is applicable to all systems. The general problem of artificiality is that of the unavoidable limits on any attempt to construct a machine. By definition, a machine must have a physical structure and therefore a set of invariant internal links. Without these rigidities, the machine would have no reality whatever. But with them, the machine will exhibit an imperfect practical rationality. It is clear in what way the sciences of the artificial are empirical ones. The theorist of a purely rational machine never runs up against the problem of limits because, for every function that has to be discharged, he simply invents a theoretical "apparatus" solely defined by the ability to carry out, by whatever means, the work in question. In other words, the internal complexity of the system is not the theorist's concern, since he assumes that, for every new situation requiring that the system adapt, the system will adopt the organization the environment imposes. But real or empirical machines are only well adapted to certain types of outer environment. The empirical problem posed by a science of the artificial is thus one of recognizing those variations in the surrounding environment that exceed the adaptive abilities of the machine. This notion of functional rationality can be summed up in a simile: a rational system is in its surrounding environment like a fish in water; an irrational system is in its surrounding environment like a fish in a fisherman's net.

Every analysis of a machine must have three dimensions: (1) that of the *function* to be discharged (the dimension of finality); (2) that of the *construction* of the system through an assemblage of parts (the dimension of the inner environment); (3) that of the *external conditions* of its use (the dimension of the outer environment).[10]

For example, Simon explains, a clock considered from the point of view of its function is a machine to tell time.[11] This function can be discharged in several ways: a sundial, a mechanical clock, and an electronic clock all have the same function. From the perspective of natural science, however, these three types of system have nothing to do with one another. Only from a functional perspective and without considering their internal mechanisms can they be put in the same class. Next, we need to know the conditions in which the machine is supposed to be used: in this case, natural science will tell us which device can function in a given environment. As the author puts it, a sundial works well in Phoenix, Arizona but is of no use at all in the Arctic. Natural science thus intervenes twice, once to describe the inner environment of the device and a second time to describe the outer environment. The sciences of the artificial, by contrast, deal with the *interface* of these two environments.

Simon remains sufficiently close to the traditional philosophy of science to avoid using the term "natural science" to refer to anything other than the discipline that explains things by means of "natural laws."[12] By this view, natural sciences by definition never make reference to functions or purposes but only to general terms under which the particular phenomenon in question can be classed. That is why, as we will see, a science that introduces the point of view of adaptation can only be a "science of the artificial." A clock is made to tell time in certain conditions. As soon as this perspective has been introduced, the inner and outer environments can be distinguished from one another. The inner environment of a mechanical clock allows it to tell the time in "normal" conditions of use (i.e., those stipulated by its instruction manual). For example, the clock tells time when placed on a bureau. This same clock would not function on, say, a boat.

This provides us with a first conception of functional explanation: functional explanations exist everywhere we find it useful to draw a distinction between the inside and the outside. This is the major idea put forward in Simon's lectures, an idea whose numerous consequences he proceeds to develop. It is therefore crucial that we clarify the principal sense of a distinction between the interior and the exterior.

Rather than being a distinction between two realms (one of nature and another of artifice), this is a distinction between two points of view. We can study a natural thing as if it were an artificial system (and therefore possessed of a use and a purpose). But we can also study an artificial thing as if it were natural. A theory of airplanes must involve natural science in order to explain their inner environment (for example, the engine) and to explain their outer environment (the properties of the atmosphere at a given altitude). Yet natural science has nothing to say about the interface of the two: it does not raise the question of whether a motor with a particular inner environment will be able to function in a given outer environment. In fact, natural science does not even recognize this distinction between two environments, and therefore has no way of asking which of them must adjust to the other. But, similarly, a theory of birds can also be framed from two points of view: as a theory of a natural thing that obeys natural laws and as a theory of a flying machine.[13]

The reconciliation of "natural" and functional explanations comes about when we are able to point out the mechanism by which the adaptation is carried out. Simon gives the following example: functional explanation will tell us that if polar bears are "rational systems," they will acquire white fur.[14] In one sense, this explanation is tautological: the creatures best adapted to survive in an environment are the creatures who survive best in that environment. But it is not *entirely* tautological. The explanation does not merely say that white bears get along better in the snow and ice because they are better adapted. It also says how (or why) they are better adapted. Of course we must still find the *mechanism* by which this adaptation occurs. Nevertheless, the functional explanation does serve to delimit the phenomenon in need of mechanical explanation (in this case, the mechanical explanation will mention "natural selection"). We thus discover that the two explanations—which, in philosophy manuals, would be called "efficient causality" and "final causality"—are not mutually exclusive but complementary. The functional explanation tells us *what makes* the polar bear better adapted to Arctic conditions than the brown bear would be, and the mechanical explanation tells us *how* this advantage came to be that of the polar bear. Thus, our functional explanation does not consist in empty proclamations that the winners are those who have proven themselves to be the best. The reason for their superiority is indicated: it lies in the happy correspondence between their inner and outer environments. As a result, notes Simon, it is possible to predict the system's behavior without having to study its internal mechanisms: the postulate of rationality allows one to say what the animal's behavior must be, given that it must accomplish a certain function (for example, survival) in certain external conditions.[15]

This teleological explanation of the polar bear's white fur is perhaps not wholly convincing, since the finality of white fur, if indeed it exists, appears only in the course of speculation about the polar bear species. The example does not assume that a brown bear transported into the snow and ice would rationally seek to camouflage itself by whitening its fur. The notion of adaptation might appear to introduce an interpretation on the part of the observer. Here it will be useful to look at another example, taken from Richard Sorabji's study of explanation in Aristotle. A certain species of animal shivers from time to time when the weather is cold.[16] Let us suppose that we know in detail the mechanism of this shivering. We still have another question to ask: Why does the animal shiver? The teleological explanation is far from being either empty or redundant: the animal shivers so as to raise its body temperature. It is therefore not some secondary reaction devoid of function. Moreover, we can compare this method of adjustment to ambient temperature with other such reactions and other such mechanisms that attain the same result. Here it is clear that mechanical explanation does not completely cover the domain of our legitimate curiosity. Not only is the explanation in terms of function meaningful, but it opens the way to a comparison of internal structures by opening up the possibility that the same function might be carried out in other ways by other species or in other situations.

We are left with the following definition: The sciences of the artificial are those disciplines that study adaptive systems, i.e., systems for which the norms of rational functioning can be defined. But the idea that such sciences exist immediately gives rise to several philosophical objections.

One objection can be dispensed with right away, since it rests on a misapprehension. The objection is as follows: this definition of a rational system appeals to norms of rationality and thereby to ideas extraneous to a pure description.

This objection obviously appeals to the familiar opposition between facts and values. Values are held to be extraneous to description, for there are no values *in themselves*, there are only values *for us*. In order to answer this objection, one need only point out that the norms in question are those of the system under consideration and not those of the observer. The principle according to which the values of the observer must not dictate the description is therefore complied with. This division between description and evaluation is entirely justified in virtue of the following precept: we must not introduce into our description of reality elements that do not belong to reality itself but only to *our* reality, i.e., to our experience or to our needs (whether these needs are practical or speculative). The opposition between the descriptive and the normative means that we insist on the distinction between what a thing is in itself and what it is for us. To make such a decision is to become a naturalist, in a sense of that word consistent with its origins, i.e., a natural historian, a describer. For example, a naturalist must avoid judging some natural things unworthy of study because they happen to be ugly, or ridiculous, or inferior, etcetera. For him—for his naturalist's eye—all that exists is equally worthy of being classed and explained. The study of natural things must thus not be approached from the limited or provincial perspective of the creatures we happen to be. But it is evident that such naturalism in no way rules out the description of natural systems. When a naturalist provides a functional description of a bird, he does not impose our human norms on the bird: birds do not fly in order to please us, and it is not an interpretation to say that their wings allow them to fly or to note that some of them are better equipped than others in this respect. In other words, the point of view that allows us to study a system does not concern itself with the rationality that the system exhibits *for us*, but with the rationality that the system exhibits *in itself*. Later we will have an opportunity to assess the consequences of this distinction.

You may well claim that your philosophy does not allow such finality to be seen as anything other than mere appearance. In that case, it is your philosophy, and not the rigor of your description, that imposes this restriction. Your philosophy requires that you divide your description into two parts: a description of appearances and a description of reality. You have thereby adopted a new set of *norms* governing description (or, rather, you have made a distinction of value among the results of a description of phenomena). On account of these norms, part of the raw description is disqualified, and for reasons that are entirely speculative.

There is another, more interesting, objection contained in the following argument: The expression "sciences of the artificial" obviously contrasts with "natural sciences." But how can there be explanations other than those provided by the natural sciences? The explanations provided by the natural sciences appeal to laws rather than to purposes or functions. Simon himself reminds us that teleology is foreign to physics. It would seem then that the word "artificial" takes us not only out of nature, but out of science as well.

Simon's answer is a shrewd one. The artificial is not opposed to the natural as one realm might be to another, but as one perspective is to another. Everything artificial is also natural and must receive an explanation in the terms of natural science (and thus, "in the final analysis" as they say, it must be explained in the terms of physics). For example, an airplane is without a doubt a man-made machine, but, even so, airplanes are not foreign to nature, and they can only perform the services we require of them by "obeying" natural laws. How, then, can the functional point of view clarify matters for us and make us perceive something that could not be appreciated from the perspective of natural science? The principle behind the answer is that the functional point of view inheres entirely in the distinction between the two environments, the inner and the outer. Natural science, however, dispenses with this distinction.[17] If we choose to make this distinction, then by this very fact we have adopted the functional point of view. Such a distinction is not just for the products of human craft. Whenever one considers a natural system, one also considers an interface between the inside and the outside. In short, what the label "sciences of the artificial" leads to is the following conclusions: everything artificial (i.e., fabricated) is also natural (i.e., subject to nomological explanation); there are thus natural things amenable to functional description (specifically, those devices created by human craft), and what makes these systems functional ones is not the fact that they have been fabricated but the fact that they are adaptive. It is a fact that they are constructed as they are by engineers so as to be adaptive. For example, when the airplane manages to fly, it can in this regard be said to be the equivalent of a natural system. This is why the functional point of view can be extended to adaptive natural systems.

This response may satisfy the concerns of the natural philosopher who raised the objection, but it remains incomplete. In order to make the distinction drawn by Simon more convincing, something more will have to be added to his argument.

The distinction between the natural and the artificial would appear to have grown unstable. We started with a stark distinction between *phusis* and *technè*: on the one hand there are birds, on the other there are airplanes. Airplanes do not sprout up by themselves; we make them. Yet the theory of flight is the same for everything that flies, whether bird or plane. As a result, in some ways natural systems fall under a science of the artificial. Better still, only from this point of view can they interest us as systems that function, i.e., as systems whose parts have a purpose when looked at from the perspective of the aims of the whole. What, then, is the meaning of "artificial," since it is the case that a bird is a functional and adaptive system despite not having been fabricated (i.e., despite the fact that it is a natural system)? The answer is that the artificialism in the title of Simon's lectures is what allows him to speak of (teleological) natural systems where he could not do this were he to limit himself to what he and all modern philosophers call natural science. Because natural science does not provide teleological explanations and because one must provide such explanations the moment one seeks to discuss systems, there was no choice but to call "sciences of the artificial" those disciplines that take up systems from the point of view of their functions.

Thus, the difference between the natural and the artificial is first introduced in the usual way, as a distinction between things fabricated by man and those that sprout up on their own. But this everyday distinction is then rectified so as to satisfy our modern conception of nature according to which everything produced, everything that changes, and, in the end, everything, must have a natural explanation: i.e., an explanation in terms of the laws of nature. This is naturalism of a modern sort, which arose in the eighteenth century when Malebranche's idea of a General Will of the Author of things was transformed into the idea of an immutable and inflexible order of laws. The decisive point of this nomological naturalism is worth noting: it is a naturalism *without natures*. A bird that cannot fly because it is sick or deformed is just as natural as a bird that does fly. There are no *denatured* systems, by which I mean systems that have lost their natural powers. Thanks to this properly modern naturalism, the devices we build are just as natural as are the things produced with no intervention on our part. A disordered system is just as natural as a well-functioning one. This is so only because naturalism, once it has come to be defined solely by the nomological order of things, must exclude all teleology.

As a result, nomological naturalism can only provide an impoverished notion of system, one by which there is a system if somewhere several entities interact or come together in such a way that they can be isolated from their environment. For example, an armchair forms, on a human scale, a system, since we can lift it and move it to another room: the seat, the back, the feet, etcetera all move together and prove as a group to be separable from the other material objects that surround the chair where it happens to be now (provided, of course, that these objects are not attached to it). Which is to say that, in this view, there is only one system, the material system: a system is a portion of matter that forms a unit.

The rationale for what Simon calls the "sciences of the artificial" is thus to provide a richer concept of system than the material conception. The material system could be said to be defined by a *negative* relationship to its surrounding environment: there are things around it, but the system in question is not attached to them. The armchair is the same, whether it is in the living room or the attic. By contrast, an adaptive system cannot be indifferent to its surrounding environment, since that is where it must work. The adaptive system takes its environment *into account*. If it does not, it is doomed to decline or perish. It follows that the most characteristic trait of a system, in the full sense of the term, is not its cohesion, but the fact that it can seek to fit into its surrounding environment. Mere cohesion is compatible with utter indifference to the outside world. This is just the opposite of rationally adaptive—intelligent—behavior.

7.3. The Architecture of Complexity

The sciences of the artificial are thus the sciences of the interface between the interior and the exterior. We are now in a position to explain this somewhat elliptical proposition. It means that the distinction between the two environments, inner and outer, makes a double abstraction possible. Here is how Simon summarizes this idea:

> Central to their description [i.e., that of artificial systems] are the goals that link the inner to the outer system. The inner system is an organization of natural phenomena capable of attaining the goals in some range of environments, but ordinarily there will be many functionally equivalent natural systems capable of doing this.
>
> The outer environment determines the conditions for goal attainment. If the inner system is properly designed, it will be adapted to the outer environment, so that its behavior will be determined in large part by the behavior of the latter, exactly as in the case of "economic man." To predict how it will behave, we need only ask, "How would a rationally designed system behave under these circumstances?" The behavior takes on the shape of the task environment.[18]

What we have been calling an "interface" is not like a boundary or a barrier. An interface is a zone where the communication between two environments takes place. The specific nature of this communication inheres in the fact that the inner environment is not cut out from the outer environment (it is not one of its parts), but is nonetheless *in* the outer environment. This inclusion is not simply of a spatial nature. Can it be made more precise?

There is a primacy of the outer environment over the inner one. The outer environment is determinative. Like any privilege, this privilege of the outer environment might seem arbitrary and, from a nomological point of view, it *is* arbitrary: as we have seen, the clock that runs slowly obeys the natural order just as surely as does the clock that functions properly. But, from the functional point of view, the inner environment is mistaken whenever it fails to produce an adaptive behavior. This does not mean that it is mistaken in a causal sense (i.e., that poorly adapted systems will be eliminated) but that it is mistaken in a teleological sense: it fails to do what it must do given the aims with which it was constructed.

What must we take into consideration in judging the conditions of this adaptive relationship? This is where the double abstraction comes into play.

For the inner environment, the same result can be obtained using different physical equipment. What differentiates "airplanes and birds, dolphins and tunafish, weight-driven clocks and spring-driven clocks, electrical relays and transistors,"[19] to use Simon's examples, is their inner environment. But when we undertake an empirical study of the behavior of an adaptive system, we need not enter into the details of its internal structure. Simon provides an example from his initial area of study, the behavior of corporations. The behavior of a corporation whose aims are known (for example, to earn the greatest profit in the short term), when it is confronted with a change in its outer environment, can be predicted. To make such a prediction, one need only be able to assume that it will respond rationally. By this, Simon means that one need not know with any precision the internal structure of the corporation, or the workings of its decision-making apparatus. This possibility of abstracting from the internal structure and the nature of the components is nothing other than the dematerialization of description characteristic of functionalism. The consequence for the study of intelligent systems is precisely the one that Searle found so objectionable: the important thing is not the physical nature of the components, but their organization.

For the outer environment, there is a similarly remarkable abstraction. If the machine is well designed, it should be constructed so as to withstand the effects of any external variation. In other words, only some of the characteristics of its environment will concern it. Simon here refers to the cybernetic notion of "homeostasis" (i.e., a teleological mechanism by which a system tends to conserve a state of equilibrium while the outer environment moves through varying states). Everything works as though the external world were reduced to a few of its aspects. We will return to this crucial point.

In short, there are several levels of description and explanation. The notions of simplicity and complexity do not have absolute meanings, but are relative to the level of explanation one has chosen. If the level chosen is that of a part of the system, only some of the properties of the outer environment will be relevant to the description of that part. For example, in homeostasis of the teleological mechanism known as a thermostat, the physical environment is reduced to the variations in temperature. The reason for this is that the outer environment for a *part* of the system is not the same as the world in which the *whole* system must attain its goals. Rather, the part's outer environment is that in which it cooperates with the other parts of the system: namely the inner environment of the whole system whose parts they are.

Conversely, if we place ourselves on the outside, we doubtless do not perceive a simple system. If the system were nothing more than a single physical point, it might be able to be moved, but it could not have the behavior of a system in control of its modifications. The system must therefore be articulated into parts. Nevertheless, we need not study the structure of each of these parts unless it noticeably affects the conduct of the entire system, i.e., if it appears in the structure of the behavior of the organism or machine. For example, in order to know whether a car is going to take the next turn or, on the contrary, crash into a tree, we need only know if its behavior is rational; we have no need to know whether the car has front-wheel drive.

Why is it legitimate to abstract (provisionally) from the real complexity of a thing? Here we will do well to turn to Simon's famous 1962 lecture on "the architecture of complexity," which has since become the last chapter of his book on the sciences of the artificial.

Functional explanation is hierarchical: it does not proceed from the bottom up but from the top down. The point of departure is the function that the system is meant to perform. What allows a system to fulfill this function? The way in which it is organized. This assumes that the problem to be solved or the function to be discharged is divisible into stages or distinct operations to be carried out simultaneously. One thus moves from a global function to the coordination of partial functions. The analysis of the global system into its functional parts is effected through the breakdown of the system's operation into the coordination of partial operations assigned to various subsystems. The model is that of the division of labor. To carry out such an analysis, one must obviously be in a position to identify the operation of the system. Otherwise, there is nothing to be analyzed.

The material nature of the components is not here of interest to the designer. All that is required is that each of the pieces that make up the system be able to carry out the operation assigned to it. How is the component able to carry out its operation? Our analysis will have to be repeated at this level, treating the subsystem as a system, explaining the ability to carry out the global operation by the internal structure of the assemblage of components. This implies that the study of complex systems is an exercise in *holistic* analysis. To subordinate the part to the whole and stipulate that the system is real is to assume that "the whole is more than the sum of the parts."[20]

Seemingly uneasy at having to go so far, Simon indicates in a footnote that his holism is methodological.[21] But his efforts to restrict the scope of his thesis seem like purely formal concessions made only to avoid upsetting the physicalist orthodoxy. Indeed, these concessions clearly have no effect on his analysis, and simply amount to solemn proclamations that certain principles have been respected when, in fact, they have long ceased to govern much of anything.[22]

The fact of organization guarantees that the interesting interactions will be those of the parts within the whole. The interactions between the sub-parts of part A and the sub-parts of part B can therefore be disregarded.

> In hierarchic systems we can distinguish between the interactions *among* sub-systems, on the one hand, and the interactions *within* subsystems—that is, among the parts of those subsystems—on the other. The interactions at the different levels may be, and often will be, of different orders of magnitude.[23]

According to the example given by the author, normally there are more interactions between two employees in the same department of a corporation than there are between two employees from different departments.[24] This is why reality can be studied piece by piece: it is organized in such a way that the researcher can (provisionally) abstract from the complexity of things at levels below the ones he has chosen to study and of which there are three: the *environment* in which the system operates, the *system* as such, and the *parts* that make up this system. One is obliged to see the whole as more than the sum of its parts whenever this whole exhibits organization. If it were not organized, or if its organization could be disregarded, we could not study it *as a system*.

This answer forestalls the classic objection that if holism were true, it would be a very bad thing, since it would mean that we could not undertake to analyze anything at all by breaking it down into its components. Indeed, we do not study everything when we study a whole, as if there were only one whole. We study a hierarchy of totalities integrated into one another or contained within one another.

The idea of a "hierarchical structure" is one that opens up possibilities of analysis for the researcher. One need not immediately proceed to breaking down a system into its basic elements (assuming one can find them). One can, if the analysis requires it, describe a "subsystem" as if it were a basic element. Vulgar holism refers only to the Whole and its Parts, thereby conceiving the relationship between part and whole as established once and for all, absolutely, as if something that is a whole from one point of view could not at the same time be a part from a different point of view. Philosophers educated in the Kantian tradition are accustomed to writing exercises on the subject "Totality and Totalization." The corrections of such exercises typically follow a familiar pattern. They begin with a reminder that the claim to discuss a totality is the definition of "Metaphysics" (as a purely rational speculation that aspires to scientificity). They then go on to show that our "Understanding" is never confronted with an authentic Whole and that there is thus something equivocal about any thesis on the Whole of things: it is indeed possible to show, based on undisputed principles, that the Whole of things has a beginning and that it has no beginning, that it is made up of basic elements and that it is infinitely divisible, and so on. Conclusion: The Whole must be constructed, and it can be shown *a priori* that the totalization of experience will never be completed.

By contrast, in Simon's proposed theory of hierarchy, the relationship between a whole and its parts is relative to the level of abstraction at which it is considered.

Simon's article on the architecture of complexity inspired Arthur Koestler's theory of the "Janus-faced entity" or *holon*, according to which a single thing, considered as a totality, has two faces. When the "holon" is looked at from below, it resembles a self-contained whole. When the "holon" is looked at from above, it resembles a dependent part.[25] Koestler explains that the reason for introducing this neologism, "holon," is to counteract the tendency to speak about the relationship between wholes and parts as one that is fixed for all time and therefore absolute. That would be the case if we were always forced to choose between x being a whole or a part. In reality, the relation of whole to part is relative to the level at which we take it up: the same thing, x, can be a whole relative to another thing, y, that is one of its parts, and it can itself be a part of another whole, z.

7.4. Psychology as a "Science of the Artificial"

Simon includes psychology among the sciences of the artificial. How are we to understand this? Psychology is the study of the conduct of what Simon calls "behaving systems."[26] It is a science of the artificial because it does not study the phenomena of the inner environment, but the behavior of the system in its outer environment. Everything that takes place in the inner environment is the province of neurophysiology and, in general, will not appear within psychological descriptions. This is where Simon derives his thesis: the needs of psychological explanation require that we treat the system as if it were (relatively) simple. Of course, the word "system" makes clear our awareness that the living thing whose intelligence we are studying is not a simple being. Nevertheless, its internal complexity, which constitutes the object of study for anatomists and physiologists, is of little interest to the psychologist of intelligence. Simon explains his thesis through a story about men and ants. His point of departure is an ant walking on a beach trying to get back to its anthill. Its path along the beach can be traced as a complicated line, the zigzags of which require an explanation:

> I show the unlabeled sketch to a friend. Whose path is it? An expert skier, perhaps, slaloming down a steep and somewhat rocky slope. Or a sloop, beating upwind in a channel dotted with islands and shoals. Perhaps it is a path in a more abstract space: the course of search of a student seeking the proof of a theorem in geometry.[27]

This example assumes that what is curious about the ant's path is necessarily its apparent inconsistency. Why is it not just straight? But our curiosity itself requires justification. Why should the line be straight? Why does a zigzag line require an explanation while a straight one does not? The answer is of course that we have from the start seen the line as one describing the path of something mobile—a skier, a boat, a student—that seeks to reach a goal. Why doesn't the ant just go straight? Our point of view is thus that of the "artificial," i.e., the point of view of ends to be attained. From this point of view, the answer is that the ant, despite appearances to the contrary, *is going straight toward its goal*. The zigzags of its itinerary do not represent adventures undertaken along the way but, rather, detours imposed by the variations in the surrounding terrain. This amounts to saying that the example presupposes that the ant has but one aim and that it cannot be distracted on the way. So it is that we come to appreciate the rationality of a device whose functions are highly specialized, for the only thing it has to do is return home.

Simon offers this example as an illustration of his thesis, which he puts as follows:

> The ant, viewed as a behaving system, is quite simple. The apparent complexity of its behavior over time is largely a reflection of the complexity of the environment in which it finds itself.[28]

The complexity of behavior must be entirely attributed to the outer environment, which means that the behavior reflects the complexity of the outside world and not the complexity of the internal one. This is an important thesis that must be correctly understood.

First of all, this attribution of complexity to the external world is not a causal attribution. We are not looking for a "natural constraint." On the one hand, the outer environment does not act mechanically upon the ant (as a strong gust of wind might); the ant itself takes detours in order to solve its problem, which is to get home despite such obstacles. On the other hand, the ant takes detours only because there is an obstacle in its path and not because something in its internal structure compels it to do so. We know that the ant is a very complex organism. But, from the viewpoint that interests us here (i.e., the intelligence of its behavior), it is "relatively simple" in the sense that we need not concern ourselves with the physiological machinery that allows it to solve the problems it encounters. "That is why an automaton, though completely different at the microscopic level, might nevertheless simulate the ant's gross behavior."[29] The abstraction by which we turn the ant into a teleological system and the environment into a pure obstacle course allows us to foresee functional explanation taking the quasi-empirical form of a simulation of the ant's behavior by a mechanical equivalent. This first point allows us to conclude that psychological explanation and neurophysiological explanation are separate. This is the immediate consequence of having put into a functionally equivalent class the systems meant to execute the program of returning home.

Second, Simon goes on to extend his functionalist thesis to man. "A man, viewed as a behaving system, is quite simple."[30] Here again, the complexity of behavior is a reflection of the complexity of the problems given externally rather than of any complexity of internal organization. The parallel that Simon draws between men and ants requires two comments which, in their turn, require that we move from the elucidation of Simon's view to an interpretation that seems inevitable but that he did not put forward himself. If he had, he would not have announced in 1958 that the development of systems like the General Problem Solver would soon allow the simulation of every human operation.

(1) Ants are stupid, while men seem intelligent. Indeed, the ant attacks obstacles one at a time and without organizing the succession of detours. By contrast, a man will show himself to be more astute than an ant by drawing up in advance an itinerary from his point of departure to his goal. In other words, the man's outer environment must include, beyond present obstacles and resources, *possibilities that are not yet actualized.* An obstacle in his path represents an immediate impossibility of moving straight ahead. In such a case, a move to the side offers an immediate possibility of moving around the obstacle. Human travelers, however, have the ability to envisage from the very start possibilities that are not yet present. For example, a traveler might choose at the outset to take a wider detour in order to make things easier later on. In short, human travelers must be credited with the ability to resolve *general* problems instead of passing from one immediate problem to another.

It would clearly be absurd to claim that if a flesh and blood human *seems* to proceed more intelligently than an ant, it is because he in fact does the exact same thing the ant does but does it *in his head*, trying out each of the possible detours on a "mental map" he has drawn up of the area to be traversed. What matters is just as much the generality of the problems solved as the generality of the problem-solving apparatus.

(2) The relative simplicity of the mobile system depends in both cases on an abstraction in which the real being is replaced by a purely functional system, i.e., by a machine with a fixed goal. This system is animated by a single project and has but one behavior in its repertoire. Human systems are indeed simple if they have only a single goal. Yet, as we know, humans allow themselves to be distracted: among the obstacles that explain Odysseus's detours one finds not just winds and storms but all of the various seductions of life. It is true, however, that this complexity remains external, since it is the complexity of a problem of movement from one point to another in a difficult world. The complexity is not neurological or mentalistic.

Simon displaces *memory* into the outer environment. It is part of the environment to which one must adapt rather than of the adaptive system itself (p. 57). This is a legitimate position: the system's outer environment is enriched by everything the system has learned through experience. This allows us then to say that, in one sense, the system *perceives* not just smoke but the fire of which the smoke is the sign, even when the flame is not presently visible. Similarly, when the sign "tree" comes under my gaze, there is no reason not to say that I *perceive* a word rather than mere physical marks that must be interpreted as a written English word. At the same time, the *imagination* of what is possible must also be displaced into the outer environment inasmuch as a rational system must adapt to the world as it is, and the world as it is for a system capable of anticipation cannot be reduced to the actual world but also includes the inactual, yet foreseeable, world. An intelligent subject prepares by foreseeing events presaged by various indicators, and it also takes into account events that, although not (yet) inevitable, are nonetheless possible. Each change in the actual state of the things around it makes certain outcomes possible that hitherto had not been, while excluding other outcomes that had been possible but must now be ruled out.

It is now time to draw the philosophical lessons of this comparison.

The first lesson is that mind has in some sense been "decerebralized." Simon writes at the end of his chapter on "The Psychology of Thinking":

> One of the curious consequences of my approach—of my thesis—is that I have said nothing about physiology. But the mind is usually thought to be located in the brain. I have discussed the organization of the mind without saying anything about the structure of the brain.[31]

What is the meaning of this "disincarnation of mind"? It will rightly be said that this thesis is precisely the contribution that the Artificial Intelligence model makes to the philosophy of mind. Functionalism consists in separating the mind from the brain in much the same way that the computer scientist separates questions concerning programs from questions concerning the electronic circuits of the machine. Rather than referring to a disincarnation or dematerialization, however, we should perhaps refer to a "decerebralization," thereby avoiding confusing the fact that thought is attached to a brain with the fact that it is attached to a living system.

This dematerialization has nothing to do with any sort of "spiritualization," i.e., the substitution of an immaterial part (the soul) for the material part under consideration. It is simply a way of expressing the fact that, as Aristotle puts it in the text that serves as the epigraph to this chapter, the *formal cause* is more important than the *material cause*.

The second lesson is that psychology deals with systems integrated within their outer environment, meaning that it is only within that environment that they have goals to attain or obstacles to surmount. It follows that a purely logical machine has no psychology unless it has an outer environment. What is a formal automaton? It is, we are told, a machine for calculating results in accordance with rules that are applicable to symbols based only on their physical form and without taking their content into account. As long as an automaton is formal in this sense, i.e., as long as the formulas it manipulates are devoid of signification for it, we have not yet entered the realm of the psychological, let alone the mental realm. In this regard, one notion that is worth noting is what Simon calls a "task environment." If we want to compare a computer to a subject bringing his thought to bear on a problem, we must provide this computer with an outer environment. Simon writes, for example, that

> computer programs designed to play games or to discover proofs for mathematical theorems spend their lives in exceedingly large and complex task environments. Even when the programs themselves are only moderately large and intricate (compared, say, with the monitor and operating systems of large computers), too little is known about their task environments to permit accurate prediction of how well they will perform, how selectively they will be able to search for problem solutions.[32]

It seems to me that when the author writes that the computer systems in question "spend their lives in exceedingly large and complex task environments," the phrase should not be seen as a mere stylistic figure. Unless, that is, the idea of a psychology of Artificial Intelligence is also to be taken in a figurative sense. Every being whose psychological behavior can be described has, by definition, problems to solve in the environment in which it lives. One must then choose: computers must be, if not living, then at least provided with the equivalent of a *life environment* if the question of their intelligence is to arise. Barring this, they have no behavior whatever and, having no behavior in any but an inconsequential and figurative sense, they have no opportunity to demonstrate their intelligence, e.g., to pass or fail a Turing test.

The third lesson to be drawn is this: a psychology of thought that is conceived as a science of the artificial will be a science of the systematic means by which human beings attempt to resolve general problems. In our example, the ant's conduct is rational and it has a psychological life, but it has no mental life, since it engages in no intellectual work, and the mental presupposes intellection. Things are quite different in the case of an astute traveler. A human being planning his itinerary is attempting to solve a general problem, and in two senses. On the one hand, his problem goes beyond the task presently at hand, since this problem is not the simple overcoming of a single obstacle but rather of a series of them that separate him from a distant goal. There is thus a need to find the path, or, as it is called in Greek, the *method* that leads to the goal. On the other hand, the traveler's problem is general because it is endowed with a form that can be abstracted. As a result, it is possible to apply to a given problem proven methods from other cases. It might also be possible to transpose ingeniously a procedure for solving a problem from one domain to another. This is what allows us to say that the student seeking to find the answer to a mathematical problem resembles a traveler in that he, too, traces out an itinerary within an abstract space.

What would an empirical psychology of intellectual work then look like? It would be the study of the methods that subjects spontaneously bring to bear when they are confronted with the problem of having to deal with a complex situation. In this perspective, the psychology of the intellect is to be defined as the science of the solutions invented and transmitted from generation to generation. So defined, it is not above all the search for natural universals, as the Chomskyan school believes.[33] Psychology is a *social science*, a science of behavior that must be learned, and learned in accordance with the mores and habits of a group. Simon seems to subscribe to this view when he writes: "Insofar as behavior is a function of learned technique rather than 'innate' characteristics of the human information-processing system, our knowledge of behavior must be regarded as sociological in nature rather than psychological."[34] From this I draw the following conclusion: the psychology of intellectual functions must take on the problem posed by institutions that are properly intellectual, by cultural styles of thought, and by techniques for reflection and meditation. It will have to be a *historical* psychology. As for the study of the "human information processing system," it is not psychological but physiological.

If psychology wanted to consider natural systems, what might it study? A natural psychology would study the structures of the inner environment insofar as they limit the practical rationality of the system. Psychophysiology would thus study the ("irrational") limits of mental functioning, measuring, for example, short-term memory capacity, the thresholds of perception, disturbances of linguistic functioning, etcetera. It goes without saying that the limits discovered would not be the mental limits of the mental, but the physiological limits of the mental.

All of this leads us toward a conception of psychology that bears little resemblance to the paradigm put in place by mental philosophy. If the adjective "cognitive" were not already overladen with mentalist connotations, one might say that psychological functionalism amounts to a *cognitive ecology of mind*.

It is an ecology because intelligent systems ought to be studied in their life environment (rather than in laboratory settings, as if they were ideal rational machines). Here the word "life" has nothing to do with vitalism or the introduction of obscure forces, contrary to what certain polemicists pretend to believe, acting as though every appearance of the word "life" betokened a *vitalist* conception of things. The word serves only to determine the phenomena to be considered: the systems we are interested in are those that prosper only if they are well integrated within their outer environment and if they are able, in some measure, to adopt the form of behavior required for such integration. The environment itself does not mechanically produce this form of behavior: it is a consequence of integration having become a problem for the system to solve.

This ecology is a *cognitive* one in the following sense: these systems spend their time extracting from their outer environment information that interests them. This information is extracted from the environment and not from sense-data; otherwise the life environment would be the inner environment and we would be studying the behavior of an organ internal to the system. Information is "processed" in the following sense: the current environment is enriched by the consideration of the memorial dimension of the world as well as of the imaginable dimension. The first dimension corresponds to the addition of "memory" and the second to the addition of "anticipatory imagination." All of this is required if we are to be able to say that the system exerts a cognitive or intelligent control over the way in which the structure of the external world is expressed in its behavior.

.   .   .

Has our examination of the concepts of the interior and the exterior begun to delineate a concept of mind? We know that the division between an external world and an internal one organizes the entire conceptual apparatus of the mental philosophy that we have inherited from the philosophical tradition. In fact, all of the traditional oppositions will have to be revised in light of the functionalist idea according to which animation is a phenomenon of the processing of complexity by a system capable of apprehending such complexity.

The most general question of a philosophy of mind can be put as follows: What is it to have a mind (*mens*)? More modestly, one might ask, what decisive trait must a being possess in order for the presence of mind to become an issue? Our discussion of functionalism has taught us that the presence of mind cannot be characterized either by *interiority* or by *subjectivity* or by *rationality in the execution of an operation*.

Interiority is not a sufficient condition of mind. It is not sufficient because an interiority must be conceded to every functional system, whether natural or designed by an engineer. Every system, as long as it is "rational" or adaptive, has an inside and practices an abstraction from its outer environment in conformity with the capabilities provided by its inner environment. The division between the interior and the exterior is a division between two kinds of changes: the changes that require the system to adapt and the changes by which that adaptation takes place. The former correspond to the outer environment and the latter to the inner one.

It might be said that the psychological interiority to which reflexive philosophers refer is not the sort that could be used in speaking of, say, a clock, but is rather the interiority that confers a sense of self. The interior is conceived as the *self*, while the exterior is the foreign or *other than self*. Psychological interiority would then have to be conceived as a subjectivity. Yet *subjectivity* is not sufficient either, if by subjectivity one means *being for oneself*, or what philosophers call "egoism" (*all that exists is for me*). Pascal says that the self is unjust because it makes itself the center of everything. However, this sort of ego cannot suffice to define mind, since every living system is subjective or, if you like, egoistic in that its interiority provides it with a function of selecting what is important *to it* (rather than to someone or something else).

Castoriadis has pointed out that contemporary discussions of subjectivity have been rendered cloudy by the confusion between this sort of natural subjectivity, the fact of being for oneself, and the mode of being that is proper to the human subject, which he calls *autonomy*. Subjectivity suffices only to define automatons. These days, automatons tend to be conceived on the model of the machine, but this is not the best conception one might have. An automaton is above all a being that is capable of moving around on its own, by itself, without external impulsion. The paradigm case of an automaton is therefore a living being. Cybernetics, if it seeks to produce automatons, cannot but seek to simulate the conditions of life of an organism ("art imitates nature"). Now what defines an automaton, precisely because it moves on its own, is to have a *self* and to be for itself: when it moves, it does so from a self-centered perspective. It follows that the concept of an automaton is that of a subjective system, i.e., a system that constructs a world of its own out of what it finds outside of itself. It is therefore correct to emphasize that every living thing exists for itself, right down to the cell and the immune system.[35] Being for oneself does not constitute mind or even consciousness, but only a certain sensitivity to the difference between harmful external elements (aggression) and helpful ones (conservation). We cannot, therefore, be satisfied with a definition in terms of subjectivity or the care of the self.

For this very reason, fundamental physics does not admit the existence of automatons. Castoriadis thus takes a different route to the same conclusions that Simon framed in artificialist terms. What Simon calls "artificial systems" are in fact the same as Castoriadis's "subjective systems":

> Too little attention is paid to the fact that cybernetics implicitly relies on a concept of the automaton that is, strictly speaking, without any meaning for physics. . . . The rigor of the arguments of the *Principia Mathematica* is of no concern to the mites in the British Museum library. The room's lighting is not relevant to the functioning of a computer. Radio waves carry no information to the living beings of the Earth, with the exception of modern man.[36]

These examples illustrate the necessary distinction between two points of view. According to the one, there *are* no systems, whether living organisms or manufactured machines: the distinction we have sought to draw between the inside and the outside, between favorable and dangerous situations, is devoid of meaning and seems arbitrary or "unjust" as Pascal would put it. According to the other point of view, there are such systems and therefore there is also the difference between that which represents something to the system (what brings it relevant information, information to which it is sensitive) and that which represents nothing to it.

It might be said that, in these conditions, a system's own world is not its outer environment but a representation, the "World as Representation" of idealist philosophy. In cognitivist terms, it would be the world as it is represented by images and symbols present within the system and whose regulated transformations constitute its mental life. But to maintain this is to fall prey to a sophism. To posit a system's own world is not to posit a representation or an internal image of the world that could be opposed to an external reality. Rather, it is a selection. The subjective system retains only those things that interest it. It does not follow from this that the elements that the system retains and that make up its *Umwelt*, its outer environment, only exist because it has retained them. A selection is made from among what exists. A system that is sensitive only to the presence of food is not interested in the *representation* of food but in the fact *that there is* food present. Let it not be claimed that it is interested by the representation of the existence of food, unless one means by this that it is interested by external representative signs or *traces*. So, a truffle hunter is interested in the presence of a certain species of fly, not because these flies are of any interest in themselves but because they are often found over truffle beds. One might then say that the truffle hunter is interested in what represents the presence of truffles for him. And what interests him is indeed that there be a visible external sign of the exquisite entities hidden in the soil.

Rationality in the execution of an operation and, in particular, the ability to calculate, which is a particular case of the capacity to operate rationally, is also not sufficient to constitute mentality or to endow the operator with a mind. Indeed, according to one of the current definitions of calculation, it can be said of a system that manipulates physical figures in accordance with an algorithm that it is carrying out operations of calculation, without requiring us to say that it calculates. The notion of calculation has been formalized and thereby purified of all intentionality. A mechanical calculator calculates; it does not, however, calculate something. A formal automaton is able to carry out operations on pure symbols, independently of any interpretation these symbols might be given. But in this case, the formal automaton is not in the process of solving a problem, because problems must be defined in the outer environment that they comprise, the task environment. Even if this environment might occasionally exhibit a somewhat abstract character, it is nonetheless exterior. Because formal automatons have no life environment, they also have no behavior. Without behavior, they have no opportunity to exhibit intelligence. They therefore do not have minds.

What, then, are we to take as the salient characteristic of mind? The preceding remarks suggest that we must distinguish the notion of *psychic life* or animation, which corresponds to the different traits just enumerated (existence for oneself, finality, and calculating power), from the notion of *mind*, which should only be applied to what is properly mental, i.e., intellectual.

Since rationality of execution is not a sufficient condition for mind, we are left with saying that the sufficient condition is rationality in the determination of what is to be done. Mind will then be characterized by autonomy, i.e., by the ability to determine one's own goals and not merely rationally to attain goals already set. It will perhaps be objected that such rationality has more resemblance to *irrationality*: how can one rationally set oneself goals other than on the basis of other goals that have already been defined? But to assume this basis would be to allow the imposition of a particular definition of rationality as the utilization of means to attain ends that have been determined elsewhere.

Let us return to the difference between an ant and Odysseus. The difference is no doubt that the ant moves from one obstacle to another until it reaches its goal, whereas the human actor will attempt to plan his journey, perhaps beginning (if he has time) with the collection of information about the environment to be crossed and the methods already tried in similar cases. Until now, it has been possible to maintain that the difference between the two is simply a difference of degree in the complexity of the problem posed and, therefore, in the conduct derived in response to this problem.

In truth, the difference is that the goal of the human agent is not given but rather presupposed by the analysis of the methods used or invented by our traveler. At any moment, Odysseus might decide that it is too tiring, or too dangerous, to continue his attempt to return to Ithaca. There is therefore a profound indeterminacy of the goals of a human enterprise, one that is not a matter of degree or of greater flexibility in the choice of means.

In our tradition, Odysseus is the classic example of a certain form of intelligence. Odysseus, the man of a thousand ruses, the *polumetis*, is skilled at inventing ways of getting around obstacles. But the endurance and the tenacity of Homer's hero are also part of the humanity that he exemplifies, and even of his intelligence. A detour is a way of heading toward a goal by first heading away from it. At first, a traveler making a detour cannot be distinguished from one who has changed his mind and decided to go somewhere else. This is no doubt one reason why some insist on interiority: if we stick to appearances, if we observe from the exterior a traveler beginning his detour and another one who has changed his destination, we perceive no difference. There is not (yet) any manifestation of the fact that they are not doing the same thing. The result is that the difference between them, which is a mental one, seems to have reality only beyond visible appearances, in the realm of their innermost thoughts. Needless to say, this concept of interiority presents no particular philosophical difficulties and comes down to little more than a manner of speaking. It is simply a way of expressing the fact that our understanding of the traveler's action is incomplete for as long as we do not know how to extend the initial observed movement toward one or the other goal. As a result, within the context of a competition, a detour is as good as a ruse: the opponent has nothing to go on, and might let himself be taken in. Indeed, it cannot be assumed that the Achaeans have not abandoned the idea of taking the city of Troy, nor can it assumed that Odysseus has not abandoned the idea of returning from exile. When Odysseus pretends to have abandoned a goal, the ruse works because it is always possible that he *has* given up a quest judged to be too difficult.

In order to simulate the rational behavior of an ant, we must assume that it has but one goal: to return in one way or another to its anthill. Is this idealizing abstraction totally acceptable from an ethological point of view? It is, in any case, legitimate, if only as an approximation. By contrast, in the case of a human being, it would be an egregious error to count on our adversaries' obstinacy. We esteem endurance in those who demonstrate it precisely because we recognize that it is not part of the makeup of every human being. In thinking about a particular case, we may provisionally act as if the goals of men were determined outside of the domain where they put their intelligence to use. But it goes without saying that the goals of an agent are not detached from his thinking. Quite the opposite. In order to simulate the behavior of a human being, his functional equivalent will have to be constructed in such a way that, among the means for attaining its goal, it might enumerate the following: redefining the goal; maintaining the goal in principle while postponing its attainment ("these grapes are too green"); translating the goal into another language, for example, by deciding that the goal one has set ought to be understood in a moral rather than a material sense; subordinating the goal to other, more urgent or elevated, ends; and so on. It is thus not the ability to plan complicated itineraries that distinguishes men from ants (to remain within our example). In order to see the real difference, the argument based on the tale of the man and the ant will have to be expanded. Our ant would really appear to be a *rational being* in the properly human sense of the word if we were to discover that it had come to the decision that, in the end, returning home does not necessarily mean returning to the anthill and that it had set itself to elaborating a kind of reflection that would allow it to give new meaning to the idea of *being at home*.

CHAPTER 8

Mechanical Mind

Many a wheel takes the place of all the world's mind.

—La Fontaine, *Discours à Mme de la Sablière*

WE HAVE still not reached an understanding of how the analogy with the computer came to be seen to support the materialist philosophy of mind. The program of Artificial Intelligence, if it is understood in the functionalist way proposed in the previous chapter, would tend rather to *dematerialize* the mind, separating the question of the structure of mental operations from those pertaining to their physical support. We insisted in the previous chapter that this in no way amounts to making mind a reality separate from matter: to distinguish formal causes from material ones is not to maintain that the form in question is anything other than a form taken by matter. We simply noted that mind's properties are not linked to the fact of being the form of any particular matter: the same form can be realized in different materials, in much the same way that the same sentence can be written in black ink or in red pencil. Searle points out (and deplores) the fact that, with functionalism, the identity of the physical and the mental ceases to be a respectable dogma. The very statement of this identity becomes dubiously meaningful, since it is apparent that the logic governing mental description differs from that of physical description, with the result that it can be deemed a category mistake to seek to make mental and physical states coincide with one another.

The lesson of functionalism (the one that renders psychology a "science of the artificial") is the following: if our aim is to study the intelligence of a system—to study the form and limits of the rationality of its behavior—we have no need to know what goes on inside the system. We know by other means that this internal environment contains the most delicate sort of complex machinery, but investigation of this internal structure tells us nothing about the intelligence of the method chosen by the actor to resolve its problem. The internal environment is what neurophysiology describes. But psychology's concern is what happens in the external environment.

This is another way of saying that we have still not understood what kind of psychological explanation would be both causal and naturalistic (in the nomological sense). What does the analogy with the computer lack that keeps it from providing the hoped-for solution? According to the cognitivist, it has failed to raise the problem of the mechanics of mind. Only if this question is raised can the Artificial Intelligence paradigm provide the conceptual mediation needed in order to move from the physical to the mental as well as, in the other direction, from the intentional to the natural. The mechanical question about the mind is this: How might ideas have physical effects corresponding to their meaning? We have seen that there is no point in replacing the immaterial ideas of Cartesian philosophy by physical signifiers: such a materialization of ideas fails to move things forward, for the physical effects of a sign are the effects of its physical qualities and not those of its intention (see above, § 5.4). What we are after, then, is a conceptual mediation between the semantic and physical descriptions of a sign. An intermediate level of description must be found, one that will allow us to say: A physical thing is X, anything X is semantic, and this property X is such that the physical effects of the sign are exactly those required by its semantic value. The appeal to the analogy with the computer is meant to provide this intermediate level.

8.1. From Simulation to Mechanical Explanation

As Zenon Pylyshyn explains, the analogy with computers is sometimes understood in a limited way, sticking to the idea of a *simulation* of intelligent behavior by a machine.[1] Yet the cognitivist theory cannot content itself with a mere simulation: it hopes to find in computers the literal model of the phenomena of mind, or at least those that can be placed under the general heading of cognition. The metaphor of the computer makes it possible to envisage a causal explanation of intelligent behavior. The mental abilities of human beings will have the same sorts of explanations as those of the computer: they are calculating abilities, i.e., symbol manipulation. Cognitivist psychology will be a computational one.

So the idea of calculation, in the sense of a rational transformation of symbols, is meant to provide the required intermediate level. Calculation is understood to be a sequence of rational operations performed on symbols. The sequence is rational because it is rule-governed: each step in the calculation gives a result that is either correct or incorrect. The operations bear upon symbols in that they consist in transforming formulas. The final formula provides the result of the entire operation. If the procedure to be followed to obtain the correct result from a finite series of transitions is specified in entirely formal terms, so that at each step one knows what the next transformation to be carried out will be (without having to guess or look for it), then the procedure can be determined by an *algorithm*, in which case, it must be admitted that the procedure can be automated in virtue of the mathematical theory of the decidable.[2]

A computer is a material device able to calculate. What makes such a system a *calculator*? A mere physical description of the machine cannot provide the answer, for such a definition takes only the machine's physical states into account. The sequences of these physical states can be explained by natural mechanisms. One must therefore move to a different level of description if one is to discuss the calculator that this machine also is. The same sequence of states that has just been described and explained at the physical level may now be taken up from a different point of view: some of the states of the machine can be characterized as symbolic states, and the sequence of states then appears to be a calculation. This new level of description is in one sense still physical, for what distinguishes two symbolic states is a physical difference. But it also presupposes a massive abstraction, since not every physical difference between states of the machine at different times is counted. Only some of these differences are relevant. The entire calculation allows a move from the "input" to the "output," from the problem to be solved to its solution, from the argument to the value of the function to be calculated for that argument. Finally, the machine's calculation itself can be given a semantic interpretation: the machine will be said to be solving an arithmetical problem or, to return to our example, to be playing chess.

In the end, the description of the machine will have to take place on three levels, which might be called the physical level of the material machine, the symbolic level of calculation, and the semantic level of representations.[3] The three levels are independent of one another: to be familiar with the machine's physical behavior is not yet to know the calculation being worked upon, and to know the formal program being executed does not allow one to say what the machine is doing in intentional terms: is it arithmetic or a chess problem? But these three levels are articulated with one another: symbolic calculation is the mechanical realization of intellectual work on representations, and the physical processes are the causal realizations of a formal calculation.[4] We are left with the following remarkable fact: when a calculation is carried out, the computer works without taking into account the fact that the symbols are representative of a certain reality. If, for example, it calculates the function "PLUS" for the argument "2, 3" and if it gives as a result the symbol "5," the computer itself has no need to know that it is adding numbers. For it to do its work, it is necessary and sufficient that the symbols be identifiable through their configurations (their physical morphology). Yet (and this is what interests the cognitivist), the process carried out is assuredly a calculation: if the symbols are given their correct arithmetical interpretation, the operation is that of addition.

The question that is now in need of an answer is a simple one: How does any of this elucidate our psychology? What do these distinctions among the levels of description of a computer's functioning have to do with the psychological explanation of intelligent behavior? It is now time to state clearly what is presented as a cognitivist hypothesis but which is really the philosophical thesis that underlies the entire doctrine. This thesis is that thinking is a process of calculation. We are able to think only because we have the means to operate in a rule-governed way upon symbols that are physically inscribed in our cerebral system. In the physical work that we, like the computer, carry out, the meaning of the symbols is not taken into account. And yet, that meaning is respected.

That is, according to Fodor, the ingenious idea underlying the entire cognitivist revolution:

> The trick is to combine the postulation of mental representations with the "computer metaphor." Computers show us how to connect semantical with causal properties for *symbols*. . . . In this respect, I think there really has been something like an intellectual breakthrough. Technical details to one side, this is—in my view—the only aspect of contemporary cognitive science that represents a major advance over the versions of mentalism that were its eighteenth- and nineteenth-century predecessors. Exactly what was wrong with Associationism, for example, was that there proved to be no way to get a *rational* mental life to emerge from the sorts of causal relations among thoughts that the "laws of association" recognized.[5]

Fodor here makes clear that he has taken on board the aims of associationism, which were to propose laws of mental mechanics. He has also adopted its metaphysics, according to which mental life is made up of combinations of elementary psychic units ("ideas" or "representative states"). But Fodor departs from the views of his predecessors when it comes time to propose a model of these mental mechanisms. The model of the computer provides precisely what the model of attraction could not: a mental mechanics that respects the rationality of our intellectual activity.

8.2. The Causality of Ideas

Let us return once again to the central issue of this entire theoretical enterprise: there will be a true scientific psychology when we are able to provide psychological explanations of a mechanical sort. In order for this to happen, we must uncover what I earlier proposed to call "psychical causality." Recall that ordinary mental causality—the sort used, for example, in psychological explanations giving rise to a rhetorical act (narration, plea, etc.)—was insufficient for this role. Ordinary mental causality is at work on the level of events in the histories of individuals: for example, person A angers person B by refusing to adopt toward B the deference to which B feels entitled. Psychical causality would have to exist between an internal event of mental life and another such internal mental event. In associationist psychology, this causal power was attributed to "ideas" and to "representations." An idea calls forth or evokes another idea according to a few basic principles.[6] But, as Fodor notes, associationism never managed to reconstitute anything resembling a chain of thought, a *logical* sequence of thoughts. The "laws" of the association of ideas are incapable of making a distinction between a chain of reasoning and a non sequitur. Moreover, a mechanics of mental association might well be able to claim to have produced a semblance of mental life, but it cannot account for the passage to action. These are two problems with which the doctrines of psychical materialism have always been burdened. The appeal of a psychology on the model of the computer is that it seems able to solve both of these problems, which might be called the "Sherlock Holmes problem" and the "Brentano problem." The first of these is the problem of giving a plausible psychological explanation of someone's mental life. The second is the problem of explaining the effect ideas have on behavior.

Let us begin with the general problem, i.e., with the problem that some American philosophers refer to as the "Brentano problem." Note that the "Brentano problem" was precisely not a problem for Brentano himself, but only becomes one for philosophers with a naturalistic orientation. It is not a problem that Brentano set for himself but rather became a problem for materialist or naturalistic philosophers from the moment that they heard of the "Brentano criterion" and were thereby put on notice (usually from having read Quine's *Word and Object*) that psychology cannot claim to be a real science as long as it only provides explanations that take into account the content of opinions and desires. This is because a description of someone in terms of his intentions explains what the person is doing by means of factors that have no causal force: ideas, motives, aims.

Causal explanation takes the following form: what happens to a thing makes something else happen. The explanation for a change in the state of a thing is sought in a prior change in the state of that thing. For example, if someone pushes me into the ocean, my behavior has a causal explanation understood by everyone. Things are much the same if I fall into the ocean after having slipped on the dock. By contrast, if my behavior consists in diving into the ocean for a dip, then my conduct is explained by an intentional object, namely, the dip in the ocean that I wish to take. The fact that the dip seems desirable to me explains my dive. What we call an "intentional object" is the content of my mental state, *what* it is that I

desire or believe. But an intentional object does not have the causal properties that explanation requires. If the intentional object is a goal to be attained, then it does not yet exist and therefore cannot influence my action.
The same thing goes for beliefs and opinions. I wish to go for a swim
because I have just learned that the water temperature is above 70 degrees,
a threshold below which ocean swims lose their appeal to me. This information explains my behavior despite the fact that the temperature of the
water has no way of exerting a causal influence on my conduct.

The mechanistic psychologist's preoccupation is to find a way of recon-
ciling his mental philosophy with his natural philosophy. He means to
preserve the value of intentional explanations, in which one explains what
one has done by providing some sort of goal or reason, but at the same
time he wants to see this explanation integrated into a "physicalist" vision
of things. This is where he encounters a thorny difficulty. It is as if, or so
he thinks, there were physically unconditioned causal forces, not unlike
what happens in the battles between Homeric heroes: the warriors strike
mighty blows, but these are not the actions by which the battle's outcome
is decided. For there are other, invisible forces that contend above their
heads, as it were, and that give victory to one side over and against the
other, without it being possible to say (in prosaic terms at least) how they
do it.

The traditional solution is to replace powerless intentional objects with
effective representations. It is not the goal, it is claimed, that influences
my conduct; it is the *representation* of the goal. This solution would be a
merely verbal one if it did not introduce a mechanical model. And here we
encounter two difficulties. The first is one already familiar to us: the problem of the causality of ideas upon things. How can a representation in my
mind cause a movement of my body? This problem, of the interaction
between the mental and the physical, arises for every mental philosophy.

The other difficulty is the causation of a mental entity by another mental
entity: How can an idea cause the appearance of another idea or of a desire?
This difficulty might be called the "Sherlock Holmes problem," by analogy
with the "Brentano problem." Here again, this is not a problem that the
detective himself raised in any of his adventures, but rather a problem put
to mechanistic psychology by Conan Doyle's character. In general, at the
end of one of the Sherlock Holmes stories, Dr. Watson recounts Sherlock
Holmes's explanation. Here is how Holmes managed to identify the crimi-
nal: a certain detail made him think of a certain circumstance, which gave
him an idea, etcetera. Watson's summary is a psychological narrative, a
description of Holmes's "train of thought." And these short narratives are
precisely those cited by Fodor as the epitome of a cognitive mental process
of the sort that behaviorists were unwilling to consider.[7] But this train of
thought is also a form of reasoning, an argument that will be more or less

solid, more or less convincing. In the past, mechanical psychology proved unable to account for the rationality of such episodes in mental life.

But if rational thought could be considered a process of calculation, i.e., a manipulation of symbols, then the mental functioning of an intelligent being would be comparable to that of a computer. We know that symbols have (causal) physical properties and (intentional) semantic properties. Therefore, our thinking might also be at one and the same time a rational train of thought and a mechanical sequence able to give rise to a behavior of the body. Fodor explains the idea as follows:

> Contemporary cognitive psychology is, in effect, a revival of the representational theory of the mind. . . . [T]he mind is conceived of as an organ whose function is the manipulation of representations and these, in turn, provide the domain of mental processes and the (immediate) objects of mental states. That's what it is to see the mind as something like a computer.[8]

The comparison is thus made between two systems: on the one hand, the machine considered as a device for transforming formulas; on the other, mind considered as an organ whose task is to manipulate representations. The transformation of formulas into other formulas in a rule-governed way is calculation. By providing interpretations of the formulas by which the machine calculates, we raise the computer to the level of a semantic machine, i.e., a machine for transforming *representations* into other *representations* (or meaningful formulas into other meaningful formulas). Now, the regulated transition from one representation to another is what the representational theory of mind calls "mental life." To have a mental life is to move from one idea to another. To think is to move rationally from one idea to another. The innovation is thus that we can give a natural (i.e., mechanical) model of such mental life, a model that respects its rationality (and note that mind is held to be an *organ* of the person).

It is remarkable that, in the text cited above, Fodor continues his explanation with a parenthetical comment:

> (Or rather, to put the horse back in front of the cart, that's what it is to see a computer as something like the mind. We give sense to the analogy by treating selected states of the machine as formulæ and by specifying which semantic interpretations the formulæ are to bear. It is in the context of such specifications that we speak of machine processes as computations and of machine states as intensional.)[9]

For Fodor, one puts the cart before the horse if one acts as if the proposed analogy said this: It would be illuminating to compare human beings, from a psychological point of view, to computers. For the computer, by itself, offers no point of comparison for as long as it does not have the equivalent of a psychology. In fact, the relationship is the reverse: computers are first compared to human calculators. The cognitivist asks us to go beyond the mere comparison of external behavior and consider the work performed within artificial and human calculators respectively. But (and this is the decisive point, one that Fodor understands better than many cognitivists), the computer is not being compared with any old thinking subject, but with one endowed with a Cartesian or neo-Cartesian mind, a representing mind, replete with internal symbols. Just as a computer manipulates formulas (rather than objects in the external world, about which it knows nothing), the mind manipulates representations (rather than objects in the external world, about which it knows nothing beyond what those mental representations provide). In order for computers to provide the physical and mechanical model of the mind in the way the cognitivist program hopes they will, it is essential that the computer itself be conceived according to the philosophical model of the representing mind put forward by Descartes and his heirs. Here again we see the accuracy of the idea that today's cognitive revolution presupposes that of the seventeenth century.

It follows that the cognitivist's analogy presupposes a philosophy of mind, precisely the philosophy that we presented earlier under the name "mental philosophy" and according to which, to have a mind is to be the seat of mental processes that mobilize representations.

The analogy with the computer serves to naturalize the notion of a *representing mind*. If the human mind is a representing mind, then the model of the computer might allow one to harbor serious hopes for a mechanical psychology. But this analogy begins by comparing the computer to the Cartesian or Lockeian thinking subject. This is not an idea that the analogy can provide; rather, it is the idea that grounds the very use of the analogy.

8.3. The Homunculus Objection

Since the issue is the restoration of representationism (a Good Old Theory, as Fodor calls it), one may well ask how cognitivist psychology has managed to overcome the difficulties confronted by previous versions of this philosophy of mind.

Representations are needed when one wants to explain behavior by means of intentional objects. This is the moment when one moves from:

(1) I am going out to buy the paper.

to:

(2) The desire to buy the paper (combined with the belief that papers are sold at the corner newsstand) makes me go out.

What can possibly be the justification for such a transcription? In what way is the second formulation more explicit than the first? All that can be said is that the first formulation bears no resemblance to a causal explanation, because it does not relate two entities or two events. By contrast, the second formulation seems to endow intentional objects with the ability to act through the intermediary of their representation in the mind. On its own, the newspaper to be purchased has no way of acting on the movement of my legs. But the desire to buy a newspaper that is represented as available at the corner newsstand can explain the movement of my body (provided that this desire is physically located in the appropriate place, i.e., in contact with the centers that control the motor nerves). What is at issue in all of this is not Artificial Intelligence, but the metaphysics of explanation. How can events in the world be explained by ideas or thoughts? How can thoughts take the form required by explanations?

We might begin with an example given by Peirce. Peirce frequently adopts forms of description that seem to be dictated by the natural philosophy of classical mechanics: an action must be expressed as a relation between two events. In his essay on "What Pragmatism Is," Peirce maintains that *universals* are not only real, but effective, i.e., that they have physical effects. This would seem to imply a causality of ideas. True, but how does Peirce express this? He writes: "Aside from metaphysical nonsense, no sane man doubts that if I feel the air in my study to be stuffy, that thought may cause the window to be opened."[10] In this sentence, only the form of expression is a bit odd: the causality of the thought works upon the window. There is, first of all, the fact of a physical change to be explained: the window opens and it does not open by itself. This change is explained by another change, this one a mental change: a thought came to someone ("if I opened the window, the air in this room would be replenished"). What is odd about Peirce's way of expressing the relationship between the two changes is that he attempts to fit into a "causal statement" consistent with the dominant philosophy of his time—*an event causes an event*—an action that would normally be expressed through the use of a causal verb: someone, feeling the air in the room in need of ventilation, opens the window. In this latter case, the causality Peirce attributed to thought is attributed to a thought armed with an *agent of execution*—which means that there is no paradox of symbolic efficacy and no mysterious action of the mental on the physical. As Peirce himself might say, thought becomes effectual by being provided with a *judge* and a *sheriff*. By contrast, if one does not include the physical world within the order of meaning, then natural laws and human ideas become comparable to tribunals with no police officers to carry out their judgments.[11] Here we have run up against the fundamental problem of all mental mechanics: How can mental representations (ideas) act without an agent of execution?

This was also a problem for the associationist theory of ideas. We have seen that Fodor cites the precedent of the laws of associationism in order to illustrate the idea of a mechanics of representations. He refers to these so-called "laws of association" not because he believes in them but because he wants to remind us that mechanical laws will have to associate ideas without regard to their representational content. This is perhaps why Fodor mentions only association by contiguity. For example, pepper makes me think of salt: the association is one of contiguity, brought on by the fact that one usually sees the pepper shaker next to the salt shaker.[12] It is well known that there are two such principles of classical associationism: other than association by contiguity in experience, there is association by resemblance.[13] But resemblance is of no help whatsoever to a mechanical psychology, since it is an association of content, of meaning: to present association by resemblance as a mechanism is to commit the error of appealing to an *intelligent mechanism*. This is precisely the "homunculus" that has been widely mocked in the debates about mechanistic theories of the mental. The theorist describes the machinery meant to produce the phenomena of mind, pointing out its various elements. But when his demonstration is scrutinized more closely, it turns out that the function of one of the mechanisms he has postulated is to apply rules (that it must therefore be able to understand) and to decrypt signs (that it must be able to read). Instead of explaining the cognitive abilities of an animal by means of internal mechanisms, one is in a ridiculous situation where the functioning of these mechanisms is in turn explained by the cognitive abilities of certain of their elements. In fact, the old associationist theories were discredited for two reasons: the reason mentioned earlier (the mechanism produces a train of thought but not a rational train of thought) and the one that has just come to light (the mechanisms adduced are in fact pseudomechanisms).

The difficulty here is the familiar philosophical "problem of the subject." How does mental mechanics eliminate the subject? Dennett has recognized this problem, which he calls "Hume's Problem."[14] In his view, Hume sought to solve this problem by getting rid of the self in psychology. The problem, Dennett notes, arises for any psychology that postulates the existence of internal representations or cognitive mental entities (ideas inside the head). There must be someone present to read the mental sentences, to see the mental images, and to contemplate the representative ideas. If there are images in the mind, who is it that sees them? Could it be me? But this function of the self is not explained in mechanical terms. If there are sentences inscribed within the brain, whose job is it to read them? There must be a reader. This reader is a homunculus.

Dennett takes it to be established that there is no psychology without the postulation of internal representations. He is thus led to formulate the following dilemma: psychology without homunculi is impossible, while psychology with homunculi is without explanatory value.[15] Without homunculi, no psychology of internal representations, but with homunculi, no explanations.

How have these difficulties been dealt with? A first solution that is often proposed ought to be mentioned, although it strikes me as a simple diversionary maneuver that clarifies nothing. It is proposed that the solution should be sought in the idea of cognitivist analysis: the cognitive abilities of the system are explained by the set of subsystems that, in their turn but at a lower level, process signals and produce intelligent results. The idea is that breaking down the problem faced by the intelligent processor will necessarily allow for the progressive elimination of all intelligence in the programmed treatment of the problem.

Another proposed solution has been derived from the idea that a conceptual mediation between the semantic and the physical has been discovered: between trains of thought and neuronal activity lies the syntactic level of the internal activity of physical systems able to carry out calculations. The homunculus is thus nothing but an appearance.

I will consider each of these two proposed solutions in turn.

8.4. The Debraining of the Homunculi

As Neisser pointed out, the analogy with the computer is often used by mechanists to reassure their readers: the work carried out by a machine is certainly mechanical! The hypothetical internal processors may *seem* intelligent, but this is only an illusion. In reality, they are not. Rather, their apparent intelligence is a property that "emerges" when they are skillfully combined, whence the response to those who object that the attribution of a person's intellectual performances to the internal manipulations of mental representations requires the installation of intelligent mechanisms within the person. It is true, goes the reply, that the mechanisms assumed to carry out this work are intelligent ones, since they process representations, and treat representations in different ways according to their content. In this sense, a homunculus has indeed been placed within the "black box" or "module" meant to carry out a given mental function. But the presence of this little man is only temporary. Only at a provisional stage of our analysis of the entire performance do we need such intelligent mechanisms. The greater our success in breaking down the work in question, the easier the partial operations assigned to the modules will be to carry out. At the end of the entire process, we will come to a set of elementary operations that make no appeal to intelligence.

Dennett uses a humorous illustration to clarify this point.[16] He explains that the cognitivist explanation consists in the first place in hiring a group of little men or homunculi. A complex operation is then broken down into different parts. Each part of the overall problem is assigned to a box that is functionally defined: the box is there to solve a particular part of the problem. Because the working of the box and the procedures employed have not been specified, it is as if a homunculus has been placed in the box. If the analysis stopped there, nothing will have been explained. But it does not stop there. It is as if the homunculus had been replaced by an entire team made up of competent homunculi, each of which is assigned a less complex operation. In the end, when the level at which the operations require no intelligence has finally been reached, it is as if the homunculi had been given their walking papers: the explanation no longer needs them, for it has attained the level of mechanisms without intelligence that was its goal from the beginning.

Remaining in a figural register, the same idea can be expressed by an absurd image: the homunculi will have to be "debrained," since they were originally planted in the brain to explain the intellectual abilities of a person. This comical formula, however, has the salutary effect of reminding us that, although the discussion seems to concern issues in higher cybernetics, in reality it revolves around purely speculative devices and mechanisms invented by philosophers. It is therefore wise to bear in mind how little it takes to slide from enlightening analogies to the most outlandish metaphors.

Dennett's fiction suggests we distinguish two types of transition between levels of explanation: (1) the division of labor, which entails a transition from the more complex to the less complex; (2) the reduction of the intentional to the mechanical, which entails crossing the border beyond which the mechanisms posited by the model no longer depend upon cognitive explanations by means of rules and representations, but instead appeal to purely physical explanations.

The first transition does not take us out of the world of rules and representations, but remains within the order of intelligent mechanisms. If we grant to mechanical psychology that the notion of an "intelligent mechanism" makes sense, the image of a division of labor among homunculi might serve to illustrate the *construction* of mental life out of elementary processors applying their rudimentary cognitive resources to symbols. Of course, the difficulties with the very concept of an "intelligent mechanism" remain, whatever its postulated level of intelligence.[17] If mechanical psychology expects intelligence to be what emerges from this machinery, its chain of workers has to be made up of processors devoid of all cognitive competence, i.e., mechanisms that operate without rules or representations. According to a financial metaphor used by Dennett, as long as the theorist practices transitions of type 1, he is in debt by one explanation, for he has asked for authorization to place, provisionally ("on credit"), an intelligent operator in each of the different subsystems of the mental machinery. Only a transition of type 2 will allow him to "pay back the loan": the homunculi will then be out of work.[18] In the last analysis, the cognitive superstructures will all have to be explained by mechanical infrastructures. At the level of the rudimentary processors, there will be no rules to apply, no representations to recognize, no information to process, and no problems to solve. In short, there will be no intellectual work to be done.

It might be pointed out that the image itself reveals the incoherence of the argument. This image appeals to one of the main sources of our functional models: the division of labor. But the division of labor—within an administration, for example—applies to functions and not to operators. The jobs are divided up, not the employees themselves. A secretary is replaced by a typist, an operator, a filing clerk, a receptionist, etcetera. Moving in the other direction, Harpagon replaces his entire domestic staff by a jack of all trades. In other words, as was already suggested by Herbert Simon's arguments regarding the architecture of complexity, the subdivision can be continued infinitely: there is no reason to think of a job as inherently simple or complex, because simplicity and complexity are relative. Even the operations discharged by menial laborers, street sweepers, and assembly-line workers can be divided up among several employees.

To put this another way: it is true that assemblages (like machines) are built out of individual pieces. But this sort of construction must not be confused with the functional *differentiation* of a whole into its parts. These parts are not individuals, but rather functions. By definition, an individual is indivisible, and this is why the image of the homunculus is so telling: it refers to a part of a man that, instead of being a human part (an organ), is in fact a small man, i.e., a smaller whole.

In fact, the argument by way of this sort of breakdown, if it lends itself to any philosophy whatever, would seem to support a version of panpsychism. If it were possible to move gradually from intelligence to unintelligence, the absence of intelligence would only be the ultimate degree of stupidity.[19] This in turn would mean that the rudimentary mechanisms postulated by the cognitivist explanation are merely of *very low* intelligence. Far from naturalizing intentionality, we would succeed only in mentalizing nature.[20] If the transition were a gradual one, it could be carried on infinitely, and we would have to say that mechanisms are always intelligent to some degree.

There has been a mistake regarding the nature of the problem. The mechanist thinks he needs to construct, whereas the difficulty at hand requires *differentiation*.

Why this need to postulate a little man inside the head? Why do we require, beyond the rule that says what to do, a little man to interpret the rule? We are told that it is because the operation to be carried out has not been broken down completely. Yet the complexity of the task did not create the need for the homunculus; it was the fact that the task requires dealing with *representations*. To stress this point is not to proclaim dogmatically that the philosophy of mind must, as is said, "posit a subject." Indeed, the problem is not so much one of having a subject as of having an *intentional relation*, the very condition of signs as such. Subjectivity, in the sense of being for oneself (i.e., considered from the perspective of the system's own teleology), in no way suffices to provide this intentional relation. Even if the theory brings together a sign and a system endowed with existence for itself, it has still not accounted for the semiotic value of the sign, for its ability to represent something for the subject. What must be posited for the representation (or the rule) to apply to a subject's behavior is not a subject, but an *intentional subject*, i.e., a subject able to *use* the sign to determine its own conduct. To use Peirce's terminology, what counts is not the existence of an observing subject able to see that the sign represents the object (as is assumed by representational theories of meaning for which the relation between a sign and the thing signified is dyadic). What is required is a subject equipped with the habits of thought necessary to interpret the sign as determining a second sign relative to an object (a triadic relation). The prints in the sand are not signs of Friday (a dyadic relation), they are the signs that Friday has passed this way (triadic relation). More generally, the semiotic relation does not take place between a representation and a thing represented, or between a signifier and a signified. It is a relation that requires the establishment of three functions: x is the sign of y only if z is posited as the interpretant of x, i.e., the sign applicable to y if x is given. This print on the ground is the sign that applies to Friday if another sign, the predicate "has passed this way," applies to Friday. If this thing on the ground is a trace of Friday, then Friday must have passed this way. The passage from one sign to another does not take place in a psychic medium by a law of association. It takes place in a mind, which is a way of saying that it occurs in virtue of a *rule*, a principle of inference, or a habit of thought: here we see a footprint, *therefore* someone has passed this way.

Dennett perceives all this when he writes, in a review of one of Fodor's books, that "nothing is intrinsically a representation of anything; something is a representation only *for* or *to* someone; any representation or system of representations thus requires at least one *user* or *interpreter* of the representation who is external to it."[21]

This can be understood as follows: signs are signs if they have a function in the *external* behavior of a user, and this means in the behavior of someone in his external environment. Let us bear this first conclusion in mind. We will return to it.

8.5. The Manipulation of Symbols

We have now come to the second purported response, the only one that deserves to be taken seriously: thought is a process of calculation, i.e., one that has a "formal" or "syntactic" aspect.[22] The interposition of such a syntactic process makes possible a comprehensible articulation of an intentional process and a physical one within the mental machinery.

The symbols that the representational theory places in the mind are primarily cognitive entities: their presence in the mind accounts for the person's cognitive abilities. The representation in someone's mind of a newsstand allows him to have the idea of going there to get the newspaper. It is admitted that symbols or mental representations qua cognitive entities have no causal effect on the system's physical processes. But these same symbols are also physical entities and therefore have all the natural efficacy provided by their physical constitution. It happens that some of their physical properties serve to individuate them as entities belonging to certain syntactic types. And we know that the sequence of syntactic states described by an algorithm is compatible with the semantics of the operation, even though the calculation is carried out without taking the meaning of the symbols into account. Let us assume that the calculation has been given a logical interpretation: if every step of the calculation is understood as a step within a chain of reasoning, the sequence of these transformations will correspond to a valid inferential scheme from a logical point of view.

The analogy with computers here boils down to comparing the *functioning* of the mind with the *functioning* of a computer. This analogy is meant to assure us that there is no question of there being homunculi within systems of natural intelligence, any more than in those whose intelligence is artificial.

This purported solution immediately raises the following question: Reference has been made to the manipulation of symbols, but *whose* symbols are they? To whom do they belong? Or, to put it another way: To what behavior are we to ascribe the manipulation of symbols that constitutes mental processes? To which system does the behavior of transforming symbols belong? We must bear in mind that the flaw of the Chinese Room argument was not to have taken this aspect into account: in order to grant that an operator engages in symbolic activity, it is not enough that it manipulates symbols. It must also *use* those symbols when it manipulates them (see above, § 6.4).

At first glance, the proper response would seem to be: The symbols belong to the thinker. The symbols in question are those that have been introduced precisely so as to provide psychological explanations. Let us imagine that the behavior to be explained is that of a chess player, whether human or programmed: the symbols processed must represent the chessboard and the pieces.[23] Indeed, we hope to explain how a player's thought—e.g., "I must protect my queen"—can interact with other representations and produce movement on the player's part. Symbols (or internal representations) are thus representative of the world outside of the player: e.g., the chess board, the pieces, the opponent, the clock, and so on. As a result, the manipulation of symbols seemingly must be a behavior of the player, of the person who is playing chess, and who uses symbols to think various thoughts regarding the games he is playing.

Yet things are not so clear. The principle of the entire theory is that several descriptions of the same activity will be provided. One of these descriptions is physical. Yet the physical activity to be described is, strangely enough, not that of a chess player moving pieces on a chessboard, nor that of a chess player wondering what move to make. It is rather the physical activity of a *brain* moving from one state to another. It is within the brain that symbols, taken as physical entities, will play a causal role. If this is so, the morphological (or syntactic) redescription of this activity will also have to bear upon a process that takes place in the brain. And it is this calculation that, in the end, will have to be interpreted as the line of reasoning that leads the chess player to decide to play as he does. It is thus well and truly in the player's brain that physical symbols are manipulated, and it is there that those symbols constitute the player's thoughts.

We are thus meant to conclude that the thinker in this case—i.e., what intellectually organizes the player's participation in the chess match—is not the player but the player's brain. The thinker is a brain and the symbols are thus the brain's symbols.

This conclusion is all the more inevitable since, as we noted earlier, the system of symbols can be given an interpretation only if it is considered to be *external* to the operator. Symbols are manipulated in the external environment of the manipulator. Fodor seems to say much the same thing when he writes that computers "just *are* environments in which the syntax of a symbol determines its causal role in a way that respects its content."[24] Fodor means by this that the machine is absolutely not concerned with the meaning of the symbols and that its work is to transform symbols in virtue of their physical form. Yet the machine is constructed in such a way that the transformations it carries out correspond to what would be done in an intelligent transformation that takes the meaning of the symbols into account. Notice the way Fodor formulates the point: The machine is the *external* environment in which symbols are transformed.

It would therefore seem to be impossible that the symbols manipulated in the course of a calculation are those of the person or, if you will, that the transformation of these symbols is a behavior on the part of the person. Just as the machine is the external environment in which the symbols used in mechanical calculation are transformed, the person is the external environment in which mental representations are manipulated. The manipulation in question is therefore necessarily carried out by a part of the person. And it is carried out by the brain, or perhaps by a part of the brain. The symbolic behavior of thinking will then have to be attributed to the brain (or to a part of the brain).

We should have been alerted to this by the expressions Fodor used in introducing his version of the computer analogy. He spoke about comparing the *mind* to a computer. When the mind is compared to a computer, he claimed, the comparison is made in the light of an idea that governs the entire analogy: like the computer, the mind is an organ or an apparatus for manipulating representations.[25] As a result, the analogy with the computer is no longer the one we began with. Until now, the comparison has always been made between an intelligent subject—a chess player, for example—and a computer. The terms of the analogy in its initial version were, as we saw in our discussion of the Turing test, on the one hand, the machine with its cognitive abilities (as, say, a chess player) and, on the other, us with our mental abilities. Now the terms of the analogy have become: on the one hand, the machine and its transformations of symbols and, on the other, our mind and its intellectual operations upon representations. What has happened to the chess player? In the new version of the computer analogy, everything suggests that the chess player is *his mind*. What can this possibly mean? The response is likely to be that the proposed theory is a materialist one and that by "mind" it means a quite concrete reality, namely the brain. But how can a brain play chess when the chessboard is in the person's *external environment* while, for its part, the brain's external environment is the organism's *internal environment*?

Our question is then this: How can the brain's symbols be used in the game the person is playing? In what way do the processes that take place in the player's brain constitute the player's reasoning? These questions might be considered obscure. Indeed, they are obscure, but that is because they reflect the obscurity that has come to envelop the entire theory according to which the mind is like a computer. We cannot hope to do better than to ask that the theory be clarified.

One might attempt to get out of the difficulty in the following way: Yes, the brain manipulates symbols that are the person's symbols, but this does not create any difficulties, because the brain is precisely the *organ* of the person's thoughts. The situation is much the same as that of Alexandre Dumas's telegraph employee, who manipulates signals sent from the prefect to the minister. The employee's physical work allows the minister to remain informed. Similarly, there is a part of the person that carries out the physical work by which the person is put into this or that cognitive state. Yet this comparison solves nothing. If things were as it describes, we would have to conclude that the brain's work is solely physical and that the intellectual work is carried out elsewhere, in much the same way that, in Dumas's novel, the intellectual work is done in the prefecture and the ministry. The doctrine that we are here seeking to understand maintains that thoughts and lines of reasoning are cerebral events, that what we call intellectual work is nothing more than a redescription of physical work.

What is the source of the difficulty here? It is that, in the course of considering the comparison, we have lost the bearings initially provided when we were asked to derive a psychology from the model of the computer. The cognitivist explanation requires us to say that what plays chess is the player's mind. Does this mean that we must attribute the player's behavior to a part of his person? Or does it mean that the mind (the brain) is not merely a part of the player, but its center, that it is the player himself minus a few accessories, like eyes and arms?

The analogy by which the computer is taken as a model for the study of our cognitive abilities turns out to be more and more disconcerting. Our initial understanding was that we were comparing a *person* calculating to a *machine* able to carry out this same calculation, or comparing a chess match against a human opponent with one against an automaton. The Turing test is the outgrowth of this understanding of the comparison. But it happens that, for cognitivism, the comparison is no longer between man and machine, for this would render the analogy a mere simulation. Instead, we are asked to compare the mind (the brain) with a computer. But in this case, the terms of the analogy have changed in the course of the argument, with all the risk of equivocation that that implies. In general, the mind consists in the *person's abilities*. For example, most of us have memories of vacations at the beach, and it is certainly a mental ability to be able to remember having gone swimming in the ocean. The cognitivist version of the analogy takes place between the computer and the brain. But which of the brain's abilities are at issue here? It would seem more than a little difficult to ask a brain to remember having been at the beach and having gone swimming. Does the analogy maintain that the computer has the same psychology as does a person or, rather, does it maintain that it has the same psychology as a brain? If the latter—i.e., if the computer provides a *psychological* model of the brain—it will have to be explained what the psychology of a brain is.

Perhaps the computer provides a useful model of the physiological functioning of the brain. This is for neurology to determine.[26] Perhaps the computer provides a useful model of a person's intellectual activity. Clearly one will have to choose between the two: the computer cannot provide, simultaneously and in the same way, a psychological model of the person and a physical model of the person's brain. Here it might be objected that precisely what the analogy does not require is that we make the "dualistic" distinction between the psychology and the physical. This objection really misses the point, for the entire difficulty in understanding the cognitivist analogy stems from the fact that it saddles us with an unintelligible dualism of the thinking brain and the person.

There is one response that cannot be accepted for any of these questions: that of a philosopher who would claim that, for his part, he can see no difference between the mental abilities of Mr. Dupont and those of Mr. Dupont's brain. It is nevertheless not unusual to come across theorists who seem oblivious to this distinction between part and whole. It is incumbent upon me then to convince them that this is not an optional or speculative distinction, but rather a simple condition on the meaningful use of the vocabulary of abilities. I will show that the conceptual slippage that moves from the person to the mind, and from the mind to the brain, reveals once again a lack of attention to the conditions upon the meaningful attribution of the status of *whole* and *part* to the realities we seek to describe or analyze.

8.6. Philosophy of the Suppositum of Operations

Contrary to what is often said, reflection upon the *conditions of meaning* of the attribution of an action to an agent are not part of a "linguistic philosophy," if by this one means the invocation of ordinary language or the study of what is and is not said in a given language. Ordinary use has no bearing upon philosophical discussion, which generally considers questions that people do not ordinarily ask, at least not in the terms in which philosophers ask them. What is at issue here, as we shall see, is the metaphysics of wholes and parts: Can the verb describing an operation be transferred from the whole to one of its parts? In other words, what are the conditions of meaning of the attribution of an action?

These conditions can be brought together under a principle that might be called "the principle of narrative intelligibility." From the perspective of a poetics of narrative composition, every comprehensible episode of a story determines, precisely in virtue of the tale told, different possible chains of events, in the direction of both the past and the future. First, the episode brings forward a determinate past. If the hero remembers having gone swimming in the ocean, he must have gone swimming in the ocean, or it must at least be conceivable that he has. Next, the episode recounted partially determines the way the story can subsequently develop. By recounting the hero's actions, we open a horizon of suspense in which not just anything can follow. And this can only be the case if the verbs that we use to describe the actors' intentional activities (including their purely intellectual activities) are meaningful not in themselves but within the conceptual systems that they comprise.[27] The principle is that psychological attribution imposes a historical context: a particular past must have taken place, a particular future must be conceivable, barring which, the present attribution is quite simply inconceivable. If, for example, the hero of the story is remembering something, he must be remembering things that have happened to him. This is why it is impossible to move from "I remember having gone swimming in the ocean" to "my brain remembers having gone swimming in the ocean." Nor is it possible to move from "I intend to go swimming in the ocean" to "my brain intends to go swimming in the ocean." But can it not be claimed that my brain remembers swims that I have taken or that it plans my vacations for me? Even in this case, we would have to be able to endow this memorialist or planner with the past and the future of a memorialist or a planner. Here again, certain conditions of intelligibility must be respected. Where, though, do all these conditions come from?

In order to answer this, we will do well to consider a passage from the *Theodicy* in which Leibniz attempts—unsuccessfully—to reconcile the dualism of the soul and the body with the fact of the unity of personal behavior. In the course of his discussion of the notion of free will, Leibniz seeks to explain the difficulty confronted by all Cartesian philosophers. Contrary to what Descartes assumed, there can be no physical communication between the soul and the body.[28] Having failed to define clearly the laws governing the communication of movement from one body to another, Descartes thought that the soul could intervene by changing the *direction* of a body's movement without having to make use of a (physical) force. But he was wrong about this: energy must be expended to change the direction of a movement, just as it must to accelerate or decelerate the movement of a body. The influence of the soul on the body, as Descartes imagines it, is really physical. It thereby entails a violation of natural laws, unless one supposes that the soul is material. This is evident, Leibniz claims, in the analogy that is often put forward according to which the soul is to the body as the horseman is to his steed. The horseman does not produce the horse's movement, but he does direct it. True, but that is done "by means of the bridle, the bit, the spurs and other material aids."[29] If we deprive the soul of all of its physical instruments, we also deprive it of any power over the material course of things. This objection is often what motivates theorists in their view that the soul posited by Descartes must in some way be a "material soul," for otherwise it would lack the equipment required for the mental causation of bodily movement.

The failure of the solution Descartes derived from a speculative physiology has led some to propose supernatural solutions that refer to the Author of all things. Leibniz quickly dispenses with Malebranche's occasionalist solution (§ 61) in order to propose his own: There is in reality *no* action of the body upon the soul, nor is there action of the soul upon the body. What does that mean? The body does not act on the soul any more than the soul does on the body. But the soul and body are constructed in such a way that the soul on its own represents what happens to the body at the very moment that it happens, whereas the body "must do of itself that which the soul ordains."[30] The communication between these two parts of the person is thus a matter of synchronization between two sequences of states.

The preestablished harmony that is applied to the problem of the apparent interaction of the soul and the body is illustrated by the analogy of a master and his servant:[31]

> [I]t is just as if he who knows all that I shall order a servant to do the whole day long on the morrow made an automaton entirely resembling this servant, to carry out to-morrow at the right moment all that I should order.[32]

If my body is set into motion at the very moment that the soul wants me to go for a walk, then the body is like a valet who is so well disciplined that he automatically carries out my instructions at the moment of their conception. What is remarkable is that the master (who speaks in the first person above) must first have transformed himself into a sort of "spiritual automaton," but, says Leibniz, without prejudice to his freedom.[33] The system of preestablished harmony generalizes the situation of this example. Because God knows in advance the orders that the master will give, He has adjusted the master's body (the automaton that serves him) in advance so that the orders will be carried out "at the right moment."[34] It follows that the master discovers that he has an order to give to his valet thanks to an automatism every bit as regular as that which leads the valet to conclude that he has an order to carry out.

The difference between the Cartesian and Leibnizian solutions is therefore as follows: the horseman's action upon the horse is a physical one, but the relationship between the order the master gives and the order carried out by the valet is not physical, since the order given is a mental event on the master's side (i.e., he wants something) while the order carried out is a physical event on the valet's side (i.e., he provides something). In this way, the "phenomena" can be "saved." Leibniz writes that, by means of this "metaphysical communication," the combination of the soul and the body make up a single and whole person:

> [M]any moderns have acknowledged that there is no *physical communication* between soul and body, despite the *metaphysical communication* always subsisting, which causes soul and body to compose one and the same *suppositum*, or what is called a person.[35]

But this position seems tenuous at best, which is why the "mind-body problem," which all good Cartesians have had to take up, seems less a problem in need of an ingenious solution than a symptom of a certain conceptual confusion. An adage that Leibniz sometimes pertinently cites says that what we call a "person" is a "rational suppositum," because a person is a subject of action able to subordinate his actions to the principles of rationality.[36] "Suppositum" means: *subject of attribution of an action or a passion*. Leibniz's chosen example—the relation between master and servant—which is meant to illustrate his notion of metaphysical communication, shows that the person, i.e., a composite made up of a soul and a body, is in fact a *twosome* made up of two supposita, one for mental actions and passions, the other for physical ones. There appears to be only one subject of action, one to which both physical and psychological descriptions are applied. In fact, though, if dualism is to be taken seriously, the whole human is in fact made up of two parts that must both be held to be subjects of action (or supposita).

A word of explanation is needed here regarding the content of the principle by which action is attributed to an entire concrete subject, or suppositum.[37] Where does this principle come from and why must it be acknowledged? The principle asks us to distinguish two uses of action verbs. In their figural use, these verbs can have as their grammatical subjects signs that designate something other than supposita or concrete individuals. But this is just a way of speaking, without ontological implications.

> Acts are done by whole and complete substances [*actiones autem sunt suppositorum et totorum*], not, properly speaking, by parts and forms and powers; except by analogy we do not speak of a hand striking or of heat making hot, but of a man striking with his hand or of fire making hot through its heat.[38]

Although Thomas Aquinas, in this text, draws a consistent distinction between what is commonly said (*proprie loquendo*) and what is not, his aim is not to offer a linguistic observation on the correct use of Latin words. The explanation he provides is not a linguistic one tied to a given language, but is rather part of the philosophical grammar of the concept of action, i.e., of the conditions of meaning of an action verb in any language, whether real or possible. Only in a figural way can a part or a faculty be represented as acting. The proof is precisely the price that one pays for treating such a part as the suppositum of the action of the whole: as soon as I claim that my hand strikes a blow, I have stripped that hand of its status as an organ and turned it into an independent entity able to move on its own. The same is true of a faculty: to speak of it as an entity with its own behavior is to make of it a concrete subject.[39] The first case, in which the action is attributed to an organ rather than to the entire animal, results from a misapprehension of the *integration* of part and whole, an integration that is upheld, however, by the ordinary use of the instrumental complement ("to strike a blow with one's hand"). In the second case, the status of a power or faculty or form has been misunderstood: through an unfortunate reification, we treat as a new subject of action something that was meant to indicate the abilities of a first subject of action. This is perhaps the same confusion targeted by jokes about the dormitive virtues of opium: the action is attributed to the agent's power to act.

The terminology (of scholastic origin) that has just been introduced allows us to make clear something that still seems bizarre in the moral model proposed by Leibniz. We can accept that a perfectly trained servant of a master with well-established routines might be able to satisfy the latter's needs immediately. At the very moment when the master thinks that a cup of tea might be nice, the valet arrives with a cup of tea. The scene is like one between an English gentleman and his butler that might appear in a novel by Jules Verne. The moral model of communication without causal mediation is thus an intelligible one, but only if we do not forget that two people are involved.[40] Each of them is equally a suppositum: the function of the servant is to do what the master would have to do himself were he not being served. In our example, the master has had the servant serve as his *replacement* in the task of preparing tea.

A servant is not one of his master's organs. He is an auxiliary. The same is true of Leibniz's automaton. What I mean is that the valet in our example must have the same metaphysical status as his master, since his entire duty is to replace that master. The status of an organ is entirely different. An organ must be conceived as a part of the suppositum (i.e., of the subject of attribution of the activity in question), as a component whose activity is physically (rather than "metaphysically") controlled. We would not say that by entrusting my hands with the task of preparing tea (rather than attempting to carry out the task using different organs), I charge them with the task of which I discharge myself. Everything is still done by me. My hands are active, but they are not the suppositum of the action.

This is precisely the difficulty for every mental philosophy: How can the attributions of a personal subject be transferred to a part of that subject? The very notion of a suppositum is meant to prevent this transferal, in virtue of the distinction between the organism (the whole) and the organ or instrument (the part). Consider the following situations:

I am writing a letter.
I am having my secretary write a letter.
I am writing a letter by hand.
My hand is writing a letter.
My brain is having my hand write a letter.
My brain is writing a letter.

By virtue of the principle of the intelligibility of narrative sequences spoken of earlier, the last three statements must be seen as increasingly obscure stylistic figures. When I charge my secretary with replying on my behalf, I am asking him to write *my* letter to *my* correspondent. My secretary puts his talent and his pen to work for me: he replaces me. When my hand writes a letter, the question does not arise whether it is writing my letter to my correspondent or to its own correspondent. This is just an innocuous figure of speech. It could of course be said that my hand is writing a letter dictated by someone else. But in that case, I am the one playing the role of secretary. Are we ready to claim that my hand can write by itself through "automatic writing"? The Surrealist experiments in this area proved at least one thing: that the very idea of automatic writing is ambiguous, since it really applies to ingenious literary exercises but is often held to suggest that the phenomenon is one of "channeling," as if the attempt to interrupt the intentionality of the process of writing must also provide an opportunity for some obscure power to express itself in the writer's place. At which point, if my hand starts writing a letter that I have nothing to do with, it must be controlled by some other power and it will be as if my hand has ceased, for as long as the exercise continues, to be my own.

When we turn to the brain, the application of the verbs "to write" and "to have someone write" becomes unintelligible. Do we mean to say that I charge my brain with composing and formulating a letter in my stead (i.e., that my brain is a suppositum serving as my auxiliary)? What, then, is the difference between this and the role played by my brain in cases where *I am not* replaced in my writing activity?

It is true that there are cases worth considering that are intermediary between auxiliaries, like my valet, and the organs of my personal activities, like my hand. For example, my stomach is an organ, but one whose activity I do not control: it takes it upon itself to digest without asking for either my permission or my instructions. Of course it cannot be said that it digests in my stead. Should the brain perhaps be thought of as an organ from whose activity I benefit rather than as a natural instrument? Just as the stomach takes care of the digestion of the food I eat, perhaps the brain takes care of "cognition," i.e., all of the internal processes necessary to my intellectual activities. If this is granted, how is the work carried out by my brain to be expressed? When I digest, my stomach is really doing the digesting: I merely benefit from its labor. Is the situation the same in the case of the brain? Does it do the calculating when I calculate? But if there is an error in my calculations, the error will be attributed to me and I will be the one reminded of the rules for the calculation in question. It follows that the brain can only be the subject of attribution of my mental activities through a figure of speech substituting part for whole.

These remarks on the difficulties of classical dualism have brought out a lesson regarding the analogy between people and computers (between natural and artificial intelligence). Is the metaphysical status of the computer that of a suppositum of intellectual attributes (i.e., of mental capacities)? If the computer is an auxiliary that can be assigned "cognitive" tasks—an automatic secretary rather than an automatic valet—then it is certainly an intelligent being. Or, if you like, it is an intelligent being exactly to the extent that it can replace me. It happens that we do charge computers with carrying out work that is often tiresome for us. But we must not overlook the following: the secretary who writes my letters for me is able to do so because he is also able to write letters to his own correspondents. If he were unable to do so, he could not offer me his services in this regard. Similarly, the valet is able to prepare the tea in his master's place because he is also able to prepare tea for his own consumption. This is why the question concerning the machine's status reduces to this: To what extent are the problems that it solves problems it has made its own, and to what extent are the "internal symbols" that it manipulates its own symbols?

The answer is that the machine manipulates formulas, but our interpretation gives them the status of symbols: not the symbols of a machine language, but symbols in a system that is our own. Those who insist that intellectual activity is symbolic activity are right: to think, for a subject, is to use symbols. But whose symbols? Symbols in someone else's language or symbols in a language effectively used by the subject? The fact is that I am able to think using a system of symbols set up by others, and that this is what most of us do most of the time, but only if we have *adopted* this system and made it our own. In other words, the typing monkeys in Emile Borel's famous myth about chance may well accidentally type out the text of the *Aeneid*: *Arma virumque cano* . . . They are nevertheless not using characters to write a text, nor are they using Latin words to recite a poem. The symbols that they are manipulating in the course of playing with the typewriter keyboard are not their symbols, which is a way of saying that there is nothing symbolic or intellectual in their activity. The same would be true even if the apparatus formed by the monkeys and the typewriters were governed by a mechanical constraint so that each of the monkeys' actions on the keyboard produced the text of the *Aeneid*.

To put this another way: what prevents a thinking machine from being the auxiliary of my thoughts—and thereby a thinking subject in its own right—is the *instituting ability* by which someone can treat different things as symbols, making possible the communication of a thought about other things. In order for the manipulation of symbols to be a symbolic activity, it must participate in the institution by which these symbols *are* symbols.

CHAPTER 9

Cerebroscopic Exercises

I was not yet used to giving myself a rigorous account of the
phenomena of my mind, by means of the methods recommended
by philosophy.

—LAUTRÉAMONT, *Les Chants de Maldoror*, Song II

INTENTIONALITY, the mentalist philosopher tells us, is a property of some
of a person's states. One therefore ought to be able to do the same thing
for a person that one does for exterior and public cognitive entities like
posters and signs: one ought to be able to describe both the physical state
of the support and what it represents. The same should be true for states
of mind. From a physical point of view, states of mind are states of the
brain. But, from an intentional point of view, they are representative states.

Let us assume that believing is really an internal state of mind. According to this hypothesis, it ought to be possible to know whether or not
someone believes something through an examination of his person similar
to what one does when assessing his state of health. Yet the claim goes even
further: the application of different tests is held to mark an incontestable
advance over the method we actually use, which is to look at our interlocutor's expressions of his state of mind, or, if he is not present or able to
respond, to consult his past declarations, or, finally, if he has not made any
such declarations, to see whether his deeds and actions speak in his stead.
The methods we use are those of a biographer and consist in bringing
together all of the available documentation. Needless to say, these documents are to be found in the surroundings of the person being studied,
among his effects, among those of his friends and associates, indeed everywhere that he may have been active. By contrast, when the examination
bears on a person's state, it must limit itself to that person rather than his
relatives, neighbors, and so on. In other words, the state in question here
is an internal state, which means that its properties are in no way dependent on the states of other people or other things in the vicinity. In order
to know whether your stomach is functioning properly, the doctor must
examine your stomach and not your wife's stomach or your congressman's.

If we add that the state of believing is a physical one, a state of the organism, it follows that the examination could be, in principle, a physical one. In other words, as Fodor rightly points out, the omniscient god of the cognitivists is a "physicalist" one who knows what is in our heads because he knows the details of our brains right down to the molecular level.[1] On this point at least, the would-be psychological scientist's position comes to resemble that of the hermeneutic theorist: the necessity of interpretation is a result of human finitude.

The theory of "brain sentences" maintains that mental representations are firmly situated in the mind and that they are therefore in the brain. They are in the brain in the form of brain sentences, meaning that they have been inscribed in the brain by means of a (hypothetical) code called "the language of thought." To have a particular belief is to have the sentence that expresses that belief appropriately transcribed in brain language and put into a place where its presence provides the organism with the belief in question.

How can the presence of a sign in the brain have effects that its presence in a book within arm's reach could not? What is the significance of this cerebral interiority?

Here is a simple explanation offered by Fodor. Let us assume that to have an intention is to have the intention to make a certain proposition true. This way of speaking allows us to redescribe intention as a relation between the subject and a certain proposition expressed by the sentence "p." What then happens in the subject's head is the following: he takes into his head a symbol "p" meaning that p, a symbol that says in "mentalese," for example, that the window is open, and he moves this symbol into an intention box within his head. This intention box is a system for processing the symbols inserted into it so as to change them into instructions with a motor force. The end result is that the subject behaves in such a way that p becomes true. He rises and opens the window.

> So, for example, suppose I intend to raise my left hand (I intend to make true the proposition that I raise my left hand). Then what I do is, I put in my intention box a token of a mental symbol that means "I raise my left hand." And then, after suitable churning and gurgling and computing and causing, my left hand goes up.[2]

A philosopher of consciousness might say that this model is too crude. But this misses the point of the comparison. Fodor has happily and deliberately stressed the resemblance between his "intention box" and an everyday vending machine. In fact, the model's simplicity is one of its virtues and would work in its favor if only we could understand *what* the model is supposed to model. We can understand that the model of modular boxes in the mind is meant to represent the different possible positions of a symbol within a system, and that each of these positions is to account for a relation between a subject and a sentence. The only unclear part of this model is when the person is required to place sentences in one or another of the boxes: in the real theory of cerebral entities, this task must be carried out by the "modules" themselves and not by a homunculus.

But none of this justifies considering intention as a relation of a subject to a sentence. Rather, the entire model presupposes the notion of an intentional state.

The classical expression of the idea that our head is full of cognitive entities without which we would have no mental life can be found in Fodor's "hypothesis" of a language of thought, a code used by the brain to inscribe our representations.

The peculiarity of the theory of "brain sentences" is brought out well in Daniel Dennett's amusing speculations regarding "brain writing."[3] As a complement to historical epigraphy, which studies the inscriptions on ancient monuments, one might well imagine a psychological epigraphy, which would study what is inscribed in subjects' heads.

The goal of such speculation is not, of course, to come up with a patented procedure for mind reading. It is to find out whether the expressions "mental discourse," "cerebral discourse," and "cerebral code" are comprehensible. In this case, we are examining the notion of a "mental discourse" endowed with a material reality. The novelty of this theory is not in having postulated a "mental discourse" or even a "mental language." The distinction among three kinds of discourse (written, oral, mental) appears very early on among Aristotle's commentators.[4] The novelty lies in the speculation regarding the inscription of mental discourse in the subject's cerebral matter. For every one of a person's thoughts, there would have to be a sentence written in "mentalese" in his central nervous system. If, then, the brain contains text, it might be possible for a researcher to decipher this text, in much the same way that archeologists were able to discover the code in which the Linear B tablets were written. Consideration of this fantasy will allow us to bring out precisely what is so disconcerting about the notions of mental states and internal symbols.

Dennett begins by telling us his reaction to this sort of speculation:

> What are we to make of the popular notion that our brains are somehow libraries of our thoughts and beliefs? Is it *in principle* possible that brain scientists might one day know enough about the workings of our brains to be able to "crack the cerebral code" and read our minds?[5]

As Dennett indicates, the question is not whether such a thing will one day be possible (given the progress of neuroscience), but whether we even understand what such a thing might mean. Is such a thing possible in principle? In other words: Can we even understand the claim that might one day be made by a neurologist, that the secret code used by the brain to register our thoughts has been discovered?

Dennett seeks to stake out a moderate position between those who are too quick to accept the possibility of this principle and those who claim not to understand what such a principle might mean. As a representative of the latter group, those who feel the hypothesis masks a nonsensical idea that the philosopher must bring to light, Dennett rightly chooses Elizabeth Anscombe. Although Anscombe never explicitly rejected this sort of speculation in the book to which Dennett refers, she does implicitly reject the idea of thoughts being physically identified.[6] For Anscombe, the only way of determining the thoughts and desires of someone on a particular occasion is to draw up his biography. Even if we had an incomparably more detailed neuronal description of the person than today's science can provide, we would still know nothing more about this person's intentions and desires. If I told you that Mr. Martin is in the mental state made up of brain state XYZ, you still would not know what Mr. Martin is thinking.[7] But if I told you his life's story, you might begin to have an idea of his mindset.

For Anscombe, psychological explanation is thus historical, not neuronal or, more generally, mechanical.

Like a lawyer in one of Courteline's comedies, Dennett takes up both sides of the argument in turn. The reader comes to understand that Dennett sees the absurdity of the hypothesis of a cerebral language but that he seeks to formulate his critique of this philosophical fiction in such a way as to spare the idea out of which it springs, the notion of an "internal representation" in the literal sense of representations that exist in our heads. Here are the two fictions put forth by Dennett. The first is meant to illustrate our reaction when we refuse to credit this hypothesis; the second is meant to illustrate our reaction when we find it tempting and illuminating, i.e., intelligible at the very least.

FIRST FICTION

Let us imagine that Jack Ruby was put on trial and that he pleaded not guilty. The entire world saw him shoot Oswald (since the crime took place in front of television cameras), but he nevertheless maintains that he believed his gun was not loaded. Who is the jury going to believe: the witnesses for the prosecution who testify as to Ruby's character based on his biography and the company he keeps, or the expert in *neurocryptography* who, thanks to his mind-reading machine, the *cerebroscope*, claims to have read in Ruby's brain that, indeed, Ruby believed that the gun was not loaded? Nobody, according to Dennett, would reject the clear findings of a historical inquiry into someone simply on the basis of an analysis of his cerebroscopic dossier.

Yet Dennett does not maintain, as Anscombe would, that *we would not understand* what the expert is supposed to have done when he claims to have read the accused's brain. Dennett is careful to claim only that *we would not believe him*. We would not accept his expertise because we would be unwilling to treat as equally valid the whole of the biographical information at our disposal (when this whole points clearly to a certain answer) and the isolated declaration of an observer who claims to have "read" such an improbable belief. In other words, the reasons for Dennett's skepticism are entirely epistemological and relate to the way in which we adapt our new observations to our view of things in general. Normally, a single isolated observation is not sufficient to undermine a coherent theory, since its very singularity precludes it from offering a different coherent theory and thereby providing serious competition for our initial conclusions. The situation here is very much like that faced by a newspaper editor: he rejects out of hand certain rumors, news, dispatches and the like as mystifications and groundless assertions, and he does so simply because they are improbable.

In this case, Dennett's response to the expert's claims is not that he has no idea what the expert is talking about (i.e., that a belief is not something that devices can detect). His response is that even if the expert did read Ruby's brain, he must have misread or misinterpreted what he read: every possible translation of a cerebral sentence in Jack Ruby's head will have to ascribe to him the belief that the gun was loaded. Quine's philosophy of radical translation, to which Dennett here appeals, can be illustrated by a comparison. A professor of ancient Greek correcting a student's translation has no need to consult the original text to know that the proposed translation is inaccurate if it makes assertions that an ancient author could not possibly make. If a student has translated a sentence in the original as "Socrates took a taxi to Piraeus," he has made a mistake. As a result, what is ruled out is not that it might be possible to read someone's brain, but that the messages read might utterly overturn our ordinary psychological explanations, which are historical in nature.

As a result, Dennett does not even mention, let alone respond to, a more radical philosophical response to the "cerebroscopic hypothesis." This radical response maintains that the so-called expert's view is simply irrelevant and can be disqualified regardless of what he claims to have read. Even if his interpretation were to confirm the conclusions reached by investigators working with historical documents, his testimony would be of no value whatsoever. All of the "readings" he claims to have done are nothing more than mystifications. More generally, according to this view, a belief is not the sort of thing that can present itself to us in the form of a brain state. All speculation about the "cerebral code" is the result of a conceptual mistake. Though Dennett wants no part of this radical critique, the appeal in favor of cerebral codes put forward in the following part of his text may well be, despite what Dennett thinks, a vivid demonstration of the incoherence of the entire analogy between ordinary texts (written in a language that is really used) and cerebral ones (written in some innate language).

Is it only a lack of imagination or theoretical audacity that leads one to put forward the radical response? But science fiction, of course, need not present authentic conceptual inventions in order to entertain and amuse us. In fact, if the cerebroscopic expert had been presented as a kind of haruspex, able to interpret the signs of defendants' guilt not by applying various procedures to entrails, as the ancients did, but based on an examination of the brain, we would surely have no confidence in his claims, but we would at least be able to understand them. Among them is the claim that he possesses a superior method of investigation. Even if the expert himself cannot provide us with reasons why his method works, we can at least envisage that there might be a correlation between two apparently disparate phenomena (in the same way that we need not believe in the sorcerer's magic wand in order to understand his claims about its powers). In the case of cerebroscopy, we do not understand what the expert is supposed to be able to do. Indeed, we should take heed of the fact that the hypothesis requires that the sentence to be read be of a very special kind. If, to our great surprise, we were to find upon opening the defendant's head not a brain, but the text of a written confession properly formulated in English, we would not say that we had read in the accused's head that he had admitted his crime. The fact that the confession was found in the defendant's head rather than in his pocket is of no significance: the only question would be to determine whether the confession was *his*. The sentence that the expert is supposed to be able to read is one that no one else can read, not even the defendant himself (whose only way of "reading" the sentences written in his brain is to *believe* what they say).

SECOND FICTION

Taking up a different role, Dennett takes it upon himself to argue in favor of the hypothesis of "brain writing" by inventing a case where it no longer seems so absurd to talk about the neurological detection of someone's intentions. Let us now suppose that an art critic named Sam, whose judgment has hitherto been recognized as both refined and reliable, begins to sing the praises of some mediocre paintings. These paintings happen to be the work of his son. There are two possible hypotheses:

    a) in fact, this critic believes the paintings to be of poor quality but wants to help his son, who is trying to establish himself as an artist;

    b) the critic believes that the paintings are good because his paternal love blinds him and prevents him from seeing their poor quality.

We seek to choose between these hypotheses through an examination of the critic's biography. Let us now suppose that the biography is inconclusive and Sam's past is equally compatible with the hypotheses that he is lying or that he is blinded by his love. By definition we cannot count on a confession from the critic in which he would confirm for us hypothesis (a): critical lucidity accompanied by familial loyalty. The example is constructed so that Sam's psychology is "underdetermined" by the facts of his biography. For his part, the historian is condemned to study the documents if he wants to fill this gap in our knowledge. Otherwise, he will have to admit that there are indeterminate mental states.

The question is then whether to endorse the view that what the art critic really thinks of his son's paintings is indeterminate or, on the contrary, to maintain that he really holds one of the following two opinions: (a) "my son's paintings are second-rate"; (b) "my son's paintings are excellent."

Let us consider the case in which the art critic does have a definite opinion. If we have trouble deciding whether to ascribe opinion (a) or opinion (b) to him, this cannot be because he has somehow managed to be in neither of these states but simply because we do not know what is going on in his mind. We do not know this because none of the things we do know about Sam (about his deeds and actions or about his behavior as it might be reconstructed by a historian) rules out his having mental state (a), but nothing rules out his having mental state (b) either. Is it forbidden, in this case, to imagine that the facts our historical investigation would need in order to decide the question might become available if we only had additional means of investigation? It is, of course, not forbidden and, up to this point there is nothing problematic. We might, for example, come up with some new witnesses or the correspondence between Sam and his son. But our example is constructed on the hypothesis of our historical ignorance: the investigators charged with coming up with intentional explanations cannot reach a conclusion. The question is whether additional facts might in some way be "added to the file" by a neurocryptographer.

Using an approach similar to that of Champollion decrypting the Rosetta Stone, the neurocryptographer, thanks to his cerebroscope, is able to decipher the system that Sam uses to store his beliefs. Finally, we can read the contents of Sam's mind. According to the advocate of a language of thought and brain writing, this idea is not inconceivable.

Are the claims of the expert in brain epigraphy in principle absurd, or are they only absurd for technical reasons? Dennett himself does not defend the "mentalese" hypothesis of a natural language of thought, nor does he uphold that of a brain inscription by which thoughts would come to be written in our neurons. He does raise several objections. Yet his objections are those of an engineer who tells us that the proposed machine cannot work as it has been vaguely described. For example, he raises the question of volume: How much space is needed in the cerebral "library" to store all of someone's beliefs, not only those that he actively holds but also those he in fact has without ever thinking about them? In the end, Dennett expresses his reservations about various points, but he above all avoids saying that cerebroscopy is an *absurdity*. Nevertheless, his discussion is extraordinarily instructive, since it makes clear the presuppositions of all speculation regarding the presence of cognitive entities in people's heads.

What are we looking for in the brain? Is it the cerebral counterpart of a declaration that Sam might have made to himself in the depths of his conscience but that he would have kept to himself to his dying day: "I do not like my son's paintings"? In that case, our goal would be to uncover his secret, and we naively believe ourselves able to do so in virtue of a psycho-physical parallelism: if there is a mental act on Sam's part, it must have a cerebral counterpart, or rather, there is a cerebral version of this act. This might be called the theory of the cerebral carbon copy: every activity, every incident, every variation in one's mental life leaves a trace, since there are always two sheets of paper to be considered, the original upon which thoughts are expressed in a semantic or intentional mode, and the cerebral duplicate upon which the same thoughts are inscribed but in a physical mode. For the materialist philosopher of mind, the two sheets are merely two descriptions of a single sheet. In the end, peering out from behind the science-fiction story is the method used by intelligence services in cases like the Dreyfus affair: rummaging in wastebaskets so as to find the carbons of otherwise secret thoughts. But this very analogy reveals why the idea of cerebroscopic detection is a poor model rather than a bold hypothesis. The carbons that secret agents find in wastebaskets may well have been put there in order to sidetrack them. They are not entirely trustworthy. Why, then, should we trust brain inscriptions? Let us suppose that, rather than doubting that he knows what he is talking about, we take the cerebroscopic expert at his word when he tells us that he *has read* one or the other of the two sentences in Sam the critic's brain: (a) "my son's paintings are second-rate"; (b) "my son's paintings are excellent." Under this hypothesis, we do not doubt him for an instant: he saw this cerebral sentence and it is inscribed in Sam's head. Yet we have still not made any progress, because we have not yet answered the question we would have to ask if we were reading one of the sentences not in Sam's brain, but in the diary he keeps in the leftmost drawer of his bureau. A literary critic writing the biography of a writer takes note of what he reads in the author's private papers, personal notes, journals, etcetera, but that does not mean that he takes all of it at face value. And this is precisely Dennett's conclusion: whatever the neurocryptographer might have read in Sam's brain, he is still not able to probe his heart of hearts. We still do not know what Sam really thinks of his son's paintings but only what he says about them, whether in public, in his diary, or in his conscience. Here Dennett, who is no doubt mindful of Ryle's teachings, introduces a new distinction between beliefs, which are mental states, and *judgments*, which are episodes.

But the "mental states" that interested us were meant to be "belief states": judgments, which are acts that one might well imagine leave traces of one kind or another, were precisely not what was at issue. Dennett observes that a neurocryptographic system for detecting judgments would tell us nothing about beliefs. It is conceivable that someone could pronounce a judgment in his heart of hearts that would in no way be an expression of his beliefs. This leads Dennett back to a *historical* conception of explanation through beliefs and intentions whose attribution must allow us to explain and also to predict to a certain extent. If the attribution of (a) and the attribution of (b) to Sam are equivalent, then nothing is clearly written in his brain on this matter.

The distinction between judgments and beliefs leads Dennett to reject the idea that a person's beliefs take the form of *sentences*. Yet he nevertheless continues to maintain that they are states that may be forms of transcription or attestation. In fact, his example shows the superiority of an authentically dispositional analysis: a critic's belief about a painting is not a *state* of this critic (meaning, not an internal state), one that is intrinsic to him and that does not depend on his past or future. His belief is more a style of response, a general orientation, a line of conduct and therefore a reaction of a conditional sort. In Dennett's example, there is a conflict between two moralities: that of the critic, which requires an (impartial) professional judgment, and that of the father, which requires a more indulgent judgment. The critic does not have a belief but rather two systems of reference with which to formulate an opinion on the painting, systems that are here in conflict.

Two things a brain certainly cannot do is appreciate the responsibilities of a father (for the brain is not the artist's father) nor those of an art critic (for the critic's brain is not itself a critic and signs neither expert appraisals nor reviews in the press). As for a biographer, he cannot hope to do more than see whether one of the two systems clearly wins out over the other.

Dennett concludes that beliefs (if we distinguish them from expressed beliefs, i.e., judgments) quite simply do not exist: "are we sure there is a difference between his really and truly believing his son is a good artist, and his deceiving himself out of love while knowing the truth in his heart of hearts?"[8] This conclusion would be incontestable had it been more specific about the places where such beliefs are to be sought and about the period of time that they have in which to manifest themselves. Beliefs do not exist if we seek them as one might look for mushrooms in the woods of Fontainebleau: no matter how hard we look, all we find are judgments. Nor do they exist if we insist that they present themselves as real entities might, entities which are either present or not at the moment of inspection. And this is why the very idea of seeking out Sam's beliefs not only does not arise, but is devoid of sense, anywhere but in the context of a biography of Sam. Whatever we may find in Sam's head, it is not a belief. A belief must have a belief's consequences. For example, to say that Sam believes his son's paintings are good *because* he is blinded by paternal pride is to say that he would judge them normally—i.e., harshly—if he were to learn subsequently that the paintings he had taken to have been done by his son were in reality the work of a talentless con-man who had made off with the remarkable paintings that the young painter had sent to his father. In a general way, to attribute beliefs to someone is to sketch out certain scenarios and to rule out other such scenarios. In no case is it the practice of a form of inspection of something actually given.

Dennett's philosophical fiction is interesting in that it draws our attention to one of the strategies of mentalist philosophy: it has to get us to include within our metaphysics the concept of an internal state of mind, so as to make the notion of a "psychological law" plausible. The consequence of this is immediately obvious. If to believe something or to desire something were to be in a particular state, it would be legitimate to imagine procedures for inspecting the content of someone's head. Even better, the same would be true of the subject of these beliefs and desires himself. In order to know what I believe, I would have to *have access*, as cognitivists say, to my belief states. But in that case, a strange reversal has taken place where the subject who is asked to declare what he believes about a matter is obliged to form an opinion, not about the question asked, but about his own state. He will have to examine himself in order to see whether he finds the belief in question within himself. The theory may well seem strange, but it is not so strange as to be without its defenders.

There follows from this a reshuffling that clearly reveals the confusion behind all such speculation. When I want to know whether somebody believes a certain story, I do not in the main ask myself whether the story itself is believable, whether there are reasons to believe it. I ask myself whether it is believable for the person in question, given what I know about his ideas and dispositions. In other words, I ask myself if it is plausible that this person, with his "psychology," should find this story credible enough to believe it. Things are no different for the attribution of desires. Does the child want this cake? I do not ask myself whether the cake is good, whether there are reasons to find it appetizing, but only whether there are reasons to consider that the child finds it appetizing. By contrast,

if I am considering myself rather than someone else, the asymmetry between the third and the first person that is characteristic of psychological
verbs means that now my own reasons are what is at issue. In order to
know whether I believe the story you've told me, I ask myself whether the
story is plausible, not whether it is plausible that I be in the state of believing it. I look to see whether there are reasons to believe the story, not
whether there are reasons to think that I believe it. The same is true for
desire: I need to know whether the thing is desirable, not whether the state
in which I find myself is one of desiring it.

Only in the case where I want to know not whether I believe your story,
but whether I am not mistaken to believe it, will I have to think of myself
in the third person so as to ask, not whether the story seems believable to
me, but whether the fact that I find it believable (or, as the case may be,
unbelievable) has more to do with my "psychology" than with the weight
of the reasons that my reflection has given me for believing in it (or not).

This idea, that belief is an internal mental state and therefore possibly
also a brain state, is the expression of a decision to give the mind the
metaphysical constitution of a physical thing. The notion of a state gets
its initial meaning in the context of practices like explanation and examination. The mentalist is someone who wants to trade upon the first series
of associations. If there has been an automobile accident, it must be because the vehicle's brakes were in a poor state: we explain events by means
of states. But one must also find room for something like an inspection. In
order to know the state (of health) I am in, I will have myself examined
(by a doctor). But what can the inspection of someone's state of belief
possibly be?

CHAPTER 10

The Metaphysics of Mental States

Thinking, imagining, having an opinion, planning, wanting, desiring: these are commonly held to be examples of a person's states of mind. But little can be concluded from this vague classification, for the ordinary notion of a "state" has not been given a determinate definition. A glance at the lexicon of the phrase "state of mind" is enough to reveal its flexibility. Depending on who is writing, a state of mind can be a mood (gaiety, melancholy), an attitude (resolution, indecision), a level of activity (torpor, excitation), and it can also be a "mental state" in the sense of a state of health or disorder.

Among philosophers, I believe one can distinguish two different acceptations. In a neutral sense, the notion of a state of mind indicates only that one has moved into the order of psychological description: the use of the phrase does not serve to classify the vocabulary of that order of description. However, the notion is also used in an acceptation that might be called "predicamental," insofar as it seeks to introduce category distinctions, particularly the opposition between processes and states.

Let us first consider the neutral sense. It may so happen that the fact of speaking of a mental state in this sense betokens no particular philosophy of mind beyond this: someone is in a mental state if there are psychological facts about him, if there are descriptions using psychological verbs that apply to him. We have still not said anything about the psychological reality that distinguishes the person to whom this description applies from the person to whom it does not. We have merely ruled out the possibility that sentences presenting themselves as intentional descriptions might be devoid of all descriptive value. The only philosophy of mind excluded is thus one in which people have no opinions, inclinations, preferences, habits, or projects. Up to this point, the notion of a state is philosophically empty. As Putnam notes, one can decide to posit that a psychological state is a state studied by psychology, in which case every psychological study of your person becomes a study of your psychological states.[1]

Suppose it is claimed that the difference between two people, A and B, is that A wants to win whereas B does not. A psychological difference between A and B has been posited. Will a philosopher insist that this difference be expressed as a difference between A's *mental state* and B's *mental state?* If he does, we should ask him what makes this way of speaking anything more than a stylistic variation of the previous declaration. Is the introduction of an idiom in which people's psychological properties have been renamed "states" meant to be of philosophical interest? Does the word "state" tell us something about the mental, allowing us to make clear the mode of being of what we attribute to people? If so, we have moved to the predicamental meaning of the notion of a state: indeed, a classification has been introduced by which whatever is conceived to be a state of a subject is thereby immediately excluded from being an act or a relation of that subject, and so on.

Wittgenstein emphasizes that in this way of proceeding, everything is decided long before one declares one's allegiance to a given philosophical doctrine.[2] Everything is decided by the simple fact of having agreed to talk about mental processes and mental events (and, one might add, mental states). The mentalist's trick is to have put in place a metaphysics of states and processes modeled on the natural philosophy of physical processes and of things that are in a particular state.

One frequently finds in Wittgenstein's writings observations like the following: "Seeing isn't an action but a state (A grammatical remark)."[3] What is the point of such a "grammatical" remark? It is to attract our attention to a category distinction. If a verb signifies a process or an operation, we can ask when it occurs, with what regularity, and whether it is under our control. But if it signifies a "state," the questions to be asked are different. Here we must distinguish someone's mental *states* from the *episodes* of his mental life.

Nevertheless, this initial distinction is not sufficient, since another distinction will have to be made among different kinds of states, i.e., among those forms of mental life that are not present acts or processes. The distinction between episodes and states—which is essentially that drawn by Gilbert Ryle in his *The Concept of Mind*—above all serves to deny that certain psychological verbs signify the acts of a subject or an episode of his mental life. The other class, states, seems at this point to be a sort of catchall. In order to introduce the beginnings of a classification among all of the words that are not episodic, Wittgenstein takes as his criterion the temporality proper to each psychological verb. Among the verbs corresponding to psychological states are: fear, sadness, joy, anger.[4] In ancient rhetoric, these would have been called "passions." What makes them states are their temporal traits. One of these traits is the mode of presence (from a chronological point of view) of the pathos in question: we may well remain angry for an entire day, from the moment when we are told a certain irritating bit of news up until another incident saddles us with a different object of concern. It is thus natural to speak of a state with regard to anger: a state must begin, take hold,[5] last (whether continuously or intermittently), and then come to an end. It follows that intellectual verbs like "to consider," "to believe," and "to think" are generally not verbs describing states. One cannot be *continually* (i.e., without interruption) in something like a state of belief or in a state of planning something. Not that we stop believing one thing when we begin thinking of another; just that the continuity of belief is not that of a state.

Neither of the two senses of the word "state" provides us with the acceptation required by the psychology put forward by psychical materialism. The reason for this was brought to light in an important article by Putnam on "the meaning of meaning."[6]

Putnam's article is above all about semantics. But, semantic and, more generally, logical questions have traditionally been confused with psychological questions, so that it is normal that a discussion of semantics have consequences for the philosophy of mind.

Putnam has discerned two prejudices governing classical theories of meaning. The first holds that to know the meaning of an expression is to find oneself in a psychological state. The second holds that the meaning of a word (what one might find in a dictionary) determines its extension (the set of things to which it is applied).

In his texts from around this time, Putnam is especially interested in refuting the second prejudice: the meaning does not determine the extension but rather the converse, according to his "causal theory" of the meaning of proper nouns. Generic nouns receive a usage through their application to samples taken from nature. Their meaning must evolve along with our progress in the knowledge of the properties of the things that make up the genre corresponding to the sample to which the noun was first applied.

Putnam presents a few ideas about psychology as a way of overturning the first of these two prejudices. He notes that traditional philosophy's psychology is generally solipsistic. A psychology is solipsistic when the mental properties it posits are such that it would not be contradictory to endow a given individual—let us call him Paul—with these properties even if he were the only existing creature. Needless to say, the vast majority of ordinary psychological attributions are not of this nature. If Paul sees a dog, or remembers his dog, there must be someone (Paul) to do the seeing or remembering, and someone (the dog) to serve as the object of these mental acts. From a grammatical point of view, we might say that the only psychological verbs liable to be of a solipsistic sort are monovalent (or intransitive) verbs like "to suffer," "to be pensive," "to be bored" (taken in an intransitive sense). Solipsistic psychology requires that all psychological verbs be *reconstructed* as monovalent verbs or verbs expressing a state. For example, the verb "to see" will have to be reconstructed as a verb attributing to a subject the state of having a visual representation of something (but without the object having to exist anywhere but within this representation). The attribution of a state must respect the presupposition of the subject's isolation and solitude. This psychology is familiar: it is none other than mental philosophy, which sees the mind as isolated and detached (and does so as a way of considering its *content* in the explanation of the course of events).

Putnam offers the following illustration.[7] Consider the psychological state that consists in being jealous. In ordinary usage, Putnam claims, we will use an expression that requires us to admit the existence of more than one person. The schema, which represents a familiar three-person psychological situation, takes the triadic form: *x is jealous of y's regard for z*. Traditional psychology practices what Putnam calls, following Carnap, "methodological solipsism": the state attributed by a predicate of the above form is not considered to be a psychological state in a sense acceptable to mentalist philosophy, for it involves several people. In the ordinary sense of the word, though, the state in which the jealous person (*x*) finds himself is not a state of jealousy unless there is a rival (*z*) of whom he is jealous and someone else (*y*) who is the motivation for his jealousy. As a result, *x*'s state is dependent on what is happening around him, and we have thus left the mental sphere we sought to isolate.

Putnam proposes that we say that psychological states, in the ordinary acceptation of these terms, are states "in the wide sense" and that, for methodological reasons, traditional psychological theory requires that we reformulate them as states "in the narrow sense." Jealousy, taken in a narrow sense (or, as is sometimes said, taken as a *narrow state*) need only involve a single individual. In this case, we would have to imagine someone flying into a jealous rage about a rival who may be imaginary and with regard to an object of his affections who may also not exist.

The procedures by which philosophers of the mentalist tradition detach the mind—hallucination, suspension of belief, phenomenological reduction—have in common that they substitute an experience for a relation. Normally, the attribution of jealousy involves a relation: who is jealous, of whom, and about whom? But the logical form of the attribution of a feeling of jealousy allows a distinction to be drawn between the relations among the people involved and the jealous person's lived experience.

Having distinguished mental states in the broad sense from mental states in the strict sense, Putnam attempts to show that knowledge of the meaning of a word cannot be a mental state in the strict sense. His argument consists in pointing out that a mind detached from the world (a mind to be described in accordance with the "solipsistic method") *does not know what it is talking about*, as can be shown through several examples. And if it does not know what it is talking about, it also does not know the semantic value of the words it uses. Therefore, the knowledge of the meaning of words cannot be a "psychological state" in the sense claimed by traditional psychology, i.e., a state in the narrow sense. The semantics of ordinary language must be "externalist."

This argument has been illustrated by means of various fictional examples that have been taken up again and again in contemporary philosophical debate. Putnam himself put forward the story of two twin planets that are at first glance indistinguishable but where, unbeknownst to the inhabitants of each, the real chemistry of certain substances is in fact different. For example, everything would be phenomenally identical on Earth and Twin Earth, except for a physical difference that nobody knows about (Putnam's story is meant to take place before the advent of chemistry): water is H_2O on Earth and something else on Twin Earth, with the result that people are referring to different realities on the two planets when they use the word "water." On Earth, the word "water" is used to speak about water (H_2O), while on Twin Earth the meaning of an otherwise entirely similar word "water" is totally different, since the word is applied to something which, hypothetically, is chemically not water.

All of these fictions appeal to fantastic cases of doubling or twinning because in all cases the idea is to construct a situation of the following sort: two people are, in the invented story, in the same mental state in the narrow sense, even though they live in worlds that are in fact different. What interests us here is the principle of the argument. A mind detached from the world is one whose states are narrow: it does not therefore know what it is talking about. Indeed, this mind takes situations that *seem* identical to be identical, or rather, this mind draws similar conclusions from similar experiences, even when the experiences that it takes to *be* identical occur in circumstances that, unbeknownst to it, differ from one another. One need only construct a logically conceivable situation in which two different realities, A and B, give rise to the same epiphenomena. The detached mind does not know if it is talking about A or about B. It has no way of knowing and, moreover, has no particular reason to suspect that there may be two realities where it only sees one.

If to know the meaning of words is to know what one is talking about, there can only be two ways of knowing the meaning of words. The first is to have complete and final knowledge of everything. The second is to have relations of a physical sort with the things that one talks about, so as to be able to point out an example of the sort of thing one means and say, regardless of the ultimate verdict of science on the real essence of the thing: "this is what people mean when they use this word." Whence Putnam's conclusion, which has become a famous slogan: *Meanings ain't in the head.*[8]

What has Putnam shown? That, contrary to what certain cognitivist propaganda would have us believe, one need not be an antimaterialist in the philosophy of mind to reject the idea of a science of internal psychological states. This point has nothing to do with the dispute regarding the material out of which mental entities are made. To suggest that it does is a simple diversionary tactic. What, then, is at issue? The argument shows that *a state cannot be both intentional and internal*: if it is internal, it cannot be semantically evaluated, but if it can be semantically evaluated, it is not internal (Putnam here understands "intentionality" in a semantic sense: a thought is a thought about water if the thing it bears upon is water).

Because its importance was recognized immediately, Putnam's argument gave rise to enormous amounts of discussion. If this argument were to carry the day, then the "theoretical and conceptual breakthrough" of the new mental philosophy of mind would find itself reduced to a mere passing fancy. It is consequently fascinating to recollect that Putnam himself was responsible for launching several of his students on the path of a psychology of the functional states of a logical machine based on a distinction between hardware and software.[9]

Putnam's argument is useful in that it allows us to recognize, beyond the vogue for certain "paradigms" derived from this or that technical development, the philosophical motives for so-called "methodological" solipsism. We now understand that this solipsism is not *methodological* at all. Of course it is not an ontological solipsism either, since its partisans do not doubt for an instant the existence of a world outside the subject, nor do they imagine that this subject has doubts about the matter. Yet to call this solipsism "methodological" suggests that psychological understanding will be furthered—or made possible—if we treat the subject as though it were the only individual in the world. But it quickly becomes apparent that the issue is not the determination of a method for psychological research as it is actually practiced. The aim is to prescribe a method for psychological research as it *ought* to be practiced in conformity with the canons of mentalist philosophy.

So-called methodological solipsism has been imposed on us by a metaphysics according to which psychological states must be taken in the narrow sense, not in order to be *psychological* states, but in order to be *internal* states of the subject or organism or system under discussion. The requirement that we reduce the psychological reality of jealousy or perception to what persists even when the external environment is different is a dogmatic requirement, one imposed by the system and not by the things themselves. Putnam makes this quite clear in his reminder of how the technical term "state" should here be understood. In the sense of this term that matters to us, a state is "a two-place predicate whose arguments are an individual and a time."[10] Putnam provides several examples of states: being five feet tall, being in pain, knowing the alphabet, being a thousand miles from Paris. There is an immediately obvious disparity here: among the properties that we attribute as *states* to things, some can play a role in causal explanation while others cannot. We can explain why a piece of furniture cannot be moved through a doorway: it is too big. We can explain why an animal recoils when coming into contact with an electric fence: it feels the pain of an electric shock. But the property of being far from Paris does not *causally* explain why, at this very moment, the streets are wet here, a thousand miles from Paris, while they remain dry in Paris (where no rain has fallen). By themselves, spatial relations have no causal role. All of which boils down to a distinction between internal (or intrinsic) states and states that constitute what are called "extrinsic denominations" precisely because they do no more than allude to the reality of the thing by presenting its relation to things external to it.

In the just-noted series of examples given by Putnam, I deliberately left aside the psychological example. In what way is knowing the alphabet a state? Seen in light of the distinction between the intrinsic and the extrinsic, it is an intrinsic mental state: if someone knows the alphabet, he knows it wherever he may be. To know the alphabet is to be able to decipher the letters (during an eye test, for example). When we analyze this ability, we must distinguish the conditions to be met by the subject himself (he must be able to recognize the letters) and the conditions to be met by the circumstances (letters must be presented, they must be large enough to be recognizable, there must be sufficient light, and so on). It would seem then that knowledge of the alphabet is more a state than a relation. True, but is it a state whose expression takes the logical form of "a two-place predicate whose arguments are an individual and a time"? What sort of explanation do we offer when we invoke knowledge of the alphabet? One might say, for example: this tourist is able to find his way in Athens because he knows the Greek alphabet, while a different tourist is unable to decipher the names of the streets. In such case, we appeal to a difference between the two tourists, one which is not to be sought in the circumstances but in their "internal conditions." Should we call this an explanation by means of an intrinsic state? Would that not be similar to explaining the effects of opium by its dormitive virtue? Here we can begin to discern a category distinction between the two psychological examples: knowledge of the alphabet cannot be a state in the sense in which pain is a state. I cannot be in the state of knowing the Greek alphabet in the same way that someone can be in the state of feeling a pain in his left leg.

Even if knowledge of the Greek alphabet is classed among a person's intrinsic states, it is still not a state in the way in which a state of the body is a state (e.g., my body is dehydrated), nor is it a state in the sense in which a person's lived or experiential state is a state (e.g., I feel thirsty). One major difference is the temporal profile of these states. Physical states, both intrinsic and extrinsic, must be understood as states *at a particular moment*. What is the size of this piece of furniture at the present moment? There is an answer to the question. The piece of furniture's size can also be changed relatively rapidly. Similarly, pain can appear and disappear at a moment's notice. But can I say that at time *t* I know the Greek alphabet? Of course, if I know the Greek alphabet, I know it now although I did not know it before I learned it. Yet it is quite obvious that the temporality of knowledge is not the same as that of the dimensions of a body (which can be changed in less time than it takes to describe it). Likewise, it has little resemblance to the temporality of pain (which appears, disappears, can be interrupted, and varies in intensity). One cannot point out in a subject's biography the moment that divides the period in which he did not know the alphabet from the period in which he does. That does not mean that knowledge of the alphabet is atemporal: as with all apprenticeships, there comes a moment where the pupil is able to say "now I know" and to prove it through the correct recitation of the letters. The recitation of the alphabet is an act accomplished in real time, time that can be measured by the circular movement of the hands of a clock. At such and such precise instant, the student had recited the alphabet up to the letter *lambda*. But the acquisition and personal espousal of this knowledge is not measurable in the same way. We might ask whether, at the moment before he utters the letter *alpha*, the student is in the process of reciting the alphabet. The answer is no: he has not yet begun. But what would be the sense of asking whether the student knew the alphabet at the instant just preceding his declaration that "now I know the alphabet"?

What lessons should we draw from Putnam's demonstration? I think that the thesis itself should be taken as proven ("meanings aren't in the head") but that the limits of this externalism (as this doctrine has come to be called) must also be acknowledged.

Putnam's stories about twin planets and doubles have brought to light the fact that underlying the traditional philosophy of mind lies a will to model the form of psychological attribution on that of physical attribution. Physical attributions proceed through the determination of a state, i.e., a current state, one determinable at that very instant. In much the same way, traditional philosophy of mind attempts to conceive of the mental as made up of the states of a thinking thing, states that must be intrinsically determinable at every instant.

Let us replace the examples out of science fiction with some more familiar and less questionable cases. Consider a case of industrial duplication: two cars of the same make and model, built on the same day in the same factory. In their industrial form, the cars are hypothetically identical. The principle of their individuation is clearly provided by their matter. The

materials out of which they are made are of course only similar to one
another and not exactly equivalent. They will never be entirely equivalent,
but we can imagine that the differences are quite minimal, in which case
the two cars are equivalent from a practical point of view. One year later,
both used cars are for sale. They are no longer equivalent from this same
practical point of view. They have a past, one that will be of interest to
their prospective purchasers. One of them has had an accident while the
other has not. The prospective buyer will want to know which one.

We are interested in these machines' *history*. But the historical explanation of the differences between the two vehicles (between their respective
performance and dispositions: e.g., their roadworthiness, tendency to stall,
etcetera) is not the last word on the reality of the two cars. As their prospective drivers, we will be interested in the history of the vehicles insofar as
it affects their mechanical constitution. In other words, we disregard other
historical aspects that have no bearing on roadworthiness, for example,
the fact that one of the cars is of great symbolic value, since it belonged to
a movie star.

Historical explanation of differences in exhibited behavior is authentic
causal explanation. But it is not the ultimate explanation. It might be said
that car "A" tends to drift to the right ever since its accident. But physical
tendencies and dispositions and abilities inhere in the *current* state of the
car's physical systems, at the present moment. Its history tells us nothing
that a sufficiently rigorous mechanical inspection could not. Even better,
a mechanical inspection can tell us the extent to which the car's history
has affected its physical reality. Knowing the car's past history, all we can
say is that our curiosity has been aroused and we will seek to determine
whether the car has suffered as a result of its past misfortunes, i.e., whether
they have left any lasting traces. The bumps and shocks that the car has
been through were real physical traumas. They were not psychological
episodes.

Now let us consider the role of past history in the case of two dogs of
the same breed and age. We will want to know how they were trained. The
psychological theory that sees the animal as a machine hopes to model the
dog's psychology on the mechanical functioning of a car and conceives of
its acquired tendencies as mechanisms. Is there a chance that this psychological theory will be able to discover such mechanisms? A distinction is
here needed: a tendency is certainly not a mechanism, but one can easily
imagine science explaining the formation of tendencies in an animal by
means of its neurophysiological configuration. It is, moreover, a purely
empirical question whether and how the animal's psychophysiology accounts for the habits it has formed and the abilities it has acquired.

Finally, consider the case of two twins raised by different parents. We
will want to know what has happened to each of them in order to appreci-

ate their "personalities." Common sense (as expressed by everyday rhetoric) is satisfied in this regard by a reconstruction of their pasts. How were they educated? The past provides a motivation that illuminates their conduct in general terms. For example, one of the adolescents thinks that "the world owes him a living" while the other is vengeful. We do not ask for more than that history. We do not expect to know how these "character traits" have been "inscribed" in the subjects' mental machinery. The burden of proof thus rests with mechanistic psychology. It is not true that we treat personality traits as "states at time t." It may well be claimed that psychology has the right to hypothesize that certain traits have a support and are thereby linked to states of the person. Yet, even under the hypothesis that such states have been discovered, we will still have to distinguish personality, whose temporality requires a multiplicity sufficient to underpin a narration in multiple episodes, from states that are such at a given moment in time, as measured by the chronology of natural movements.

Nevertheless, the limits of Putnam's externalist demonstration deserve to be mentioned. His brand of externalism concerns only the referential determination of the terms comprising the nomenclature of natural kinds (e.g., water, maple trees, elm trees, etc.). To say that meanings are not in the head means that we must study things (samples) and not representations (current definitions) in order to know what we are talking about when we use these words. In other words, meanings must not be confused with representations in the head. The argument does not, however, bear upon these representations in the head. There are, then, such things as narrow mental states.

In short, Putnam has transposed into modern terms the nominalist argument drawn from the idea of divine omnipotence. The aim of this argument is to push the dissociation between appearance and reality as far as possible. It is possible, *de potentia Dei absoluta*, that I might have the experience of intuitively perceiving a horse in front of me when, in fact, there is no horse in front of me. Since this entails no logical contradiction, there are no grounds for the view that such a state of affairs could not happen if the Almighty so willed it. Today, what is almighty, at least in the examples given by philosophers, is the science of the future. It is conceivable that, one day, some mad scientists might remove a man's brain (unbeknownst to him) so as to preserve it in a laboratory vat where they can stimulate it by means of sophisticated equipment, giving him, for example, the same cerebral state he would have if he were on a beach in California. In these conditions, the brain in the vat thinks it is sunbathing and looking at the waves of the Pacific Ocean. In reality, it is in a vat in a laboratory and sees neither the waves of the Pacific nor the blue sky.[11]

In other words, appearances are the same for the subject in the vat and the subject on the beach, but only the latter has thoughts relative to a beach and the Pacific Ocean. In this version of the fiction, we may continue to speak of the brain in the vat as though it were a psychological subject (endowed with "lived experience"), for, according to the story, this is all that is left of the man whose brain it is. There is therefore continuity, at least in this version of the story. Yet the argument is also often applied to a brain whose entire life has taken place in the vat (and which has thus never been part of a human organism's nervous system). In this case as well, the argument grants mental life to the brain in the vat. The brain does not speak of a tree when it thinks it sees a tree in front of it, because there is no historical (causal) link between it and trees. Therefore—and this is Putnam's conclusion—the brain in the vat also cannot think and say that it is a brain in a vat, for the word "vat," when used by the brain, does not refer to what we call vats.

Putnam does not claim that the brain in the vat has no mental states. He grants it a *narrow* mental life. From the perspective in which appearances are removed from all links to reality or, what amounts to the same thing, from the perspective of a psychology of narrow mental states, we could well be brains in vats.

Putnam thus leaves in place the possibility of a World of Appearances. The brain in the vat is like a Husserlian Ego that has bracketed the natural world.[12] This subject would have the same lived experience we have. As a result, this argument has been made to serve the philosophy of consciousness. Thus, Searle can write:

> The brain is all we have for the purpose of representing the world to ourselves and everything we can use must be inside the brain. Each of our beliefs must be possible for a being who is a brain in a vat because each of us is precisely a brain in a vat; the vat is a skull and the "messages" coming in are coming in by way of impacts on the nervous system.[13]

It is clear that one result of Putnam's argument is to disgrace methodological solipsism, yet it fails to bring out its absurdity. All that it establishes is that such solipsism must abandon all talk of semantics as well as of psychology, in the ordinary sense of the word. But it can still talk about the appearances to which the subject is given over, even if it cannot say anything about these appearances, since to do so, one would have to use our language, whose semantics is both public and externalist.

Putnam's conclusion is an externalist one. At the same time, he denounces the illusion inherent in the mentalist program. In order for a theory to be able to formulate psychological laws in the sense in which natural sciences formulate laws, it would have to adopt a closed psychic system so as to define that system's internal states. The laws would consist in determining the conditions under which these states are obtained.

But if psychological states only become intrinsic states on the condition that we treat psychic life as a closed (solipsistic) system, then the most important thing has eluded us. For three centuries, this sort of "mentalist" psychology has been sought: "three centuries of failure," according to Putnam.

Fodor, not without a certain measure of panache, takes up Putnam's challenge. For him, the three centuries of failure to which Putnam refers are three centuries of theoretical fecundity. If, by thinkers who have failed, Putnam is referring to "everybody from Locke and Kant to Freud and Chomsky,"[14] then, Fodor says, he would not be unhappy to fail as they have. The disputed point here is quite substantial if it requires us to judge unfavorably all philosophy of mind from Locke to Freud and Chomsky, and especially if we take into account the considerable differences among the thinkers mentioned. One of the merits of the current debate is to have revealed how, behind what is often presented as a scientific program linked to recent developments in neurology and computer technology, in fact there lies a philosophical decision. Mental philosophy has chosen to maintain that the mind would have no reality if it did not have the reality of a closed system. The mind of a person makes its effects felt when we imagine it detached from circumstances.

CHAPTER 11

The Detachment of the Mind

A PSYCHOLOGY of mental states is a solipsistic psychology. By raising this objection to the psychology of the computer-mind, Putnam made clear that it was also an objection to the psychology of philosophers in the tradition running from Locke to Freud. If a theory requires that meanings be given in the head, it is solipsistic and cannot claim to provide psychological descriptions in the ordinary sense.

Jerry Fodor has valiantly taken up the challenge to his school put forward by Putnam. According to Fodor, far from being a flaw in cognitive psychology, the embrace of a "solipsistic" method is one of its strengths. Only a solipsistic psychology can lay claim to a fully scientific status among the "special sciences." For Fodor, Putnam's *objection* is merely a *condition* on psychology. In short, a psychological explanation is not a scientific and causal explanation unless it explains by means of a person's narrow states. Fodor's article on "Methodological Solipsism Considered as a Research Strategy in Cognitive Psychology"[1] is a crucial document for our discussion because it explicitly lays claim to the heritage of what I am proposing be called "mental philosophy."

Once more, the aim is to find a way of justifying the idea of a science able to offer explanations that would be at once psychological, causal, and natural. For Fodor, then, the key is to demonstrate that one can define the mental by Brentano's criterion, yet still be both a causalist (because our psychology must be scientific) and a materialist (because our psychology can only be scientific if it is a natural science). This might seem about as easy as squaring the circle. Let us recall the meaning of these doctrinal labels. Accepting Brentano's criterion means accepting the claim that intentional action is explained by the content of an intention, by what is proposed in a proposal, what is aimed at in an aim, what is desired in a desire. To be a *causalist* is to claim that the psychological explanation of action and behavior must be by means of an efficient cause, i.e., by indicating a prior state whose occurrence is sufficient to produce the action or behavior to be explained. If one wants to explain an action by an intention, the intention must be a prior state of the intentional system, which is of course the sticking point of causalism. To be a *mentalist* is to claim that the causes of action are mental, for if they are not, the explanation offered is not psychological. To be a *materialist* is to claim that mental causes are real because they are also physical.

The entire argument revolves around the notion of *mental content*. It is important to mentalists that the phrase "mental state" be applied only to narrow states, for this is the basis of their causalism. The motor that makes my car able to move must be part of my car and must be linked to the car's wheels by a set of appropriate mechanisms. If the motor were located anywhere other than within the car and so linked, it could not explain the vehicle's movement. The same is true of the mind conceived as the motor lying behind behavior. The existence of a rival is external to the jealous man's person and can therefore explain nothing. By contrast, a representation of this rival *is* able to play this role, provided it is present in the correct place (in the "belief box"). In short, the rival himself cannot be located in that part of the world where the person's physical movements are decided, but the representation whose content is that "Mr. X is a rival" can be located there. This is how mental content is held to be able to play a (causal) role in the course of things. But how are we to understand this presence in the mind of an entity endowed with a causal power, i.e., a representation?

There is clearly an innocuous sense in which we speak about mental content in much the same way that we refer to the content of a doctrine or a discourse. We might say, for example, that two people who do not have the same ambitions do not have "the same thing in mind." We seem to accept that the difference between them, from a psychological point of view, is a question of content, of what is in their minds. This is, of course, only an image. In the vague and figurative sense in which we refer to the content of a mind, what this mind contains can be taken from any and every ontological category. The well-made head and the well-filled head to which Montaigne refers[2] do not contain the mentalist's "representative ideas." They contain reflections, preoccupations, and calculations, but also memories, habits, things read, abilities, recipes, prejudices, rules, information, beliefs, principles, etcetera. In other words, the ordinary notion of the content that fills our heads is a kind of catchall, and the things included on the list do not necessarily take the form of things that must at this very moment be *present to mind*. In what way can habits or abilities be said to be inside our heads? Surely not in the form of present representations.

On the other hand, mentalism wants to speak about the content of a mind in both a literal and spatial sense. The content must be made up of representations, and it must be located in the very place where mechanisms must be sought, i.e., inside the machine. If these mechanisms were outside rather than inside, we would end up embracing the sort of behaviorism condemned by everyone, in which behavior is directly controlled by the external environment.

Does the requirement for mental content go without saying, or is it the result of a philosophical decision? It goes without saying if we mean by it that, for example, jealousy involves more in a jealous person than the simple fact of having a rival. It is correct to say that this condition—which we might call "phenomenological" if this adjective did not already legitimately belong to a school of philosophers—opens up certain possibilities for lunacy and delirium. Someone can be jealous when he has no reason to be. Yet the key point is this: ordinarily, thanks to the distinction between lucidity and delirium, we deem there to be a *psychological difference* between a man who is jealous because he has a rival and one who is jealous and has no such rival. The two are not in the same mental state. The first is lucid, the second is deluded. Yet, according to the mentalist, there is no difference between their mental states. And this conception of a mental state endowed with a content is certainly not the one that goes without saying and that nobody can do without. It is a particular conception that requires explanation and justification.

Fodor's article is an attempt to transform into a "research program" the obstacle that Putnam set before psychological theories of meaning. Fodor's defense consists in showing the affinities between the computational theory of mind and the traditional representational theory of mind. A cognitive psychology must take on board both the analogy with the computer and the stance of traditional mental philosophy. The latter has good reasons to be solipsistic. Fodor's text is thus especially meant for other cognitivists: he hopes to convince them that the representationist and even idealist psychology of traditional philosophy fits better with their conception of a computational mind than does a naturalistic psychology. The concurrence of the two theories requires an explanation, since they were developed independently. This is the first point in Fodor's demonstration.

In order to explain what the solipsistic psychology of traditional philosophy and solipsistic computational psychology have in common, Fodor introduces a condition on any specification of mental states. By this he means, a condition on our holding two mental states to be either different or identical. He calls it "the formality condition."[3] The computational theory of mind explicitly posits this condition and, according to Fodor, so did the mentalist psychology of traditional philosophy, though in its own terms: these two psychologies are therefore related. Their affiliation stems from the idea that to posit "the formality condition" is to adopt solipsism as one's method. It then remains to be shown that both psychologies are right to do so. This is the second point in Fodor's demonstration.

Before discussing Fodor's argument, we should note that he is above all interested in the psychology of the intellect. The psychology that concerns him is not one that could explain the differences between people by means

of their ill-tempered or lethargic nature, by their mental vivacity or slug-
gishness. The only psychological distinction that is of interest to him, and
to us here, is that between someone who believes something and someone
who does not believe it. For example, I am going to open the door because
I believe someone is knocking on it. If I did not believe that—if I believed,
say, that someone was knocking on my neighbor's door—I would not be
on the way to opening *my* door.

Let us begin with the formality condition.

First thesis: A psychological explanation must be intentional. Or, more
to the point and to use Fodor's language, it must be an explanation in
terms of mental content and not in terms of external circumstances.

The conclusion immediately drawn by Fodor is the same as that drawn
by the phenomenologists. Fodor distinguishes two schools in the history
of psychology, "naturalistic psychology" and "rational psychology."[4] His
thesis is that an authentically psychological explanation cannot be naturalistic. It follows that there is a dissociation between the mind and the
world, similar to the separation advanced by the "rational psychologists"
through the operations of universal and methodical Doubt or the phenomenological *Epochè*. Fodor develops this dissociation under the label of "the
representational theory of mind": to have a representation of something—
that the bakery on the corner is closed on Mondays, for example—is not
to be in a relation with the bakery; it is, as Fodor would say, *to be in a
relation with a representation* of the thing represented. His theory is thus
consistent with the strictest representationist orthodoxy.

Second thesis: If a psychological explanation must be a causal one, it
must also be unconcerned with semantics, for the semantic properties of
thoughts and representations have no causal force. Fodor points out that
by an expression's "semantic properties" he means all of the properties
that the expression has in virtue of its relations with non-linguistic entities.
In the context of this article, these semantic properties are: a sentence's
property of being true or false, a name's property of referring to the object
whose name it is. Semantic properties cannot form part of the explanation
of behavior, because they are extrinsic.

These two theses allow Fodor to present the heralded formality condition, a condition that is, according to him, the dogma that both cognitivists
and the traditional philosophers of "rational psychology" have in common.

What does the theory of computational mind claim? That systems comparable to computers do not distinguish two symbols unless they exhibit
a formal difference. On the other hand, they do distinguish two symbols
if the two symbols have different forms. This is the formality condition:
such systems only take account of formal differences and not of differences
in content or meaning (keeping in mind that the "form" to which this

theory refers is an external configuration, a morphology, so that the formal difference between two symbols will be a difference in their spelling).

As a simple illustration of what is involved, consider what the user of a poorly designed database goes through. A poorly designed system treats the names "Pierre Dupont," "Pierre-André Dupont," and "P. A. Dupont" as separate entries. If the database entry clerk has simply recorded the identity of the author of each book just as it figures in the reference he has been given, he risks recording the works of a single author under different names or the works of different authors under a single name.

Let us now consider the theory of representational mind. It identifies mental states by their represented content. The introduction of the notion of representation indicates that we are taking into account the possible disparity between things as they are and someone's subjective point of view on them. For the psychologist, what distinguishes thoughts from one another is not reality *per se* but rather reality *as it is represented.* There can thus be a difference in represented reality for which there is no corresponding real difference in things. Or, conversely, there can be a difference in reality that is not represented.

The classic example of the difference between meaning and denotation will serve to illustrate this first point: a difference in representations without a real difference. To simplify the example, here are the thoughts that can be attributed to two people, A and B. A believes that the Morning Star rises in the east. B believes that the Evening Star rises in the east.[5] These two thoughts have the same semantic features, since the semantic profile of their expression will have been fully determined once we have specified: (1) which things are at issue (the referent); (2) how these things are characterized or described (the predicate). Now, A and B are discussing the same thing (since the Morning Star is the Evening Star) and they characterize it in the same way. Yet they do not have the same thought. Indeed, A may well come to a conclusion regarding the Morning Star yet have no opinion whatever on the Evening Star, which is an object of B's thoughts.

Conversely, Putnam's examples illustrate the possibility of people having the same thoughts even though they are in fact confronting different things: the semantics of their thoughts is different, but the intentional content is the same. This can be illustrated through an example that is somewhat less fantastic (and therefore less fragile) than those of Twin Earth or the Brain in the Vat. Suppose a friend comes to visit me and, not finding me at home, waits for awhile, learns that I will not be back until the next day, and leaves, taking with him my copy of the magazine *Bonnes Soirées.* The next day, he sets out for my house but notices on the way that he has forgotten to bring with him my copy of *Bonnes Soirées* to return it to me. He buys a copy at the newsstand, arrives at my house before I do, and places the newly purchased magazine in the exact spot where my copy had been. The two copies are identical with regard to their type (so-called "type identity"). Moreover, I had not yet read my copy. In these conditions, I make no distinction between my apartment as I left it, with *my* copy of the magazine that I intended to read upon my return, and my apartment as I find it, with *another* copy of the magazine, one indiscernible from the first. Yesterday, my desire to read *Bonnes Soirées* upon my return home bore upon a copy that is now at my friend's house. Today, my desire to read *Bonnes Soirées* as soon as my friend has left bears, unbeknownst to me, upon a different copy of the magazine. The two copies of the magazine are ontologically independent. If, after having returned to his house, my friend throws the copy he took from my house on the fire, nothing happens to the copy in my house with which he replaced it. The two copies are two distinct existences, but the physical and ontological difference between them is not reflected in my "representation." In other words, in the context of this story, I make no distinction between the copy purchased yesterday and the one purchased today. Let it not be said that what is really happening is that I make no distinction between yesterday's representation and today's representation, for this is a distinction that I *am* able to make (yesterday's representation is the one I had yesterday, whereas today's is the one I have today). Let us instead claim that I have no representation of the difference between yesterday's *Bonnes Soirées* and today's *Bonnes Soirées*, which means that the difference that really exists between them escapes my notice.

Fodor has thus established the first part of his demonstration. Cognitive psychology entails solipsism just as does the rational psychology of Cartesians and empiricists. Both are concerned with what is in the subject's head and not with what is in the world around him. It remains to be demonstrated that they are right to embrace solipsism. This is Fodor's second argument.

Fodor's reasoning goes as follows: narrow states are what matter in psychology. It matters little that meanings are not in the head, as Putnam claims, since, in any case, they have no role in the mentalist explanation of behavior through the causality of states of mind. This was true for traditional mentalists and it remains true for materialist versions of contemporary mentalism. When our aim is psychological explanation, there is no difference between a true opinion and a false one, as long as those who hold the false opinion do not deem it to be false. Similarly, there is no difference between an attainable desire and an impossible one, as long as those who have the latter do not know that its satisfaction is impossible in the world as it is.

Fodor offers an interesting example that we can present as follows:[6] Imagine that we have given instructions to our stockbroker that, "if p, then sell," where p is a particular state of the market. We do not tell him: "if you believe that p, then sell." Yet psychology is unable to take into account the real distinction between "if p, then sell" and "if you believe that p, then sell," because that would suggest that there was another possibility, "if p, and even if you don't believe that p, then sell." From a psychological point of view, the instruction to act in a certain way if it is true that p can cause our stockbroker to execute a trade only if he himself takes p to be true, i.e., if he believes that p. What matters is not the state of the world, but the broker's state of belief.[7]

This first argument assumes that there is a psychology of belief, but no psychology of knowledge or perception. Specifically, it rejects a distinction—one made by ordinary language but not by mentalist philosophy—between merely believing that p (for various reasons that are more or less solid) and ascertaining that p. Fodor concedes the point: there is neither a psychology of knowledge nor a psychology of perception.[8] In his view, all that we can hope to develop is a psychology of beliefs.

In short, the detachment of the mind consists in saying that psychological explanation—one that accounts for the mind—must make reference to a subject's beliefs but need not ask whether these beliefs are true.

The residents of the New York region who were fooled by Orson Welles's infamous radio broadcast announcing the Martian invasion believed the hoax because they heard it on the radio. The false news bulletin caused a panic. The psychological force of false information arose from people believing it to be true, not in its actually being true. Semantic correctness thus has no psychological force.

It follows, according to this view, that we have a Cartesian, representational, mind. Our mental states, taken as *mental* states, are narrow states.

How are we to evaluate these representationist arguments for the thesis that mind is detached? Can we justify representationism solely in terms of the needs of psychology without setting in motion the whole machinery of methodical doubt and the *cogito*? It is not enough to point out that to err is human to prove that our mind is of a Cartesian sort. It is also not enough to point out that appearances can be deceiving: one must account for this possibility by means of the representational nature of the mind. I will now attempt to isolate the truly Cartesian elements of the proposed theory.

There is nothing particularly Cartesian (or representationist) about declaring that there is no difference between someone who believes that p and happens to be right and someone who believes that p and is wrong. Everyone grants this. To say that there is no difference is not to say much. It is merely a different way of saying that subjects are sometimes wrong and that they would never be wrong if false opinions had the outward appearance of Error and Blindness (just as the error of the synagogue is indicated on the cornice of Strasbourg Cathedral by the fact that the figure representing it wears a blindfold). The very notions of error or false opinion presuppose that, for example, a false sentence is syntactically and semantically identical to what it would be if it were a true sentence. The difference between a true sentence and a false one is not inscribed within the sentence itself but must be sought without, in the reality in which one of them describes what is and the other what is not. By definition, a false sentence is one that has a meaning and that could therefore, from a logical point of view, be true. Yet if we take a historical perspective on things, there is a distinction to be drawn: there is certainly a difference between someone who is *always* or *frequently* wrong, and someone who is *rarely* wrong, and this difference is, in certain cases, well and truly "psychological" in the "cognitive" sense. For example, someone who is constantly wrong may not have the knowledge or discernment of someone who is rarely wrong.

What is Cartesian about the argument in favor of solipsism is that it posits no difference, from the cogitative perspective of what is present to the mind, between someone who sees a sheet of paper and someone who believes he sees a sheet of paper. Perception then ceases to be direct and becomes an act of cogitation. The perceiving subject is not in relation with a sheet of paper but is only having the experience of seeing one, and therefore cannot come to any conclusions about the matter. *A new concept of representation has thus emerged*: the idea that there is a common core to the representation of someone who sees a sheet of paper and the representation of someone who merely believes he is seeing one. This is the solipsistic, narrow conception of a mental state: one can see a sheet of paper without there being a sheet of paper in much the same way that one can be afraid of the bogeyman when no bogeyman is present. In both cases, there is a thing represented (the sheet of paper given as present to one's gaze), and the difference is merely one of the "semantic correctness" of the act or the object by which the thing represented is presented to the mind.

As soon as one insists that a cogitation is shared between someone who sees and someone who merely believes he sees, one inevitably dissociates the subject of mental operations from the subject of transitive actions. From that point on, there are two subjects, resulting in a dualism of supposita. As we know, Descartes adduces this duality in his attempt to prove the immateriality of the subject of mental operations. But one is no less dualist for insisting that both supposita are material.

The subject of mental operations receives signals from the external world, but receives them through the intermediary of the organs and has no direct access to the source itself. It responds by giving instructions to the organs but, once again, only by passing through the intermediary of the motor centers. Indeed, it does not know what really happens when an order is given. What is Cartesian in all this is thus the dissociation between the *theater of operations* and the *command center*.

One is reminded of the Shakespearian situation of the aging dictator who has been isolated from the external world by his entourage. The old dictator thinks he is still leading the country: he issues decrees and receives reports. Whole newspapers have been fabricated so as to maintain him in his state of illusion. Apparently, Salazar's last days were spent in a similarly constructed illusion. Such a dictator is a "Cartesian mind": his encounters are not with the external world but only with representations of that world, and he lives his life as if in a dream.

Representationism maintains that there is no intrinsic difference between someone who sees and someone who believes he is seeing. One is tempted to respond that the truly interesting psychology is the psychology of error. A psychology that treats knowledge as outside its scope also gives up the possibility of discussing error (opposites having but a single science). But without a psychology of error, there can be no psychology of the correction of errors and therefore no psychology of apprenticeship nor of the formation of habits. One may well wonder whether everything interesting in psychology has not been cavalierly thrown overboard in order to make room for the calculating mind.

Yet there is a difference between traditional solipsism and the new solipsism that is associated with the psychology of the computer: in the Cartesian conception, a representational mind has representations that *represent*. Fodor's representational mind has representations that represent nothing and cannot but remind us of the signifiers without signifieds posited in the psychical materialism of certain French structuralists. Fodor thinks he is expressing a tautology when he remarks that, after all, "it is in the nature of representations to represent"[9] and that he in no way seeks to deny that the semantic relations between thoughts and the environment will subsequently have to be reconstituted. Yet this tautology is precisely one that Fodor's "strategy" does not respect: he proposes representations whose nature is *not* to represent.

What is missing from Fodor's reconstruction is the moment of *appearances*: it is by no means clear why the brain should believe that it exists in a world. In order to illustrate the relationship between the two psychologies that are devoid of a semantics—the cognitivist and the representationist—Fodor says that they both bear on a system that "has access" to its own representations but not to what it is they are meant to be the representations of. He provides a nice illustration: Winograd's computer program is meant to show that a computer can carry out the mental operations necessary to recognize cubes according to their forms and colors and then to move them according to its instructions. This program never had to be put to use. Instead, it was made to function in a simulation, since the construction of a robot to carry out the movements would have added little to the demonstration. From an external perspective, the program was manipulating nothing whatever. Fodor claims that, for the computer, there is no difference between such a simulated manipulation and a real one. Here again, we find the indifference to the external world that gave rise to the fiction of the Brain in a Vat.

> Of course, it doesn't matter to the machine that its beliefs are false since falsity is a semantic property and, qua computer, the device satisfies the formality condition; viz., it has access only to formal (nonsemantic) properties of the representations that it manipulates. In effect, the device is in precisely the situation that Descartes dreads; it's a mere computer which dreams that it's a robot.[10]

Here, Fodor openly professes the dualism he seeks to uphold, a dualism of the computer (mind-brain) and the robot (body). But, at the same time, he refers to a computer that dreams. That amounts to cutting corners. Why should the robot believe that it is a robot manipulating cubes? Why should *our simulation* appear to it to be reality? The situation that Descartes staged was that of a man who could be being tricked by appearances. For such a man, there is therefore something given, namely: appearances. But are there appearances for a formal automaton? Later, Fodor admits that there are not: the machine that provides answers to questions "doesn't know what it's talking about, and it doesn't care; *about* is a semantic relation."[11] But in that case, the machine does not dream. What is fascinating about dreams is that when we dream, just as in waking life, we care about what happens to us. Dreams are not mere sequences of images or of indifferent oneiric thoughts, like a boring television program that one leaves on without really watching it. Fodor has confused the reduction of the outside world to appearances (which is the classic Cartesian operation) with the reduction of the external world to nothing (which is a "formalizing" operation, in the sense that it is a canceling of all content).

Consider a gallery of portraits. The paintings that comprise it have semantic properties (in the extensionalist sense used by Putnam and Fodor): each of them is the portrait of somebody. It will either be true or false if someone says: "this portrait of a young woman is of my great-grandmother."

If we perform an operation of abstraction on these portraits, one that brackets their semantic properties, we end up with Cartesian representations. Under the solipsistic hypothesis, the portrait of my great-grandmother is not a portrait at all, for there is nothing to portray. It is then nothing more than a *painting* that represents a young woman. Such a painting makes no ontological claim. The pictorial representation of a young woman need not, in order to be the representation that it is, have a semantic relation to a real young woman. In other words, it does not require, in order to exist as an image, that there be a young woman whose portrait it is.

Thus, Cartesian *cogitationes* have properties that survive the suspension of semantic relations of truth or reference, and this is why a Cartesian mind does in fact have "narrow mental states." For such a mind's relations are with representative ideas, which can represent without "denoting" or "referring." Cartesian philosophers insist on the fact that ideas (i.e., what the mind is concerned with) refer to nothing at all.

> Now ideas considered in themselves, and not referred to something else [*si solæ in se spectentur, nec ad aliud quid illas referam*] cannot strictly speaking be false; whether I imagine a she-goat or a chimera, it is not less true that I imagine one than the other.[12]

If my idea of a she-goat is to have a semantic relation as this notion is defined above, it will have to enter into a relation with something. By imagining a she-goat or, if you will, in using the word "she-goat" (or the Latin word *capra*), I am placed in relation with a species of animal, and this is true whether I want to be or not, whether I know it or not. The semantic relation takes place independently of the prejudices of the speaker or representing subject. But the representative Cartesian idea of a she-goat, taken as a mere painting and before any act of judgment, no more puts me in a relation with things that are she-goats than my idea of a chimera puts me in a relation with things that are chimeras.

When Fodor carries out the abstraction by which mental entities become pure morphological ("syntactic") units, he does not thereby turn the portrait gallery into a gallery of genre paintings, but into a gallery of "abstract" (i.e., non-figurative) paintings. *Nothing is represented.* There are only surfaces on which there are lines and colors "assembled in a certain order," as Maurice Denis put it.

Imagine, then, two art galleries. One contains historical paintings. All of the images in it are iconographic documents: portraits of people, landscapes, or historical scenes. (The day when it is discovered that a painting that had been thought to represent a historical person in fact represents a fictional character, the painting is banished from the gallery, in much the same way that saints are removed from the Christian calendar when it is discovered that they did not exist, or the way that encyclopedias are corrected by removing passages that gave false information.)

Then there is the second gallery. It is a Cartesian gallery: every image that is put into it loses its semantic properties. Even if you place within it the portrait of your great-grandmother when she was twenty-five years old, the spectator visiting the gallery sees only the portrait of a young woman.

The difference between the two galleries allows us to bring out the principle underlying the difference between the presence of a young woman in the world and the presence of a young woman in the intellect.

It is impossible to give anything a place in the intellect without giving it the status of a type or a universal, moving for example from the representation of a given person (who can be pointed out) to the representation of a young woman. And, in the world, there is nothing like the form of a young woman that is not also the form of a given person. In other words, one cannot point out just a *young woman*, for to do so is to point out one particular young woman or another.

The representational theory of traditional philosophers conceived of mental signs according to the model of iconic signs rather than linguistic ones. But, as Peirce reminds us, iconic signs have affinities with predicates rather than with singular terms. In order for a portrait to be the portrait of my great-grandmother as a young woman, it must at least be the portrait of a young woman. The appearance of a young woman can be detached from the young woman whose appearance it is, and can, within a representation, be given separately, without it being implied that it belongs to a particular young woman.

Fodor has not explained how the introduction of a symbol into someone's head would allow the mind to have at least a *notion* of what the symbol is supposed to symbolize. He has not raised the question of mental content from the perspective that becomes unavoidable when one returns to a theory of representations considered as mental signs: the problem of universals.

The entire discussion presented in this chapter can be brought together in a question: Are a subject's cognitive resources Cartesian ideas or are they instead concepts? The Cartesian subject has ideas, i.e., *archetypes*. As is well known, Descartes appropriated the word "idea," which until then had been reserved for the contents of the Divine Creator's understanding, precisely because he wanted to talk about the representations that might be available to a solipsistic subject. To announce that the representation of a she-goat is an idea is to maintain that the fact of being able to represent a she-goat must presuppose nothing about the world in which the subject who has this power lives. The question is whether human subjects have ideas in this sense. Do they not instead have *concepts*, by which is meant mental abilities to classify things and their aspects, to recognize, to construct, to locate, and so on? Abilities are defined through their exercise, and an exercise is defined by its effective content, i.e., by what must be carried out in order for the exercise to take place. One may well wonder, then, whether a subject's mental content—its intellectual equipment—can be described once one has abstracted it from the world in which this subject is called upon to use it in the variety of its practices.

CHAPTER **12**

The Historical Conditions of Meaning

THE NOTION of an intentional state of a physical system is the keystone of the mentalist construction meant to house the scientific psychology of the future. The brain, we are told, represents the world (to itself) and even, as some theorists audaciously claim, represents the world in which it lives, by which they mean not the organism's inner environment but the same world in which we conduct our affairs. The question is whether such a notion is not culpable of what is called a "contradiction in terms." This is certainly the opinion of those who maintain the opposite thesis, "anthropological holism," according to which a person's intentional states should be understood as states he has in his anthropological world, one that includes his own history and education.

12.1. Anthropological Holism

In his article on solipsism, Fodor was not concerned with establishing the intelligibility of his notion of a "narrow semantic content of mental states." He did not take into account Wittgenstein's arguments against any such notion. True, he does mention these arguments on one occasion, but he does not deem it necessary to take them into consideration. In the text of his article he labels as "Wittgensteinian" arguments that are more reminiscent of Oxonian ordinary language philosophy: if Macbeth in fact had a dagger in front of him, it would be incorrect to say that he was "hallucinating," because the word to be used in such cases is "to see."[1] In the response that he offers to Peter Geach's comments on his article, Fodor more relevantly points out that, for Wittgenstein, "contextual properties of thoughts *must* be the ones which determine their content."[2] No doubt Fodor is here thinking about the type of argument found in the oft-cited section 337 of the *Philosophical Investigations*: if there did not already exist a practice of playing chess, it would not be possible to say of someone that he intended to play a game of chess. By attributing an intention to someone, we presuppose an entire context made up of institutions and customs. The intention to play chess is the intention to play a well-defined game, with its own rules. The rules of chess are fixed, they are imposed on individuals, and they are transmitted through instruction: they thus have the characteristics of a social institution. If this institution did not exist, nobody would have the intention to play chess. The impossibility here is not, of course, empirical, as if the claim were simply that nobody would think to play chess, that the idea would not occur to one. The impossibility here is a logical one: no matter what idea occurs to one, it cannot be the idea of playing chess unless chess has an institutional presence in one's world.

Fodor seems to think that such an argument is too vague to be appreciated and rebutted. Fortunately, though, we find in Geach's objections to his paper all of the elements of a full exposition of the argument. Elsewhere, Fodor gives this argument the name "anthropological holism" (which should be understood as meaning "anthropological holism of the *mental*").[3] Fodor immediately recognizes the Wittgensteinian motivations of Geach's objection (one that is, for him, "counterintuitive"). The merit of Geach's objection is to suggest, with decisive concision, a way in which Wittgenstein's argument might be made against the solipsistic perspective of mental philosophy that Fodor and the cognitivist school are attempting to revive.

There are two stages to Geach's argument. He concedes that the content of thought is not directly determinable from the immediate context, but refuses to disassociate it entirely from a historical and institutional context.

First stage: There are indeed general thoughts whose meaning does not depend entirely upon context. A distinction is then introduced between two ways of determining whether two or more thoughts are the same or not: some thoughts are the same *because* they have the same truth conditions, while others are the same *even though* they do not have the same truth conditions.

The first case is the very one that explains what we mean by a "thought," "the meaning of a thought," etcetera. Take, for example, a test of two high-school students' historical knowledge: their answers to a question are the same if the sentences are true or false in exactly the same conditions. It is in an analogous way that two people can be said to have had the same thought.

By contrast, things are different for thoughts that are expressed in the first person. Geach gives the example of the following thought crossing someone's mind: "It is nearly 3 P.M., I must get some cash out of the bank before it closes."[4] If two people have this thought, they have the same thought or, if you will, their thought has the same content, the same object, even if each of them is only thinking about himself. This identity of their thoughts must obviously be distinguished from the case where Mr. Dupont thinks "I must get to the bank before it closes" and Mr. Martin thinks "Dupont must get to the bank before it closes." In the latter case, the two thoughts are similar with regard to their extensional semantics (they have the same truth conditions) but they have different intentional contents.

The distinction between these two ways of comparing thoughts is linked to a crucially important consideration regarding the objects of thought.[5] A purely intelligible content is something abstract: two people may have the same thought, and thus "the same thing in mind," even if these thoughts bear in reality upon different things. When Mr. Dupont thinks that he must go to (his own) bank, he thinks with regard to himself exactly what Mr. Martin thinks regarding *himself* if and when he also thinks that he must go to *his* bank. Each of them is thinking about himself, but what they think is identical. The abstraction by which we may maintain that the two mental acts have the same content even when these acts in fact have different conditions of execution, means that a thought can in some ways be detached from the context provided by the history of its thinker. It does not entirely depend on its thinker, nor on the things in the world on which it bears.

This point becomes even clearer if we adopt the "stylised logical language" that Arthur Prior and Kit Fine call "Egocentric."[6] In Egocentric, thoughts are expressed as "thoughts without a subject," not because they are not somebody's thoughts but because everything expressed in Egocentric characterizes the person thinking or expressing himself. For example, the statements "Stand up!" and "It's time to go!" are exhortations addressed to oneself by the speaker. Similarly, in Egocentric, the response "Present," when it is made by speaker A, means the same thing as "A is present" in everyone else's language. In such an egocentric idiom, the thought that provides Geach with his example is even more obviously identical in all of the heads in which it occurs: "It is nearly 3 o'clock; time to go to the bank." This would mean on every occasion that the person who is having this thought must go to his bank.

Geach therefore concedes something to solipsistic psychology. There is indeed a way of giving an "opaque" description of someone's thought, one that does not allow a referential value to be discerned through the terms used to express the thought. In our example, if we know only the content of the thought but nothing of its context, we know only that it is thought that someone must go at 3 o'clock on an unspecified day to an unidentified bank. In its intelligible content, this thought bears in general upon people, 3 o'clock in the afternoon, and banks. It does not say precisely of someone that he must go to the bank, nor of a bank that someone must go there, nor of a certain moment in history that it is the moment for this person to go to his bank.

Now for the second stage of the argument. Even when the distinction is made between the thought as it presents itself in the mind of someone and the semantic content of this thought, it is not possible that the description of a thought be entirely abstracted from every semantic relation with the environment.

It [the above description] would be wholly unintelligible if it purported to describe the thought of someone in a culture where there were neither clocks nor cash nor banks nor even any tales about such things. There are those who hold that even in such a milieu thought of this type might run through a man's head: if, let us say, he were struck by lightning and the electrical impulses in his brain were shaken into the right pattern. I want to say such an ascription is *absurd*; and if some research projects in current psychology are predicated upon the contrary assumptions, so much the worse for them.[7]

Geach's objection is thus one that falls into what Fodor calls anthropological holism. Content cannot be attributed to a mental act in complete abstraction from a context. Now, it is remarkable that this context is not limited to natural circumstances as it is in most externalist arguments (as, for example, in the fictions of a Twin Earth, where the liquid that resembles our water is not water). Nor is the context reduced to a purely linguistic matter, as it is in Putnam's causal theory of names. It is, rather, an entire historical context, one that includes a practice like the measurement of time, and institutions like money and banking establishments. Here again we find Wittgenstein's idea that strictly linguistic activities (speaking) cannot be separated from other symbolic practices (like those of measurement and the calendar). This is precisely the meaning of the reference, which Fodor deems obscure, to "forms of life." Generally, psychological notions are unable to fix the state of a subject at a given moment: most of these notions apply to the configuration of behavior, to its structure. It is therefore appropriate to take heed of the temporal condition of the manifestation of the psychological attribute under consideration.

Geach's argument plays on the incompatibility, one that frequently comes to light in narratives, between the thoughts attributed to a character and the conditions put in place by the story. We might here be reminded of the infamous impossible sentence with which a silly historical serial supposedly began: "We, the knights of the Middle Ages. . . ." This is a paradox, because the historical conditions of the subject's existence militate against the content of the attribution by which the story hopes to begin. It is worth pointing out that our reasons for seeking to ascribe a particular thought to a subject struck by lightning are purely speculative ones: whoever is in the physical state of Mr. Dupont when Mr. Dupont thinks that he must go to the bank, must be thinking that he or she must also go to the bank (and even if he has never heard of a bank in his entire life).

Geach's example could be complemented by another, where the anachronism would take place in the supposed relation between the subject and the content of his representation. At the beginning of Alexandre Dumas's novel *The Queen's Necklace*, the old marshal Richelieu is hosting a dinner for several people, including Monsieur de Cagliostro, who claims to possess a youth potion. As a result, this man who seems in fine fettle professes to have been born more than four thousand years ago and to have been present for all of the significant events that have taken place since. He remembers having been present at the battle of Crécy as well as the battle of Actium and to have been a witness to the Trojan War. Moreover, Cagliostro brags of being able to predict the future, and tells each of the other guests of his or her fate: Condorcet will poison himself, Mme Dubarry will be decapitated, and so on.

Under the hypothesis of methodological solipsism, nothing seems to prevent Cagliostro from remembering the future as he remembers the past. One can well imagine that the potion inserts brain sentences into his memory module (in his "recollection box") that correspond to his prognostications regarding the other guests. Every brain sentence present in this box gives rise to a memory. As a result, nothing in the mechanics imagined by the psychology of narrow mental states can prevent Cagliostro from remembering the fall of the Bastille in 1789, even though the dinner is supposed to have taken place at the beginning of April 1784. Being a discriminating novelist, Dumas is careful not to mix mental functions. When dealing with the past, Cagliostro remembers having been there. When dealing with the future, he reads the telltale signs in a crystal glass filled with water.

What, then, is the basis of the disagreement between the theorist of methodological solipsism and his critic? The difference between them is radical, since Fodor, in his response, claims that Geach is the one whose thesis is "counterintuitive."

In Geach's view, Fodor has left open the possibility that a subject might think thoughts that are necessarily unthinkable for him. Imagine a Cro-Magnon man suddenly struck by lightning, and imagine that the electrical discharge makes his neuronal state identical to that of someone remembering that he has to go to the bank. According to the postulates of the materialist theory of mind, this Cro-Magnon man must have the thought that he must now go to the bank. What happens when this thought occurs to him? Are we to say that he understands this thought, since it is, we are assured, his "intentional state" to represent himself as having to go to the bank? To do so is to assume that the lightning has given him supernatural abilities. Are we then to say that he does not understand the thought he is having? This latter response is more tempting, but amounts to saying that this prehistoric man is thinking a thought such that thinking this thought boils down to thinking nothing.

By contrast, for Fodor, Geach is asking us to imagine that two subjects can be equivalent ("down to the last molecule"[8]), and yet manifest real differences. If the subject and his double are in every way identical, then they are in the same mental state. But Fodor is no doubt assuming that Geach has granted him that the two subjects are in every way identical. Geach might well respond that they are not, since they have not lived in environments that are similar with regard to their customs and history. Here, then, is the basis of this dispute: for Fodor, two subjects are necessarily, at a given instant, in the same mental state if they are in the same physical state; for Geach, two subjects cannot be in the same mental disposition if they have histories as different as those assumed by our example, *regardless of what their physical state is at a particular moment*. In short, for Fodor, physicalism requires us to say that physical identity suffices to determine mental identity, whereas for Geach, the fact that the determination of thoughts is contextual prevents us from subscribing to the physicalist dogma. Fodor continues to work for the separation of the thinking subject from its environment in order to turn it into a closed system able to manifest nomological regularities. Geach denies that someone's physical state can be described without taking his history into account, so that a state of mind, by definition, cannot be a narrow internal state.

12.2. Physicalism and the Principle of Supervenience

Certain arguments in favor of physicalism appeal to our "intuitions" and common sense. I suppose that such arguments are addressed to those who are already convinced of the doctrine's validity. There is an argument that would appear to be more respectable: Philosophers should avoid claiming that they already know, thanks to philosophy, what the limits are in domains that have not yet been sufficiently explored by empirical research. In other words, one must avoid hindering the freedom of scientific inquiry with philosophical speculations that seek to decide in advance what can and cannot be found *in fact*. I believe this to be an excellent principle: it is not possible for a philosopher to know in advance things that researchers in the empirical and theoretical field have not yet established.

Using a principle of this sort, one by which we recognize the contingent nature of concrete reality, a physicalist philosopher might attempt to discredit the objection drawn from anthropological holism to the very idea of a narrow mental state. His reasoning in defense of mentalism might go as follows: "you are doing something everyone recognizes as illegitimate, namely intervening as a philosopher within the province of an empirical science; you are in effect claiming to determine through a purely philosophical argument what it is that a brain is capable of doing. This is something for neurophysiology to decide, not you."

This line of defense is the result of a confusion. In fact, the holist argument presented above has no bearing on what the brain sciences may or may not one day find. Perhaps it will one day be discovered that it is impossible for a creature constituted as humans are to carry out the mental act whose intentional content is expressed by the sentence "It is 3 o'clock; I must go to the bank," unless its brain takes the configuration XYZ. We will have then discovered a physical or, more precisely, neurophysiological condition on the ability to think this thought.[9] This discovery would allow us to predict that someone whose brain cannot take the configuration XYZ, *ipso facto*, will be unable to think the specified thought. Bear in mind that this modality should be understood in a physical sense (exactly like the impossibility of swimming across the Atlantic, which is a "medical" impossibility, as Russell might say, and not a logical one). Similarly, someone who is dazed, or drugged, or intoxicated cannot read the *Critique of Pure Reason* as he might in his normal state: but we will not go so far as to claim that such an observation, however well-established, is some sort of step forward in the chemical analysis of philosophical reasoning.

All that the philosophical argument seeks to establish is that such a discovery, regardless of its own worth, would not be a *psychological* discovery. In other words, it would tell us nothing of use for psychological explanation.

In order for there to be a causal psychological explanation, one would have to be able to discover a *sufficient* condition: just as the mere mention of a certain subject is sufficient to make me irritated, the cerebral state XYZ would have to be sufficient for someone to have the thought in question. But, as we have seen, such a psychological discovery poses serious problems, since it would require us to accept the natural possibility of a supernatural state of affairs: a primitive living peacefully on his Pacific island would have the inexplicable ability to think a thought that ought to be unthinkable for him. By contrast, the neurological discovery mentioned above, if it were to be made, would bear on a *necessary* condition. But enumerating the necessary conditions for the exercise of an activity does not necessarily play any part in the explanation of the forms that this activity takes.

In fact, none of this discussion has anything to do with neurology. It is a discussion among philosophers: those who are materialists are so for philosophical reasons and not because they have more extensively researched these issues than others have. More precisely, we should note that the subject of discussion is not the *cerebral* state of the thinking subject, but its *state*, whether we call it cerebral or something else.

The anthropological holist thesis holds that someone's state of mind cannot be a brain state. The reasons for this thesis are not that philosophy can tell us in advance things that neuroscience has only partially established: what a brain consists in and what its functions are. The impossibility at issue here has nothing to do with the particularities of the brain but with the metaphysical difference between two meanings of the word "state." The brain states to which some refer are internal states, states that can be determined without taking the external world or history into account, whereas intentional states are precisely states that are a function of the historical world of which the subject is a part. An armchair is in the same state until a carpenter or an upholsterer repairs it, whether it is in the shop or at my house. But a person's mental content depends on his history and cultural references.

States of mind are historical states and, one might say, civil states. This proposition can be developed in two directions.

(1) If we know that someone is in a certain state of mind, we must accept that he has a history compatible with this state and therefore a past and a future destination that are intelligible in the light of his present. If the primitive wants to play chess, he must have been in a position to learn the rules or to hear about the game in some way or another. Here we again encounter the principle of the intelligibility of narrative sequences (see above, § 8.6).

(2) If we know that someone is in a certain mental state, we must accord him a civil state compatible with the content of his mind: this person has a status in civil society. This civil state must be understood not just in the narrow sense of a position in a kinship system (filiation and alliances) but more generally as a position in a social system.

One might object that this view fails to take into account the principle according to which the relation of the mental to the physical is one of *supervenience*.[10] Perhaps, but what *is* a relation of supervenience? In reality, it is impossible to provide a definition of the word "supervenience" that fits all of the contemporary uses of the term. Many philosophers seem to think that the principle of supervenience expresses a physicalist philosophy. But I believe it would be more accurate to say that this principle, properly understood, explains why every reduction of a physicalist sort is impossible.

The word "supervenience" was part of the English-language philosophical vocabulary before it came to be used for the relation between the physical and the mental. It has been pointed out that the word had already appeared in the English translations of a difficult passage in the *Nicomachean Ethics*, where Aristotle is explaining the relationship between pleasure and activity.[11] The English word in that text is modeled on the Latin, which is a literal transposition of the original Greek. It is worthwhile calling our attention to this passage in Aristotle, for in it we find the idea of traits to be brought together, of a relation between two realities, one of which emerges [*survient*] when the other is given.

Aristotle is attempting to explain how pleasure comes to be added to an activity. Pleasure endows the activity with a certain perfection: for example, the use of one's vision may be pleasing. But pleasure is not added to the activity as a *habitus* or intrinsic determination or disposition would be. "The pleasure perfects the activity, not as the fixed disposition does, by being already present in the agent, but as a supervening perfection, like the bloom of health in the young and vigorous."[12] The words "supervening perfection" are a translation of the Greek *epigignomenon telos*, which Guillaume de Moerbeke's Latin translation renders literally as *superveniens finis*.

In this text the core of the concept of an ontological relation of supervenience is already evident: on the one hand we have a reality that is fully constituted, whose description has been exhaustively provided once one has enumerated all of its intrinsic properties; on the other hand, there are additional properties that also belong to this reality, but about which one might well ask what they add, since they were not part of the first description. The element that is *superveniens* is added to something that it cannot complete. According to Aristotle's analysis, this is the case with experienced pleasure. When an activity is performed in the conditions it requires in order to be fully performed, this activity becomes pleasing. One might say that wherever there is an unhindered activity, there is pleasure: pleasure *supervenes*, is added, but it is not added in the way that one thing can be added to another. Rather, it is added simply as a result of the fact that the activity has been fully performed. According to Aristotle's comparison: there is beauty wherever human beings attain their fullest form, their *acme*, simply as a result of this full form being given. The whole problem of the element that supervenes is that it hovers between two statuses, that of something additional and that of something superfluous. If it is something additional, how can it arise from the sole fact that something else (the activity) is given? Must not the pleasure be separable from the activity and have its own reality? But if pleasure had a reality that could be discerned separately, one could easily imagine the same activity being performed in the same conditions without pleasure supervening. Conversely, if pleasure does not add a reality to the reality of the activity itself, is it not superfluous even to mention it? The fact that pleasure supervenes adds nothing to what was already there: the supervenient element then begins to look like a mere epiphenomenon. Today, the notion of supervenience is used to articulate two descriptive vocabularies, A and B (for example a physical vocabulary and a psychological one), in the following way:

1) There can be no difference of order B between two things x and y without there also being a difference of order A;

2) On the other hand, it is conceivable that there be a difference of order A that need not result in a difference of order B.

In analytic moral philosophy, these principles are applied to moral vocabulary, so that it is impossible that two things x and y which are identical when described in vocabulary A, the vocabulary of natural science, also be appreciated differently in vocabulary B, which is the vocabulary of evaluation. This principle seems obvious and even somewhat vacuous. For example, suppose that a book is morally evaluated to be an "obscene book." It follows that another book that is an exact reproduction of the first must also be held to be obscene. To hold that there is a difference between the two is incomprehensible.

What, then, of the supervenience of mental differences on physical differences? Depending on whether the stress is placed on the negative point 1 or the positive point 2, the idea of supervenience is given a different doctrinal flavor. Point 2 guarantees that supervenience is not a materialist reduction: if every corporeal difference had a mental difference as its consequence, then every mental difference would be reduced to a pure and simple corporeal difference. The mental difference would then be merely epiphenomenal. But the point here is that the two vocabularies are distinct and serve to describe different aspects of reality.

By contrast, point 1 seems to lead to physicalism. This is how Quine understands it: physicalism, he writes, does not require a "utopian" reduction of mental events to physiological or microbiological events. Such reduction would be utopian because it would assume that there is always a correlation between a type of mental state and a type of physical state. This is something that a philosophical argument cannot ask for. But all that a physicalist requires is that there be "no mental difference without a physical difference."[13]

The very notion of a reality that "supervenes" has something undeniably paradoxical about it. One could focus on this and accuse "metaphysical dualism" of giving rise to all manner of paradox, including this paradox of supervenience. Western metaphysics, so it is said, has endlessly divided things and set them in opposition, but it is up to us to overcome these oppositions, either by conceiving a unity of the opposed terms or by seeing the two things not as opposed but as different aspects of a single reality. Yet to claim this is to miss the important point. The denunciation of the traditional "grand dualisms" is a rhetorical prescription that sometimes has an effect on readers but that clears up nothing. Here, as elsewhere, paradox is an indication of a need for further analysis.

In the two cases of supervenience considered by contemporary philosophy, the moral and the psychological, the paradox arises when one views the "supervenient" properties as *adding* something to what must already be given in order for them to supervene. Yet, if that were the case, if they added some determination, moral description would have to be that of an inherent property and therefore of an intrinsic quality, and, similarly, intentional description would have to be that of an internal state, and therefore also of a physical state of the system. In reality the paradox arises if we seek both to mark a difference in orders (by means of one of the acceptations of the notion of supervenience) and, at the same time, to erase that difference (thanks to the other acceptation of the notion of supervenience).

If it means anything, the notion of supervenience must primarily serve to underline the irreducibility of one order to another. Consider once again the use of the term in moral philosophy. What does it mean that the quality of goodness is "supervenient" on natural properties? It means, first and foremost, that goodness is not a natural property: the so-called naturalistic interpretation of moral adjectives is thus put into serious difficulty. Ordinary grammar makes no distinction between the adjectives for intrinsic natural qualities (for example, "liquid," "metallic") and adjectives of moral character, but the logic of the predicates expressed by these adjectives is different. If the fact of being good were reduced to a natural quality, the property of goodness would have to be included in the naturalistic description. The list of the natural qualities of the thing would remain incomplete until one has stated whether the thing is good or mediocre. As a result, the notion of supervenience is applicable where we want to indicate a *change of order* in the concepts applied to a thing. Take the example given by Plato in the *Laches* (191ac): among the Scythians, to retreat rapidly before one's enemy is not a form of cowardice, because this is how they fight. We will therefore have to say that the moral quality of bravery must take the physical comportment of the warriors into account, but that it cannot be identified with a particular type of physical comportment: for example, it does not everywhere and always consist in standing up to one's enemy without retreating an inch. On the other hand, it would be incomprehensible to maintain that one Scythian warrior is brave and another is cowardly when they are doing the exact same thing: shooting their arrows while falling back. Yet this example shows that moral qualities do not supervene purely and simply when a certain physical conduct is given: they supervene when the physical conduct is given in a particular moral context. In order for bravery to "supervene" when warriors retreat before the enemy, one must take into account the context of Scythian mores.

The principle of supervenience, taken as marking the heterogeneity of two groups of properties, can be illustrated through an example that is entirely separate from debates about moral naturalism and materialist psychology. In an essay on Frege's philosophy of number, Geach writes the following: "It is incidental to or supervenient upon any given kind of things, how many things of the kind there are."[14] Geach immediately applies this observation to traditional philosophy, pointing out that one of Descartes's arguments regarding divine perfection rests on a mistaken conception of number: unity cannot be a divine attribute because it is clearly a supervenient property.[15] It is clear that the supervenient property is neither an appearance (i.e., a superfluous epiphenomenon) nor a systematic effect of what the thing upon which it supervenes intrinsically is. It is a supervenient property of a thing that there be only one thing in its genre, and this is a result of what is around it. If an athlete is the only one to have arrived at the finish line at a given time, it is not because of his intrinsic properties but only because his competitors have not yet arrived.

Searle has observed that the principle of supervenience does not necessarily imply materialism, and this is why he insists that the causal version be adopted.[16] We can easily recognize that what he means by a relationship of causal supervenience is different in everything but the chosen vocabulary: he means a relationship in which (ideological) superstructures are determined by (material) infrastructures. But this relationship is a notoriously obscure one: historical materialism has always wavered between the idea of a total dependence in which the superstructure *reflects* the infrastructure, and the idea of a mysterious dialectical causality in which the superstructure is accorded a "relative autonomy" from the infrastructure, i.e., its own reality and a retroactive causality.

Does Geach's argument against Fodor entail a rejection of the principle of supervenience? This is no doubt Fodor's perception of the matter. Does not Geach's objection require us to accept that two people might be in the same physical state while being in different mental states? For example, one person is a caveman and has never heard of banks and therefore has no thoughts about them, while the other is one of our contemporaries remembering that he must withdraw some money from his bank. There would then seem to be a mental difference between them without a physical difference.

One might first respond that the thought in question supervenes when a *world* is given and not simply when a physical individual is given. The difference between the caveman and our contemporary is not immaterial. It only seems immaterial when one sets up the comparison so as to minimize the relevant material differences and retain only the two physical individuals, whose matter is unable to manifest the difference in question. It is as if one claimed that there is no difference between depositing and withdrawing money from a bank since, at a given moment, the client depositing and the client withdrawing are in an identical situation "down to the last molecule," at least as regards this operation: both are standing in front of a teller and a stack of bills lies in front of them (in the one case because it is being given to the teller, in the other because it is being given to the customer). One need only point out that the material difference exists, but that it should be sought slightly further afield, for example, in the employee's ledger (where the money has been recorded either in the "debit" or the "credit" column of the customer's account). The situation is much the same as with the supervenience of the attribute of being first in a race relative to the times of all of the participants (and not simply in virtue of the rapidity of the winner taken by itself).

Secondly, it has not yet been explained what the principle means when it claims that "a state is given." When is the state given and how do we estimate its duration? A given state must have at some point begun to be given. The principle according to which there is no mental difference without a physical difference also means: no change in mental states without a change in physical states. Using what chronology do we corroborate the correspondence between the two changes? The chronology that allows us to say when someone has begun *reciting* the alphabet and when he has finished his recitation is not the same chronology that we use to say that, before, he did not know the alphabet and now he does. Thus, once again, the philosophy of mental states seeks (here by means of *its* version of the principle of supervenience) to reduce all "states" to a single category, a metaphysical category within which we might subsequently distinguish or identify the mental and the physical.

Consider a psychological difference that affects a single subject: his mental state has changed. We are asked: How can his mental state have changed if his physical state has not? Without a physical change, the mental change would be unreal, extrinsic (or would have to take place in a spiritual substance). But this entire argument presupposes that the word "state" is meant in the same way. If we ask a physicist to observe the changes in a person's physical state so as to discover the change that corresponds to the change in his mental state, the physicist will ask us to tell him precisely when the mental change begins. But most psychological changes cannot be timed in this way. As Wittgenstein points out, one can say that someone felt sharp pain for a second, but one cannot say that someone felt deep grief for a second.[17] The problem, of course, is not whether this is what people say or whether this phraseology is correct, but whether it is comprehensible, whether this psychological concept can be used without a more substantial story, one where a motive and an organization can be discerned in the variety of events.

12.3. The Enumeration of Thoughts

The principle of supervenience is not what the anthropological holist and the methodological solipsist disagree about. What then is the ground of this dispute? I think it must be sought in the opposition between holism and atomism. Atomism is here the project of counting the units of mental life one at a time. It is not by chance that Fodor uses the vocabulary of *individuation* when he asks how to distinguish two mental states or how to recognize that two people are in the same state. In the end, the disagreement is about the conditions of identification of thoughts. How are we to distinguish one thought from another?

Mentalists propose that we individuate mental entities, especially beliefs, *as if* they were distinct entities. But, for them, the "as if" is not even needed. Fodor wants to maintain that beliefs are literally individual entities, since he has turned them into localized and material cognitive entities: the content of a belief is a brain sentence, and the state of believing is a relation of the organism to this sentence.

In this regard, today's mentalist philosophy has the merit of giving its position a metaphysical clarity that was lacking in the nineteenth-century version. *No entity without identity*, it claims, following Quine. For mental entities to be referred to, their conditions of individuation must be determined. Traditional mental philosophy was profoundly atomistic. It proposed to construct the entirety of mental life in all its complexity out of simple operations of association among elementary units (primitive ideas). How did it derive the plurality of its representational units? By conceiving of representations as intrinsically significant mental entities: ideas resemble the things of which they are the representations, and this resemblance is intrinsic to them. The representative idea was not conceived as a linguistic sign but rather as a figurative painting. Such a model *ought* to allow one to conclude that the meaningful entities have been individuated in the same way that paintings can be.

Following Descartes, then, ideas are like paintings. We should understand this as meaning that the semantic properties of these mental entities are to be conceived according to the model of iconic signs. Imagine that my castle has a portrait gallery. This gallery contains no paintings that are not portraits. It may contain several portraits or it may contain only one. It is even conceivable that, at certain times, it contains no portraits at all (either because the gallery has just been opened and the portraits have not yet been hung, or because, later on, the portraits will all have to be sold to pay for the repair of the roof). The acquisition of paintings might then represent the empiricist model of concept acquisition as something done *piecemeal*. To see a horse and remember what it looks like—i.e., to acquire through experience the concept of a horse—is like hanging the portrait of this horse in one's mental gallery.

In this view of what thought is, it is conceivable that an *atomistic* procedure for identifying units of meaning (whether the semantic units of a language or units of mentality, i.e., the elementary units of mental life) be applied to mental life.

The conditions of individuation of mental entities would then seem to be clear. On the one hand, the portraits are distinct from one another. Each painting must be acquired individually (even if I buy a collection of several paintings at once). On a list, each of them would be clearly distinct from the others. On the other hand, the "semantics" of these portraits is also atomistic: each portrait is indifferent to the presence or absence of the others. I may have but a single portrait in my gallery: a portrait of Napoleon. This portrait represents the same person whether it is by itself or surrounded by other portraits. The semantic value of an iconic sign does not depend upon its placement in a series or in a system. The fact that I possess three portraits of Napoleon may have an effect on my critical interpretation of these paintings, but it does not reinforce or affect in any way the semantic properties of each of them. Moreover, my portrait of Napoleon is no less or more a portrait of Napoleon if I hang it next to a portrait of Admiral Nelson.

Thus, the presence of a painting in my gallery neither requires nor excludes anything else: each painting is an atom, in the sense that each of them is distinct and counts as a unit of the genre in question. A painting is still a painting whether it is by itself or surrounded by others. The relations between these paintings are external to the physical reality, as well as to the pictorial and the semantic reality of each of them. Fodor would like to recover these conditions of individuation for the mental entities that he asks us to posit. Beliefs could then be counted one at a time, and it would then be possible to have a unique and isolated belief, because the identification of this belief would not be dependent on the possession of other beliefs.

However, the lovely clarity of the traditional doctrine of representational mind vanishes when we remember that in it, representative ideas are only *compared* to paintings. Like paintings, they present to the mind something to be found elsewhere (if it is to be found anywhere at all). But representative ideas cannot be images of a mental sort. Indeed, the entire representationist doctrine depends on the principle that is constantly invoked: in order to think of something in category *A* (whether she-goats or chimeras)—for example, when I encounter an *A* in the countryside or when I dream about one or even when I speak about one—my mind must in itself already possess a representation of an *A*. It follows that the internal representation cannot be a mental painting, i.e., an iconic sign made up of mental rather than physical material. If it could be a mental painting, it would be possible to make a distinction, as we do with paintings painted on stretched canvas or wooden plaques, between the physical properties of the support and the figurative properties of the representation itself. For example, a painted portrait might be fragile (due to its physico-chemical constitution) and in the classical style (owing to its figurative constitution). One would have to be able to recognize what is represented in the mental sign in the same way that one recognizes Napoleon's traits in a stretched canvas on a frame. But there would obviously be an infinite regress, since possession of the idea was held to be the condition for recognizing the content represented on the surface of the physical painting.

The question of identity at which we have arrived may seem difficult or overly subtle. I aim to show why it is central for any discussion regarding the metaphysics of states of mind. At the same time, I will present the set of questions to be addressed in my book *Les institutions du sens*.

Let us begin with the following question: In asking for an identity criterion for thoughts, have we presupposed that thoughts are individuals, that they must be individuated? In that case, it might seem that physicalist philosophy has already won the day, since it would be impossible to say whether two people are thinking the same thing without implying that their thoughts are individuals. But how can thoughts be individuals if they are not *physical* individuals?

It does indeed seem that we have available to us two overarching paradigms for our concept of an individual: numbers and physical objects, for example, sheep. Numbers are the epitome of well-individuated objects. One might say that that is what they are made for: to be entirely distinct from one another. But they are formal or ideal objects. Thoughts cannot be individuated as numbers are. Indeed, unlike numbers, thoughts have a place in history. For the partisan of mentalist psychology, their place is a causal one. But, even if we reject the idea that their place is a causal one, we still believe that thoughts have a historical place: the entire argument of anthropological holism seeks precisely to remind us that the content of an act of thinking (content by which it resembles or differs from other acts of thinking) depends on a social and historical context. Thoughts would thus appear not to be able to be individuals in the way numbers are.

"Therefore," the advocate of an atomistic identification of thoughts concludes, "thoughts are rather like sheep which are also amenable to exercises in enumeration. We may not know where one cloud ends and the next begins, but we definitely do know where one sheep ends and the next one begins: the passage between them is not gradual."

But here we must consider an objection raised by Cornelius Castoriadis: we can tell how many goats there are on a road but not how many representations there are in a dream.[18] We can say what the sum of two goats and two goats is. But how would we count the representations present in a dream or a story? If there are two paternal figures in a dream, is that two occurrences of the signification "father" or two different significations? If one of them has a beard and the other a hat, how many significations are there?

This objection must, in my view, be taken into account: significations cannot be counted. Those who unthinkingly imagined that it could be done were counting something other than significations, or else what they were saying was unintelligible. In fact, Castoriadis raised this objection against structuralist metaphysics or, more precisely, against the metaphysics of what was earlier called "psychical materialism." This brand of structuralism held that whatever the symbolic domain, one should divide it up into elementary units (according to the model provided by linguistic phonemes) so as to derive, through their combination, the increasingly complex "syntagmas" that are speech, dreams, myths, dramas, and civilizations. These theories claimed to *count* significations: this claim alone is enough to refute them.

The real is amenable to a certain extent to an extensional analysis, if one means by this an analysis that holds coextensive terms (predicates that apply to exactly the same things) to be equivalent. But this is not true of the order of significations: in a story or a dream, there are masses of significations, but this mass is not amenable to being analyzed as a set. Its multiplicity cannot be exhausted by drawing up a list of its elements, for the multiplicity of significations cannot be expressed by us as a "collection into a whole of defined and distinct objects."[19]

More generally, Castoriadis criticizes an intractable prejudice of philosophers and of all those whom they (often unknowingly) inspire: that everything that exists exists in a *determinate* form. Everything that exists is precise, determined, and apprehensible. If by chance something exhibits indetermination, haziness, or vagueness, then that thing has shown itself to be, if not utterly illusory, at least of inferior status.

For my part, Castoriadis's critique leads me to the following conclusions:

First, the prejudice according to which the truly real is determinate must be rejected. It is true that this dogma has a place within the philosophical tradition and that some thinkers accord it the status of a principle of reason. For these thinkers, who are *determinists* in the true sense of the term, it may well happen—indeed, it unfortunately happens quite frequently and perhaps always—that our representations of things are imprecise, vague, or indeterminate. But this flaw can have no effect on the things themselves: they are what they are to an entirely determinate degree. To these determinists, we might respond: indetermination is conceived as less determination, by contrast with greater determination. But what are we talking about when we contrast greater and lesser determination? We are talking about more or less determined *representations*. The principle of the determination of things thus rests on an illegitimate transfer that, on the basis of a difference that is relevant when one is comparing two representations of reality, derives a thesis on the general relationship of representations to reality, by means of a confusion between reality and a postulated exhaustive representation of reality. A representation that is given to us can be entirely determinate or remain indeterminate in one or another regard (relative to the questions that we have asked). Reality, however, is neither determinate nor indeterminate.

Second, the critique of the traditional concept of identity is a salutary task as long as this critique is understood as a critique of the illusion of a general metaphysics.[20] A general metaphysics would have to take up unity and plurality, identity and difference, the individual and relations, all without taking any particular domain into consideration. In particular, it would have to make plain how the words "being" and "identity" are to be understood before philosophical inquiry is divided into "regional ontologies," including the ontology of nature and the ontology of mind. Such a project can only lead to an impasse: How can one inquire into conditions of identification without taking into account the type of things one seeks to identify? Rationalist "formal ontology" is a mirage.

Third, it nevertheless goes without saying that this indispensable critique of the philosophical prejudices we have inherited takes none of the importance away from a question like: Do two people think the same thing, or do they think differently? And if this question is meaningful, we will have to propose a criterion for identifying thoughts.

Let us return to the example of the task of enumerating the representations or significations contained in a dream. Or, rather, in order to fulfill the principle of the exteriorization of the mental, let us replace the dream by a grand figurative painting: *The Raft of the Medusa*. It is quite impossible to say how many significations or representations there are in Géricault's painting. But why? It cannot be done because in order to do so, one would have to be able to enumerate the *things* represented in the painting. The impossibility thus has nothing to do with the fact that the representations are indeed representations and not things. For the same impossibility would confront us if we had to enumerate the things in a part, even a tightly circumscribed part, of the world. We cannot say how many things (entities, distinct existences) there are in the historical event of the shipwreck of the *Medusa*. As a result, in one or the other case, the impossibility has to do with the concepts themselves. It is impossible to count things, not because there are not several of them or because things are essentially fleeting, but because the concept "thing" is not meant to be applied in an exercise of enumeration. The same is true of the concept of "signification." This concept manifests no identity criterion.

This reflection leads us back to Frege's philosophy. The main lesson of a philosophy of arithmetic like Frege's is that arithmetic concepts have a different status than descriptive ones. We speak about "quantity" as if it were just another category, along with quality, relation, etcetera. But whiteness is a property of the tablecloth, and the fact of being smaller than the person on his right is a property of the man in the photograph. By contrast, the fact that there are two people visible in the photograph is neither a property of these people, nor a property of our representation. In short, as Frege says, the conception of number can be neither "physical" nor "psychological."[21] Frege's solution inheres in what he calls the "principle of context": do not ask about the meaning of words by themselves (for example, those that serve to designate numbers), but look at their role in a proposition. With regard to numbers, we might look to statements of numerical equality: there are as many things of type A as there are of type B. But this solution makes evident that we can only enumerate things if we have already made clear the sort of things we are counting.

It remains to be shown how these ideas about identity and enumeration can be applied to our problem: determining whether two thoughts are identical or different. Geach has provided the following clarification of Frege's lesson, in a text that bears quoting at some length:

> In the past, great advances of thought have been made because people exchanged the question what an *A* IS for the question what it is to be the same *A*. The Euclidean treatise on proportions contains one definition telling us what a ratio IS; this is perfectly futile and is never used; and then there is another definition giving the criteria of identity for ratios, which is a masterpiece, and shows how to deal with irrational ratios.[22] Frege knew his Euclid well, and I feel this must have inspired him to cut short centuries of futile nattering about what a number IS by considering rather the criterion of identity for numbers. This is the way forward. I once read a complaint that some writing about Fregean *Gedanken* [thoughts] failed to supply "a philosophical account of what thoughts ARE";[23] but if only we had a good criterion of identity for *Gedanken*, we could probably do without such an account.[24]

In this text, Geach generalizes the lesson drawn from Euclid and Frege, maintaining that one always gains by avoiding the essentialist question: What is a thing of type A? By mischievously writing the verb "to be" in capital letters, he clearly means to show that he sees a link between the traditional form of questioning that is held to be eminently philosophical (What is the BEING of numbers?) and the form of those of Euclid's definitions that have no purpose and clear up nothing. For Geach, a true definition, not only for mathematicians but also for philosophers, is like those used in demonstrations: such definitions really tell us *what makes* something a number, i.e., what formally constitutes number as such.

The Euclidean procedure did not disappear in the subsequent history of philosophy. Leibniz explicitly refers to it when he needs to define "a place": he explains that one cannot say what a place is, but only what it is for two things to be in the same place.[25] Yet Leibniz seems to think that this procedure is a simple stopgap measure, a stand-in for cases where we cannot give a definition in due form.

The idea that one accounts for the thing one is talking about by proposing an identity criterion has general implications. Geach's critique bears upon a certain way of conducting philosophical inquiry, one that invites philosophers to turn their attention to an essential kernel of the thing to be defined.[26] According to this traditional view, the philosopher's task is to render the tenor of this eidetic kernel in general terms. What is a number? As long as the philosophy of arithmetic has not provided an answer, arithmeticians do not know what they are talking about. What is a thought? What is the meaning that must be understood in order to understand a sentence? As long as the philosophy of language has not expressed the answer to these questions in a definition, logical analysis will remain irresponsible, for the logician will be unable to define the object of his analysis. It might be worth noting that in criticizing this view, I am not criticizing the use of the *word* "to be" itself, as if it were a harmful word to be avoided or erased. The object of this critique is the illusion that philosophy's task is eidetic. It is true that we are used to reading that philosophy is defined by "the question of Being."[27] But the word "Being" is not the crucial part of the question: it is easy enough to translate the question asking "what is it to be an *A*?" into a question about the identity criteria of things that are *A*, i.e., about what it is for a thing, *x*, to be the same *A* as another thing, *y*. I am criticizing "the question of Being" not because being should never be a question for philosophy, but because the very style of the question—"what is it for an *A* to be an *A*?"—is both misleading and paralyzing: it asks us to provide an answer but also implies that every possible answer is rejected in advance, except one. The only acceptable answer is one that expresses the tenor of a "donor intuition" of the thing itself. In vain do we seek this experience of contact with the essence of the thing itself, for we are not even sure of understanding what this intuitionist description tells us we would have to possess in order to know what the thing IS.

In the text cited above, the search for an identity criterion concerns Fregean thoughts, i.e., objects of thought and not acts of cogitation.[28] But the question at hand is precisely one of knowing whether two people expressing their judgments in sentences with the same semantic content (i.e., sentences with the same truth conditions) have performed the same mental act, whether they have the same thoughts in their heads, and whether their mental acts are the same.

It is suggested that beliefs can be identified by counting mental sentences, the units of meaning. But what units are we to count with? How many beliefs are there in a *credo*? It would be absurd to claim that there are as many as there are sentences. How many beliefs are collected in one article of a *credo*? It would be absurd to claim that there are as many as there are words, or even as there are words with a semantic value. In fact, the enumeration of thoughts bears more resemblance to the enumeration of functions to be carried out in a complex system than it does to the enumeration of rabbits in a rabbit hutch. If we count rabbits, the level of individuation is fixed once and for all by the concept of the species. A rabbit can be divided into rabbit pieces, not into little rabbits. It never happens that a thing that has just been counted as an example of the rabbit species, when considered from another point of view, requires that we take it to be a pair of rabbits, or appears to be an integral part of a higher-order rabbit. In other words the identification of thoughts takes place in conditions that are entirely different, since a thought can be divided into several thoughts in exactly the same way that a responsibility in a collective endeavor can be divided into several responsibilities to be apportioned among several different people. It would seem, then, that the identification of thoughts must be made holistically, by means of differentiation through contrast.

.   .   .

If mental philosophy were able to engender a scientific psychology, that psychology would be solipsistic. But its partisans hasten to reassure us: this is a methodological solipsism rather than an ontological one. The method they describe is the one that mental philosophy wants to impose on the sciences of the mind. In fact, the solipsism of narrow states of mind is an expression of the decision to give the disciplines that study the phenomena of mind the same metaphysics as the natural sciences.

The consequence of this, as we have just seen, is that such a natural psychology is unable to tell us about the mind, i.e., about thoughts. Mental vocabulary is deeply historical, which is another way of saying that there are historical conditions of meaning. A subject's words and thoughts have the meaning that they must be given in his world and cannot be dissociated from that world.

Such a conclusion is likely to be judged worrisome by those philosophers inclined toward philosophical atomism. And it should be admitted that some of the motives behind their concerns are justified, even and perhaps especially if one does not share their atomist prejudices. Does anthropological holism not essentially maintain that a subject's thoughts cannot be identified by someone who is unfamiliar with the world in which that subject lives? The world that must be known in order to know what the subject thinks is not just a natural world. If it were a natural world, we could perhaps refer its determination to the omniscient jurisdiction of a future physical science, as in "externalist" doctrines of meaning. But anthropological holism has expressly emphasized the historical and human character of this world: it is a cultural world, one that contains institutions like the calendar, money, banks, and the game of chess.

By providing thoughts with the historical context of a set of institutions and a formative past, the holist might well think that he has done nothing more than distinguish the sciences of the mind from the natural sciences. But has he not rather ruined any possibility of an *empirical* science of the mind? The contextualization of the mind may well confront an alternative where it amounts either to a relativism or to an absolute idealism. It is a relativism if the context of others' minds turns out to be the context of the researcher's mind. It is an absolute idealism if we are in fact witnessing the disappearance of the difference between a study of the concept of mind and a study of the effective reality of the mind.

The objections of atomists to holism are ways of pointing out certain consequences of the refusal to identify significations by individuating them.[29] These consequences are well known and were already pointed out by Hegel, for example, when he wrote: "Individuality is what *its* world is, the world that is its *own*."[30] As soon as one seeks to understand a historical individual, one is referred to the world in which he is the individual that he is. Unfortunately for the Understanding (*Verstand*), which seeks to be able to explain the individual by his world, in much the same way that Hippolyte Taine claimed to do through his triad of race, milieu, and moment, the same thing that is true of the individual is true of the world: as soon as one seeks to apprehend the world in which the historical individual is what he is, one finds that one has apprehended the world of an individuality. Hegel writes that "*what* is to have an influence on the individuality, and what *kind* of influence it is to have—which really mean the same thing—depend solely on the individuality itself; to say that by such and such an influence this individuality has become *this specific individuality* means nothing else than that it has been this all along."[31] In fact, this mirror effect might remind us of research into the causes of a unique event, for example, the causes of the First World War. Analysis of these causes uncovers a generative mechanism so special that it could not have worked more than once: the particularities of the causes reproduce the particularities of the effect to such an extent that one ends up saying that one is really talking about two different aspects of a single thing. The world that produced the First World War is, in reality, the world of that war, the world determined by it. We were looking for circumstances— contingent elements—yet everywhere we look we seem to find only necessity, a necessity that needs to be attributed: Is it in history itself, or in the historian's interpretation, i.e., in the way he apprehends his material? Is it a necessity derived from the concept of mind, or is it a necessity derived from the conceptions of a particular researcher, who is asserting his subjective perspective?

Thus, my reflection on the conditions of mind ends, provisionally, in an expression of perplexity. This is no doubt preferable to pointless speculative exultation, but it follows that my inquest must be declared to be incomplete. We have been able to take stock of the force of the holist argument against the presuppositions of mental philosophy. Yet we are not yet able to turn this critical result into a solution of the difficulty we have encountered. If representations or thoughts cannot be identified, then they are unreal. The mentalist, the physicalist, and the atomist are entirely correct to insist on this: if we cannot state what the difference is between what person A thinks and what person B thinks, then we also cannot state what the difference is between the fact of thinking as A does and the fact of thinking as B does. But if we cannot state this, we must accept the consequence: there is no difference between having the one or the other thought. In this case, thoughts are of no importance whatever, since nothing can be determined in the mental order. It goes without saying that, under this hypothesis, the claims of an inquiry to being a moral *science*, a science of the mind, are unacceptable: there could be no knowledge worthy of the name in this domain, since we are unable to identify what we seek to discuss.

It therefore seems impossible to abandon the idea of identifying thoughts. But how are we to identify them without individuating them? As long as the partisan of mental holism has not explained this, he will be reproached with having provided little more than a hollow formula. He will be told that, practically, his position is indistinguishable from that of a mental "nihilist," i.e., someone whose skepticism would have the following expression: we know nothing about what people think or believe; all that we know is, if you will, the spelling or voice that they give to them, the letters and sounds that they use when they write or speak their thoughts.

The holism of the mental (or of meaning) has a poor reputation. And it must be acknowledged that this disrepute is partly deserved. Yet it is noteworthy that the confused ways in which the holist position has been put forward are often the result of the fact that the thinkers involved are really closet individualists doing little more than expressing the limits of their atomism. For them, an analysis must involve decomposition into atoms. If it so happens that such decomposition into individual units is not possible, one can only, in their view, resign oneself to this or call this failure of analysis "dialectical." A perhaps caricatured example of this turn from dogmatic atomism to the most extreme holism can be found in a passage where Sartre is discussing language. If language were analyzable, it would have to be analyzable in material—i.e., inert—units. This is partly true, according to Sartre, who adds that this has the following fateful consequence: the meaning of a word I use is modified each time that someone else uses it. "Words live off the death of men, they come together through men; whenever I form a sentence its meaning escapes me, is stolen from me; meanings are changed *for everyone* by each speaker and each day; the meanings of the very words in my mouth are changed by others."[32] But language is not inert matter, it is also a human activity. As a "praxis," language is a whole, which Sartre explains as follows: "the sentence is an actual totalisation where every word defines itself in relation to the others, to the context and to the entire language, as an integral part of a whole. To speak is to modify each vocable by all the others against the common background of the word [*verbe*]; language contains every word and every word is to be understood in terms of language as a whole; it contains the whole of language and reaffirms it."[33] The very least that can be said is that this holism of the "total word" is no more convincing than the atomist view of words that it is supposed to rectify.

In the present work, which here comes to an end, I have attempted to show that a mentalist theory of mind is necessarily incoherent and that it is vulnerable to a decisive holist objection: when one wants to identify someone's thoughts, one cannot abstract from the historical context. So let us suppose that one wants to take the context into account: would we then be able to identify anything at all? The procedure of identification through the individuation of entities that are independent from one another does not allow us to identify *thoughts*. It remains to be seen whether mental holism does not in its turn rule out the discrimination of thoughts due to an inability to *distinguish* one thought from another. It therefore remains to be demonstrated that, if mental atomism is indeed incoherent, mental holism can be put forward in a coherent way.

INTRODUCTION

1. See Vincent Descombes, "An Essay in Philosophical Observation," trans. Lorna Scott-Fox, in *Philosophy in France Today*, ed. Alan Montefiore (Cambridge: Cambridge University Press, 1983), pp. 67–81.

2. On "immanent critique" as the traditionally dominant mode of French philosophy, see Vincent Descombes, "Introduction: Analytical versus Continental Philosophy?" in his *Objects of All Sorts*, trans. Lorna Scott-Fox and Jeremy Harding (London: Blackwell, 1986), pp. 1–14.

3. Vincent Descombes, *The Barometer of Modern Reason: On the Philosophies of Current Events*, trans. Stephen Adam Schwartz (New York: Oxford University Press, 1993), p. 76.

4. See, for example, Luc Ferry and Alain Renaut, *French Philosophy of the Sixties: An Essay on Antihumanism*, trans. Mary H. S. Cattani (Amherst: University of Massachusetts Press, 1990); Luc Ferry, *Homo Aestheticus*, trans. Robert de Loaiza (Chicago: University of Chicago Press, 1993); Alain Renaut, *Kant aujourd'-hui* (Paris: Aubier, 1997).

5. Vincent Descombes, *Modern French Philosophy*, trans. Lorna Scott-Fox and Jeremy M. Harding (Cambridge: Cambridge University Press, 1980), p. 3.

6. Olivier Mongin, *Face au scepticisme: Les mutations du paysage intellectuel ou l'invention de l'intellectuel démocratique* (Paris: La Découverte, 1994).

7. Descombes, "Analytical versus Continental Philosophy?," p. 9.

8. Descombes, *The Barometer of Modern Reason*, p. 64. This is a reference to a passage in Baudelaire's "The Painter of Modern Life" in *Selected Writings on Art and Artists*, trans. P. E. Charvet (Cambridge: Cambridge University Press, 1972), p. 397.

9. Descombes, "Vers une anthropologie comparative des démocraties modernes," *Esprit* no. 263 (May 2000), pp. 157–58.

10. On the *intensification* or rush to extremes characteristic of Romantic thought (as well as typical of the Heideggerian style of doing philosophy), see Descombes, *The Barometer of Modern Reason*, pp. 98–102 as well as p. 123. See also Louis Dumont, "Are Cultures Living Beings? German Identity in Interaction," *Man* (NS) 21 (1986).

11. Clément Rosset, *Le réel: Traité de l'idiotie* (Paris: Minuit, 1977), p. 82.

12. Descombes, "An Essay in Philosophical Observation," pp. 69–70.

13. Descombes, "L'identification des idées," *Revue philosophique de Louvain* 96: 1 (February 1998): 86–90.

14. Descombes, *Proust: Philosophy of the Novel*, trans. Catherine Chance Macksey (Palo Alto, Calif.: Stanford University Press, 1992).

15. Descombes, *Les institutions du sens* (Paris: Minuit, 1996), p. 96.

16. Descombes, "L'identification des idées," p. 88.

17. Ibid., p. 86.

18. Marcel Proust, *La fugitive* (*A la recherché du temps perdu*, vol. 3), (Paris: Gallimard/Pléiade, 1954), p. 450.

19. See, for example, his "Nietzsche's French Moment" in *Why We Are Not Nietzscheans*, trans. Robert de Loaiza, ed. Luc Ferry and Alain Renaut (Chicago: University of Chicago Press, 1997); "The Interpretative Text" in *Gadamer and Hermeneutics*, ed. Hugh J. Silverman (London: Routledge, 1991), pp. 247–68; as well as "L'identification des idées," previously cited.

20. Fodor and LePore, *Holism*, p. 2.

21. Robert B. Brandom has argued in favor of a similar principle ("inferential" in his vocabulary, and not "narrative") in his recent books *Making It Explicit* (Cambridge, Mass.: Harvard University Press, 1994) and *Articulating Reasons: An Introduction to Inferentialism* (Cambridge, Mass.: Harvard University Press, 2000): "Grasping the *concept* that is applied in such a making explicit is mastering its *inferential* use: knowing (in the practical sense of being able to distinguish, a kind of knowing *how*) what else one would be committing oneself to by applying the concept, what would entitle one to do so, and what would preclude such entitlement" (*Articulating Reasons*, p. 11). It is in much the same spirit that Descombes claims, following Peirce, that "to think is not to bring one's attention to bear on objects, it is to derive consequences" ("L'esprit comme esprit des lois," *Le débat* no. 90 [May–August 1996], p. 85).

22. Descombes, "An Essay in Philosophical Observation," p. 74.

23. Ibid., p. 75. See also *The Barometer of Modern Reason*, pp. 38 ff, and "Philosophie du jugement politique," *La Pensée Politique*, 2 (1994), esp. pp. 147–49.

24. Descombes, "Philosophie du jugement politique," p. 148.

25. Descombes, "An Essay in Philosophical Observation," p. 75.

26. Descombes, "The Philosophy of Collective Representations," trans. Anthony Cheal Pugh, *History of the Human Sciences* 13:1 (2000), p. 39.

27. Indeed, the relation between Descombes's way of doing philosophy and that of the immanentist is analogous to the relation between what he calls, following Hegel, "l'esprit objectif" (objective mind) and "l'esprit objectivé" (objectified mind). These are two views of how the past is present for us:

> "*Objectified mind* corresponds to the fact that we live in a world that was inhabited by others before us (these others are at first foreign to us). By contrast, *objective mind* is the opposite: it is not the trace, within our field of perception, of those who are absent, but the presence of the social in each of our minds. Not at all a relation to foreigners (that we would have to reacquaint ourselves with, whose thoughts we would have to restore based on documents we have). On the contrary, it is a relation to those who are familiar and who I need not reacquaint myself with or interpret because they are already present in my innermost being, in my language and my thought. [*Les institutions du sens*, p. 289].

28. Descombes, "L'esprit comme esprit des lois," p. 82. Or, as Lévi-Strauss put it, the goal is "the reintegration of culture in nature and finally of life within the whole of its physico-chemical conditions" (Lévi-Strauss, *The Savage Mind* [Chicago: University of Chicago Press, 1966], p. 247; cited below, page 62).

29. Descombes, *The Barometer of Modern Reason*, p. 152.

30. The French title of *Objects of All Sorts* was *Grammaire d'objets en tous genres* (Grammar of All Sorts of Objects).

31. Hilary Putnam, "The Meaning of 'Meaning,'" in *Mind, Language and Reality (Philosophical Papers, Volume II*, Cambridge: Cambridge University Press, 1975); and Tyler Burge, "Individualism and the Mental," *Midwest Studies in Philosophy* 4 (1979), 73–121.

32. Descombes, "L'esprit comme esprit des lois," p. 83.

33. Descombes, *Les institutions du sens*, p. 308.

CHAPTER ONE
THE PHENOMENA OF MIND

1. [Translator's note: French and German both have a single word, *esprit* and *Geist* respectively, where English has at least two: "mind" and "spirit." This fact forces the translator to choose in ways that are often less than satisfactory. Hegel's English translators, for example, have had to choose between rendering his *Phänomenologie des Geistes* as either *The Phenomenology of Mind* or as *The Phenomenology of Spirit* and there are indeed translations of the book under both of those titles. Descombes's use of the term "*sciences de l'esprit*" here is a literal rendering into French of the German *Geisteswissenschaften*. This latter term is usually translated into English, when it is translated at all, as the "human sciences." But it could just as easily be (and, indeed, has been) rendered literally in English as the "sciences of the mind."

Throughout what follows, I will usually translate the French "esprit" by the English "mind," in order to emphasize that Descombes's claims bear upon what, in English, is called "the philosophy of mind" ("la philosophie de l'esprit" in French). But it is important to recognize that the other meaning of "esprit," *spirit* (as in Montesquieu's *Esprit des lois* or *Spirit of the Laws*), is never far from Descombes's concerns. For one of the aims of Descombes's recent work, including this book, might be seen as bringing together the two English meanings of "esprit," by defending the holistic and externalist thesis that the individual *mind* is inconceivable outside the impersonal *spirit* of the institutions of meaning, i.e., that these are its necessary conditions.]

2. Mallarmé, *Œuvres complètes*, p. 374.

3. Goethe, *Faust*, p. 161 [translation modified].

4. In chapter 3, I make the claim that within the moral sciences, structuralism is indeed a theory of impersonal mind. But I will also show that this impersonality has been construed in contradictory ways. If this is so, it is no doubt a mistake to

assimilate the structuralist approach as such to the strain of postwar French thought that put forward the ideas of subjectless process and the structural unconscious.

5. In order to comply both with current parlance and the legitimate need for clarity of expression, I will adhere to the following convention: a *subject of predication* is a linguistic sign, specifically the linguistic sign that, when combined with another sort of linguistic sign—a predicate—results in a third sort of linguistic sign called a proposition; a *subject of attribution* is something to which a predicate is attached by means of a proposition that will be either true or false depending on whether the predicate describes the thing as it is or fails to do so. Thus, in the sentence "Socrates is walking" the subject of predication is the name Socrates (in other words, the *word* "Socrates"), while the subject of attribution is Socrates: if the proposition is true, Socrates is doing the walking, not his name.

6. Fodor, *Representations*, p. 26.

7. The term "representationism," which is a good short form to replace Fodor's turn of phrase for this philosophy ("the representational theory of mind"), was applied by Ravaisson to the doctrine put forward by Renouvier. See Ravaisson's *Rapport sur la philosophie en France au XIXe siècle* (1867) in *De l'habitude*, p. 162. The term can indeed be extended to cover any theory, whether classic or contemporary, that sees ideas as representational, i.e., what the French Philosophical Society's *Vocabulaire*, published by Lalande, aptly characterizes as follows: "a doctrine generally accepted by Cartesians according to which the mind does not directly know real objects but only the *ideas* which are their signs" (*Vocabulaire technique et critique de la philosophie*, article "Représentatif," p. 920).

8. Mill, *A System of Logic*, book VI, chapter 4, § 2.

9. There is a duality in psychology by which some psychologists claim to study creatures in possession of a psychic life and thus of a particular mode of integration into their surrounding environment, while others claim to study creatures endowed with a flux of consciousness or a representational apparatus and thus mentally indifferent to the "external world." This duality is recognized by Fodor in the distinction he draws between the "rational psychology" of classical philosophers and the "naturalist psychology" of American pragmatists (*Representations*, p. 228).

10. Bréhier captures this wavering in a passage in which he compares the systems of the seventeenth century with eighteenth-century treatises: "The beginning of the 18th century was characterized by the rapid decadence and collapse of the great systems in which the intellectual heirs of Descartes had sought to unite the philosophy of nature and the philosophy of mind." The two authorities of the century of Enlightenment were Newton and Locke. Newton never really put forward anything but a natural philosophy, and his views on the mind have no systematic relationship with his physics. Locke, on the other hand, propounded "a philosophy of mind not directly related to the contemporaneous development of mathematical and physical sciences in the hands of Boyle or Newton." Of course Locke's successors sought to expand the notion of "attraction" to give it applications in the philosophy of mind. Yet, as Bréhier concludes, there is nothing in such ideas that allows anything like the systematic Cartesian unification of all areas of philosophy. The theory of attraction is "a simple metaphor in which the image of mind corresponds

to the model of nature as revealed by Newton, for the illusion persisted that it was possible to achieve in sciences of the human mind success as remarkable as that achieved in natural sciences" (Bréhier, *The History of Philosophy*, vol. V, pp. 1–2).

11. Wittgenstein, *The Blue and Brown Books*, pp. 24–25.

12. Readers of Hegel will recognize here a particularly clear expression of the idea associated with the ancient apologue: *Hic Rhodus, hic saltus* (cited in the preface to the *Philosophy of Right*). Has the braggart who claims to have made a prodigious leap at Rhodes got the strength for such a leap? If so, he must be able to do it again here, as if he were at Rhodes.

13. Of course nothing prevents us from assuming that the ability to translate a page of text in Latin, as this ability is *logically* manifested in the act of translating, might also be *empirically* manifested by symptoms of a cerebral type. This is an empirical hypothesis. It is the province of science and not philosophy to form such hypotheses and, even more so, to explain how one can move from the symptom to the reality that it indirectly manifests.

14. [Translator's note: The following passage is my English translation of the French translation of Descartes's original Latin text. The salient point here is that Descartes's French translators seem to have deliberately chosen not to avail of the French word *conscient* (conscious) to translate its Latin equivalent: the Latin *ut ejus immediate conscii simus* is translated as *que nous en sommes immédiatement connaissants* (that we are immediately cognizant or aware of it). Were it not so awkward in English, the word "*connaissants*," used here instead of "*conscients*," could literally be translated by the English word "knowing" (i.e., that we are immediately knowing of it). A published English translation of this passage reads as follows:

> *Thought*. I use this term to include everything that is within us in such a way that we are immediately aware of it [*ut ejus immediate conscii simus*]. Thus all the operations of the will, the intellect, the imagination and the senses are thoughts. I say "immediately" so as to exclude the consequences of thoughts; a voluntary movement, for example, originates in a thought but is not itself a thought (Descartes, "Objections and Replies," Second Set of Replies, p. 113].

15. Descartes, *Méditations métaphysiques, Secondes Réponses*, Definition 1 of the *Exposé géométrique* (ed. J.-M. et M. Beyssade), p. 285.

16. Descartes, "Objections and Replies," Fifth Set of Objections, p. 180.

17. Ibid., Fifth Set of Replies, p. 244.

18. The same wavering between Cartesian and naturalistic conceptions of cognition exists today. For example, Dan Sperber and Deirdre Wilson write that "some authors (e.g., Dretske) use the terms 'information' and 'inform' to talk only of the representation and transmission of facts; for them, all information is by definition true. We will use the terms more broadly, treating as information not only facts, but also dubious and false assumptions presented as factual" (*Relevance*, p. 2). The authors subsequently adduce reasons taken from cognitive psychology to explain their decision: "From a cognitive point of view, mistaken assumptions can be indistinguishable from genuine factual knowledge, just as optical illusions can

be indistinguishable from true sight. Just as illusions are 'visible,' so any assumption, whether true or false, may be manifest to an individual (ibid., p. 39). It is not inconsequential that the analogy here is one, as it is for Cartesians, between thought and perception.

19. Changeux, *Neuronal Man*, p. 227.

20. Ibid., p. 168 [translation modified].

21. A single example will suffice to illustrate the uselessness of mental objects in an account of mental life. The example is linguistic comprehension. Changeux provides the following sentence as an example: "The Mona Lisa visits Japan" (*ibid.*, p. 127). This phrase might be held to be ambiguous, but in fact everyone understands by it that Leonardo da Vinci's painting has been sent to Japan for an exhibition. This painting is, of course, one of the most famous in the history of painting. Changeux writes that "one can readily conjure up the image of this intriguing woman, with her enigmatic smile, her hands crossed in front of her" (*ibid.*). Apparently, this mental image is supposed to account for our understanding of the sentence. Changeux also claims that "when one hears 'Mona Lisa' one has a *mental image*, an 'inner vision' of Leonardo's painting, months or even years after having seen it at the Louvre. To recall this image is a personal, introspective event" (ibid.). In fact, no mental image can account for the way the words "Mona Lisa" allow the reader of the sentence to know which object it is that is supposed to be traveling to Japan. In order for the image to play this referential role, it would first have to be related to the object of which it is the iconic sign, which presupposes that the problem of reference raised by the sentence has been resolved. To see this, one need only ask what difference there would be between the mental image evoked in the sentence Changeux gives and the mental image that would be evoked by a different sentence according to which "an excellent copy of the Mona Lisa has been sent to Japan." The two mental images are almost certainly indiscernible. The psychological theory according to which we understand words by the images they evoke would therefore have to hold that these two sentences are equivalent. Yet the museum in Japan will surely insist that the original painting be sent to them rather than a copy, however excellent.

22. Husserl, *Cartesian Meditations*, § 14.

23. See his *Intentionality* as well as *The Rediscovery of the Mind*.

24. See below, § 2.2.

25. "For medievals the *intentio* of a term was what was intended by the mind in the use of the term, *quod anima intendit*" (Geach, *Reference and Generality*, p. 181).

26. "Every mental phenomenon is characterized by what the Scholastics of the Middle Ages called the intentional (or mental) inexistence of an object, and what we might call, though not wholly unambiguously, reference to a content, direction toward an object (which is not to be understood here as meaning a thing), or immanent objectivity" (Brentano, *Psychology from an Empirical Standpoint*, p. 88). Further on, one finds a general formula: "We can, therefore, define mental phenomena by saying that they are those phenomena which contain an object intentionally within themselves" (ibid., p. 89). This formula generalizes from a series of examples that have just been given: in representation, something is represented; in judgment, something is accepted or refused; in love, something is loved, etc.

27. The philosophical problems raised by intentionality are considerable and have given rise to numerous debates. I will not be able to enter into those debates here but hope to offer at some later time an analysis befitting the subject's importance.

28. Phenomenologists have developed the (apparent) transitivity of psychological verbs into a doctrine of the "transcendence" of conscious beings. In doing so, they go against scholastic doctrine, which distinguished two sorts of action, immanent action (*actio manens in agente*) and transitive or physical action (*actio transiens in obiectum*). On this point see the remarks made by Anthony Kenny in *Action, Emotion and Will*, pp. 193–97.

29. Sartre, "Intentionality: A Fundamental Idea of Husserl's Phenomenology." This essay was originally published in the *Nouvelle revue française* in 1939.

30. On the application of the Russellian theory of definite descriptions to the problem of intentionality, see Arthur Prior, *Objects of Thought*.

31. A brief clarification of the unity of the problem of intentionality can be found in G.E.M. Anscombe's article on the intentionality of sensation in her *Metaphysics and the Philosophy of Mind*, pp. 3–20.

32. Dennett, *Content and Consciousness*, p. 23.

33. "On the proposed test of the mental, the distinguishing feature of the mental is not that it is private, subjective, or immaterial, but that it exhibits what Brentano called intentionality. Thus intentional actions are clearly included in the realm of the mental along with thoughts, hopes, and regrets" (Davidson, *Essays on Actions and Events*, p. 211).

34. If Husserl's and Merleau-Ponty's interpreters object that these difficulties have in fact been overcome by phenomenology, in ways close to those I have set out here, thanks to new concepts like *the horizon, habituality*, and *the institution*, I can only welcome the new support given to the intentionalist position. My aim here has only been to explain the reasons that intentionalism, in the sense in which I am using it here, cannot be confused with the doctrines derived from the philosophy of representational consciousness.

35. Hobbes, *Leviathan*, chapter 5.

36. Leibniz, "Principles of Nature and of Grace," § 14, p. 202. Leibniz is here alluding to the Old Testament verse (*Omnia in mensura et numero et pondere disposuisti*. Wisdom 11:21) that was often expressly cited in the seventeenth century by the advocates of the new physics.

37. Montaigne draws the relevant contrast as follows: "it is a more common fault for theologians to write too humanly than for humanists to write too untheologically" (Montaigne, *Essays*, p. 234 [Book I, chapter 56]). The theology that Montaigne has in mind here is revealed theology. Philosophy for its part cannot lay claim to means of expression other than the forms of "human speech" (ibid.).

38. See, for example, Heidegger's *Being and Time*.

39. Emmanuel Lévinas described the transition from Husserl to Heidegger (or from the analysis of "consciousness" to the analysis of "Being-In-The-World") in the following terms: Husserl maintains that all thought is thought *of* something at the same time that he maintains that to think is to exist. It follows, then, that *to exist is to exist something*. "Thought is not just an attribute of Being; to be is to think. Consequently, the transitive structure of thought also characterizes the act of being. Since thought is thought of something, the verb 'to be' must always have

a direct object: I *am* my pain, I *am* my past, I *am* my world. . . . The act of existing is at that point to be conceived as an intention. To be sure, for Husserl, transitivity is not the only characteristic of thought that will determine existence. . . . But the transitivity introduced into the notion of Being prepared the way for the conception of existence in use since Heidegger or, in France, since Sartre" (Lévinas, *En découvrant l'existence avec Husserl et Heidegger*, pp. 98–99).

40. "On the level of categories, the innovation of the philosophy of existence seems to me to have been the discovery of the transitive nature of the verb 'to be.' One does not merely think something; one exists something. Existence is a transcendence." Ibid., p. 100.

CHAPTER TWO
TWO SCIENCES?

1. Mill's work, *A System of Logic Ratiocinative and Inductive, Being a Connected View of the Principles of Evidence and the Methods of Scientific Investigation* (1843), was translated into German as early as 1849.

2. Dilthey, *Introduction to the Human Sciences* (originally published 1883).

3. [Translator's note: The Institut de France was the result of a reorganization of the existing Academies (the *Académie Française*, the *Académie des Inscriptions et Belles-Lettres*, and the *Académie des Sciences*).]

4. Gouhier, *Maine de Biran par lui-même*, p. 106.

5. Ibid., p. 109.

6. Ibid., p. 115.

7. Von Wright, *Explanation and Understanding*, p. 95.

8. What follows is a short summary of a complex debate that has exercised most philosophers since Descartes. The reader will forgive its unavoidably cursory nature.

9. Von Wright, *Explanation and Understanding*, p. 9.

10. These sorts of classification of contemporary philosophies into currents and tendencies are always approximate and debatable. I should perhaps say a word about how I understand the question of whether a philosophy is or is not analytic. It seems to me that a philosophy is analytic if it conceives of philosophical activity as an attempt to treat questions through logico-linguistic (i.e., conceptual) *distinctions*. This is clearly not the case for all of the philosophies of the past or present. In this large and vague sense of the term, any philosophy that makes use of the *distinguo* is analytic. We may therefore say that Scholastic philosophy is analytic but also that Descartes is sometimes analytic, for example in his *Responses* to the objections raised regarding his *Meditations*. In the contemporary sense of the term, only philosophers who systematically take their distinctions from modern logic and the philosophy of language that it has engendered are analytic philosophers. The philosophers today who remain outside the grasp of the analytic style are those who do not see the need to fall into the Frege-Russell line. Under this description, the "second" Wittgenstein is just as analytic as the "first."

11. See, for example, the contributions to the Royaumont colloquium of 1958 which were published as *La philosophie analytique*.

12. Anscombe, *Intention*; Taylor, *The Explanation of Behaviour*.

13. Von Wright, *Explanation and Understanding*, p. 181, note 86.

14. Raymond Aron, *Main Currents in Sociological Thought*, vol. II, pp. 225–26 [translation modified].

15. The description of an action may be called "intentional" if it presents the agent as having deliberately done what he does. An *intentional explanation* will explain why the action has been done deliberately: it will provide the reason that the agent acts as he does.

16. Nomological explanation consists in pointing out that the phenomenon to be explained is a particular case of a general truth having the status of a law. The relation between the event to be explained and the law is that between a singular truth (like "Socrates is mortal") and a general one (like "all men are mortal").

17. Aron, *La philosophie critique de l'histoire*, p. 244.

18. Dretske, "Laws of Nature," pp. 248–68. Dretske makes clear that he does not seek to defend a realist philosophy of science in his short article, but merely to insist that nomological explanation is empty outside of such a philosophy. Analogous arguments can be found in works with a realist orientation: Hacking, *Representing and Intervening*; Harré, *Varieties of Realism*.

19. Notice the passage from the indicative mood ("every F is a G") to the subjunctive mood ("It is a law that every F be a G").

20. Dretske, "Laws of Nature," p. 255.

21. Von Wright, *Explanation and Understanding*, p. 140.

22. Ibid., p. 2. Von Wright refers to an article on the modes of explanation in biology and psychology published by Lewin in 1930 in the first issue of the journal *Erkenntnis*.

23. "Generally, it is 'undeniable' that Teleology, i.e., the 'determination' of the Present (which is determined by the Past) by the Future is a *Phenomenon*. . . . But it is just as undeniable that this Phenomenon is imposed upon us not as a living Organism or a Work of Art, nor, indeed, as natural Beauty, but as (negative or creative) Action of human Struggle and Toil" (Kojève, *Kant*, p. 92).

24. Richard Sorabji reminds us that in Aristotle, teleological explanation does not require the attribution of desires: neither the elements nor plants have desires (*Necessity, Cause and Blame*, p. 164).

25. This point will be addressed in greater detail in chapter 7.

26. See von Wright, *Explanation and Understanding*, pp. 60 ff.

CHAPTER THREE
THE ANTHROPOLOGICAL INVESTIGATION OF THE MIND

1. On the failure of the semiological program in the social sciences, see Pavel, *The Feud of Language* and Sperber and Wilson, *Relevance*, chapter 1.

2. Sperber, *On Anthropological Knowledge*, pp. 1–8.

3. Ibid., p. 2.

4. See Aristotle, *Categories*, chapter 5.

5. Sperber, *On Anthropological Knowledge*, p. 3.

6. Ibid., pp. 29 ff.

7. Ibid., p. 91.

8. Lévi-Strauss, for example, refers to the spirit of an institution (*Structural Anthropology, Volume.* 2, p. 19).

9. "This work takes as its subject the laws, customs, and various usages of all the peoples of the earth. It might well be said that its subject is immense, since it includes all institutions." Montesquieu, *Défense de l'Esprit des lois* in *Œuvres complètes*, p. 813.

10. [Translator's note: Descombes is here again raising the question of the possible relationship between Montesquieu's use of the word "esprit" in his masterwork, *L'esprit des lois* (*The Spirit of the Laws*), and the use of this word in the French translation of the English term "philosophy of mind" ("la philosophie de l'esprit"); for this word means not only "spirit" (in its multiple senses) but is also the ordinary French term for "mind."]

11. Montesquieu, *Mes pensées*, No. 398 (ibid., p. 895).

12. Lévi-Strauss, *The Elementary Structures of Kinship*, pp. 75 and 84.

13. Ibid., p. 99.

14. Ibid., p. 100.

15. Ibid.

16. Ibid., pp. 100–101. Lévi-Strauss goes on to say, with regard to institutions like the strictures regarding the marriage of cross-cousins or that of the dualist organization of the group, that one should not attempt to explain them historically (by asking which of the two is the origin of the other), but rather structurally. According to him, structural explanation consists in the invocation of "the apprehension, by primitive thought, of those completely basic structures in which the very existence of culture inheres" (ibid., p. 101 [translation modified]). A bit earlier in the text, Lévi-Strauss indicated that the idea is to seek, beneath the institutions, "certain basic mechanisms which we believe to be universally subjacent" (ibid., p. 100). The structures of the mind are thus explicitly characterized as psychological mechanisms.

17. Lévi-Strauss does use the word "infrastructure" in a passage from the same work in which he draws a surprisingly psychologistic contrast between, on the one hand, the logical and grammatical rules formulated by theorists and, on the other, the laws that are the real infrastructure of thought and speech. This text makes no distinction between rules to be followed and laws to be discovered by observation, thereby showing the extent to which Lévi-Strauss tends to assimilate the *unconscious* and the *infrastructural* in the materialist sense of the word, i.e., in the sense in which the infrastructure determines at a lower level what can and cannot occur at a higher level. "The Logic of the Schoolmen was the work of thinking people who believed that they had discovered the laws which their own thinking obeyed. Despite the fact that in certain cases thought develops consistently with the models of classical logic . . . it is known today, through closer observation, that in most cases, the processes of thought are governed by very different laws. The grammarians of Port Royal believed they had discovered the true laws of speech, but we have since learned that syntax and morphology rest on an infrastructure which has very few points in common with the frameworks of traditional grammar" (ibid., p. 110 [translation modified]).

18. Lévi-Strauss, "French Sociology," pp. 503–37.

19. Ibid., pp. 508–9.

20. Durkheim, Author's Preface to the Second Edition, *The Rules of Sociological Method*, p. xlix.

21. Ibid., p. lii.

22. Durkheim notes the alliance of teleology and psychological individualism in the following terms: "If society is only a system of means instituted by men to attain certain ends, these ends can only be individual, for only individuals could have existed before society" (ibid., p. 97).

23. Lévi-Strauss, "French Sociology," p. 518 [translation modified].

24. Ibid.

25. The brand of functionalism defended in this text is explicitly linked to Malinowski (ibid., p. 517). In later works, Lévi-Strauss will insist on the differences between structuralism and functionalism.

26. Ibid., p. 528.

27. Ibid., p. 520 [translation modified].

28. These are Lévi-Strauss's terms. Durkheim not only claimed that social facts had to be studied as things, but also stressed that these social facts are collective representations. According to Lévi-Strauss, this antinomy between things and representations can be resolved using the notion of unconscious structures. "The solution to Durkheim's artificial antinomy lies in the awareness that these objectified systems of ideas are unconscious, or that unconscious psychical structures underlie them, and make them possible. Hence their character of 'things'; and, at the same time, the dialectical—I mean un-mechanical—character of their explanation" (ibid., p. 528 [translation modified]).

29. Bourdieu, *The Logic of Practice*, p. 39.

30. Ibid., p. 41.

31. See Lévi-Strauss, *The Savage Mind*, p. 252.

32. Regarding the distinction between psychology and sociology, Durkheim writes: "I owe it above all to my teacher, Monsieur Boutroux, who, while I was at the Ecole Normale Supérieur, often told us that each science must seek to explain things through 'its own principles,' as Aristotle put it: psychology through psychological principles, biology through biological principles. Swayed by this idea, I applied it to sociology" (Durkheim, *Textes*, vol. I, *Eléments d'une théorie sociale*, p. 403). On the role of the ideas of emergence and a hierarchy of structures at the end of the nineteenth century, see Ian Hacking's commentary in *The Taming of Chance*, pp. 157–59.

33. Durkheim, *The Rules of Sociological Method*, p. li.

34. Lévi-Strauss, *Structural Anthropology, Volume 2*, p. 25.

35. Durkheim, *The Rules of Sociological Method*, p. 90.

36. Louis Dumont, *Homo Hierarchicus*, p. 22.

37. Ibid., p. 23.

38. Ibid., pp. 22–23.

39. The model of translation is at the heart of contemporary reflection about the mind. I discuss this in my *Les institutions du sens*.

40. Dumont, *Essays on Individualism*, p. 3.

41. Ibid., pp. 3–4. In this passage, the word "ideology" refers to an entire set of representations and collective values.

42. See, for example, *Structural Anthropology*, pp. 11–14.

43. Lévi-Strauss, *Structural Anthropology, Volume 2*, p. 9.

44. Lévi-Strauss, *The Savage Mind*, p. 247.

45. Ibid., p. 354. On this same page, Lévi-Strauss refers to information theory.

46. This is pointed out by Sperber: "In the 1940s and 50s, many scholars set great store by the development of a unified science of communication integrating semiotics, cybernetics, and information theory. This science would bring together the study of language, culture, and society with that of the human brain and mind" (*On Anthropological Knowledge*, p. 90). Lévi-Strauss believed that his own work would form part of this new science, which might explain the allusive nature of his references to a (mostly future) science of the mind's unconscious activity.

CHAPTER FOUR
THE NEW MENTAL PHILOSOPHY

1. See, for example, Daniel Andler's introduction to the collection he edited, *Introduction aux sciences cognitives*, p. 12.

2. In the philosophical vocabulary of the English-speaking world, the cognitive is often opposed to the conative. This distinction corresponds to that commonly made in the French-speaking world between the faculty of representation and the faculty of the will. In French, the word "cognition" was rare until fairly recently and is ordinarily used with the cognitivist meaning.

3. Neisser, *Cognition and Reality*, p. 6.

4. Ibid., p. 7

5. Gardner, *The Mind's New Science*.

6. More modestly, the cognitivist could limit himself to separating the work in linguistics, psychology, and sociology that fits within his "paradigm" from work that is insufficiently solid to do so.

7. See Dennett, *Content and Consciousness*, p. 39.

8. As Wittgenstein writes: "To have an opinion is a state. —A state of what? Of the soul? Of the mind? Well, of what object does one say that it has an opinion? Of Mr. N. N. for example. And that is the correct answer" (*Philosophical Investigations*, § 573). He adds: one should not expect to be enlightened by this answer to the question, even if it is above reproach. Indeed, this is the materialist's opinion: such an answer has yet to explain anything. True, but the goal was not to explain anything but to indicate, by a grammatical remark, that questions about his opinions are questions to be asked about Mr. N. N., his sources of information, the quality of his judgment, etc. rather than questions about something whose *state* could be inspected in the way that one inspects the roof of one's house.

9. "I suppose, therefore, that whatever things I see are illusions" (Descartes, "Second Meditation" in *Philosophical Writings*, p. 66).

10. This point was eminently cleared up by Anthony Kenny in "The Homunculus Fallacy" and "Language and the Mind" in *The Legacy of Wittgenstein*. This will be discussed in chapter 8.

11. Peirce, *Collected Papers*, vol. 7, § 364. Regarding this passage, see Christiane Chauviré's comparison of Peirce and Wittgenstein in "Quand savoir, c'est (savoir) faire."

12. Ibid., § 367. Similarly, Wittgenstein writes that it is misleading to say that one thinks "in one's head" or "with one's head." To say these things means only that there is a relation or connection between thinking and the head. But, at the same time, these expressions suggest that the head harbors processes that are invisible from the outside. An entire philosophy is thereby erected on the basis of this image (Wittgenstein, *Philosophical Grammar*, § 64).

13. "Neurophilosophy" should not be confused with the philosophical reflections a neurologist might have regarding his discipline.

14. Fodor, *Psychosemantics*, p. 135.

15. Ibid.

16. One can only applaud this prudent restriction of the philosopher's competence to matters of meaning and intelligibility. At the same time, one might have doubts that this restriction is wholly honored in a program that, as usually presented, includes philosophy among the cognitive sciences and calls on philosophers to construct empirical hypotheses and models.

17. Fodor, *Psychosemantics*, p. 106.

18. "How does the philosophical problem about mental processes and states and about behaviourism arise? —The first step is the one that altogether escapes notice. We talk of processes and states and leave their nature undecided. Sometimes perhaps we shall know more about them—we think. But that is just what commits us to a particular way of looking at the matter. For we have a definite concept of what it means to learn to know a process better. (The decisive movement in the conjuring trick has been made, and it was the very one that we thought quite innocent)" (Wittgenstein, *Philosophical Investigations*, § 308).

19. In the present context, the word "metaphysics" may give rise to a misunderstanding. See the "Note on the Concept of Metaphysics" at the end of this chapter.

20. Fodor, *Psychosemantics*, p. 135.

21. Chomsky, "On the Nature, Use and Acquisition of Language," p. 632.

22. Ibid., p. 629.

23. Wittgenstein, *The Blue and Brown Books*, p. 64.

24. See Letter to Elizabeth, May 21, 1643 in *Philosophical Writings*, pp. 276–76. These notions are further discussed in articles 48 to 67 in the first part of the *Principles of Philosophy*, excerpts of which can be found on pages 190–94 of the same volume.

25. Kant, *Critique of Pure Reason*, Transcendental Aesthetic, § 2.

26. Russell, *My Philosophical Development*, p. 117.

27. Guéroult, *Descartes selon l'ordre des raisons*, vol. I, *L'âme et Dieu*, p. 102. An English translation is available in *Descartes' Philosophy Interpreted According to the Order of Reasons*, vol. I, *The Soul and God*, p. 62.

28. See Geach, *Mental Acts*, p. 3, and Kenny, *The Legacy of Wittgenstein*, p. 116.

29. See Harré, *Social Being* and *Personal Being*.

30. "There are no transregional categories" (Castoriadis, *The Imaginary Institution of Society*, p. 253). I discuss several of the texts in which Castoriadis makes this critique in my article "Un renouveau philosophique."

CHAPTER FIVE
THE DOCTRINES OF PHYSICAL MATERIALISM

1. In the naturalistic sense of a science of mental mechanisms. This is the only sense pertinent to the present discussion.

2. Fodor, *A Theory of Content and Other Essays*, p. 156.

3. Fodor, *Psychosemantics*, p. xii.

4. Ibid., p. 7.

5. In much the same way it is sometimes proposed that a distinction be drawn between morality and ethics.

6. Jacob, "Le problème du rapport du corps et de l'esprit aujourd'hui: Essai sur les forces et les faiblesses du fonctionnalisme," p. 516. Jacob's article provides a very clear presentation of the state of debate among theorists seeking to resolve "the mind-body problem," but he expresses no reservations about this formulation of the problem.

7. Heidegger once rightly pointed out that if we take the word "psychology" in the now-ordinary sense of knowledge of character and motives, then Aristotle's "psychology" should be sought not in his *De Anima* but in his *Rhetoric*. See Heidegger, *Being and Time*, p. 178.

8. Aristotle defines anger as the desire to do something that will *appear* as vengeance in response to something that *appeared* to be an insult (*Rhetoric*, 1378ᵃ30). The Greek word in both cases is the participle of the verb *phainomai*, "to appear."

9. The lecture was published in 1947 in the journal *L'evolution psychiatrique* and subsequently reprinted in the French collection of Lacan's writings, *Ecrits*, pp. 151–93.

10. In his book *The Lacanian Delusion*, François Roustang shows how Lacan's entire speculative endeavor is governed by the hope of finding a way of making psychoanalysis into a science, where the word "science" is taken to imply the possibility of translating the laws and connections of the domain studied into a mathematical notation.

11. It is striking that, in his text, Lacan applies the notion of a "structural description" to the positions he is criticizing (Lacan, *Ecrits*, p. 156). It is apparently precisely the structural aspects of Ey's positions on the hierarchy of levels of vital integration that prompted Lacan's criticisms. There are in fact two incompatible conceptions of structuralism, one that sees it as a means to reduce complexity to a combination of basic units and one that sees it as a means to account for organizational phenomena (see below, § 5.5).

12. Ibid., p. 154.

13. Lacan points out that he has borrowed this expression from the text by Ey that he is discussing. At the same time, he criticizes Ey's understanding of "psychical causality" as referring to the free and intentional activity of a subject.

14. Ibid., p. 161.

15. Ibid.

16. Lacan, *Ecrits: A Selection*, pp. 297–98.

17. In the psychological evolution of human beings and during transitional periods in their development, certain images (like the image of oneself in a mirror) have a role to fill in reorganizing the entirety of the subject's expectations, attitudes, desires, etc. in much the same way that, among female pigeons, the image of the partner plays a role in initiating ovulation (a comparison made by Lacan, *Ecrits*, p. 161). If this is so, psychical causality would be nothing more than the efficacy of the image in the activation of an instinctual disposition. The difference is that in humans such psychical causes do not set in motion behaviors that are in some way already programmed into the organism. Rather, they serve to disorganize vital relations or perhaps to substitute for the well-adapted instinctual economy that man lacks (according to the theory of premature birth).

18. Lacan, "Actes du congrès de Rome," p. 243. Notice that Lacan seeks psychical matter *outside* the organism and, especially, outside the brain.

19. Kenny, *Aquinas on Mind*, pp. 10–11.

20. Paulhan, "Les enfants du siècle (entretien radiophonique)," p. 443.

21. Bouveresse, *Wittgenstein Reads Freud*, p. 39 [translation modified].

22. Ortigues and Ortigues, *Œdipe africain*, p. 291.

23. Tesnière, *Eléments de syntaxe structurale*, p. 291.

24. This article was first published in 1949 and subsequently reprinted in *Structural Anthropology*.

25. Lévi-Strauss, *Structural Anthropology*, p. 191.

26. Throughout the article, Lévi-Strauss refers to a "cure." But the condition that is cured is not a stomach ulcer, a poisoning, or the flu but the difficulties a woman experienced while giving birth. Lévi-Strauss continually speaks of this as an "illness" or a "physiological disturbance," thereby preparing the way for the parallel he seeks to establish between the psychical treatment of organic disorders (by the shaman) and the psychical treatment of psychical disorders (by the psychoanalyst).

27. Ibid., p. 191.

28. Ibid., p. 192 (emphasis in original).

29. Ibid., pp. 197–98 [translation modified].

30. Ibid., p. 204 [translation modified].

31. Ibid., p. 199 [translation modified].

32. Ibid., p. 201.

CHAPTER SIX
THE PSYCHOLOGY OF COMPUTERS

1. Fodor, *Psychosemantics*, p. 135.

2. Turing, "Computing Machinery and Intelligence," *Mind* (1950), pp. 433–60. Republished in *The Philosophy of Artificial Intelligence*, ed. Margaret A. Boden, pp. 40–66.

3. Turing writes: "We now ask the question, 'What will happen when a machine takes the part of A in this game?' Will the interrogator decide wrongly as often

when the game is played like this as he does when the game is played between a man and a woman?" (ibid., p. 41). This elliptical formulation does not clearly exclude the possibility of understanding the new game, as John Haugeland does (*Artificial Intelligence*, p. 6), as consisting of a machine trying to pass itself off as a woman without player C being told that one of the players is in fact a machine. Yet the rest of Turing's article seems to indicate that we have moved from a game of "man or woman?" to a game of "human or mechanical?" Turing writes that the machine will simulate "the behaviour of a man" (Turing, p. 42). Here, "man" is clearly to be understood in its anthropological sense.

4. This principle does nothing more than make explicit the contents of the traditional idea of nature and, as such, could hardly be more classical. Thomas Aquinas, who is close to Descartes on this point, writes for example that it can be proven that something is a human being if it proves able to reason about any subject whatever. He gives the principle governing this inference as follows: *quando aliquod particulare opus proprium est alicuius agentis, tunc per illud particulare opus probatur tota virtus agentis* ("Whenever some particular work is proper to some agent, then the entire power of that agent is demonstrated by that particular work" [Thomas Aquinas, *Summa Theologiæ*, Tertia Pars, Question 43, Article 4, ad 3um]).

5. See Pylyshyn, *Computation and Cognition*, p. xii: "cognizers" have in common that they act based on their representations.

6. See Haugeland, "Semantic Engines: An Introduction to Mind Design," p. 31. "Semantic engines" are those beings whose behavior can be systematically described as intelligent: generally, all those whose behavior is organized by practical syllogisms.

7. "Conversation" should here be understood in the French sense: as a rambling interview, one that must be constantly renewed, of the sort that might take place among people meeting in a sitting room or among travelers who happen to occupy the same train compartment. There is an *art* of conversation such that not every linguistic exchange counts.

8. Turing's formulation of this is remarkable: "The human computer is supposed to be following fixed rules; he has no authority to deviate from them in any detail" (Turing, "Computing Machinery," p. 43). Thus, he is not free to choose his method of calculation if it happens that there are several ways of going about it (for example, multiplication could be carried out using a multiplication table or through a series of additions). But what, in that case, does he have the authority to do? Turing, it seems, asks us to believe that the operator knows how to read the rulebook, find the applicable rule, and apply it correctly. The operator would then be like a customs agent who has no authority to decide what can and cannot be imported tax-free—he consults the code that decides such things—but who is charged with deciding whether your personal effects fall under this or that category of the regulations.

9. Turing himself speaks of a compliance to be transformed into mechanism: "It is the duty of the control to see that these instructions are obeyed correctly and in the right order. The control is so constructed that this necessarily happens" (ibid., p. 44). Automatic control thus replaces a supervisor.

10. In the terms of Aristotle's *Politics*, we would have to claim that an enslaved worker or an animate instrument (*empsuchon organon*) is indistinguishable from an automatic and inanimate instrument (*apsuchon organon*), which is absurd. This reference ought to be enough to indicate why the difference between a human worker and a mechanical one is irreducible (See *Politics*, 1253^{b}).

11. Wittgenstein, *The Blue and Brown Books*, p. 13.

12. Ibid., p. 4.

13. Ibid., p. 15.

14. Fodor, "The Appeal to Tacit Knowledge" (1968), reprinted in *Representations*, pp. 63–78.

15. Searle, "Minds, Brains, and Programs," in *The Behavioral and Brain Sciences* 3 (1980): 417–24, reprinted in Boden (ed.), *The Philosophy of Artificial Intelligence*, pp. 67–88. I will cite the latter edition.

16. Ibid., p. 73 (Searle's emphasis).

17. Dennett, "The Milk of Human Intentionality," pp. 428–30. This article, comprising Dennett's commentary, appeared directly after Searle's text in the review in question.

18. Ibid.

19. Dumas, *The Count of Monte Cristo*, p. 622. The scene takes place in chapter 61, entitled "The Bribe."

CHAPTER SEVEN
THE INSIDE AND THE OUTSIDE

1. Putnam, *Mind, Language and Reality*, p. xiii.

2. Ibid., p. 433. His example: pain is not a physical or chemical state of the brain, but "a functional state of a whole organism."

3. See, for example, Putnam's articles from 1960 (ibid., p. 368), 1963 (p. 328), and 1967 (p. 431).

4. "Behaving systems" (or systems endowed with a psychic life) can be understood as those whose movements in the outer environment are explained by motives like "fleeing the enemy" or "running after prey," and not by the action of the physical forces of that environment.

5. See Newell and Simon, *Human Problem Solving*.

6. See the criticisms made by David Marr in "Artificial Intelligence: A Personal View" (1977) and by Drew McDermott in "Artificial Intelligence Meets Natural Stupidity" (1976), both reproduced in Haugeland, *Mind Design*, pp. 129–42 and 143–60, respectively.

7. In Simon, *The Sciences of the Artificial*, pp. 2–29 and 193–229, respectively.

8. Ibid., pp. 6–7. The vocabulary of the team at MIT, he claims, won out over that of his own team at the Rand Corporation and Carnegie-Mellon University.

9. Ibid., pp. 10–11.

10. The English word "environment" (like the German *Umwelt*) seems to have acquired its current technical meaning precisely as a way of translating the French word "*milieu*," a word which itself came into being in the eighteenth century in order to translate the Latin word *medium* as used in Newton's work (see Leo Spitz-

er's study on "Milieu and Ambiance" in his *Essays in Historical Semantics*). Note that although the English term "inner environment" seems at first glance to be paradoxical, it was also the case that the term "milieu extérieur" seemed illogical to French speakers (see the article "Milieu" in Lalande's *Vocabulaire technique et critique de la philosophie*). As Spitzer shows, there is no real paradox involved: the history of the word "milieu" is that of a constant oscillation between two poles: on the one hand, the assimilation of the "internal milieu" to a circumstance that is determinative in the way that the circumstances of the external milieu are supposed to be; on the other, the redefinition of the external world as an ambient one, an *Umwelt*, i.e., the opposite of a Newtonian mechanical *medium*.

11. Simon, *The Sciences of the Artificial*, pp. 8–9.

12. According to Gardner (*The Mind's New Science*, p. 23), Simon studied with Rudolf Carnap in Chicago in the 1940s.

13. Simon, *The Sciences of the Artificial*, p. 10.

14. Ibid.

15. Ibid., p. 11.

16. Sorabji, *Necessity, Cause and Blame*, p. 165.

17. One might add by way of confirmation that a mechanistic theory of the environment is precisely one that dissolves the individuality of the system or organism into its environment and does not accept the validity of the distinction between inside and outside. On this subject, see Georges Canguilhem's study of living things and their environment in *La connaissance de la vie*, particularly the neo-Lamarckian texts cited on page 135.

18. Simon, *The Sciences of the Artificial*, p. 15.

19. Ibid., p. 11.

20. Ibid., p. 195.

21. This footnote (ibid., p. 195, n. 5) is perhaps clearer than the declaration of principle in the text itself. In it, Simon observes that it is a mistake to think that "scientists" are necessarily reductive and that "humanists" are necessarily holists. Since holism is nothing but the appropriate way of approaching the study of organized systems, there is just as much need for holistic analyses within the natural sciences as within the arts and the human sciences.

22. Of course, Simon claims, the foundations of his analysis are physical. Yet it also so happens that the edifice of science is built from the top toward the foundations (ibid., p. 20). Simon posits that, in principle, everything must be explicable through laws applied to elementary particles. But what are these elementary particles? "Physics makes much use of the concept of 'elementary particle,' although particles have a disconcerting tendency not to remain elementary very long" (ibid., p. 196).

23. Ibid., p. 209.

24. Here it would perhaps be better to refer to more interaction between the *functions* of these employees rather than of the people occupying those functions, since people might well have several functions.

25. Koestler, *The Ghost in the Machine*, p. 48. The idea of a holon has been taken up in the theory of ecosystems (see, for example, Allen and Starr's *Hierarchy: Perspectives for Ecological Complexity*). Louis Dumont, in his *Essays on Individualism* (pp. 249–50, n. 23), points out that something related to the holon appears in François Jacob's work, *The Logic of Life*. Jacob calls Koestler's *holon* an *integron*:

"Living beings thus construct themselves in series of successive 'parcels.' They are arranged according to a hierarchy of discontinuous units. At each level, units of relatively well defined size and almost identical structure associate to form a unit of the level above. Each of these units formed by the integration of sub-units may be given the general name 'integron.' An integron is formed by assembling integrons of the level below it; it takes part in the construction of the integron of the level above" (p. 302).

26. Simon, *The Sciences of the Artificial*, p. 95.

27. Ibid., p. 63.

28. Ibid., p. 64.

29. Ibid., p. 65.

30. Ibid.

31. Ibid., p. 97.

32. Ibid., p. 25.

33. Ibid., p. 90.

34. Ibid., p. 76.

35. Reflection about the difference between information in the Information Theory sense of the term and what is relevant information for an automaton shows that . . . "the automaton can never be thought except from within, that it constitutes its own frame of existence and of meaning . . . in short, that to be alive is to be for oneself, as some philosophers have for a long time asserted" (Castoriadis, *Crossroads in the Labyrinth*, p. 183 [translation modified]). Castoriadis is alluding to the classical thesis that goes back to Aristotle (*De Anima*, 415^{b}13) according to which every living being seeks as much as possible to preserve its being, and that this teleology accounts for all of its vital operations. This thesis was subsequently reinterpreted in modern philosophy, particularly German idealism, in terms of "subjectivity."

36. Castoriadis, *Crossroads in the Labyrinth*, pp. 182–83 [translation modified].

CHAPTER EIGHT
MECHANICAL MIND

1. Pylyshyn, *Computation and Cognition*, pp. xiii–xiv.

2. See for example, Boolos and Jeffrey, *Computability and Logic*.

3. Pylyshyn presents these distinctions, which have been proposed under different names by different theorists, as "the basic assumption of cognitive science" (*Computation and Cognition*, p. 131).

4. Ibid., p. 132.

5. Fodor, *Psychosemantics*, p. 18.

6. In fact, the infamous "laws of association" were themselves derived from rhetoric, since contiguity and similarity are, in reality, stylistic figures by which the author of a discourse "develops" his position in a direction that has been anticipated or prepared in advance in the minds of his audience by the very words he has used.

7. Fodor, *Psychosemantics*, p. 13.

8. Fodor, *Representations*, p. 203.

9. Ibid.

10. Peirce, *Collected Papers*, vol. 5, § 431.

11. Peirce compares a "law of nature left to itself" to a court without a sheriff. The law, he explains, describes what must occur if there is to be a regular order of natural phenomena. Thus, all bodies must respect the law of gravity. At this point the law is nothing but "a mere formula establishing a relation between terms": we must still convince a stone to respect it. "All other stones may have done so, and this stone too on former occasions, and it would break the uniformity for it not to do so now. But what of that? There is no use talking reason to a stone. It is deaf and it has no reason" (ibid., vol. 5, § 48). If the positivist is a nominalist, he must accept that the law is valid only for cases that have already been observed. If this positivist believes that the law allows one to predict what is going to happen when a stone is released above the ground, then he will have to admit that there is a real connection among things, and that this connection explains the regularity that the natural law merely transcribes. The positivist will then have ceased to be a nominalist and will believe in the "reality of universals," i.e., in the reality of a natural order.

12. Fodor, *A Theory of Content and Other Essays*, p. 24.

13. If we add the principle of association by contrast, there would then be three psychological laws of the composition of mental life.

14. Dennett, *Brainstorms*, pp. 101–2 as well as p. 122.

15. Ibid., p. 122. The second part of this assessment is still too lenient. It would be better to say that "psychology with homunculi" is without any value whatsoever. Dennett, however, wants to claim for it the figurative value of a way of speaking.

16. Dennett, *Brainstorms*, p. 81. Like many of the ingenious ideas that have been taken up by other cognitivists, the solution to the problem of the homunculus through the division of labor seems to have first been put forward by Fodor in his article on the analysis of tacit knowledge (see *Representations*, p. 64). In *Content and Consciousness* (p. 87), Dennett provides a clearer view of matters, mocking theories that seek to explain by means of a team of homunculi what cannot be explained by a single little man in the brain.

17. The problematic notion of an "intelligent mechanism" is used to mean a mechanism that applies rules and that takes into account what is represented to it through signs. Of course, reference to an intelligent machine is not at all problematic if one means such things as workers who are expected to execute operations without thinking about them, like Turing's human calculator or Alexandre Dumas's telegraph employee (see above, chapter 6, n. 10).

18. Dennett, *Brainstorms*, p. 81.

19. Stupidity is not a pure and simple lack of intelligence. It is the result of a "limited mind" (Littré dictionary, article "bêtise" [stupidity]). Stupidity is then the *opposite* of intelligence; it is not its *loss*, let alone its pure and simple *absence*. A pebble cannot demonstrate stupidity any more than it can be taciturn or mute.

20. Some philosophers appear to have reached precisely this conclusion. See Boden, "Escaping from the Chinese Room," p. 97.

21. Dennett, *Brainstorms*, p. 122.

22. "Syntactic" should here be understood as referring to physical morphology or, if one prefers, to the orthography of the symbol. This notion of syntax evidently differs from that used by a linguist like Tesnière (cited above, § 5.5). Linguists study languages used for communication, not what logicians call "formal languages."

23. See Fodor, *Psychosemantics*, p. 25.

24. Ibid., p. 19.

25. Fodor, *Representations*, p. 203.

26. Apparently, the view of neurologists is that it is not such a model. See Changeux, *Neuronal Man*, pp. 126–27.

27. See Wittgenstein, *Philosophical Investigations*, § 281, on the fact that psychological attribution must respect certain anthropomorphic conditions: for example, only beings that manifest pain in a way similar to ours can be said to suffer. This is a principle familiar to fabulists. See also Wittgenstein's *Zettel*, § 567 ff on the necessity of historical context for any intentional description of action.

28. Leibniz, *Theodicy*, § 59.

29. Ibid., § 60.

30. Ibid., § 62.

31. Leibniz says he took this example from a certain Jaquelot, a controversialist of the time.

32. Ibid., § 63.

33. "The human soul is a kind of *spiritual automaton*" (ibid., § 52).

34. Ibid., § 66.

35. Ibid., § 59.

36. See the *Discourse on Metaphysics*, § 8: "Actions and passions properly belong to individual substances (*actiones sunt suppositorum*)." Leibniz here has in mind the traditional definition of a person, which goes back to Boethius's interpretation of the Greek *hypostasis*: "*naturae rationabilis individua substantia*" [individual substance of a rational nature] (Boethius, *The Theological Tractates*, p. 85).

37. This principle is one that Anthony Kenny puts forth, yet without explicitly referring to it, in his critique of the illusion of the homunculus (see his "The Homunculus Fallacy" in *The Legacy of Wittgenstein*). The connection between this principle and the Wittgensteinian principle according to which verbs require a narrative context should be obvious.

38. Thomas Aquinas, *Summa Theologiæ*, Secunda Secundæ, Question 58, Answer 2. Although Aquinas illustrates the second sort of mistake with an example taken from an outmoded physics (fire warms through its heat), his observation is not dependent on that physics. It would be easy to replace his example with others taken from current texts.

39. As Leibniz puts it: "Faculties or qualities do not act; rather, substances act through faculties" (*New Essays on Human Understanding*, bk. II, chapter XXI, § 6).

40. *Mutatis mutandis* the same thing goes for the mechanical model of harmony: two clocks set to chime the hour at the same time. Two clocks will be required.

CHAPTER NINE
CEREBROSCOPIC EXERCISES

1. Fodor and Lepore, *Holism*, p. 129.

2. Fodor, *Psychosemantics*, p. 136.

3. Dennett, "Brain Writing and Mind Reading" (1975), reprinted in *Brainstorms*.

4. This was as a result of a misreading of a page of *De Interpretatione*, as Kretzmann points out in his article on the history of semantics in *The Encyclopedia of Philosophy*, vol. VII, p. 367.

5. Dennett, *Brainstorms*, p. 39.

6. See Anscombe, *Intention*.

7. It matters little what meaning is given to the letters XYZ, since the argument put forward by materialist philosophers of mind postulates nothing more than a cerebral counterpart of every mental state, or rather, a redescription in physical terms of what has already been described in intentional terms.

8. Dennett, *Brainstorms*, p. 49.

CHAPTER TEN
THE METAPHYSICS OF MENTAL STATES

1. Putnam, *Mind, Language and Reality*, p. 220.

2. Wittgenstein, *Philosophical Investigations*, § 308 (cited above, chapter 4, n. 18).

3. "Sehen ist keine Handlung, sondern ein Zustand (Grammatische Bemerkung)" (*Remarks on the Philosophy of Psychology*, vol. I, § 1). Wittgenstein also refers to "state of mind" [*Seelenzustand*] (vol. II, § 722) and "mental state" [*Geisteszustand*] (v. II, § 247).

4. Ibid., vol. II, § 177.

5. Ibid., vol. II, § 388.

6. Putnam, "The Meaning of 'Meaning'" (1975), reprinted in *Mind, Language and Reality*, pp. 215–71.

7. Ibid., p. 220.

8. Ibid., p. 227.

9. Putnam explains his functionalist past and his current objections to it in *Representation and Reality*.

10. Putnam, *Mind, Language and Reality*, p. 219.

11. Putnam, "Brains in Vats," in *Reason, Truth and History*, pp. 1–21.

12. Putnam, *Reason, Truth and History*, pp. 28–29.

13. Searle, *Intentionality*, p. 230.

14. Fodor, *Representations*, p. 247.

CHAPTER ELEVEN
THE DETACHMENT OF THE MIND

1. The article originally appeared in the journal *The Behavioral and Brain Sciences* 3 (1980), pp. 63–73, accompanied, as is usual in this journal, by the comments of more than two dozen psychologists and philosophers, along with the author's replies to these comments. Fodor later included the essay in his book *Representations*. It is to this latter version that I will refer.

2. Montaigne, *Essays*, p. 110 (bk. I, chapter 26).

3. Fodor, *Representations*, p. 227.

4. Ibid., p. 228.

5. Fodor, *Representations*, p. 234.

6. Ibid., pp. 242–43.

7. The interesting thing about this example is that it could also be used to support the opposite thesis. Even if our aim in giving our broker instructions is to stress his personal responsibilities ("sell only if you *believe* it to be the right moment"), we still produce nothing more than a stylistic variant. For the broker, to act if he believes that *p* is to act if *p*. The broker cannot turn away from the question of knowing what the real situation is so as to concentrate all his attention on the real state of his beliefs on the matter. He cannot say to himself: "I don't need to know whether *p*; all I am asked to know is whether I believe that *p*." In the first person, to ask oneself whether one believes that *p* and to ask oneself whether *p* are entirely equivalent (see above, chapter 9).

8. Fodor, *Representations*, p. 228.

9. Ibid., p. 233.

10. Ibid., p. 232.

11. Ibid., p. 233.

12. Descartes, *Meditations on First Philosophy*, in *Philosophical Writings*, p. 78.

CHAPTER TWELVE
THE HISTORICAL CONDITIONS OF MEANING

1. Fodor, *Representations*, p. 229.

2. Fodor's responses were published with his article following the commentary of other philosophers and psychologists in *The Behavioral and Brain Sciences*, no. 3 (1980). Geach's commentary, "Some Remarks on Representations," is on pp. 80–81; Fodor's response to Geach is part of "Methodological Solipsism: Replies to Commentators," p. 102.

3. See Fodor and Lepore, *Holism*, p. 6.

4. Geach, "Some Remarks on Representations," p. 80.

5. See chapter 19 of my *Les institutions du sens*, entitled "L'esprit objectif."

6. Prior and Fine, *Worlds, Times and Selves*, pp. 30–31.

7. Geach, "Some Remarks on Representations," p. 81. The italics are, of course, Geach's.

8. Precise instruments are generally quite expensive. Yet physicalist arguments frequently appeal to a precision in their comparisons that costs philosophers nothing, since nobody seems to be concerned with how we determine the synchronic identity of a person "down to the last molecule."

9. Regarding the distinction between an *ability* and a factual *condition* on the possession of this ability, see § 4.2, above.

10. Pascal Engel provides a survey of the theories that appeal to the notion of supervenience in his *Introduction à la philosophie de l'esprit*.

11. See Lewis, "Is the Mental Supervenient on the Physical?"

12. Aristotle, *Nicomachean Ethics*, bk. X, chapter 4, 1174^b31–32.

13. "Facts of the Matter" (text from 1979, cited by Hookway, *Quine*, p. 71). To the best of my knowledge, Quine does not use the word "supervenience" to explain

the tenor of his physicalism, but that does not detract from the interest of his remark for our problem here.

14. Geach, "Frege," p. 159.

15. "That there is one and only one being who has certain attributes is something supervenient upon those attributes, and cannot itself be one of those attributes." Ibid.

16. Searle, *The Rediscovery of the Mind*, pp. 124–26.

17. Wittgenstein, *Philosophical Investigations*, part II, § i.

18. Castoriadis, *Crossroads in the Labyrinth*, p. 33 (see also p. 216).

19. Cantor, cited by Castoriadis (ibid., p. 208).

20. See the "Note on the Concept of Metaphysics" that follows chapter 4, above.

21. Frege, *The Foundations of Arithmetic*, § 106.

22. Geach is here alluding to definitions 3 and 5 of Book V of Euclid's *Elements*. In definition 3, a ratio (*logos*) is defined as a kind of quantitative relation between two magnitudes of the same kind. Definition 5 is meant to answer the question: What is it for magnitudes to "be in the same ratio"? In Thomas Heath's commentary, he notes that definition 3 is not put to use in the remainder of the text. See Euclid, *The Thirteen Books of the Elements*, vol. II, p. 117.

23. The allusion would seem to be to Michael Dummett's critique of Geach in *The Interpretation of Frege's Philosophy*, p. 268.

24. This text is taken from one of Geach's responses to his critics, published in the volume *Peter Geach: Philosophical Encounters*, p. 292.

25. Leibniz, *The Leibniz-Clarke Correpondence*, Fifth Paper, § 47.

26. This invitation is more common, however, in textbooks and didactic introductions than it is in the texts where the real work of philosophy is carried out.

27. This is no doubt the result of a century of controversy regarding philosophy's point of departure: should one move from knowing to Being, or from Being to knowing? This controversy proves to be groundless when one observes that, historically, philosophy has not been limited to a single point of departure and that, in practice, each philosopher begins from the point where he happens to be.

28. "By a thought [*Gedanke*] I understand not the subjective performance of thinking but its objective content, which is capable of being the common property of several thinkers" (Frege, "On Sense and Meaning," p. 62 n).

29. See, for example, Fodor and Lepore, *Holism*. These arguments are examined in chapter 13 of my book, *Les institutions du sens*.

30. Hegel, *The Phenomenology of Spirit*, p. 185.

31. Ibid., p. 183.

32. Sartre, *Critique of Dialectical Reason*, p. 98.

33. Ibid., p. 99.

Works Cited

Allen, T. F. H. and Thomas Starr. *Hierarchy: Perspectives for Ecological Complexity*. Chicago: University of Chicago Press, 1982.

Andler, Daniel, ed. *Introduction aux sciences cognitives*. Paris: Gallimard/Folio, 1992.

Anscombe, G.E.M. *Intention*. Oxford: Blackwell, 1957.

——. *Metaphysics and the Philosophy of Mind: Collected Philosophical Papers, Volume II*. Minneapolis: University of Minnesota Press, 1981.

Aristotle. *Ethica ad Nicomachum*. Latin trans. Guillaume de Moerbeke. In Thomas Aquinas, *In decem libros Ethicorum Aristotelis ad Nichomachum expositio*. 3rd ed. Ed. R. Spiazzi. Turin: Marietti, 1964.

——. *The Nicomachean Ethics*. Trans. H. Rackham. Cambridge, Mass.: Harvard University Press, 1934.

——. *Parts of Animals*. Trans. W. Ogle. In *The Complete Works of Aristotle*, Volume I. Ed. Jonathan Barnes. Princeton: Princeton University Press, 1984. 994–1086.

Aron, Raymond. *Main Currents in Sociological Thought*. Vol. 2. Trans. Richard Howard and Helen Weaver. New Brunswick, N.J.: Transaction, 1999 (1967).

——. *La philosophie critique de l'histoire: Essai sur une théorie allemande de l'histoire*. 2nd ed. Paris: Vrin, 1950 (1938).

Boden, Margaret A. "Escaping from the Chinese Room." In *The Philosophy of Artificial Intelligence*. Ed. Margaret A. Boden. 89–104.

——, ed. *The Philosophy of Artificial Intelligence*. Oxford: Oxford University Press, 1990.

Boethius. *The Theological Tractates*. Trans. H. F. Stewart, E. K. Rand, and S. J. Tester. Cambridge, Mass.: Harvard University Press, 1973 (1918).

Boolos, George S. and Richard C. Jeffrey. *Computability and Logic*. Cambridge: Cambridge University Press, 1974.

Bourdieu, Pierre. *The Logic of Practice*. Trans. Richard Nice. Stanford, Calif.: Stanford University Press, 1990.

Bouveresse, Jacques. *Wittgenstein Reads Freud: The Myth of the Unconscious*. Trans. Carol Cosman. Princeton: Princeton University Press, 1995.

Bréhier, Henri. *The History of Philosophy*. Vol V. Trans. Wade Baskin. Chicago: University of Chicago Press, 1967.

Brentano, Franz. *Psychology from an Empirical Standpoint*. Ed. Oskar Kraus and Linda L. McAlister. Trans. Antos C. Rancurello, D. B. Terrell, and Linda L. McAlister. New York: Routledge, 1995 (1973).

Canguilhem, Georges. *La connaissance de la vie*. 2nd ed. Paris: Vrin, 1965.

Castoriadis, Cornelius. *Crossroads in the Labyrinth*. Trans. Kate Soper and Martin H. Ryle. Brighton: Harvester, 1984.

Castoriadis, Cornelius. *The Imaginary Institution of Society*. Trans. Kathleen Bla-
mey. Cambridge: Polity Press, 1987.

Changeux, Jean-Pierre. *Neuronal Man: The Biology of Mind*. Trans. Laurence
Garey. Princeton: Princeton University Press, 1997.

Chauviré, Christiane. "Quand savoir, c'est (savoir) faire." *Critique* 65, no. 503
(April 1989): 282–99.

Chomsky, Noam. "On the Nature, Use and Acquisition of Language" (1987). In
Mind and Cognition. Ed. William G. Lycan. Oxford: Blackwell, 1990. 627–46.

Davidson, Donald. *Essays on Actions and Events*. New York: Oxford University
Press, 1980.

Dennett, Daniel. *Brainstorms: Philosophical Essays on Mind and Psychology*.
Cambridge, Mass.: MIT Press, 1981.

———. *Content and Consciousness*. London: Routledge and Kegan Paul, 1969.

———. "The Milk of Human Intentionality." *The Behavioral and Brain Sciences*
3 (1980): 428–30.

Descartes, René. "Objections and Replies." In *The Philosophical Writings of Descartes*. Vol. 2. Trans. John Cottingham, Robert Stoothoff, and Dugald Murdoch.
Cambridge: Cambridge University Press, 1984. 63–383.

———. *Philosophical Writings*. Trans. and ed. Elizabeth Anscombe and Peter
Thomas Geach. Indianapolis: Bobbs-Merrill, 1971 (1954).

Descombes, Vincent. *Les institutions du sens*. Paris: Editions de Minuit, 1996.

———. "Un renouveau philosophique." *Revue européenne des sciences sociales* 27
(1989): 68–85.

Dilthey, Wilhelm. *Introduction to the Human Sciences*. Ed. Rudolf A. Makkreel
and Frithjof Rodi. Princeton: Princeton University Press, 1989.

Dretske, Fred I. "Laws of Nature." *Philosophy of Science* 44 (1977): 248–68.

Dumas, Alexandre. *The Count of Monte Cristo*. Ed. David Coward. New York:
Oxford University Press, 1998.

———. *The Queen's Necklace*. Boston: Little, Brown and Co., 1899.

Dummett, Michael. *The Interpretation of Frege's Philosophy*. London: Duckworth,
1981.

Dumont, Louis. *Essays on Individualism: Modern Ideology in Anthropological Perspective*. Chicago: University of Chicago Press, 1986.

———. *Homo Hierarchicus: The Caste System and Its Implications*. Trans. Mark
Sainsbury, Louis Dumont, and Basia Gulati. Chicago: University of Chicago
Press, 1970.

Durkheim, Emile. *The Rules of Sociological Method*. Ed. George E. G. Catlin.
Trans. Sarah A. Solovay and John H. Mueller. New York: The Free Press, 1966
(1938).

———. *Textes*. Volume I. *Eléments d'une théorie sociale*. Paris: Editions de Minuit, 1975.

Engel, Pascal. *Introduction à la philosophie de l'esprit*. Paris: La Découverte, 1994.

Euclid. *The Thirteen Books of the Elements*. 2nd ed. Trans. Sir Thomas Heath.
New York: Dover, 1956.

Fodor, Jerry. "Methodological Solipsism: Replies to Commentators." *The Behavioral and Brain Sciences* 3 (1980): 99–109.

———. *Psychosemantics: The Problem of Meaning in the Philosophy of Mind*.
Cambridge, Mass.: MIT Press, 1987.

————. *Representations: Philosophical Essays on the Foundations of Cognitive Science*. Cambridge, Mass.: MIT Press, 1981.

————. *A Theory of Content and Other Essays*. Cambridge, Mass.: MIT Press, 1990.

Fodor, Jerry and Ernest Lepore. *Holism: A Shopper's Guide*. Oxford: Blackwell, 1992.

Frege, Gottlob. *The Foundations of Arithmetic: A Logico-Mathematical Enquiry into the Concept of Number*. 2nd rev. ed. Trans. J. L. Austin. Oxford: Blackwell, 1968.

————. "On Sense and Meaning." Trans. Max Black. In *Translations from the Philosophical Writings of Gottlob Frege*. 3rd ed. Ed. Peter Geach and Max Black. Oxford: Blackwell, 1980 (1952).

Gardner, Howard. *The Mind's New Science: A History of the Cognitive Revolution*. 2nd ed. New York: Basic Books, 1987.

Geach, Peter T. "Frege." In *Three Philosophers: Aristotle, Aquinas, Frege*. Ed. G.E.M. Anscombe and P. T. Geach. Oxford: Blackwell, 1963. 127–62.

————. *Mental Acts: Their Content and Their Objects*. 2nd ed. Bristol: Thoemmes Press, 1992 (1957).

————. *Reference and Generality: An Examination of Some Medieval and Modern Theories*. 3rd ed. Ithaca: Cornell University Press, 1980 (1962).

————. "Replies." In *Peter Geach: Philosophical Encounters*. Ed. Harry A. Lewis. Boston: Kluwer Academic, 1991.

————. "Some Remarks on Representations." *The Behavioral and Brain Sciences* 3 (1980): 80–81.

Goethe. *Faust*. Trans. Walter Kaufmann. New York: Anchor, 1963.

Gouhier, Henri. *Maine de Biran par lui-même*. Paris: Editions du Seuil, 1970.

Guéroult, Martial. *Descartes selon l'ordre des raisons*. Vol. I, *L'âme et Dieu*. Paris: Aubier, 1953.

————. *Descartes' Philosophy Interpreted according to the Order of Reasons*. Vol. I, *The Soul and God*. Trans. Roger Ariew and Alan Donagan. Minneapolis: University of Minnesota Press, 1984.

Hacking, Ian. *Representing and Intervening: Introductory Topics in the Philosophy of Natural Science*. Cambridge: Cambridge University Press, 1983.

————. *The Taming of Chance*. Cambridge: Cambridge University Press, 1990.

Harré, Rom. *Personal Being: A Theory for Individual Psychology*. Oxford: Blackwell, 1984.

————. *Social Being: A Theory for Social Psychology*. Oxford: Blackwell, 1979.

————. *Varieties of Realism: A Rationale for the Natural Sciences*. Oxford: Blackwell, 1986.

Haugeland, John. *Artificial Intelligence*. Cambridge, Mass.: MIT Press, 1985.

————, ed. *Mind Design: Philosophy, Psychology, Artificial Intelligence*. Cambridge, Mass.: MIT Press, 1981.

————. "Semantic Engines: An Introduction to Mind Design." In Haugeland, Mind Design, 1–34.

Hegel, G.W.F. *Phenomenology of Spirit*. Trans. A. V. Miller. Oxford: Oxford University Press, 1977.

Heidegger, Martin. *Being and Time*. Trans. John Macquarrie and Edward Robinson. New York: Harper and Row, 1962.

Hobbes, Thomas, *Leviathan*. Ed. Richard Tuck. Cambridge: Cambridge University Press, 1991.

Hookway, Christopher. *Quine*. Cambridge: Polity Press, 1988.

Husserl, Edmund. *Cartesian Meditations: An Introduction to Phenomenology*. Trans. Dorion Cairns. Dordrecht: Kluwer Academic, 1995 (1950).

Jacob, François. *The Logic of Life: A History of Heredity*. Trans. Betty E. Spillmann. Princeton: Princeton University Press, 1993 (1973).

Jacob, Pierre. "Le problème du rapport du corps et de l'esprit aujourd'hui: Essai sur les forces et les faiblesses du fonctionnalisme." In *Introduction aux sciences cognitives*. Ed. Daniel Andler. Paris: Gallimard/Folio, 1992. 313–15.

Kant, Immanuel. *Critique of Pure Reason*, Trans. Norman Kemp Smith. New York: St. Martin's, 1965.

Kenny, Anthony. *Action, Emotion and Will*. London: Routledge and Kegan Paul, 1963.

———. *Aquinas on Mind*. London: Routledge, 1993.

———. *The Legacy of Wittgenstein*. Oxford: Blackwell, 1984.

Koestler, Arthur. *The Ghost in the Machine*. London: Hutchinson, 1967.

Kojève, Alexandre. *Kant*. Paris: Gallimard, 1973.

Kretzmann, Norman. "Semantics (History of)." In *The Encyclopedia of Philosophy*, vol. VII. Ed. Paul Edwards. New York: Macmillan and Free Press, 1967. 358–406.

Lacan, Jacques. "Actes du Congrès de Rome." In *La psychanalyse*. Vol. I, *Travaux des années 1953–1955*. Paris: Presses Universitaires de France, 1956. 199–255

———. *Ecrits*. Paris: Editions du Seuil, 1966.

———. *Ecrits: A Selection*. Trans. Alan Sheridan. New York: Norton, 1977.

Lalande, André. *Vocabulaire technique et critique de la philosophie*. 11th ed. Paris: Presses Universitaires de France, 1972 (1926).

Leibniz, Gottfried Wilhelm. *Discourse on Metaphysics and Other Essays*. Ed. and trans. Daniel Garber and Roger Ariew. Indianapolis: Hackett, 1991.

———. *The Leibniz-Clarke Correspondence*. Ed. H. G. Alexander. Trans. Samuel Clarke. Manchester: Manchester University Press, 1956.

———. *New Essays on Human Understanding*. Ed. and trans. Peter Remnant and Jonathan Bennett. Cambridge: Cambridge University Press, 1996.

———. "Principles of Nature and of Grace." In *Philosophical Writings*. Ed. G.H.R. Parkinson. Trans. Mary Morris and G.H.R. Parkinson. Rutland, Vt.: Everyman, 1995 (1934). 195–204.

———. *Theodicy: Essays on the Goodness of God, the Freedom of Man and the Origin of Evil*. Ed. Austin Farrer. Trans. E. M. Huggard. La Salle, Ill.: Open Court, 1985.

Lévinas, Emmanuel. *En découvrant l'existence avec Husserl et Heidegger*. 2nd ed. Paris: Vrin, 1967.

Lévi-Strauss, Claude. *The Elementary Structures of Kinship*. Ed. Rodney Needham. Trans. James Harle Bell, John Richard von Sturmer, and Rodney Needham. London: Eyre and Spottiswoode, 1969.

———. "French Sociology." In *Twentieth Century Sociology*. Ed. Georges Gurvitch and Wilbert E. Moore. New York: Philosophical Library, 1945. 503–37.

———. *The Savage Mind*. Chicago: University of Chicago Press, 1966.

————. *Structural Anthropology*. Trans. Claire Jacobson and Brooke Grundfest Schoepf. New York: Basic Books, 1963.

————. *Structural Anthropology, Volume 2*. Trans. Monique Layton. London: Allen Lane, 1977.

Lewis, Harry A. "Is the Mental Supervenient on the Physical?" In *Essays on Davidson*. Ed. Bruce Vermazen and Merill B. Hintikka. Oxford: Oxford University Press, 1985. 159–72.

Mallarmé, Stéphane. *Œuvres complètes*. Paris: Gallimard/Pléiade, 1945.

Marr, David. "Artificial Intelligence: A Personal View." In *Mind Design*. Ed. John Haugeland. 129–42.

McDermott, Drew. "Artificial Intelligence Meets Natural Stupidity." In *Mind Design*. Ed. John Haugeland. 143–60.

Mill, John Stuart. *A System of Logic, Ratiocinative and Inductive*. Ed. J. M. Robson. London: Routledge, 1973.

Montaigne. *Essays*. In *The Complete Works of Montaigne: Essays, Travel Journal, Letters*. Trans. Donald M. Frame. London: Hamish Hamilton, n.d. 1–857.

Montesquieu, Charles de. *Œuvres complètes*. Paris: Editions du Seuil/Intégrale, 1964.

Neisser, Ulric. *Cognition and Reality: Principles and Implications of Cognitive Psychology*. New York: W. H. Freeman and Co., 1976.

Newell, Allen and Herbert A. Simon. *Human Problem Solving*. Englewood Cliffs, N.J.: Prentice-Hall, 1972.

Ortigues, Marie-Cécile and Edmond. *Œdipe africain*. 3rd ed. Paris: L'Harmattan, 1984.

Paulhan, Jean. "Les Enfants du siècle (entretien radiophonique)." In *Œuvres complètes*. Paris: Cercle du livre précieux, 1969.

Pavel, Thomas G. *The Feud of Language*. Trans. Linda Jordan and Thomas G. Pavel. Oxford: Blackwell, 1989.

Peirce, Charles Sanders. *Collected Papers*. Cambridge, Mass.: Harvard University Press, 1931–58.

La philosophie analytique. Paris: Editions de Minuit, 1962.

Prior, A. N. *Objects of Thought*. Ed. P. T. Geach and A.J.P. Kenny. Oxford: Oxford University Press, 1971.

Prior, A. N. and Kit Fine. *Worlds, Times, and Selves*. London: Duckworth, 1977.

Putnam, Hilary. *Mind, Language and Reality (Philosophical Papers, Volume II)*. Cambridge: Cambridge University Press, 1975.

————. *Reason, Truth and History (Philosophical Papers, Volume III)*. Cambridge: Cambridge University Press, 1981.

————. *Representation and Reality*. Cambridge, Mass.: MIT Press, 1988.

Pylyshyn, Zenon. *Computation and Cognition: Toward a Foundation for Cognitive Science*. Cambridge, Mass.: MIT Press, 1984.

Ravaisson, Félix. De l'habitude *and* La philosophie en France au XIXe siècle. Paris: Fayard, 1984.

Roustang, François. *The Lacanian Delusion*. Trans. Greg Sims. New York: Oxford University Press, 1990.

Russell, Bertrand. *My Philosophical Development*. London: George Allen and Unwin, 1959.

Sartre, Jean-Paul. *Critique of Dialectical Reason.* Ed. Jonathan Rée. Trans. Alan Sheridan-Smith. London: NLB, 1976.

Sartre, Jean-Paul. "Intentionality: A Fundamental Idea of Husserl's Phenomenology." *Journal of the British Society for Phenomenology* 1 (1970): 4–5.

Searle, John. *Intentionality: An Essay in the Philosophy of Mind.* Cambridge: Cambridge University Press, 1983.

———. "Minds, Brains, and Programs." *The Behavioral and Brain Sciences* 3 (1980): 417–24. Reprinted in *The Philosophy of Artificial Intelligence.* Ed. Margaret A. Boden. 67–88.

———. *The Rediscovery of the Mind.* Cambridge, Mass.: MIT Press, 1992.

Simon, Herbert. *The Sciences of the Artificial.* 2nd ed. Cambridge, Mass.: MIT Press, 1969.

Sorabji, Richard. *Necessity, Cause and Blame: Perspectives on Aristotle's Theory.* Ithaca: Cornell University Press, 1980.

Sperber, Dan. *On Anthropological Knowledge: Three Essays.* Cambridge: Cambridge University Press, 1985.

Sperber, Dan and Deirdre Wilson. *Relevance: Communication and Cognition.* Oxford: Blackwell, 1986.

Spitzer, Leo. "Milieu and Ambiance." In his *Essays in Historical Semantics.* New York: S. F. Vanni, 1948. 179–316.

Taylor, Charles. *The Explanation of Behaviour.* London: Routledge and Kegan Paul, 1964.

Tesnière, Lucien. *Eléments de syntaxe structurale.* 2nd ed. Paris: Klincksieck, 1988 (1959).

Thomas Aquinas. *Summa Theologiæ.* Vol. 37. Ed. and trans. Thomas Gilby. London: Eyre and Spottiswoode, 1975.

———. *Summa Theologiæ.* Vol. 53. Ed. and trans. Samuel Parsons and Albert Pinheiro. London: Eyre and Spottiswoode, 1971.

Turing, Alan. "Computing Machinery and Intelligence," *Mind* (1950): 433–60. Reprinted in *The Philosophy of Artificial Intelligence.* Ed. Margaret A. Boden. 40–66.

von Wright, Georg Henrik. *Explanation and Understanding.* Ithaca: Cornell University Press, 1971.

Wittgenstein, Ludwig. *The Blue and Brown Books: Preliminary Studies for the "Philosophical Investigations."* Oxford: Blackwell, 1969.

———. *Philosophical Grammar.* Trans. Anthony Kenny. Ed. Rush Rhee. Oxford: Blackwell, 1974.

———. *Philosophical Investigations.* Trans. G.E.M. Anscombe. Oxford: Blackwell, 1953.

———. *Remarks on the Philosophy of Psychology.* Vol. I. Trans. G.E.M. Anscombe. Ed. G. H. von Wright and G.E.M. Anscombe. Oxford: Blackwell, 1980.

———. *Remarks on the Philosophy of Psychology.* Vol. II. Trans. C. G. Luckhardt and M.A.E. Aue. Ed. G. H. von Wright and Heikki Nyman. Oxford: Blackwell, 1980.

———. *Zettel.* Ed. G. H. von Wright and G.E.M. Anscombe. Oxford: Blackwell, 1967.